21 DEBATED

Issues in World Politics

EDITORS

Gregory M. Scott
Randall J. Jones, Jr.
Louis S. Furmanski

University of Central Oklahoma

Prentice Hall, Upper Saddle River, New Jersey 07458

Library of Congress Cataloging-in-Publication Data

21 debated—issues in world politics / Gregory M. Scott, Randall J. Jones, Jr., Louis S. Furmanski, editors.
    p. cm.
    Includes bibliographical references.
    ISBN 0–13–021980–0
    1. World politics—1989–   I. Title: Twenty one debated—issues in world politics.   II. Scott, Gregory M.   III. Jones, Randall J.   IV. Furmanski, Louis S.

D2009 .A14 1999
320.9049—dc21

99–048606

Editorial Director: *Charlyce Jones Owens*
Editor in Chief: *Nancy Roberts*
Senior Acquisitions Editor: *Beth Gillett Mejia*
Editorial Assistant: *Brian Prybella*
Managing Editor: *Ann Marie McCarthy*
Production Liaison: *Fran Russello*
Project Manager: *Marianne Hutchinson (Pine Tree Composition)*
Prepress and Manufacturing Buyer: *Ben Smith*
Cover Director: *Jayne Conte*
Cover Illustration: Illustration People on a Globe, Boris Lyubner/Stock Illustration Source, Inc.
Marketing Manager: *Christopher DeJohn*

The book was set in 10/12 Trump Medieval by Pine Tree Composition and was printed and bound by Courier Companies, Inc. The cover was printed by Phoenix Color Corp.

Printed in the United States of America

10   9   8   7   6   5   4   3   2   1

ISBN 0-13-021980-0

Prentice-Hall International (UK) Limited, *London*
Prentice-Hall of Australia Pty, Limited, *Sydney*
Prentice-Hall Canada Inc., *Toronto*
Prentice-Hall Hispanoamericana, S.A., *Mexico*
Prentice-Hall of India Private Limited, *New Delhi*
Prentice-Hall of Japan, Inc., *Tokyo*
Pearson Education Asia Pte. Ltd., *Singapore*
Editora Prentice-Hall do Brasil, Ltda., *Rio de Janeiro*

To

Jill
Shirley
Pat

Contents

Introduction

The task is awesome, the prospects poor: to find a selection of articles that will provide students of world politics with a representative sample of the issues that have recently surfaced in the international arena. Six billion people, six continents, scores of nations, hundreds of ethnic groups, and vast divergences in health and welfare, poverty and plenty, inhabit what often seems an overcrowded globe. A planet full of politics is now available at the click of your mouse.

If you are reading this preface, you are probably a college student taking a course in world politics, foreign policy, or international relations. You may already know a good deal about global politics, or you may not have paid too much attention thus far. You may be unaware of how many important issues are currently shaping the global political and economic environment. As today's citizen of the world and perhaps tomorrow's leader, you have a role in determining how these issues shape your future.

In order to grasp the importance of some of these issues, imagine a day in the life of an American president that has turned from pressing domestic concerns to problems that may have an even greater long-term effect on the nation's future. A presidential meeting with the National Security Council might feature an agenda containing the following items:

- International dispersion of sensitive materials on the Internet
- Nuclear weapons reduction treaty
- Proposal to allow Russia to join the North Atlantic Treaty Organization (NATO)
- Plan to guard against terrorism attacks against American embassies
- Resolution to reduce opportunities for Americans to become mercenaries
- Resolution to impose a tax on imported computers
- Response to expansion of the European Monetary Unit (EMU)

- Request to increase the U.S. allocation to the International Monetary Fund (IMF)
- Plan to increase economic sanctions on Iraq
- Request for a study of the strategic implications of global warming
- Request for assistance to several African countries to help reduce the spread of AIDS

The preceding items would make for a full agenda, to be sure, but they would by no means exhaust the number of foreign affairs concerns deserving attention. But where do you begin to grasp the complex web of issues that confront ambassadors, statesmen, international corporations, and nongovernmental organizations (NGOs) every day? This book can be more than just a course requirement: It can, in fact, help you get started in your quest to become familiar with the world's problems and opportunities.

Obviously this volume does not cover all the issues, nor does it address all aspects of or all sides of any particular issue. In addition, the size of the book imposes a further limitation. The text is presented in a debate format with one author on each side of each issue, whereas in reality, every major social and political issue is complex, and many sides may develop in the process of an issue's resolution. This book does, however, get you started in the right direction, by introducing you to twenty-one of the most controversial and important issues facing the world's governments today, which are discussed by some of the world's most thoughtful commentators.

It is unlikely that any single article will allow you to resolve conclusively for yourself any particular issue, but that is not our purpose. As editors we have, from the start, had in mind three objectives. The first is to pique your interest in the issues themselves. You may have already heard so much discussion on some of the issues, such as the NATO attacks on Serb troops in Kosovo, that you think that nothing of interest can still be said. If this is the case, we hope to surprise you with some creative thought and good writing.

Our second objective is to provide you with some of the basic information that is needed to begin to develop your own informed opinion. The articles here provide a great many facts and findings, as well as interpretations. Our third objective is to raise questions in your mind. Good analysis often raises more questions than it answers. We hope that after you have read these articles, you will have a wide array of new questions and that you will be more eager to begin a lifelong search for the insight needed to make the world a better place in which to live. We wish you all the best.

Greg Scott, Randy Jones, and Lou Furmanski
Edmond, Oklahoma

PART I
Entering a Global Economy

Issue 1
Globalizing the World

INTRODUCTION

Israeli political thinker Yaron Ezrahi has said that "the most arbitrary powers in history always hid under the claim of some impersonal logic—God, the laws of nature, the laws of the market. The same could happen with globalization." Whether or not the term *globalization* will fall into this category, there is no question of its having become a standard term to describe the political and economic forces current at the turn of the twentieth century.

Perhaps no term better symbolizes the forces affecting the course of international relations than does globalization. Everywhere we turn, we read or hear about its impact. The refrain goes something like this: We live in a global society, increasingly linked together by an ever more complex web of communications, economies, and other types of mutual dependencies. Thus, there seems to be no denying the term's relevance.

Neither of the two articles in this section attempts to deny that relevance. Both accept the truth of globalization, focusing primarily on its economic aspects. Where these two articles differ, however, is in their assessment of the impact of globalization on accepted understandings of political and social existence. Charles K. Wilber is highly critical of the economic forces affecting modern society, forces that have promoted "changes in the international economy [which] have led to a direct assault on the welfare state." His main criticism centers on how the increasingly competitive nature of the global economy has exerted a vicious downward pressure on wages and on the ability of governments to restrain the destructive excesses of capitalism.

Daniel Drezner's contribution is a collection of book reviews of recent "popular" treatments on the phenomenon of globalization. Collectively, the books under review all acknowledge erosion of sovereignty that comes with the globalization process. Not all the books attribute the cause to economic factors. Cultural forces are also cited, but as contributing both to globalization and to fragmentation.

As you read the articles, consider the following questions.

Discussion Questions

1. Is globalization a force for peace, or does it promise more opportunities for conflict as it brings people into closer interaction with one another?
2. Will political globalization inevitably follow economic globalization?
3. Does globalization perpetuate, and perhaps even deepen, the gap between the richer postindustrialized countries of the Northern Hemisphere and the poorer industrializing countries of the Southern Hemisphere?
4. Will globalization destroy the underpinnings of the modern welfare state and thus, ultimately, of democratic governance?

   For more on this topic, visit the following websites:

   http://www.igc.org/millennium/
   Millennium Institute

   http://epinet.org/index.html
   Economic Policy Institute

   http://www.cgg.ch/
   The Commission on Global Governance

Globalization and Democracy

CHARLES K. WILBER

Freedom for the pike is death for the minnow.
—Isaiah Berlin

In this paper, I make the following points: capitalism is a creative/destructive system; the democratic welfare state emerged to tame the destructive side of capitalism while promoting its creative side; changes in the international economy have undermined the ability of the democratic welfare state to do its job; and any attempt to re-create political economic consensus to control the destructive side of capitalism must take into account the nature of the economy as a system.

THE CAPITALIST SYSTEM

Two facts stand out from an examination of the history of capitalism. First, capitalism has been successful in producing amounts of goods and services unprecedented in history. Second, it has done so in a temporally and spatially uneven manner, i.e., capitalist development has proceeded very unevenly between countries and among regions within countries. The capitalist system developed in both North America and South America, but one more so than the other. Certain countries and regions became dynamic centers of development, while others stagnated on the periphery. Then the process shifted, and once growing areas stagnated and stagnant ones developed. And, of course, development has proceeded cyclically through booms and busts in each country and region. This process extends to individual industries and even households. These imbalances are naturally generated by the process of capitalist development. One of the great economists of the twentieth century, Joseph Schumpeter, captures this dynamic process in his concept of "creative destruction."

The price of this creation of new products, new jobs, new technologies, and new industries is the destruction of the old products, jobs, technologies, and industries. And the closing or relocation of plants with

Charles K. Wilber is Professor of Economics, University of Notre Dame. This paper was presented at the annual meeting of the Association for Evolutionary Economics, Chicago, Illinois, January 3–5, 1998.

Reprinted by permission. *Journal of Economic Issues*, June 1998 Vol. 32, No. 2, p. 465.

their loss of jobs hurts families and communities—here and now. The new plants and jobs frequently are located elsewhere and use a new generation of workers. The gains are in new and lower cost products for people as consumers.

This process of creation and destruction always has been present in the U.S. economy—the textile industry moved from New England to the South, the growth of supermarkets wiped out mom-and-pop grocery stores, petroleum replaced coal, etc. In the last 20 years, the challenges have come ever more from abroad. The textile industry has moved on from the South to various places overseas, Japanese autos and steel have captured a large part of the market from U.S. firms, etc. The result has been better products at lower prices, new technologies, new jobs, and lost jobs and devastated communities, in addition to balance of trade deficits.

During the past 60 years, citizens have turned ever more to government as the social institution with the task of softening the destructive side of these economic forces. In the domestic economy, the result was the New Deal–Keynesian consensus that reigned from the end of World War II to the mid-1970s. However, control of the destructive side of the capitalist development process in an expanding world economy has become ever more difficult as U.S. dominance has declined.

THE CHANGING INTERNATIONAL ECONOMY

A closer look at the history of the world economy is essential to understand the winds of change that have been buffeting the world and the United States in recent years. At the end of World War II, U.S. dominance of the world economy was unchallenged. The dollar became the international currency, and the United States set the rules for an international trade regime based on the nineteenth century liberal principles of free flows of capital and goods. While often violated in practice, this was the spirit animating multilateral trade negotiations—emphasis on procedures and not on results.

Naturally, as other countries began to rebuild from the devastation of war, the United States' dominant position could not survive. Japan, Germany, and others rebuilt with the latest technologies, giving them more up-to-date industrial structures than the United States. Their lower wage levels and newer plants and equipment combined to make them high-productivity, low-cost producers. The process accelerated as countries such as South Korea and Taiwan began to industrialize, combining the latest technologies with exceptionally low wage levels. The outcome has been ever stronger competition in the international economy.

Many of the major policy developments of the 1970s that finally shattered the New Deal–Keynesian economic consensus were not taken autonomously by the United States, but were forced on policymakers by external pressures. Two incidents stand out in this regard. The first was the August 15, 1971, decision of President Nixon to remove the United States from the Bretton Woods fixed exchange rate system and at the same time adopt a rigid program of wage and price controls. The key factors in these decisions were international.

This, in turn, had a major effect on the international economic system. International financial and commercial order is difficult to achieve among equals, and since the erosion of the United States' economic power after 1971, no single nation has been sufficiently powerful to impose order unilaterally. The breakdown of the Bretton Woods system resulted in floating exchange rates, which, when coupled with recession in several major nations, posed a constant threat of an international commercial disintegration and, in turn, reinforced domestic recessionary forces.

The second case of an internationally induced domestic policy change was the revolution in interest rates that took place in 1979 when the Federal Reserve Board decided to de-emphasize interest rate targets and to concentrate instead on the growth of the money supply. A key factor was the discontinuity between U.S. and international interest rates. The U.S. money supply growth rates and rates of inflation were also out of line with European countries.

This change pushed interest rates to historic highs, but even more importantly it signalled the large corporations in the economy that their wage bargains (and subsequent price increases) would no longer be ratified by the Federal Reserve through automatic increases in the money supply. Coupled with international competition, which limited their price setting behavior, this encouraged the assault on labor unions and wage roll-backs that were characteristic of the 1980s.

So in both instances of fundamental reformulation of domestic economic policy, the proximate cause was the vulnerability of the U.S. economy to foreign economic pressure and influence. This is a far cry from the hegemonic days of the 1950s and 1960s.

IMPACT ON THE U.S. ECONOMY

These changes in the international economy have led to a direct assault on the welfare state here and in other industrial democracies. The changes in the international economy enumerated above have increased the possibility of "exit" by people with large incomes and capital resources. Fearing the flight of capital from their own citizens and hoping to attract capital inflows from citizens of other countries, governments are pressured to overhaul both their tax and expenditure structures. Thus, the internationalization of capital markets is forcing countries to restructure their tax systems, which in turn is undermining the democratic welfare state. Countries as different as the United States, Canada, Sweden, and Japan, not to mention a number of LDCs, have had major tax reforms. While very different in detail, they share in common the attempt to reduce marginal tax rates on capital and high-income earners and to "broaden the tax base." The result is an increase in regressivity of tax systems.

To provide these tax reductions, governments are forced to cut back on the programs of the welfare state. It is important to note that these outcomes are less the result of demands by the electorate than decisions driven by the exigencies of international economic changes. This certainly raises questions about the autonomy of the democratic state.

The modern industrial world has seen the democratic welfare state as the answer to restraining economic forces so that society could be made a more humane place for people to live and develop as human beings. Unfortunately, international forces are undermining the ability to sustain the welfare state. Instead, we are moving toward the acceptance of a philosophy of "everyone take care of themselves and too bad if people can't cope." The society being created is one of great inequality, alienation, and even despair for many. This is not the soil in which democracy flourishes.

WHERE DO WE GO FROM HERE?

Developing solutions for the problems caused by international forces is difficult because the world economy differs from our or any country's domestic economy. In every domestic economy there is a sovereign power, the central government, that establishes the framework and rules for carrying-on economic exchange. In the United States, the Constitution empowers the federal government to regulate interstate commerce. No state can impose import tariffs on goods produced in other states. The federal government sets minimum wages, environmental regulations, payroll taxes, safety requirements, and so on that are binding on all of the states.

This is not the case in the world economy. There is no central government to set the rules. Prior to World War I, the hegemonic power of Great Britain set the rules for the international economy. During the interwar years, Great Britain was too weak, and the result was chaos in the international economy. After World War II, the Bretton Woods Agreement and the hegemonic power of the United States controlled the world economy. As the Bretton Woods system was abandoned and the power of the United States waned in the 1970s, coordination in the international economy was left to unregulated markets, supplemented with economic summits, to reestablish international coordination.

These efforts to organize the world economy on pure free-market principles—mainly by preachment—have not been successful. World economic growth has slowed; in many areas of Africa and Latin America, growth actually became negative during the 1980s. Trade imbalances have become extreme. Instability of exchange rates has become endemic in many areas. And the foreign debt borne by many countries, now including the United States, has had a constricting effect on the renewal of economic growth.

Reliance on GATT as the vehicle to promote a world economy of free multilateral trade worked as long as the United States and the Bretton Woods system set the rules for international trade and finance. International financial and commercial order is difficult to achieve among equals, and since the erosion of the United States' economic power after 1971, no single nation has been sufficiently powerful to impose order unilaterally.

The interdependent nature of international markets and of the various national economies means that individual policies regarding exchange rates, trade, capital flows, and debt issues will be more effective if set within supra-national programs that encourage and coordinate them. Just as it has been necessary for all countries, developed and undeveloped alike, to introduce various measures to control the workings of their domestic economies for the common good, it is time to extend those measures to the international economy. We cannot continue to practice one kind of economics up to our frontiers and another kind beyond them.

In addition, we as a society must face up to certain choices. Do we want a steel industry, do we want an electronics industry, or do we want whatever the marketplace gives us? Our policy has been that articulated by Richard Darman, Director of the Budget, when he said in 1985, during the Japanese dumping of semiconductors: "Why do we want a semiconductor industry? What's wrong with dumping? It is a gift to chip users because they get cheap chips. If our guys can't hack it, let them go.' Dumping—that is, selling below the home market price in foreign markets—is designed to increase market share and drive competitors out of business. Later the price rises. This used to be called predatory pricing and is illegal for U.S. firms under the antitrust laws.

There are two separate but related issues here. First is the idea of a strategic trade policy. This is where someone, presumably government, picks "winners"—that is, industries of the future that will make us more competitive with other countries. Japan, Korea, and many European countries, which do not have our simple faith in free trade, have national policies that attempt to create comparative advantages in key industries such as the airbus in Europe or supercomputers, optical fibers, and biotechnology in Japan. If done right—that is, "winners" and not "losers" chosen—and that is a big if, such a policy could keep us from falling hopelessly behind other countries, and it could put pressure on others to open up their economies.

The second issue is more fundamental. If we would rather guide our market system, through the agency of government, to give us what we consciously choose as a society, we will be forced to expand a strategic trade policy into a more comprehensive industrial policy. That is, we must decide that we want to maintain certain levels of some industries and expand others even if that requires subsidies or import restrictions. An example is the airline industry. Almost every country has a least one airline. We, along with every other country, do not allow unrestricted competition from foreign airlines on our domestic routes. Neither do we allow foreign firms to buy-up U.S. airlines. We have made a public choice to retain an airline industry because we think it is important, even if less efficient than having the service provided by foreign companies. The same type of choices must be made about other industries—steel, autos, machine tools, etc.

The great danger of an industrial policy is the possibility that it will be captured by special interests and the inefficiences hidden because they only show up in higher market prices. Clearly a system of democratic control must be developed. However, critics never face the fact that there are high costs to free trade—the people whose jobs are destroyed, the businesses that fail, and the communities devastated. If we counted the lost incomes, the abandoned schools, sewers, and other local infrastructure, free markets might not appear so efficient. Also we must remember that in the 1980s free markets gave us leveraged buy-outs with junk bonds, overbuilding in commercial real estate, and stock market speculation, in addition to rising poverty and inequality.

Finally, despite the above policies, there will still be many industries that are hurt by international competition. To soften the human suffering in those cases of massive dislocation, trade readjustment aid needs to be increased. Retraining programs for displaced workers, relocation allowances, and subsidies will help the impacted communities attract new businesses, in addition to helping to reduce human suffering and increase economic efficiency by providing access to new skills and encouraging mobility of resources. And, clearly, full employment is necessary to make these policies work.

The key issue here is that worker retraining and relocation, community investment, and other policies are necessary if we want to manage the transition from an industrial to post-industrial economy. Similar transitions in the past were, by default, paid for by the people and communities left behind by the creative-destructive changes brought about by capitalist development.

However, restructuring the world economy and our international economic policies are not enough. We also need to develop new policies, in light of the changes in the international economy, to rebuild a more equitable and democratic domestic economy.

Let me conclude by emphasizing that real political leadership is called for. The American people must be convinced that there is no painless solution. The power of special interest groups must not be allowed to thwart the needed reforms. In addition, real philosophic differences seperate the American people: free markets versus government intervention, individual responsibility versus community obligations, and so on. And, certainly, there will be conflict among nations over changes in international trading practices.

Whatever we do, old policies will not work.

Globalizers of the World, Unite!

DANIEL DREZNER

The past decade has not been kind to the nation-state. Its economic and security functions have been called into question. The advanced industrial states have lost much of their influence over the global economy, a trend epitomized in September 1992 by the collapse of the pound sterling on "Black Wednesday," when a speculator's bet proved stronger than the full faith and credit of the British Treasury. Governments today have little choice but to privatize their economies and pursue rigidly stable macroeconomic policies. Powerful multinational corporations circumvent states, conducting their own foreign affairs and international agreements (Strange 1992). If the leading industrial nations have found themselves constrained, weaker states have been torn asunder. Culture and ethnicity, thought insignificant during the Cold War, have proven stronger than state institutions in Yugoslavia and the Soviet Union. Many governments face a situation of juridical but not actual sovereignty over their territories (Jackson 1990). All told, the Westphalian system of state sovereignty looks much weaker at the end of this century than at its mid-point.

Daniel Drezner is Assistant Professor of Political Science at the University of Colorado at Boulder.
Reprinted by permission, Washington Quarterly Winter 1998, Vol. 21, Issue 1, pages 209–226.

The nation-state's eroding influence is underscored by the recent spate of books predicting its demise. Kenichi Ohmae argues that the authority invested in nation-states is devolving to regional organizations. For Samuel Huntington, the civilization is replacing the state as the primary unit in global politics. Francis Fukuyama and Benjamin Barber believe that global economic forces are creating a homogeneous world culture, making the state superfluous. Robert Kaplan is the most apocalyptic, claiming that demographic and environmental changes will lead to the end of the nation-state and the beginning of chaos.

These books split along economic and cultural lines. Ohmae, Barber, and Fukuyama focus on globalization—the cluster of political, economic, and technological changes that have reduced barriers to exchange. Huntington and Kaplan emphasize the renewed importance of cultural forces—the growing desire to be part of a tribe or civilization that excludes and barely tolerates the rest of the world. The cumulative effect is akin to a group of doctors bickering about the specific disease but nodding in solemn agreement that the patient is very sick.

Yet, what is striking about these books is not their areas of disagreement, but rather their areas of consensus. All of them echo another philosopher previously considered out of style: Karl Marx. Like Marx, all of these authors are economic determinists. They agree that the global spread of capitalism is eroding the power and autonomy of the nation-state, either through assimilation into a homogeneous global culture or the violent rejection of it. With one important modification—the replacement of class with cultural identity—the modern-day proponents of globalization echo Marx's theories of transnational capital's effect on states, cultures, and individuals developed over a century ago.

The renewed use of Marx is compelling, but ultimately it is not convincing. Undoubtedly, the forces of globalization impose stringent constraints on national governments, but they also empower them in new ways. Globalization does not imply the erosion of the nation-state's authority, but rather a change in state strategies and a redirection of state energies. Furthermore, these books share some of the less savory aspects of Marxism—in particular, the rejection of positive social science and the use of grand theories to make policy proposals. Both of these trends deserve to be resisted. The globalization thesis is seductive, but not satisfactory.

THE ECONOMIC LOGIC OF GLOBALIZATION

Accusing a book of Marxist leanings does not have the same meaning now that it did during the Cold War. None of these authors calls for a proletarian revolution or the overthrow of the bourgeoisie. Rather, they share Marx's belief that changes in political or social relations are a function of changes in the economic mode of production. Some of these books go further, echoing the Marxist mechanisms through which globalization denudes the state of any autonomy. According to Marx, the globalization of capital is detrimental to the nation-state because it weakens the autonomy of state institutions and dissolves the political bonds between the state and its populace. In *The Communist Manifesto*, Marx and Friedrich Engels note,

> The bourgeoisie, whenever it has got the upper hand, has put an end to all feudal, patriarchal, idyllic relations. It has pitilessly torn asunder the motley feudal ties that bound man to his "natural superiors," and has left remaining no other nexus between man and man than naked self-interest, than callous "cash payment." It has drowned the most heavenly ecstasies of religious fervor, of chivalric enthusiasm, of philistine sentimentalism, in the icy water of egoistic calculation. (Tucker 1978, pp. 475–476)

To some extent, Barber, Fukuyama, Huntington, Kaplan, and Ohmae all accept this logic.[1] Ironically, the most vigorous acceptance of Marx's logic has come from those on the right of the political spectrum. Fukuyama is the most explicit in acknowledging his intellectual debt to Marx, observing that his explanation is "a kind of Marxist interpretation of history that leads to a completely non-Marxist conclusion." (p. 131) Whereas Marx focused on the breakdown of institutions, however, Fukuyama concentrates on changes at the cognitive level. Because capitalism requires a universally educated labor force, as well as the mobility of factors of production, individuals lose what Fukuyama refers to as "thymos," or their need for recognition by others.

Individuals must constantly retool for new careers in new cities. The sense of identity provided by regionalism and localism diminishes, and people find themselves retreating into the microscopic world of their families which they carry around with them from place to place like lawn furniture. (p. 325)

The rational part of Fukuyama's individual triumphs over the irrational, thymotic part of the soul. (p. 185) This change in individuals leads to greater cosmopolitanism and cultural homogeneity as people recognize similar social relationships across borders. The decline of thymos and the recognition of a universal culture eliminates any desire to give one's life for some ancient hatred. The result is an audacious prediction:

> Economic forces encouraged nationalism by replacing class with national barriers and created centralized, linguistically homogeneous entities in the process. These same economic forces are now encouraging the breakdown of national barriers through the creation of a single, integrated world market. The fact that the final political neutraliza-

tion of nationalism may not occur in this generation or the next does
not affect the prospect of its ultimately taking place. (p. 275)

Stripped of any economic or patriotic purpose, the nation-state loses its
relevance. Ohmae's prediction of the nation-state's demise is based on
similar grounds but differs slightly in the outcome. He argues that the
spread of the marketplace and the rapid pace of technological change
weaken the social contract between individuals and nations. The globalization of capital leads to a homogenization of cultures, eliminating differences between nationalities or civilizations. Ohmae refers to this
phenomenon as the "Californiaization" of individual preferences, a
blending of taste that blurs differences between states and eradicates historical animosities, making interstate war less likely and thus removing
one of the nation-state's primary functions. At the same time, the spread
of global capital places new economic constraints on the state's role in
economic affairs: "Reflexive twinges of sovereignty make the desired
economic success impossible, because the global economy punishes
twinging countries by diverting investment and information elsewhere."
(p. 12)

Ohmae's original contribution is his prediction that, in the future,
the natural organizing unit will be "region-states," which can be located
within one country, such as Silicon Valley, or across borders, as in Southeast Asia. Regional variations in economic growth within the nation-state
generate political and economic conflicts. More dynamic regions start to
question the wisdom of subsidizing less dynamic regions within the same
country, whereas intraregional ethnic tensions decline: "Indeed, because
the orientation of region-states is toward the global economy, not toward
their host nations, they help breed an internationalism of outlook that de-
fuses many of the usual kinds of social tensions." (p. 94) Echoing Marx,
Ohmae predicts that the global reach of the marketplace will constrain the
nation-state and induce a cosmopolitanism that renders it irrelevant.

Barber's description of globalization in *Jihad vs. McWorld* is perhaps
the closest in spirit to Marx, although his metaphors are unquestionably
juicier. His definition of the global marketplace—what he calls Mc-
World—is that future in shimmering pastels, a busy portrait of onrushing
economic, technological, and ecological forces that demand integration
and uniformity and that mesmerize peoples everywhere with fast music,
fast computers, and fast food—MTV, Macintosh, and McDonald's—pressing nations into one homogeneous global theme park. (p. 4)

His mechanism for McWorld's erosion of the nation-state echoes
Marx as well. Globalization creates new sources of economic power and
a universal culture, stripping the nation-state of its economic and political rationales.

Jihad vs. McWorld differs from the other books in two respects. First, Barber attaches more importance to multinational corporations, particularly the media conglomerates that control the means of intellectual production. This emphasis places him closer to Marx's vision of monopoly capital than the other authors considered here. Second, Barber recognizes that the disruptive effects of McWorld will lead to an inevitable backlash within each culture; his use of "Jihad" refers to this rejection of modernization and cosmopolitanism. In the end, however, McWorld will win out, or so he says: "My prediction that Jihad will eventually (if not any time soon) be defeated by McWorld rests almost entirely on the long-term capacity of global information and global culture to overpower parochialism and to integrate or obliterate partial identities." (p. 82) In this prediction, Barber has merely updated Marx to the Information Age.

By stressing the direct economic effects of globalization, the first three books implicitly focus their energies on the developed world. In *The Ends of the Earth,* Kaplan looks at a slice of the developing world but comes to the same conclusions about the effects of the global market on the nation-state. More than the other authors, however, Kaplan examines the effect of the global market on states that resist laissez-faire policies. In most cases, he says, it erodes the state's monopoly on coercive violence. Corruption and the pursuit of government favors destroy the coherence of institutions designed to resist the expansion of the free market. He observes, "The border existed to tax the wealthy and to provide jobs and supplemental income for government bureaucrats. It was a wealth-transfer mechanism." (p. 73) In many of the areas he describes, in particular West Africa and Central Asia, little difference seems to exist today between states and armies, armies and militias, militias and criminal gangs. In the developing world, coercive power has become a marketable commodity. The breakdown of the state's monopoly on coercive violence is powerful testimony to the erosion of the nation-state.

The dominant themes in Kaplan's book involve how environmental and demographic change affects cultures and states. His source of ideas is Thomas F. Homer-Dixon (1991), an academic who stresses environmental factors as the cause of conflict. In particular, Kaplan argues that soil erosion and mass urbanization are the main causes of the nation-state's demise. This argument, he thinks, replaces "social-social" theory with "physical-social" theory. He fails to appreciate that the physical factors he mentions are the outcomes of economic causes, namely the spread of industrialization to the developing world. Kaplan's environmental and demographic mechanisms are different, but the causes are still economic and the effect remains the erosion of state power. In the end, his characterization of the modern world economy parallels Marx:

> In a sense, the world economy has become a larger version of pre-revolutionary Iran's, where in the 1960s and 1970s per capita income rose from $200 to $1,000. But the rise was unevenly distributed, and a large subproletariat was created in the process. The result was upheaval. (p. 381)

Although his causal mechanism differs, and although he never acknowledges it, Kaplan shares Marx's economic determinism. Even Huntington's *Clash of Civilizations*, though the most removed from the theory of globalization, uses some of Marx's argument. Huntington concedes that the spread of the free market has created a homogeneous set of values for the global elite. He refers to this as the Davos Culture, after the World Economic Forum held in Switzerland every year; indeed, his description of this group of people sounds eerily reminiscent of Marx's description of the bourgeoisie:

> They generally share beliefs in individualism, market economies, and political democracy, which are also common among people in Western civilization. Davos people control virtually all international institutions, many of the world's governments, and the bulk of the world's economic and military capabilities. (p. 57)

Huntington differs from the other authors only in arguing that cultural homogenization is restricted to the elite level and fails to trickle down into a more cosmopolitan outlook among non-Western populations.

This does not mean globalization has no effect in Huntington's vision of the world. Rather, he argues that it needs to be parsed into modernization and Westernization. Most of the world embraces the effects of modernization: technological dynamism and the reduction of barriers to economic exchange. Yet, the Western values associated with modernization, such as democracy and individual liberty, generate a backlash that Huntington believes strengthens civilizational, as opposed to national, identities:

> The most obvious, most salient, and most powerful cause of the global religious resurgence is precisely what was supposed to cause the death of religion: the processes of social, economic, and cultural modernization that swept across the world in the latter half of the twentieth century. Long-standing sources of identity and systems of authority are disrupted. People move from the countryside into the city, become separated from their roots, and take new jobs or no job. They interact with large numbers of strangers and are exposed to new sets of relationships. They need new sources of identity. (p. 97)

With this logic, Huntington agrees with the other authors that globalization is eroding the autonomy of the nation-state; any disagreement is over the precise mechanism through which this occurs. Ohmae, Barber, and Fukuyama stress the ability of global capitalism to reduce the nation-state's economic role and to create a genuine cosmopolitanism that erodes its political role. Huntington and Kaplan believe it is in the negative reaction to this cosmopolitanism that identities change.

THE NATION-STATE AND THE REACTION
TO GLOBAL CAPITALISM

Just as these authors share Marx's belief in economic determinism to some degree, they also (with the exception of Ohmae) share Marx's use of the dialectic. They acknowledge that the forces of globalization generate social upheaval and resistance to the free market. They further agree that these reactions create new movements led by educated urban elites and consisting of workers alienated by the callousness of capitalism. But at this point, the similarities with Marx, and with each other, end.

Marx believed that capitalism would alienate the laborers from the global economic system, creating a transnational class consciousness of workers. One hundred and fifty years after *The Communist Manifesto*, the new globalizers recognize that cultural identity remains more powerful than class identity. Because cultural identities do not match up well with existing state boundaries, the nation-state is thus caught between the cross-pressures of globalization and the fragmentation produced in reaction to it, weakening state power and sovereignty.

Fukuyama and Ohmae mention the threat of ethnic fragmentation primarily to dismiss it.[2] For them, the economic forces for cosmopolitanism are too great. Barber acknowledges the reaction in his description of Jihad, but he also believes that it is a transient phenomenon. Kaplan and Huntington, on the other hand, devote most of their books to the reaction to globalization.

Of all of the books, Barber's may be the best at describing the interplay between the forces of globalization and fragmentation. He points out that the forces of Jihad are a direct result of the forces of globalization: "Jihad stands not so much in stark opposition as in subtle counterpoint to McWorld and is itself a dialectical response to modernity whose features both reflect and reinforce the modern world's virtues and vices—Jihad via McWorld rather than Jihad versus McWorld." (p. 157) He shrewdly observes that these reactionary movements exploit the same technological advances as those in favor of globalization. Modernization enhances the ability of these rejectionist groups to mobilize. He does not think this will benefit nation-states: "Jihad, even in its most pacific manifestations, almost always turns out to be not simply a struggle on behalf of an ethnic fragment for self-determination, but a compound struggle within that fragment that risks still greater fragmentation and plenty of confusion as well." (p. 119) He makes the expected references to the Middle East and the former Soviet Union, but to show that Jihad is also a global phenomenon, he also devotes chapters to the United States and Western Europe. In an ironic counterpoint to Ohmae's *The End of the Nation-State*, Barber claims that regional entities will increase their power because of ethnic rather than economic motivations.

Kaplan sums up his empirical conclusions with the following line: "All I had learned so far was that states in West Africa, the Near East, and Central Asia were weakening, and that ethno-religious identities appeared stronger by contrast." (p. 272) Kaplan's descriptions are compelling. West Africa has seen violent ethnic conflicts and a growing resentment of Lebanese immigrants. Turkey and Iran fear the secession of Kurdish and Azeri minorities; Egypt fears the rise of Islamic fundamentalism. From his description, Pakistan is not so much a state as a collection of clans and drug warlords. Everywhere he looks, Kaplan finds states incapable of coping with the environmental and geographic implications of modernization; in their place, new identities are formed, based on religion or ethnicity.

If these observations were confined to the countries south of the equator, then Kaplan's book would have few implications for the more powerful and established nation-states. But he goes further in his conclusions, asserting that these are global problems:

> Many of the problems I saw around the world—poverty, the collapse of cities, porous borders, cultural and racial strife, growing economic disparities, weakening nation-states—are problems for Americans to think about. I thought of America everywhere I looked. We cannot escape a more populous, interconnected world of crumbling borders. (p. 436)

Yet he is extremely pessimistic that the United States or the developed world can do anything about these problems: "We are not in control. As societies grow more populous and more complex, the idea that a global elite like the UN can engineer reality from above is just as absurd as the idea that political 'scientists' can reduce any of this to a science." (p. 436) Academic aspersions aside, Kaplan's statement reveals his belief that both globalization and the reaction to it are structural changes that cannot be thwarted by policymakers.

For Huntington, the reaction to modernization and the rejection of "Western" values leads to an erosion of the nation-state's power:

> Political boundaries increasingly are redrawn to coincide with cultural ones: ethnic, religious, and civilizational. Cultural communities are replacing Cold War blocs, and the fault lines between civilizations are becoming the central lines of conflict in global politics. (p. 125)

This occurs through three mechanisms. First, states lose their identity relative to civilizations and thus reject the practices of realpolitik that govern the Westphalian world order. They have no choice but to ally with states of the same civilization. Second, many states face internal divisions because they straddle civilizational fault lines, or because their leaders tried in the past to imprint Western values upon their societies and only partially succeeded. The roster of conflicted states includes China, Germany, India, Iran, Japan, Mexico, Russia, South Africa, Turkey, and Ukraine.

Third—and this is where Huntington follows Kaplan's strategy of analyzing international relations to urge a change in U.S. domestic policy—Western civilization faces internal threats from immigration and multiculturalism:

> Western culture is challenged by groups within Western societies. One such challenge comes from immigrants from other civilizations who reject assimilation and continue to adhere to and propagate the values, customs, and cultures of their home societies. . . . In the name of multiculturalism they have attacked the identification of the United States with Western civilization, denied the existence of a common American culture, and promoted racial, ethnic, and other subnational cultural identities and groupings. (pp. 304–305)

Just as other civilizations are challenging the West, the permeability of state borders has diminished the ability of Western civilization to respond. Huntington, like Kaplan, believes that the developing world's reaction to globalization will spread, tearing apart the advanced industrial states as well.

CRITIQUING THE LAST SEDUCTION

Marxism was a seductive philosophy because it attempted to explain, well, everything. These books make the same theoretical leap, and the effect, sometimes, is dazzling. In the face of explanations that unite disparate facts and trends, it is tempting to embrace their claims. Yet, rather than join the chorus of mourners for the nation state, I contend that the arguments for economic determinism do not stand up to empirical or theoretical scrutiny. Empirically, much of the evidence provided in the books is inconclusive. Theoretically, the economic and cultural forces unleashed by globalization impose new constraints on countries, but not a straight-jacket. Globalization also creates new strategies and roles for the nation-state.

Empirically, these books leave many questions unanswered (*The End of History and the Last Man* excepted, as it is primarily a theoretical tract). These books were written for a relatively broad audience and thus skip over much of the drudgery of data collection and fact checking, which leads to some sloppiness. With so much ground to cover, each of the books have their factual faux-pas. For example, Kaplan states that the United States actually has less enmity and deeper military, economic, and educational links with Iran than either Japan or Germany. (p. 186) Fukuyama claims that Russian nationalism is neither expansionist nor a powerful force within Russia. (p. 272) Barber includes South Korea as an example of how free markets can be divorced from free political institutions. (p. 184) Huntington asserts an Islamic revival in post-Soviet Central Asia that has yet to be observed by others. (pp. 96–97) And Ohmae categorizes North Korea as having a higher per capita income than China. (pp. 90–91)

Even when the facts are correct, however, they do not necessarily corroborate the authors' claims. Kaplan and Ohmae commit this error in different ways. Kaplan "discovers" that countries with corrupt governments, stagnant economies, and short histories of statehood are falling apart. In other words, he looks only at failed states and concludes that all states are failing. He believes these trends can be generalized to the rest of the world, yet his own descriptions contradict him. In the countries where statehood has a longer tradition, such as Turkey, Iran, and Thailand, Kaplan finds a stronger state and a less fragmented populace. This distinction severs the contagion effect Kaplan wants to ascribe to events in West Africa and Central Asia.

Ohmae makes the mistake of most business gurus: In looking only at the economically successful, he analyzes a biased sample and thus reaches flawed conclusions.[3] Ohmae provides no compelling evidence that information technologies favor regional units of economic organization. Many of the traits that Ohmae describes in successful region-states are also evident in areas that have yet to experience rapid economic growth (Saxenian 1989), implying that the region is not the natural unit of organization across the globe. Furthermore, his East Asian examples present a paradox. On the one hand, he uses the Pacific Rim to show that the nation-state is losing its relevance in the borderless economy. In making this argument, he seems to have ignored the rising defense budgets of most states in the region, the collective effort to suppress internal dissent, and the sovereignty dispute over the Spratly Islands. In the part of the globe where his argument should be the most powerful, the nation-state remains a robust institution.

Barber's description in *Jihad vs. McWorld* is certainly vivid, but his evidence consists of anecdotes, film revenue reports, and rock lyrics, none of which proves his theory that capitalism erodes democracy. Indeed, Robert Putnam (1993) offers a rigorous analysis of the ingredients of a good democracy and concludes that economics has very little to do with it; the bonds of civic association are far more resilient than Barber claims. Barber contradicts himself on the ability of markets to erode state power, railing at Rupert Murdoch for his repeated concessions to the Chinese government. Furthermore, the claim that globalization strips states of their domestic autonomy does not have much empirical support; studies of economic integration suggest that governments have been able to increase their role, even in a globalizing economy (Garrett 1995; Hallenberg 1996; Katzenstein 1985).

As for cultural homogenization, Barber's references to movies and MTV are not enough to prove his point. He describes a thin gruel of global culture but ignores the richer cultural stew that all countries, the United States included, possess. In describing the aspects of culture that can move across boundaries, he fails to realize that much of what defines culture is immobile. To Barber's credit, he tries to show the forces of Jihad in the areas where it would be least expected, such as Western Europe and the United States. The problem is, he finds very tenuous support for his thesis. Even in the areas where fragmentation would be expected, such as the former Soviet Union, his knowledge is at best superficial and at worst wrong.[4]

Huntington's book is the best researched of the lot, but his evidence could be interpreted in several ways. For example, to show a resurgent Confucian civilization in East Asia, he liberally quotes Lee Kuan Yew and Mahathir Mohamad asserting the existence of distinct Asian values. Fair enough, but these two are leaders of relatively small countries—Singapore and Malaysia—trying to maintain their internal control; it is not surprising that they would use such rhetoric as a way of increasing their power and prestige. Huntington also uses the length and viciousness of ethnic conflicts as proof that "fault-line" civilizational wars are longer and bloodier than other conflicts. But not all ethnic conflicts are civilizational, as Rwanda and Northern Ireland attest. Wars based along clan lines (Somalia) or ideology (Cambodia) can be just as long and just as bloody.

This is not the first time the proponents of the globalization thesis have cried wolf. Marx's predictions about the subjugation of national governments to transnational capital did not occur in the nineteenth century. In 1907, a Prussian official complained: "In our time of international trade, the telephone and the telegram, the owners of 'mobile capital' are in no way bound to a specific residence. If the demands of the state on their performance become too large, then the danger is near that they will brush the Prussian dust from their feet and leave."[5] E. H. Carr (1945) wrote during World War II that state sovereignty "is being sapped by modern technological developments which have made the nation obsolescent as the unit of military and economic organization, and are rapidly concentrating effective decision and control in the hands of great multi-national units." (p. 39) In 1969, noted economist Charles Kindleberger argued that the nation-state "was just about through as an economic unit."[6] None of these predictions came true.

THE NATION-STATE AT THE NEW MILLENNIUM

Theoretically, the global trends described in these books should enhance both the economic and political role of the nation-state. Economically, the constraints of global finance have three positive effects. First, although states must abdicate certain responsibilities, such as the ownership of corporations and the ability to manipulate the trade-off between inflation and unemployment, most countries were never particularly successful at these tasks to begin with. Government ownership of firms rarely provides the best management, and the inflation/unemployment trade-off is a temporary expedient that breaks down over the long run. In the language of business, shedding these functions empowers states to focus on their core competencies.[7]

Second, rather than the inevitable race to the bottom, globalization can encourage states to coordinate their regulatory policies. The European Union added a social chapter that even Great Britain might join.[8] The North American Free Trade Agreement (NAFTA) imposed more stringent labor and environmental conditions for Mexico. Globally, the Montreal Protocol moved toward the ban of chlorofluorocarbons. Since 1990, the United Nations (UN) has been much more willing to impose multilateral economic sanctions for violations of international norms.[9] States clearly retain the option of interventionist policies in some areas of economic life. Although enforcement is a problem with some of these policies, it is not an insurmountable one. And although coordination can lead to reduced state powers, it can also lead to an enhanced state role (Cohen 1996).

Finally, the increased mobility of capital forces the nation-state to focus on the location of innovation rather than production. This benefits both the state and society. Economists agree that the greatest source of economic growth is technological change (Denison 1974; Abramovitz 1989; Boskin and Lau 1992). A renewed focus on innovation can only expand the economic pie for society. Furthermore, economists also agree that the state can and should play a role in fostering technological innovation. States are assigned tasks, such as the provision of public goods and the establishment of the necessary rules and institutions, that cannot be easily replicated by other actors. Economically, the globalization of markets implies the redirection, not the elimination, of the nation-state's role.

The state's political role also remains. The renaissance of cultural and ethnic identities might spell doom for some nation-states, but not for the nation-state in general. There is a sense in some of these books that ethnic and cultural conflict are the inevitable result of ancient hatreds. In fact, recent work suggests that governments successfully manipulate these ethnic identities to enhance their own power (Gagnon 1995; Chege 1996). Regretfully, this often implies war and bloodshed, but it also shows that states still provide people with their strongest identities. Sometimes this can take relatively benign forms, as in France or the United States. Sometimes, as in Rwanda, it leads to genocide. Furthermore, many ethnic conflicts are not over cultural disagreements, but rather over who controls the machinery of the state. Breakaway groups do not want to abolish the nation-state; they want their own.[10] The nation-state is not a hostage to ancient hatreds; one of its political roles is to manipulate these identities, and, one can hope, to direct them toward peaceable ends.

Globalization and its ripple effects do create new constraints for the nation-state. In part, the adaptability of national governments to their new roles explains the varying fortunes of nation-states in this decade. Paradoxically, at the same time as globalizers are claiming the end of the Westphalian system, the United States has increased its relative power and influence. It has strengthened its lead in the military applications of information technologies (Nye and Owens 1996). It has been more willing to use economic statecraft as a policy tool. Beyond its ability to project coercive power, the United States has also increased its co-optive or "soft" power, because the economic changes caused by globalization mirror the preferences of U.S. society and ideology (Nye 1990). Even the collapse of several developing world states hints at the strength of the great powers. These states collapsed in part because the United States and other former colonizers declined to intervene to prop up failing regimes. The great powers are still capable of performing this function when they choose, as in Haiti and Albania, but the end of the Cold War removed the incentive to intervene everywhere.

Finally, each author makes the mistake of assuming that state sovereignty is an absolute and indivisible commodity. Stephen D. Krasner (1995) notes that the violations of sovereignty that have been observed recently are nothing new; since its inception, the Westphalian norm of absolute state sovereignty has been consistently violated by other states. Even if the nation-state is weakening in the face of global forces, it still has a few centuries of life remaining. Its death is likely to be as slow as its birth.

SOCIAL SCIENCE AND POLICYMAKING

The final connection between the books reviewed here and Marxist philosophy is a disturbing one. Marx scorned the social philosophies of the nineteenth century, arguing that the point was not to explain the world but to change it. The result was a theory that could never be disproven; Marx's successors made amendments to explain away failures, all the while focusing on political change. What is striking about these five authors' books is the varying degrees of scorn they heap on modern social science—and, like Marx's successors, the fact that they use grand theories as a vehicle for radical policy proposals.

The disregard for political science is particularly noticeable in Kaplan and Barber. Kaplan, for example, argues, a political scientist can do little more than what a journalist does:

> Go to places where there appear to be interesting linkages . . . and see if the causal relationships exist. From this, some useful ideas or theories might emerge. To call it a science, though, is an overstatement. (p. 413)

Barber comes to a similar conclusion:

> The data are too protean to be definitive and the events too vulnerable to distortion by the very probes that effect to explain them to be detachable from the normative frames by which we try to capture them. This is the general problem with pretending that social and political theory can be "scientific." (p. 168)

The other authors are somewhat more generous about the utility of political science, but they reject the accepted theories of international relations as outdated and sterile.

It is a rite of passage for Washington policymakers to bash academics for their scientific pretensions and abstract theorizing. There is certainly enough bad political science to justify it. Nevertheless, it is a dangerous tactic, because it tarnishes a singularly useful purpose of social scientists vis-a-vis policymakers: the role of the critic. Politicians have the incentive to use dubious theories when they are politically expedient (Blinder 1987). Academics test arguments for their theoretical and empirical rigor to filter out those that may be emotionally appealing but wrong. This is useful to policymakers, because it tells them which theories should be ignored and which merit further attention. Scholarly criticism can make a difference. For example, Paul Krugman (1995) has performed an exemplary service in de-bunking theories of pop internationalism. One wonders whether the accusations against social science made in these books are not self-inoculations against academic criticisms down the line.

Why have so many grand theories been put forward? I would argue that it is a nostalgic, anachronistic search for an American grand strategy. One of the virtues of the Cold War was that the United States had an overarching framework of containment that dictated most of its foreign policy and some of its domestic policies. Many in the policy community look at the frequent chaos of U.S. foreign policy today and conclude that we need a new universal framework. All of these books attempt to provide it, but globalization is not the constraint on U.S. policy that Soviet power was during the era of bipolarity. Accepting this false analogy would lead to an artificial reduction of U.S. policy options.

CONCLUSION

These books agree with each other on at least four points. First, the nation-state is losing its influence in world politics. Second, this weakening is caused either directly or indirectly by global market forces. Some argue, akin to Marx, that economic forces directly affect the nation-state by constraining its economic functions and creating a homogeneous global culture that weakens nationalist sentiments. Others argue that economic forces are indirectly responsible, because they generate a cultural backlash that re-ignites older identities not associated with the nation-state. Third, these effects are global; they are not confined to the developed or developing world. Fourth, conventional social science cannot explain these changes.

These arguments challenge conventional paradigms and are genuinely thought-provoking. In the end, however, they are no more persuasive than the original Marxist argument. Whereas much of the description is accurate, it does not imply an erosion of the nation-state's authority, but rather a redefinition of its role in the international system. As a guide for the modern-day constraints on the nation-state, the globalization thesis can serve a useful purpose. Yet, the nation-state has faced constraints since Westphalia, and it has not withered away; some trends these authors mention empower rather than weaken states. As a framework for policy advice, or a map of the future, the globalization thesis leaves a great deal to be desired.

I am grateful to Page Fortna, Mark Lawrence, Timothy Snyder, Jeff Legro, Mary Elise Sarotte, Tim Snyder, and especially James McAllister for their advice. Any errors are my own.

NOTES

1. This has been observed elsewhere. Falk (1997) notes, "In paradoxical fashion, the Marxist account of the relation between economic and political power seems persuasive only after Marxism has lost its capacity to win adherents to its world view." (p. 135)
2. Fukuyama's tone in The End of History and the Last Man is more somber than in his original essay. In his final chapters, he warns that if capitalism leads to the erosion of civil society, individuals will resort to violence to

express their thymotic urges. Yet, this warning contradicts his earlier claim that the end of history is the victory of the rational over the thymotic part of the human soul.

3. Another example of this error is Peters and Waterman (1982).
4. For example, his description of Ukraine on pp. 199–200 is badly off; its first president was not "lethally nationalist" and its current one does not have a pro-Russian tilt. Barber clearly derived these characterizations from the 1994 presidential election between Leonid Kuchma and Leonid Kravchok, but he fails to separate campaign rhetoric from actual policies of either leader.
5. Quoted in Hallenberg (1996), p. 336.
6. Quoted in Cohen (1996), p. 294.
7. I do not want to imply a Panglossian view on globalization's constraints on the state. In the future, it is questionable whether the nation-state will be able to ameliorate the distributional conflicts caused by globalization. Rodrik (1997) provides an excellent account of how globalization can impair the state's ability to fulfill these tasks. Yet, Rodrik also concedes that the state might not be the institution best suited for this task.
8. See Rodrik (1997) for a more pessimistic appraisal of the European Union social chapter.
9. The Security Council has mandated economic sanctions seven times since 1990, as opposed to twice during the UN's first 45 years of existence.
10. The case of Moldova is instructive. Prior to World War II, Moldova was historically part of Romania. Annexed by the Soviet Union in 1945, the alphabet was changed from Roman to Cyrillic, and the republic's language was called Moldavian rather than Romanian. After the break-up, there was a push in Moldova to reunite with Romania. In the end, however, Moldova's leaders decided they did not want to relinquish political power, and therefore spurned any integration with Romania. Even though this state has little history independent of Romania, it survives.

BOOKS REVIEWED

Benjamin Barber, *Jihad vs. McWorld.* New York: Times Books, 1995.
Francis Fukuyama, *The End of History and the Last Man.* New York: Free Press, 1992.
Samuel Huntington, *The Clash of Civilizations and the Remaking of World Order.* New York: Simon and Schuster, 1996.
Robert Kaplan, *The Ends of the Earth: A Journey at the Dawn of the 21st Century.* New York: Random House, 1996.
Kenichi Ohmae, *The End of the Nation State: The Rise of Regional Economies.* New York: Free Press, 1995.

REFERENCES

Moses Abramovitz, *Thinking About Growth and Other Essays of Economic Growth and Welfare* (Cambridge: Cambridge University Press, 1989).
Alan Blinder, *Hard Heads, Soft Hearts: Tough-Minded Economics for a Just Society* (Reading, Mass.: Addison-Wesley, 1987).

Michael Boskin and Laurence Lau, "Capital, Technology, and Economic Growth," in Nathan Rosenberg, Ralph Landau, and David Mowery, eds., *Technology and the Wealth of Nations* (Stanford: Stanford University Press, 1992).

Edward Hallett Carr, *Nationalism and After* (New York: Macmillan, 1945).

Michael Chege, "Africa's Murderous Professors," *National Interest* 46 (Winter 1996), pp. 32–40.

Benjamin J. Cohen, "Phoenix Risen: The Resurrection of Global Finance," *World Politics 48* (January 1996), pp. 268–296.

Edward Denison, *Accounting for U.S. Economic Growth, 1929–1969* (Washington, D.C.: The Brookings Institution, 1974).

Richard Falk, "State of Siege: Will Globalization Win Out?" *International Affairs 73* (January 1997), pp. 123–136.

V. P. Gagnon, "Ethnic Nationalism and International Conflict: The Case of Serbia," *International Security* 19 (Winter 1995), pp. 130–166.

Geoffrey Garrett, "Capital Mobility, Trade, and the Domestic Politics of Economic Policy," *International Organization* 49 (Autumn 1995), pp. 657–688.

Avner Greif, Paul Milgrom, and Barry Weingast, "Coordination, Commitment, and Enforcement: The Case of the Merchant Guild," *Journal of Political Economy 102* (December 1994), pp. 745–776.

Mark Hallenberg, "Tax Competition in Wilhelmine Germany and Its Implications for the European Union," *World Politics* (April 1996), pp. 324–357.

Thomas Homer-Dixon, "On the Threshold: Environmental Changes as Causes of Acute Conflict," *International Security* 16 (Fall 1991), pp. 76–116.

Robert Jackson, *Quasi-States: Sovereignty, International Relations, and the Third World* (New York: Cambridge University Press, 1990).

Peter Katzenstein, *Small States in World Markets* (Ithaca, N.Y.: Cornell University Press, 1985).

Stephen D. Krasner, "Compromising Westphalia," *International Security 20* (Winter 1995), pp. 115–151.

Paul Krugman, *Pop Internationalism* (Cambridge, Mass.: MIT Press, 1995).

Joseph Nye and William Owens, "America's Information Edge," *Foreign Affairs* 75 (March/April 1996), pp. 20–36.

Mancur Olson, *The Rise and Decline of Nations* (New Haven, Conn: Yale University Press, 1982).

Thomas Peters and Robert Waterman Jr., *In Search of Excellence: Lessons from America's Best-Run Companies* (New York: Harper and Row, 1982).

Robert Putnam, *Making Democracy Work: Civic Traditions in Modern Italy* (Princeton, N.J.: Princeton University Press, 1993).

Dani Rodrik, *Has Globalization Gone Too Far?* (Washington, D.C.: Institute for International Economics, 1997).

AnnaLee Saxenian, "The Cheshire Cat's Grin: Innovation, Regional Development, and the Cambridge Case," *Economy and Society 18* (November 1989), pp. 448–477.

Susan Strange, "States, Firms, and Diplomacy," *International Affairs* 68 (January 1992), pp. 1–15.

Robert C. Tucker, ed., *The Marx-Engels Reader* (New York: W. W. Norton, 1978).

Issue 2
Globalization and the Nation State

INTRODUCTION

There is no doubt about it. A communications and information revolution has hit the world. Suppose that Rip van Winkle woke up today after being asleep for twenty years. Can you imagine the shock he would experience? He would witness people walking down the street talking on tiny portable telephones—after being beeped on their pagers. He would see computers the size of notebooks that are more powerful than most mainframes that had been in use when he dozed off. And he would discover near-instantaneous access to a mind-boggling array of information on the Internet.

In the first article in this set, Walter B. Wriston shows how these marvels in communications and information processing are limiting the ability of national governments to control what occurs within their territories. How can a dictatorship control the information that its people get when they can watch CNN? How can a government control the value of its currency when bankers move billions of dollars across the world electronically every day?

Is all of this electronic portability a threat to national sovereignty? Wriston thinks so and seems concerned about the possibility. But for him to come to that conclusion is a bit ironic. He was, after all, chief executive of Citicorp for seventeen years before his retirement in 1984. Under his leadership, that premier banking institution was in the forefront of applying information and communication technology to finance. Moreover, during Wriston's tenure, Citicorp was a major lender to Third World governments, whose sovereignty undoubtedly came into question when loans had to be rescheduled for fear of default.

The second article in this set, by Anne-Marie Slaughter, notes that some observers, working from information like Wriston's, have come to the conclusion that the nation-state is dying or is already effectively dead. That bit of hyperbole is nothing new. Forty years before Wriston's article was published, political scientist John Herz came to the dire conclusion that nuclear weapons had effectively caused the demise of the nation-state. His main point was that protecting its territory is an essential function of the nation-state and that atomic weapons make it impossible for even the most powerful countries to ensure that their citizens can be free from fear of attack. Of course, Herz later recanted after watching many new nations come into being, with the nuclear stalemate between the big powers providing some security.

Slaughter, a well-known Harvard University law professor, says that people today who argue that the nation-state is dying because of the information/communications revolution are overstating the situation. So are those who say that supranational organizations—like the United Nations or the European Union—are becoming all-powerful. Slaughter proposes a middle ground between these extreme views.

As you read the articles, consider the following questions.

Discussion Questions

1. In what ways has near-instantaneous satellite communication affected the way that governments conduct their relations with one another? Does this phenomenon better promote peace and security in the world? Is it possible for diplomatic communication to be too easy, too frequent?
2. Some observers argue that quick and easy international communications can help empower ordinary citizens in dealing with repressive governments in these countries. How might this happen?
3. Some people believe that speedy communications cause economic or political problems within countries to become contagious, spreading quickly to other countries. Do you believe that this is a problem? If so, can anything be done to prevent it?

   For more on this topic, visit the following websites:

   `http://www.strassman.com/pubs/dsb-iwd.html`
   (report of the Defense Science Board Task Force on Information Warfare, mentioned in the Wriston article)

   `http://terraserver.microsoft.com`
   (satellite photos of much of the U. S., Europe, and Asia)

   `http://wwwhost.cc.utexas.edu/ftp/pub/grg/gcraft/notes/gps/gps.html`
   (an elaborate site explaining the Global Positioning System for determining location and for navigation; by Prof. Peter Dana of the University of Texas at Austin)

Bits, Bytes, and Diplomacy:
The Third Technological Revolution

WALTER B. WRISTON

An American historian once opined, "Peace is the mastery of great forces; it is not the solution of a problem."[1] Great new forces are at work in the world, and if we are to master them, the beginning of wisdom is to recognize that the world is changing dramatically and at unprecedented speed. We are in the midst of a revolution. A revolution by definition causes old power structures to crumble and new ones to rise. The catalyst—but not the cause—has always been technological change. Now, as in revolutions past, technology is profoundly affecting the sovereignty of governments, the world economy, and military strategy.

We are now living in the midst of the third great revolution in history. When the principle of the lever was applied to make a plow, the agricultural revolution was born, and the power of nomadic tribal chiefs declined. When centuries later, men substituted the power of water, steam, and electricity for animal muscle, the Industrial Revolution was born. Both of these massive changes took centuries to unfold. Each caused a shift in the power structure. Today, the marriage of computers and telecommunications has ushered in the Information Age, which is as different from the Industrial Age as that period was from the Agricultural Age. Information technology has demolished time and distance. Instead of validating Orwell's vision of Big Brother watching the citizen, the third revolution enables the citizen to watch Big Brother. And so the virus of freedom, for which there is no antidote, is spread by electronic networks to the four corners of the earth.

History is strewn with wonderful inventions. Most of them were designed to solve specific problems: the wheel to move things, engines to supply power, clocks and compasses to tell time and direction. The inventions that made possible the information revolution were different. They changed the way we solve problems. When Johann Gutenberg pioneered movable type in Europe in 1436, and when Intel designed the integrated circuit in the 1970s, the way we record, store, access, and peruse knowledge made quantum leaps forward and affected not only how we do our jobs, but what we do.

Walter B. Wriston, former chairman and chief executive officer of Citicorp/Citibank, served as chairman of the Economic Policy Advisory Board in the Reagan administration.

Reprinted by permission. *Foreign Affairs*, Sept.–Oct. 1997. Vol. 76, Issue 5, p. 172, 11p.

These two events were just as important as they sound. Gutenberg broke the monopoly of the monks who copied manuscripts by hand and guarded them jealously. They understood that knowledge was power and sometimes chained books to the shelves. In *The Discoverers,* Daniel Boorstin cites a 12th-century manuscript inscription: "This book belongs to the monastery of St. Mary of Robert's Bridge, who ever shall steal it from this house, or mutilate it let him be forever cursed. Amen." Contrast that mindset with the ability of a researcher anywhere in the world with a computer and a modem to tap into the entire database of the Library of Congress, the Bibliothèque de France, or the British Library. In today's parlance, this change constitutes a paradigm shift.

George Gilder explains that "the key to paradigm shifts is the collapse of formerly pivotal scarcities, the rise of new forms of abundance, and the onset of new scarcities. Successful innovators use these new forms of abundance to redress the emergent shortages."[2] The enormous use of timber for railroad ties and trestles as American railroads pushed west caused Theodore Roosevelt to declare a national shortage of timber, which was soon replaced by an abundance of concrete, iron, and steel. Shortly thereafter, electricity and steam power overcame looming shortages of labor and materials. The recent alleged shortage of broadcast frequencies caused electronic engineers to expand the spectrum's useful frequencies. This cycle has continued throughout history. In the three pillars of the order that resulted from the Industrial Revolution—national sovereignty, national economies, and military power—the information revolution has increased the power of individuals and outmoded old hierarchies.

A GLOBAL VILLAGE

Sovereignty, the power of a nation to stop others from interfering in its internal affairs, is rapidly eroding. When Woodrow Wilson went to Paris to negotiate the Treaty of Versailles, he ordered his postmaster-general to assume control over all transatlantic cable lines in order to censor the news from Europe. Today no one and no nation can block the flow of information across national borders.

During the Persian Gulf War, Saddam Hussein proposed what was viewed in Washington as a phony peace settlement. President Bush had to convey that judgment to the 26 nations in the coalition. As Marlin Fitzwater, former White House Press Secretary, remembers, the "quickest and most effective way was CNN, because all countries in the world had it and were watching it on a real-time basis . . . and 20 minutes after we got the proposal . . . I went on national television . . . to tell the 26 members . . . that the war was continuing." In this and many other instances, the elite foreign policy establishment and its government-to-government communications were bypassed. No highly trained foreign service officer meticulously drafted a note, no secretary of state signed it, and no American ambassadors called on foreign ministers to deliver the message. The United States entrusted a vital diplomatic message to a private television company seen by the whole world. Wilson's strategy was to control the flow of information by fiat, while Bush realized that since he could not beat the world information free market, he had better join it.

Today special interest groups of all kinds, from terrorists to human rights activists, bypass government-based communications channels. In *The News Media in National and International Conflicts*, Andrew Arno explains that when relations sour between two countries "it is often more a matter of strained relations between centers of interest than whole countries." We have seen these forces at work from South Africa to Korea as one pressure group after another steps around national governments to further its own crusade.

The convergence of computers and telecommunications has made us into a global community, ready or not. For the first time in history, rich and poor, north and south, east and west, city and countryside are linked in a global electronic network of shared images in real time. Ideas move across borders as if they did not exist. Indeed, time zones are becoming more important than borders.

Small villages are known as efficient marketplaces of ideas. A village quickly shares news of any innovation, and if anyone gets a raise or new privileges, everyone similarly situated will soon be pressing for the same. And why not? These people are just like me, the villagers say. Why should I not have what they have? The Internet carries conversations between millions of people without regard to gender, race, or color. The impact of the global conversation, like that of a village conversation, is enormous—and it is multiplied many times.

A global village will have global customs. Denying people human rights or democratic freedoms no longer means denying them an abstraction they have never experienced, but violating the established customs of the village. It hardly matters that only a minority of the world's people enjoy such freedoms or the prosperity that goes with them; these are now the benchmarks. More and more people around the globe are demanding more say in their own destiny. Once people are convinced that this is possible, an enormous burden of proof falls on those who would deny them.

The global conversation puts pressure on sovereign governments that over time will influence political processes all over the world. The information revolution is thus profoundly threatening to the power structures of the world, and with good reason. In Prague in 1988 the first protesters in the streets looked into CNN cameras and chanted at the riot police, "The world sees you." And it did. It was an anomaly of history that other Eastern Europeans watched the revolution on CNN relayed by a Russian satellite and mustered the courage to rebel against their own sovereigns. All this has confirmed Abraham Lincoln's sentiment, expressed on his way to his first inauguration, that the American Declaration of Independence "gave liberty not alone to the people of this country, but hope to all the world, for all future time." At the time Lincoln spoke, his words were heard by only a handful of people. It is a testament to his prescience that changes he could not have imagined have brought his words, and freedom itself, to unprecedented portions of humanity.

A NEW SOURCE OF WEALTH

The flood of real-time data has also transformed the international economy. The depth of the global market renders economic theory based on national markets suspect. In the world's financial markets, sovereign governments have lost the ability to influence the price others will pay for their currency on anything but a momentary basis. When I started in the banking business, the total foreign exchange market in New York was only about $50 million. If the Federal Reserve called Citibank or Chase and instructed them to sell $10 million, an order that size could move the market. Today, the market is $1 trillion, and central bank intervention in foreign exchange becomes an expensive exercise in futility. The market is a giant voting machine that records in real time the judgment of traders all over the world about American diplomatic, fiscal, and monetary policies. It has created an information standard that is far more rapid and draconian than the gold standard ever was. Moments after a president announces a policy in the Rose Garden, the market's judgment is reflected in the price of the dollar.

Information technology has also produced a new source of wealth that is not material; it is information—knowledge applied to work to create value. When we apply knowledge to ongoing tasks, we increase productivity. When we apply it to new tasks, we create innovation. The pursuit of wealth is now largely the pursuit of information and its application to the means of production. The rules, customs, skills, and talents necessary to uncover, capture, produce, preserve, and exploit information are now humankind's most important. The competition for the best information has replaced the competition for the best farmland or coal fields. In fact, the appetite to annex territory has already attenuated, and major powers have withdrawn from previously occupied territories.

The new economic powerhouses are masters not of huge material resources, but of ideas and technology. The way the market values companies is instructive: it now places a higher value on intellectual capital than on hard assets like bricks and mortar. Microsoft, with only a relatively small amount of fixed assets, now has a market capitalization well in excess of Ford, General Motors, and Chrysler combined, all of which have huge bases. The powerful economies of Singapore and Hong Kong, countries with virtually no physical assets, demonstrate the growing irrelevance of territory to wealth. This shift requires a different management structure and mindset, and affects not only individual companies, but entire nations.

The changing perception of what constitutes an asset poses huge problems in expanding or even maintaining the power of government. Unlike land or industrial plants, information resources are not bound to geography or easily taxed and controlled by governments. In an economy that consists largely of information products, the government's power to tax and regulate erodes rapidly. Our laws and systems of measurement are becoming artifacts of another age. Bill Gates, with the skills to write and market a complex software system that can produce $1 billion of revenue, can walk past a customs officer anywhere in the world with nothing of "value" to declare, but his wife might have to pay duty on her new ring. Bad data produces bad decisions and leaves us puzzled as to why old policies no longer work. The measures of the industrial society, which count the number of railroad brakemen but do not record the number of computer programmers, highlight a growing problem in setting policy. As DNA research reveals more precise understandings about the way a living organism functions than gross observations of developed biological structures, so we need more precise measures of how nations and companies function in our new environment.

INFORMATION DOMINANCE

These changes affect not only the civilian production machine on which our economic strength rests, but also our military capabilities. In science, there used to be two ways to proceed: the first was to construct a theory, and the second was to conduct a physical experiment. Today we have a third: computer simulation. In the Persian Gulf War, for example, young, basically inexperienced Americans defeated Iraq's feared Republican Guards. A retired colonel asked one commander: "How do you account for your dramatic success, when not a single officer or man in your entire outfit ever had combat experience?" "But we were experienced," said the commander. "We had fought such engagements six times before in complete battle simulation at the National Training Center and in Germany."[3] The U.S. military today is a spectacular example of the replacement of physical assets by information. Information, to be sure, has often made the difference between victory and defeat. Where is the enemy located? How many troops are involved? How are they armed? What is new is the ease and accuracy with which such questions can be answered.

Military intelligence has become much more complex and even has a new name: "information dominance." Today Apache helicopters flying over Bosnia upload detailed pictures of action on the ground to a satellite, record them with a video camera, or beam them directly to local headquarters. Videos taken from the air verify the Dayton accords. Major General William Nash observed that in Bosnia, "We don't have arguments. We hand them pictures, and they move their tanks." This is a long way from 1943, when analysts were hunting through the stacks of the Library of Congress for maps and photographs of possible German targets for Allied bombers since few, if any, were available in the War Department. Today even the ground troops on patrol are equipped with night vision goggles and use a hand-held Global Positioning System device to pinpoint their exact position from satellites. Because the soil is strewn with mines, knowing exactly where you are is a matter of life and death even when there is no fighting. Mines that have been located by an airborne mine detection system are exploded by remotely controlled drone Panther tanks. And so in the military as in civilian life, information in all its forms is replacing hard assets.

Reliance on information technology also has dangerous downsides. The American information infrastructure, in the words of the recent Report of the Defense Science Board Task Force on information Warfare, is "vulnerable to attack" and "creates a tunnel of vulnerability previously unrealized in the history of conflict." Rogue states and groups can conduct information warfare even though they do not command a large military establishment. Today we are witnessing guerrilla warfare, ethnic conflicts, and active terrorist groups. As the Task Force notes:

> Offensive information warfare is attractive to many because it is cheap in relation to the cost of developing, maintaining, and using advanced military capabilities. It may cost little to suborn an insider, create false information, manipulate information, or launch malicious logic-based weapons against an information system connected to the globally shared telecommunications infrastructure. The latter is particularly attractive; the latest information on how to exploit many of the design attributes and security flaws of commercial computer software is freely available on the Internet.

Adversaries, both real and potential, have a lot to work with since the Department of Defense has over two million computers, over 10,000 local-area networks, and over 100 long-distance networks that coordinate and implement every element of its missions, from weapons design to battlefield management. During the calendar year 1995, up to 200,000 intrusions may have been made into the DOD's unclassified computers. These intruders "have modified, stolen and destroyed data and software and shut down computers and networks." Effective diplomacy at critical junctures in any age is backed by the knowledge that if all else fails, military force can be used to attain national goals.

Therefore, vulnerability to an attack on information infrastructure is attracting the attention of a presidential commission and numerous task forces. But with about 90 percent of our military traffic moving over public computer networks, it is increasingly hard to tell the military from the civilian infrastructure. The bureaucratic distinctions between intelligence and law enforcement, between permitted surveillance at home and abroad, may be unsuited for information warfare. There are no borders in cyberspace to mandate these distinctions. The smallest nation, terrorist group, or drug cartel could hire a computer programmer to plant a Trojan horse virus in software, take down a vital network, or cause a missile to misfire. Voltaire said: "God is always for the big battalions." In this new world he may be wrong. The United States' increasing reliance on massive networks may make it more, not less vulnerable.

It may even be unclear what constitutes an act of war. If U.S. satellites suddenly go blind and the telephone network on the eastern seaboard goes down, it is possible that the United States could not even identify the enemy. Its strategic stockpile of weapons would be of little use. There would be no big factory to bomb—only a person somewhere writing software. The possibility of an electronic Pearl Harbor has sparked a debate on how to counter the threat. The Commission on Critical Infrastructure Protection established by President Clinton's executive order is a step in the right direction and has been described in Senate testimony "as the equivalent of the Manhattan Project." It will work at the crossroads of the First Amendment and national security, at the vortex of personal privacy through encryption and the National Security Agency's desire to breach it, and at the frontier of what Sun Tzu two millennia ago described as "vanquishing the enemy without fighting."

VIRTUAL LEADERSHIP

We live in revolutionary times, as did the Founding Fathers. They exhibited a keen interest in technology—provision for copyright and patent protection was written into the Constitution itself. This provision was implemented by an act of Congress in 1790 creating a patent board consisting of the secretary of state, the secretary of war, and the attorney general. It was a prestigious group: Thomas Jefferson, Henry Knox, and

Edmund Randolph. That board is long gone and the schism between the diplomat and the scientist has grown wider at the very time it is becoming more and more important that the two understand each other. Because so much change in the current revolution is driven by technology, our task in mastering these new forces is made more complex by the difficulty of communicating across disciplines. Diplomats, trained in the humanities, often tend to validate C. P. Snow's famous lecture on "Two Cultures," in which he argued that scientists and humanists are ignorant of each other's knowledge and are content to stay that way. Many diplomatic historians have minimized or even ignored the impact of scientific discoveries on the course of history, preferring instead to follow the great man theory or look for the historical tides that carry the world along. Indeed, the indexes of many standard texts on diplomatic history do not even include the words "technology" or "economics."

An expert is a person with great knowledge about a legacy system—indeed there are no experts on the future. Henry Kissinger observed in Diplomacy that "most foreign policies that history has marked highly, in whatever country, have been originated by leaders who were opposed by experts. It is, after all, the responsibility of the expert to operate the familiar and that of the leader to transcend it." During World War I, an aide-de-camp to British Field Marshal Douglas Haig, after seeing a tank demonstration, commented, "The idea that cavalry will be replaced by these iron coaches is absurd. It is little short of treasonous." In the United States, the ridicule and court-martial of Brigadier General Billy Mitchell, when he postulated the importance of air power by offering to sink a battleship, is instructive. Secretary of War Newton D. Baker thought so little of the idea that he was "willing to stand on the bridge of a battleship while that nitwit tries to hit it from the air." Indeed this recurring phenomenon was encapsulated in Arthur Clarke's First Law, cited in his *Profiles of the Future:* "When a distinguished but elderly scientist states that something is possible he is almost certainly right. When he states that something is impossible, he is very probably wrong." In the case of U.S. national security, a refusal to take note of real change in the world is a recipe for disaster.

The new technology will not go away—it will only get better in accordance with Moore's law, which postulates that microchips will double in density and speed every 18 months. Bandwidth will grow even faster. The third technological revolution has brought about immense global prosperity. Contrary to the doomsayers who postulated that the world would run out of resources by the year 2000, it is difficult to find a single commodity that is worth more in real terms today than it was ten years ago. Knowledge, once an ornament displayed by the rich and powerful at conferences, now combines with management skills to produce wealth. The vast increase of knowledge has brought with it a huge increase in the ability to manipulate matter, increasing its value by the power of the mind and generating new products and substances unknown in nature and undreamed of only a few years ago. In the past, when the method of creating wealth changed, old power structures lost influence, new ones arose, and every facet of society was affected. As we can already see the beginning of that process in this revolution, one can postulate that in the next few decades the attraction and management of intellectual capital will determine which institutions and nations will survive and prosper, and which will not.

But despite all of the advances of science and the ways in which it is changing the world, science does not remake the human mind or alter the power of the human spirit. There is still no substitute for courage and leadership in confronting the new problems and opportunities that our world presents. What has changed dramatically is the amount of information available to our policymakers. One hopes that the data processed by the minds of trained diplomats will produce real knowledge, and with enough experience, wisdom. Wisdom has always been in short supply, but it will be sorely needed in the days and years ahead, because in the words of former President Richard Nixon, "Only people can solve problems people create."

NOTES

1. Henry M. Wriston, *Prepare for Peace*, New York: Harper & Bros., 1941, p. 237.
2. George Gilder, "Over the Paradigm Cliff," *ASAP*, February 1997, p. 29.
3. Kevin Kelly, *Out of Control: The Rise of a Neo-Biological Civilization*, Reading, MA: Addison-Wesley, 1994, p. 246.

The Real New World Order

ANNE-MARIE SLAUGHTER

Many thought that the new world order proclaimed by George Bush was the promise of 1945 fulfilled, a world in which international institutions, led by the United Nations, guaranteed international peace and security with the active support of the world's major powers. That world order is a chimera. Even as a liberal internationalist ideal, it is infeasible at best and dangerous at worst. It requires a centralized rule-making authority, a hierarchy of institutions, and universal membership. Equally to the point, efforts to create such an order have failed. The United Nations cannot function effectively independent of the major powers that compose it, nor will those nations cede their power and sovereignty to an international institution. Efforts to expand supranational authority, whether by the U.N. secretary-general's office, the European Commission, or the World Trade Organization (WTO), have consistently produced a backlash among member states.

The leading alternative to liberal internationalism is "the new medievalism," a back-to-the-future model of the 21st century. Where liberal internationalists see a need for international rules and institutions to solve states' problems, the new medievalists proclaim the end of the nation-state. Less hyperbolically, in her article, "Power Shift," in the January/February 1997 *Foreign Affairs*, Jessica T. Mathews describes a shift away from the state—up, down, and sideways—to supra-state, sub-state, and, above all, nonstate actors. These new players have multiple allegiances and global reach.

Mathews attributes this power shift to a change in the structure of organizations: from hierarchies to networks, from centralized compulsion to voluntary association. The engine of this transformation is the information technology revolution, a radically expanded communications capacity that empowers individuals and groups while diminishing traditional authority. The result is not world government, but global governance. If government denotes the formal exercise of power by established institutions, governance denotes cooperative problem-solving by a changing and often uncertain cast. The result is a world order in which global governance networks link Microsoft, the Roman Catholic

Anne-Marie Slaughter is the J. Sinclair Armstrong Professor of International, Foreign, and Comparative Law at Harvard Law School.

Reprinted by permission. *Foreign Affairs*, Sept.–Oct. 1997. Vol. 76, Issue 5, p. 183.

Church, and Amnesty International to the European Union, the United Nations, and Catalonia.

The new medievalists miss two central points. First, private power is still no substitute for state power. Consumer boycotts of transnational corporations destroying rain forests or exploiting child labor may have an impact on the margin, but most environmentalists or labor activists would prefer national legislation mandating control of foreign subsidiaries. Second, the power shift is not a zero-sum game. A gain in power by nonstate actors does not necessarily translate into a loss of power for the state. On the contrary, many of these nongovernmental organizations (NGOs) network with their foreign counterparts to apply additional pressure on the traditional levers of domestic politics.

A new world order is emerging, with less fanfare but more substance than either the liberal internationalist or new medievalist visions. The state is not disappearing, it is disaggregating into its separate, functionally distinct parts. These parts—courts, regulatory agencies, executives, and even legislatures—are networking with their counterparts abroad, creating a dense web of relations that constitutes a new, transgovernmental order. Today's international problems—terrorism, organized crime, environmental degradation, money laundering, bank failure, and securities fraud—created and sustain these relations. Government institutions have formed networks of their own, ranging from the Basle Committee of Central Bankers to informal ties between law enforcement agencies to legal networks that make foreign judicial decisions more and more familiar. While political scientists Robert Keohane and Joseph Nye first observed its emergence in the 1970s, today transgovernmentalism is rapidly becoming the most widespread and effective mode of international governance.

Compared to the lofty ideals of liberal internationalism and the exuberant possibilities of the new medievalism, transgovernmentalism seems mundane. Meetings between securities regulators, antitrust or environmental officials, judges, or legislators lack the drama of high politics. But for the internationalists of the 1990s—bankers, lawyers, businesspeople, public-interest activists, and criminals—transnational government networks are a reality. Wall Street looks to the Basle Committee rather than the World Bank. Human rights lawyers are more likely to develop transnational litigation strategies for domestic courts than to petition the U.N. Committee on Human Rights.

Moreover, transgovernmentalism has many virtues. It is a key element of a bipartisan foreign policy, simultaneously assuaging conservative fears of a loss of sovereignty to international institutions and liberal fears of a loss of regulatory power in a globalized economy. While presidential candidate Pat Buchanan and Senator Jesse Helms (R-N.C.) demonize the U.N. and the WTO as supranational bureaucracies that seek to dictate to national governments, Senators Ted Kennedy (D-Mass.) and Paul Wellstone (D-Mich.) inveigh against international capital mobility as the catalyst of a global "race to the bottom" in regulatory standards. Networks of bureaucrats responding to international crises and planning to prevent future problems are more flexible than international institutions and expand the regulatory reach of all participating nations. This combination of flexibility and effectiveness offers something for both sides of the aisle.

Transgovernmentalism also offers promising new mechanisms for the Clinton administration's "enlargement" policy, aiming to expand the community of liberal democracies. Contrary to Samuel Huntington's gloomy predictions in *The Clash of Civilizations and the New World Order* (1996), existing government networks span civilizations, drawing in courts from Argentina to Zimbabwe and financial regulators from Japan to Saudi Arabia. The dominant institutions in these networks remain concentrated in North America and Western Europe, but their impact can be felt in every corner of the globe. Moreover, disaggregating the state makes it possible to assess the quality of specific judicial, administrative, and legislative institutions, whether or not the governments are liberal democracies. Regular interaction with foreign colleagues offers new channels for spreading democratic accountability, governmental integrity, and the rule of law.

An offspring of an increasingly borderless world, transgovernmentalism is a world order ideal in its own right, one that is more effective and potentially more accountable than either of the current alternatives. Liberal internationalism poses the prospect of a supranational bureaucracy answerable to no one. The new medievalist vision appeals equally to states' rights enthusiasts and supranationalists, but could easily reflect the worst of both worlds. Transgovernmentalism, by contrast, leaves the control of government institutions in the hands of national citizens, who must hold their governments as accountable for their transnational activities as for their domestic duties.

JUDICIAL FOREIGN POLICY

Judges are building a global community of law. They share values and interests based on their belief in the law as distinct but not divorced from politics and their view of themselves as professionals who must be insulated from direct political influence. At its best, this global community reminds each participant that his or her professional performance is being monitored and supported by a larger audience.

National and international judges are networking, becoming increasingly aware of one another and of their stake in a common enter-

prise. The most informal level of transnational judicial contact is knowledge of foreign and international judicial decisions and a corresponding
willingness to cite them. The Israeli Supreme Court and the German
and Canadian constitutional courts have long researched U.S. Supreme
Court precedents in reaching their own conclusions on questions like
freedom of speech, privacy rights, and due process. Fledgling constitutional courts in Central and Eastern Europe and in Russia are eagerly following suit. In 1995, the South African Supreme Court, finding the
death penalty unconstitutional under the national constitution, referred
to decisions from national and supranational courts around the world,
including ones in Hungary, India, Tanzania, Canada, and Germany and
the European Court of Human Rights. The U.S. Supreme Court has typically been more of a giver than a receiver in this exchange, but Justice
Sandra Day O'Connor recently chided American lawyers and judges for
their insularity in ignoring foreign law and predicted that she and her
fellow justices would find themselves "looking more frequently to the
decisions of other constitutional courts."

Why should a court in Israel or South Africa cite a decision by the
U.S. Supreme Court in reaching its own conclusion? Decisions rendered
by outside courts can have no authoritative value. They carry weight
only because of their intrinsic logical power or because the court invok-
ing them seeks to gain legitimacy by linking itself to a larger community of courts considering similar issues. National courts have become
increasingly aware that they and their foreign counterparts are often engaged in a common effort to delimit the boundaries of individual rights
in the face of an apparently overriding public interest. Thus, the British
House of Lords recently rebuked the U.S. Supreme Court for its decision
to uphold the kidnapping of a Mexican doctor by U.S. officials determined to bring him to trial in the United States.

Judges also cooperate in resolving transnational or international
disputes. In cases involving citizens of two different states, courts have
long been willing to acknowledge each other's potential interest and to
defer to one another when such deference is not too costly. U.S. courts
now recognize that they may become involved in a sustained dialogue
with a foreign court. For instance, Judge Guido Calabresi of the Second
Circuit recently allowed a French litigant to invoke U.S. discovery provisions without exhausting discovery options in France, reasoning that it
was up to the French courts to identify and protest any infringements of
French sovereignty. U.S. courts would then respond to such protests.

Judicial communication is not always harmonious, as in a recent
squabble between a U.S. judge and a Hong Kong judge over an insider
trading case. The U.S. judge refused to decline jurisdiction in favor of the
Hong Kong court on grounds that "in Hong Kong they practically give
you a medal for doing this sort of thing [insider trading]." In response,

the Hong Kong judge stiffly defended the adequacy of Hong Kong law and asserted his willingness to apply it. He also chided his American counterpart, pointing out that any conflict "should be approached in the spirit of judicial comity rather than judicial competitiveness." Such conflict is to be expected among diplomats, but what is striking here is the two courts' view of themselves as quasi-autonomous foreign policy actors doing battle against international securities fraud.

The most advanced form of judicial cooperation is a partnership between national courts and a supranational tribunal. In the European Union (EU), the European Court of Justice works with national courts when questions of European law overlap national law. National courts refer cases up to the European Court, which issues an opinion and sends the case back to national courts; the supranational recommendation guides the national court's decision. This cooperation marshals the power of domestic courts behind the judgment of a supranational tribunal. While the Treaty of Rome provides for this reference procedure, it is the courts that have transformed it into a judicial partnership.

Finally, judges are talking face to face. The judges of the supreme courts of Western Europe began meeting every three years in 1978. Since then they have become more aware of one another's decisions, particularly with regard to each other's willingness to accept the decisions handed down by the European Court of Justice. Meetings between U.S. Supreme Court justices and their counterparts on the European Court have been sponsored by private groups, as have meetings of U.S. judges with judges from the supreme courts of Central and Eastern Europe and Russia.

The most formal initiative aimed at bringing judges together is the recently inaugurated Organization of the Supreme Courts of the Americas. Twenty-five supreme court justices or their designees met in Washington in October 1995 and drafted the OCSA charter, dedicating the organization to "promot[ing] and strengthen[ing] judicial independence and the rule of law among the members, as well as the proper constitutional treatment of the judiciary as a fundamental branch of the state." The charter calls for triennial meetings and envisages a permanent secretariat. It required ratification by 15 supreme courts, achieved in spring 1996. An initiative by judges, for judges, it is not a stretch to say that OCSA is the product of judicial foreign policy.

Champions of a global rule of law have most frequently envisioned one rule for all, a unified legal system topped by a world court. The global community of law emerging from judicial networks will more likely encompass many rules of law, each established in a specific state or region. No high court would hand down definitive global rules. National courts would interact with one another and with supranational tribunals in ways that would accommodate differences but acknowledge and reinforce common values.

THE REGULATORY WEB

The densest area of transgovernmental activity is among national regulators. Bureaucrats charged with the administration of antitrust policy, securities regulation, environmental policy, criminal law enforcement, banking and insurance supervision—in short, all the agents of the modern regulatory state—regularly collaborate with their foreign counterparts.

National regulators track their quarry through cooperation. While frequently ad hoc, such cooperation is increasingly cemented by bilateral and multilateral agreements. The most formal of these are mutual legal assistance treaties, whereby two states lay out a protocol governing cooperation between their law enforcement agencies and courts. However, the preferred instrument of cooperation is the memorandum of understanding, in which two or more regulatory agencies set forth and initial terms for an ongoing relationship. Such memorandums are not treaties; they do not engage the executive or the legislature in negotiations, deliberation, or signature. Rather, they are good-faith agreements, affirming ties between regulatory agencies based on their like-minded commitment to getting results.

"Positive comity," a concept developed by the U.S. Department of Justice, epitomizes the changing nature of transgovernmental relations. Comity of nations, an archaic and notoriously vague term beloved by diplomats and international lawyers, has traditionally signified the deference one nation grants another in recognition of their mutual sovereignty. For instance, a state will recognize another state's laws or judicial judgments based on comity. Positive comity requires more active cooperation. As worked out by the Antitrust Division of the U.S. Department of Justice and the EU's European Commission, the regulatory authorities of both states alert one another to violations within their jurisdiction, with the understanding that the responsible authority will take action. Positive comity is a principle of enduring cooperation between government agencies.

In 1988 the central bankers of the world's major financial powers adopted capital adequacy requirements for all banks under their supervision—a significant reform of the international banking system. It was not the the International Monetary Fund, or even the Group of Seven that took this step. Rather, the forum was the Basle Committee on Banking Supervision, an organization composed of 12 central bank governors. The Basle Committee was created by a simple agreement among the governors themselves. Its members meet four times a year and follow their own rules. Decisions are made by consensus and are not formally binding; however, members do implement these decisions within their own systems. The Basle Committee's authority is often cited as an argument for taking domestic action.

National securities commissioners and insurance regulators have followed the Basle Committee's example. Incorporated by a private bill of the Quebec National Assembly, the International Organization of Securities Commissioners has no formal charter or founding treaty. Its primary purpose is to solve problems affecting international securities markets by creating a consensus for enactment of national legislation. Its members have also entered into information-sharing agreements on their own initiative. The International Association of Insurance Supervisors follows a similar model, as does the newly created Tripartite Group, an international coalition of banking, insurance, and securities regulators the Basle Committee created to improve the supervision of financial conglomerates.

Pat Buchanan would have had a field day with the Tripartite Group, denouncing it as a prime example of bureaucrats taking power out of the hands of American voters. In fact, unlike the international bogeymen of demagogic fantasy, transnational regulatory organizations do not aspire to exercise power in the international system independent of their members. Indeed, their main purpose is to help regulators apprehend those who would harm the interests of American voters. Transgovernmental networks often promulgate their own rules, but the purpose of those rules is to enhance the enforcement of national law.

Traditional international law requires states to implement the international obligations they incur through their own law. Thus, if states agree to a 12-mile territorial sea, they must change their domestic legislation concerning the interdiction of vessels in territorial waters accordingly. But this legislation is unlikely to overlap with domestic law, as national legislatures do not usually seek to regulate global commons issues and interstate relations.

Transgovernmental regulation, by contrast, produces rules concerning issues that each nation already regulates within its borders: crime, securities fraud, pollution, tax evasion. The advances in technology and transportation that have fueled globalization have made it more difficult to enforce national law. Regulators benefit from coordinating their enforcement efforts with those of their foreign counterparts and from ensuring that other nations adopt similar approaches.

The result is the nationalization of international law. Regulatory agreements between states are pledges of good faith that are self-enforcing, in the sense that each nation will be better able to enforce its national law by implementing the agreement if other nations do likewise. Laws are binding or coercive only at the national level. Uniformity of result and diversity of means go hand in hand, and the makers and enforcers of rules are national leaders who are accountable to the people.

BIPARTISAN GLOBALIZATION

Secretary of State Madeleine Albright seeks to revive the bipartisan foreign policy consensus of the late 1940s. Deputy Secretary of State Strobe Talbott argues that promoting democracy worldwide satisfies the American need for idealpolitik as well as realpolitik. President Clinton, in his second inaugural address, called for a "new government for a new century," abroad as well as at home. But bipartisanship is threatened by divergent responses to globalization, democratization is a tricky business, and Vice President Al Gore's efforts to "reinvent government" have focused on domestic rather than international institutions. Transgovernmentalism can address all these problems.

Globalization implies the erosion of national boundaries. Consequently, regulators' power to implement national regulations within those boundaries declines both because people can easily flee their jurisdiction and because the flows of capital, pollution, pathogens, and weapons are too great and sudden for any one regulator to control. The liberal internationalist response to these assaults on state regulatory power is to build a larger international apparatus. Globalization thus leads to internationalization, or the transfer of regulatory authority from the national level to an international institution. The best example is not the WTO itself, but rather the stream of proposals to expand the WTO's jurisdiction to global competition policy, intellectual property regulation, and other trade-related issues. Liberals are likely to support expanding the power of international institutions to guard against the global dismantling of the regulatory state.

Here's the rub. Conservatives are more likely to favor the expansion of globalized markets without the internationalization that goes with it, since internationalization, from their perspective, equals a loss of sovereignty. According to Buchanan, the U.S. foreign policy establishment "want[s] to move America into a New World Order where the World Court decides quarrels between nations; the WTO writes the rules for trade and settles all disputes; the IMF and World Bank order wealth transfers from continent to continent and country to country; the Law of the Sea Treaty tells us what we may and may not do on the high seas and ocean floor, and the United Nations decides where U.S. military forces may and may not intervene." The rhetoric is deliberately inflammatory, but echoes resound across the Republican spectrum.

Transgovernmental initiatives are a compromise that could command bipartisan support. Regulatory loopholes caused by global forces require a coordinated response beyond the reach of any one country. But this coordination need not come from building more international institutions. It can be achieved through transgovernmental cooperation, involving the same officials who make and implement policy at the national level. The transgovernmental alternative is fast, flexible, and effective.

A leading example of transgovernmentalism in action that demonstrates its bipartisan appeal is a State Department initiative christened the New Transatlantic Agenda. Launched in 1991 under the Bush administration and reinvigorated by Secretary of State Warren Christopher in 1995, the initiative structures the relationship between the United States and the EU, fostering cooperation in areas ranging from opening markets to fighting terrorism, drug trafficking, and infectious disease. It is an umbrella for ongoing projects between U.S. officials and their European counterparts. It reaches ordinary citizens, embracing efforts like the Transatlantic Business Dialogue and engaging individuals through people-to-people exchanges and expanded communication through the Internet.

DEMOCRATIZATION, STEP BY STEP

Transgovernmental networks are concentrated among liberal democracies but are not limited to them. Some nondemocratic states have institutions capable of cooperating with their foreign counterparts, such as committed and effective regulatory agencies or relatively independent judiciaries. Transgovernmental ties can strengthen institutions in ways that will help them resist political domination, corruption, and incompetence and build democratic institutions in their countries, step by step. The Organization of Supreme Courts of the Americas, for instance, actively seeks to strengthen norms of judicial independence among its members, many of whom must fend off powerful political forces.

Individuals and groups in nondemocratic countries may also "borrow" government institutions of democratic states to achieve a measure of justice they cannot obtain in their own countries. The court or regulatory agency of one state may be able to perform judicial or regulatory functions for the people of another. Victims of human rights violations, for example, in countries such as Argentina, Ethiopia, Haiti, and the Philippines have sued for redress in the courts of the United States. U.S. courts accepted these cases, often over the objections of the executive branch, using a broad interpretation of a moribund statute dating back to 1789. Under this interpretation, aliens may sue in U.S. courts to seek damages from foreign government officials accused of torture, even if the torture allegedly took place in the foreign country. More generally, a nongovernmental organization seeking to prevent human rights violations can often circumvent their own government's corrupt legislature and politicized court by publicizing the plight of victims abroad and mobilizing a foreign court, legislature, or executive to take action.

Responding to calls for a coherent U.S. foreign policy and seeking to strengthen the community of democratic nations, President Clinton substituted the concept of "enlargement" for the Cold War principle of "containment." Expanding transgovernmental outreach to include institutions from nondemocratic states would help expand the circle of democracies one institution at a time.

A NEW WORLD ORDER IDEAL

Transgovernmentalism offers its own world order ideal, less dramatic but more compelling than either liberal internationalism or the new medievalism. It harnesses the state's power to find and implement solutions to global problems. International institutions have a lackluster record on such problem-solving; indeed, NGOs exist largely to compensate for their inadequacies. Doing away with the state, however, is hardly the answer. The new medievalist mantra of global governance is "governance without government." But governance without government is governance without power, and government without power rarely works. Many pressing international and domestic problems result from states' insufficient power to establish order, build infrastructure, and provide minimum social services. Private actors may take up some slack, but there is no substitute for the state.

Transgovernmental networks allow governments to benefit from the flexibility and decentralization of nonstate actors. Jessica T. Mathews argues that "businesses, citizens' organizations, ethnic groups, and crime cartels have all readily adopted the network model," while governments "are quintessential hierarchies, wedded to an organizational form incompatible with all that the new technologies make possible." Not so. Disaggregating the state into its functional components makes it possible to create networks of institutions engaged in a common enterprise even as they represent distinct national interests. Moreover, they can work with their subnational and supranational counterparts, creating a genuinely new world order in which networked institutions perform the functions of a world government—legislation, administration, and adjudication—without the form.

These globe-spanning networks will strengthen the state as the primary player in the international system. The state's defining attribute has traditionally been sovereignty, conceived as absolute power in domestic affairs and autonomy in relations with other states. But as Abram and Antonia Chayes observe in *The New Sovereignty* (1995), sovereignty is actually "status—the vindication of the state's existence in the international system." More importantly, they demonstrate that in contemporary international relations, sovereignty has been redefined to mean "membership . . . in the regimes that make up the substance of international life." Disaggregating the state permits the disaggregation of sovereignty as well, ensuring that specific state institutions derive strength and status from participation in a transgovernmental order.

Transgovernmental networks will increasingly provide an important anchor for international organizations and nonstate actors alike. U.N. officials have already learned a lesson about the limits of supranational authority; mandated cuts in the international bureaucracy will further tip the balance of power toward national regulators. The next generation of international institutions is also likely to look more like the Basle Committee, or, more formally, the Organization of Economic Cooperation and Development, dedicated to providing a forum for transnational problem-solving and the harmonization of national law. The disaggregation of the state creates opportunities for domestic institutions, particularly courts, to make common cause with their supranational counterparts against their fellow branches of government. Nonstate actors will lobby and litigate wherever they think they will have the most effect. Many already realize that corporate self-regulation and states' promises to comply with vague international agreements are no substitute for national law.

The spread of transgovernmental networks will depend more on political and professional convergence than on civilizational boundaries. Trust and awareness of a common enterprise are more vulnerable to differing political ideologies and corruption than to cultural differences. Government networks transcend the traditional divide between high and low politics. National militaries, for instance, network as extensively as central bankers with their counterparts in friendly states. Judicial and regulatory networks can help achieve gradual political convergence, but are unlikely to be of much help in the face of a serious economic or military threat. If the coming conflict with China is indeed coming, transgovernmentalism will not stop it.

The strength of transgovernmental networks and of transgovernmentalism as a world order ideal will ultimately depend on their accountability to the world's peoples. To many, the prospect of transnational government by judges and bureaucrats looks more like technocracy than democracy. Critics contend that government institutions engaged in policy coordination with their foreign counterparts will be barely visible, much less accountable, to voters still largely tied to national territory.

Citizens of liberal democracies will not accept any form of international regulation they cannot control. But checking unelected officials is a familiar problem in domestic politics. As national legislators become increasingly aware of transgovernmental networks, they will expand their oversight capacities and develop networks of their own. Transnational NGO networks will develop a similar monitoring capacity. It will be harder to monitor themselves.

Transgovernmentalism offers answers to the most important challenges facing advanced industrial countries: loss of regulatory power with economic globalization, perceptions of a "democratic deficit" as international institutions step in to fill the regulatory gap, and the difficulties of engaging nondemocratic states. Moreover, it provides a powerful alternative to a liberal internationalism that has reached its limits and to a new medievalism that, like the old Marxism, sees the state slowly fading away. The new medievalists are right to emphasize the dawn of a new era, in which information technology will transform the globe. But government networks are government for the information age. They offer the world a blueprint for the international architecture of the 21st century.

Issue 3
International Criminal Court

INTRODUCTION

The recent outrage at the atrocities in Rwanda and the former Yugoslavia served to focus the world's attention on the possibility of creating an International Criminal Court to bring to justice those who are responsible for such crimes against humanity. The initial response of the international community was the establishment, by the Unted Nations Security Council, of the Yugoslavia War Crimes Tribunal in 1993 and the International Criminal Tribunal for Rwanda in 1994. Limited in jurisdiction, these tribunals were followed by efforts to create a permanent international criminal court, efforts that culminated in the signing in Rome, in July 1998, of a treaty establishing a permanent International Criminal Court. The treaty was approved by a vote of 120 to 7, with the United States voting against, along with the states of China, Iran, Iraq, Sudan, & Libya.

The first article in this section, an excerpt from a talk given before the Commonwealth Club by D. J. Scheffer presents the case for the International Criminal Court, arguing that such a court is essential to bringing to justice "the architects of mass killings" and to "deter genocide, widespread or systematic crimes against humanity and large-scale war crimes in the next century."

The second article, a transcript of remarks made before the U.S. Senate by Senator Ashcroft [R] Missouri, questions the continuing assault on national sovereignty that this court symbolizes. Senator Ashcroft's concerns are mainly focused on the lack of the Rome treaty's recognition of the rights and guarantees that are enjoyed by U.S. citizens through the Bill of Rights.

As you read the articles, consider the following questions.

Discussion Questions

1. What conclusions might one draw from the group of countries that voted against the creation of the International Criminal Court?
2. Does the establishment of the International Criminal Court represent a further erosion of national sovereignty?
3. Does the establishment of the International Criminal Court represent a step closer to the establishment of a world government?
4. How important is it to establish respect for the rules of international law? Would the creation of an International Criminal Court further this objective?

     For more on this topic, visit the following websites:

     `http://www.un.org/icc/romestat.htm`
     Rome Statute of the International Criminal Court

     `http://www.asil.org/crmctbib.htm`
     American Society of International Law

     `http://www.hrw.org/hrw/campaigns/icc/icc-main.htm`
     Human Rights Watch Campaign to Establish an International Criminal Court

Seeking Accountability for War Crimes, Past and Future

DAVID J. SCHEFFER

It's a pleasure to be here at the Washington Institute this afternoon. As you know, we in the Administration thought we did well when Martin Indyk left here to join the Administration. Throughout the Washington Institute's 13-year history, including now under Rob Satloff's leadership, the Washington Institute has been and continues to be one of the most important sources of scholarship and commentary on Middle East affairs. Even when you take us to task, we find the Washington Institute's commentary to be incisive, thought-provoking, and highly relevant to what's going on in the Middle East today.

I want to address today two principal subjects. First, I want to describe for you the work the Clinton Administration is doing on the Iraqi war crimes issue. Second, I want to talk about the work we're doing on establishing a permanent international criminal court. Some might see these two points as different—one historic and retrospective, the other forward-looking and prospective. In fact, we see these two issues as inter-related parts of the Administration's overall efforts to build mechanisms of individual accountability for large-scale violations of the kind that were prosecuted at Nuremberg and Tokyo at the end of World War II, and that are being prosecuted today at the International Criminal Tribunal for the Former Yugoslavia in The Hague and at the International Criminal Tribunal for Rwanda, located in Arusha, Tanzania.

The term "war crimes" has become a shorthand for a body of law that arose more than five hundred years ago, though it is substantially shaped by World War II and the Holocaust. Before we can discuss the policy implications of war crimes tribunals and war crimes charges, it is important to have an understanding what these crimes truly are. The crimes prosecuted at Nuremberg, Tokyo, The Hague, and Arusha are the gravest criminal charges that could ever be brought against individuals. When the United Nations Security Council established the Yugoslavia war crimes tribunal in 1993, and followed it up in 1994 with the International Criminal Tribunal for Rwanda, it limited the jurisdiction of that tribunal to four categories of crimes.

David J. Scheffer is Ambassador-at-Large for War Crimes Issues, U.S. Department of State. His address was given before the Washington Institute for Near East Policy in Washington, D.C., on May 21, 1998.

First, these international criminal tribunals have jurisdiction over the crime of genocide. The word genocide evokes the Holocaust, as it always should. However, following the Holocaust, the crime of genocide was defined by international convention in 1948. The crime of genocide now has a specific legal description. The essence of the crime of genocide requires the specific intent to destroy, in whole or in substantial part, a national, ethnic, racial or religious group, as such, through killing, torture, or other means. The element of specific intent is a key part of the crime of genocide, and one of the toughest to prove in court.

Second, these international criminal tribunals have jurisdiction over crimes against humanity. Crimes against humanity as defined for the Rwanda Tribunal include murder, enslavement, deportation, imprisonment, torture, rape, or persecution on political, racial or religious grounds, when committed as part of a widespread or systematic attack against a civilian population on national, political, ethnic, racial or religious grounds. Crimes against humanity was recognized at, and after, Nuremberg. At the end of "Schindler's List," Amon Goeth is shown being hanged for crimes against humanity.

Third, these tribunals can prosecute grave breaches of the Geneva Conventions of 1949. These conventions provide protection, for example, to prisoners of war and to civilians.

Fourth, these tribunals can prosecute violations of the laws and customs of war. The laws of war are governed by numerous international treaties and customary international law. One of them is the 1925 treaty banning the use of chemical weapons.

I mention these four categories of crimes to shed light on three points.

First, international war crimes tribunals are meant to try the most heinous crimes known to humankind. These are crimes that deserve the universal condemnation of all civilized States.

Second, because of the seriousness of these crimes, before any accusations are ever made, we must understand the facts of a particular case, and how those facts fit against the law.

Third, because of the seriousness of these crimes, and where the facts are sufficient to justify it, these cases deserve special treatment. At the core of these crimes, particularly genocide and crimes against humanity, is mass murder. Experience in the former Yugoslavia, the Great Lakes of Central Africa and elsewhere have demonstrated to us that these crimes constitute threats to international peace and security. The Administration does not believe that every war crimes charge merits an international tribunal. We are committed, however, to examining each situation on its merits, and to working to achieve the right result—the right result both in terms of international justice and in terms of international peace and security. This has led the Clinton Administration to lead efforts to establish international tribunals for the former Yugoslavia and Rwanda, it has led us to support efforts to look at ways to bring to justice senior members of the Khmer Rouge, and it has led us—as well as countries like Israel, Egypt and Jordan—to support the establishment of a permanent international criminal court. I will return to this subject later.

Let me say a few words about the status of the Yugoslav war crimes tribunal, the first international criminal tribunal since Nuremberg and Tokyo. Initially, there were those who said that we could not get the Security Council to agree to establish a war crimes tribunal for the former Yugoslavia. Ultimately, the vote was 15 to nothing. Then people said we would not be able to bring those indicted to justice. In the last 13 months, the number of indictees taken into custody in The Hague has essentially quadrupled, from 8 to 31. Three others are deceased, and today there are only 32 publicly indicted war criminals still at large. We recognize that our work is not finished. Some of the major indictees, including Radovan Karadzic, are still at large. Their day before the Yugoslav Tribunal will come. In the meantime, though, even skeptics have had to realize the importance of a Tribunal indictment in undermining Karadzic's power in the Bosnian Serb entity. Radovan Karadzic was first indicted on July 25, 1995. His indictment led to pressure being brought by the United States and other members of the international community. Persons indicted by the international tribunal would not be recognized as leaders by the international community. This led to Karadzic being excluded from the Dayton peace process in November 1995. I don't want to over-sell the importance of the Tribunal's indictment of Karadzic in the improvement of conditions on the ground in Bosnia since November 1995. A lot of the credit goes to the hard work by the President, by Secretary Albright, and by Special Representative Gelbard. Radovan Karadzic remains a malign influence in Bosnia to this day. However, the indictment of Radovan Karadzic by the Tribunal made it clear to the international community—in a way that diplomacy alone could not—that Radovan Karadzic was not a man with whom anyone should do business. With that pointed example, let me now turn to the case of Iraq.

IRAQ

When I testified before the Senate Foreign Relations Committee in July 1997, I said that my focus would be on the former Yugoslavia, the Great Lakes of Central Africa, Cambodia, and Iraq. We are making good progress with the war crimes tribunals for Yugoslavia and Rwanda. The United States is now leading the effort to bring to justice the leading surviving members of the Khmer Rouge who were responsible for killing 1.7 million Cambodians between 1975 and 1979.

We are also focusing renewed attention on Saddam Hussein and the senior members of his regime. His record is a long one—as Secretary Albright has often said, he is a "repeat offender." It is extremely important that the pattern of Saddam Hussein's conduct be well known by the international community. That pattern of conduct has been criminal in character. It involves the actions of Saddam Hussein's regime during the Anfal campaign of the late 1980's against the Iraqi Kurdish people. It includes what he did to the Iranians during the Iran-Iraq war. It includes the invasion and occupation of Kuwait, and the torture and killing of Kuwaiti civilians, and it involves actions that Saddam Hussein's regime has taken against the Marsh Arabs in southern Iraq following the Gulf War.

Our government is working with others to pull together the record of Saddam's regime in a way that can be useful to a prosecutor. For example, some years ago, Human Rights Watch and the Senate Foreign Relations Committee helped collect 5.5 million pages of Iraqi documents captured in northern Iraq. The U.S. Government has now scanned and indexed these 5.5 million pages into computer-readable form on 176 CD-ROM disks. Our goal now is to make this information accessible to investigators and prosecutors looking into the way Saddam organized his activities in the north of his country.

One incident stands out in the horror story of the abuses Saddam Hussein visited upon the Iraqi people. A little more than 10 years ago, Saddam's forces dropped poison gas on the Iraqi town of Halabja. Halabja's story was told on "60 Minutes" through the work of a courageous British doctor, Dr. Christine Gosden of the University of Liverpool. Dr. Gosden examined hundreds of Iraqis, many of whom were children or were not even born at the time of the 1988 attack. Her observations of birth defects, cancers, neurological disease, and more show the effects of Saddam's willingness to violate the 1925 chemical weapons convention through the use of poison gas. As some of you may remember, the *Washington Post* turned its entire Op-Ed page of March 11, 1998, over to Dr. Gosden so that she could tell the world the consequences of the actions of Saddam's forces on the Iraqi people. As horrible as it was, Halabja was not the only Iraqi or Iranian town attacked by poison gas dropped by Iraqi forces. We don't yet know the full extent of the lasting damage suffered by the Iraqi or Iranian people as a result of Saddam Hussein's use of poison gas.

We know even more about Saddam Hussein's actions during the invasion and occupation of Kuwait in 1990–91. Earlier this month, I was in Kuwait, where I met with officials of the Government of Kuwait and leading experts at universities and non-governmental organizations, to see the evidence they had accumulated in their archives. I met with groups dedicated to keeping alive the memories of the civilians tortured to death by Saddam's forces. During the occupation, even having a camera in Kuwait could get you the death sentence, but courageous Kuwaitis working in hospitals took pictures to record the suffering these men and women endured, in most cases before being tortured to death. This—I need hardly say it—is a war crime.

I was extremely impressed by what the Kuwaitis have done to gather evidence of the atrocities committed against them. Block by block, they have documented Saddam's campaign against the Kuwaiti people. This record must not be forgotten.

I was also able to visit what must be regarded as a war crime scene—the oil fields of Kuwait. As Saddam Hussein's forces were forced to flee Kuwait in 1991, he ordered his forces to destroy or release into the Gulf what turned out to be between 7 and 9 million barrels of oil. 590 oil well heads were damaged or destroyed: 508 were set on fire, and 82 were damaged so that oil and gas flowed freely from them. The scene at that time can barely be described—photographs and films shot at that time show a black cloud that literally turned day into night. Kuwait has done a heroic job in restoring itself from this crime. Even so, some seven years later, the damage remains. Pools of oil remain. At one gathering station, where the oil from the wells was supposed to be processed prior to being shipped to tankers, Saddam's forces started a fire so hot it melted half-inch-thick steel like candy. These were wanton acts of destruction of property not justified by military necessity and carried out unlawfully and wantonly. If ever there was a case of a gross violation of military necessity and wanton destruction, this was the case.

Today, Kuwait is free, thanks to the action of U.S. forces, our Coalition partners, and the Kuwaitis themselves. As a result, we have access to the evidence of crimes that have been committed against the Kuwaiti people and their environment. Much of Iraq remains sealed off to international investigators, but there are substantial archives outside of Iraq that document crimes committed against the Iraqi people, as well. I wish those on the Security Council could see the evidence that I have seen. There have been many threats by Saddam Hussein's regime to international peace and security to which the international community has had to respond. The Clinton Administration recognizes that the record of Saddam Hussein's conduct under international law is deplorable. We are taking measures to insure that this record becomes better known to the world at large.

U.N. ARREARS

Let me now address a subject that is vital to the effort to bring war criminals to justice. Everyone understands that efforts to bring the most heinous war criminals to justice cost money. Yet, at the very moment in world history when the United States can make the critical difference in waging peace, by joining with others to enforce international law, advance vital national security interests, and bring war criminals to justice, our credibility and our influence with other governments is needlessly and foolishly at risk. The failure of the United States to pay its U.N. debts for years has had severe repercussions in the exercise of American foreign policy.

As Secretary Albright has said, we are the indispensable nation, but we cannot go it alone. We were pleased last year to receive bipartisan support for legislation that would put us well on the way to satisfying our obligations at the United Nations. Unfortunately, this bill as well as comparable legislation this year have been held hostage to an issue that should be considered on its own merits. At some point common sense, and U.S. national interests, must prevail. As we insist that reform at the United Nations goes forward, the United States has a responsibility to pay our debts to the U.N.

INTERNATIONAL CRIMINAL COURT

Let me now turn to the future: a permanent international criminal court which would have jurisdiction over genocide, widespread or systematic crimes against humanity, and large-scale war crimes. The Clinton Administration has supported a strong and effective International Criminal Court ever since talks began at the United Nations in early 1995, as have many other nations, including key nations in the Middle East like Israel, Egypt and Jordan. President Clinton and Secretary of State Albright have repeatedly stated their support for the establishment of an appropriate permanent international criminal court. Last September, before the U.N. General Assembly, the President called for the establishment of the court by the end of this century. In Kigali a few weeks ago, he reconfirmed U.S. support for such a court. The critical need for a permanent court, and the vital role the United States can play in its establishment and operation, compels our best efforts.

As head of the U.S. inter-agency delegation to the U.N. talks and the diplomatic conference this summer in Rome, I know well the strong commitment of our Administration to this endeavor. We have labored hard to address the myriad issues that confront any effort to build an institution of international criminal law. We hope that remaining differences among governments can indeed be resolved in Rome this summer, and that the heavily bracketed text emerging from the Preparatory Committee talks at the United Nations last month will be reduced to a statute for the court that can be embraced by the international community.

Our leadership in supporting the ad hoc tribunals for the former Yugoslavia and for Rwanda, as well as our current efforts to establish an ad hoc tribunal to prosecute senior Khmer Rouge leaders in Cambodia, demonstrates powerfully that the Clinton Administration seeks international justice for the architects of mass killings. We have learned through extraordinary hard work since 1993 that when diplomatic, economic, or military clout is needed to achieve the aims of international justice, the world looks to the United States for leadership and assistance. If one is truly seeking a strong and effective international criminal court, as we are, then it would be folly to ignore U.S. interests or seek any path that would exclude the United States from participation either in the negotiations or in the work of an established court.

The U.S. delegation has been and will continue to be guided by our paramount duty: to protect and advance U.S. interests. It is entirely consistent with U.S. interests to build a permanent international criminal court that can deter genocide, widespread or systematic crimes against humanity, and large-scale war crimes in the next century. Such a court can bring to justice those who would commit these heinous crimes against our soldiers, the armed forces of our friends and allies, and innocent civilians.

It also would be folly to exclude the U.N. Security Council from the work of the court. There is no enforcement arm envisaged for the court other than the Security Council. We have long argued that the court must be so constituted as to recognize the primary responsibility under the U.N. Charter of the Security Council to confront threats to international peace and security. There must be coordination and compatibility between the work of the Security Council and that of the permanent court.

There are other proposals which, while not embracing the U.S. approach, nonetheless recognize that the Security Council has a significant and appropriate role to play in the work of the court. After all, the crimes falling within the jurisdiction of the court typically will pertain to armed conflicts and other threats to international peace and security that can fall within the jurisdiction of the Security Council. It is essential that skeptics of the role of the Security Council not go so far as to abandon the one body that can put clout behind the court and give the prosecutor the kind of political authority he or she will need to effectively pursue war criminals.

A third folly clearly would be any system that dumps on the international court thousands of cases that should be prosecuted at the national level. The International Criminal Court is a court that will concentrate, essentially, on mass killings and other atrocities on a grand scale. It will not be a human rights court and the prosecutor should not be an ombudsman open to any complaint, small or large, from any source. The court must stay focused on the kind of cases it was meant to prosecute.

We also have long argued, and advanced with specific proposals, that the permanent court must ensure that national legal systems with the will and ability to prosecute persons who commit these crimes are permitted to do so, while guaranteeing that perpetrators of these crimes acting in countries lacking responsible, functioning legal systems nonetheless will be held accountable. Where national legal systems can assume their responsibilities, then the permanent court does not have to intervene. This principle of deferral to national judicial systems, which the negotiators call "complementarity," is central to the U.S. position.

Let me highlight six fundamental positions advanced by the U.S. Government in the U.N. talks:

1. We support a referral system whereby a State Party to the treaty or the Security Council can refer an overall matter—an armed conflict or an atrocity—to the court, following which the Prosecutor would investigate individuals responsible for the crimes within the context of the referred matter. This is the way the Yugoslav war crimes tribunal works now. We oppose creation of a self-initiating Prosecutor who could investigate and prosecute anyone, anywhere, anytime and under any circumstances without the benefit of a referral that establishes some parameters. That was never the original purpose of the court, namely to create a kind of human rights ombudsman empowered to press criminal charges.

2. We do not believe that the jurisdiction of the court should extend to a crime of "aggression." This is not to deny the legacy of Nuremberg, but simply to recognize that no broadly acceptable definition has yet been embraced by customary international law for purposes of individual criminal culpability. Discussion on this issue in Rome will make little progress unless governments begin with the requirement of a prior determination by the U.N. Security Council that a state in fact has committed aggression and a definition that, for purposes of the statute of the court, is confined to the most obvious and non-controversial acts constituting a full-scale war of aggression.

3. While the United States has reserved its position on the issue of "state consent" before individual cases can be prosecuted before the ICC, we firmly believe that a government that has not ratified the ICC treaty must consent before there can be any prosecution of any of its nationals before the court. Otherwise, you would have the absurd situation whereby failure to ratify would subject your citizens to the jurisdiction of the court. Nonetheless, we have long proposed that the Security Council be able to override a State's denial of consent using the Security Council's enforcement authority. No one expects a rogue state to sign the ICC treaty anytime soon. To get at future crimes committed by

rogue states, the Security Council would, under the United States' proposals, be able to refer cases to the International Criminal Court using the Security Council's enforcement authority.

4. Some governments and NGO's seek a treaty that would require U.N. funding for the permanent court. We strongly oppose this. The permanent court will not be a U.N. court. It will not be part of the U.N. system. It will be a treaty-based court, that is, only those states that sign and ratify the treaty will be members. We believe the court should be financed by the States Parties to the treaty, with the exception that a Security Council referral to the Court logically would give rise to some form of U.N. financial contribution to the work pertaining to the referred matter.

5. The U.S. delegation has worked hard to advance protection for women's issues in the statute of the court. We have spearheaded efforts to accurately define war crimes pertaining to sexual violence, to ensure inclusion of qualified women in the staffing of the court (including the selection of judges), and to ensure that witness protection units address sexual violence issues.

6. Finally, the permanent court must not become a political forum in which to challenge controversial actions of responsible governments by targeting their military personnel for criminal investigation and prosecution. America does not shrink from accountability, but we will resist politically motivated or frivolous complaints against our armed forces.

In Rome, a common ground must be found on the fundamental issues still open in the international criminal court treaty. It will not be easy, but neither is this challenge an impossible one. The United States and its allies approach the Rome conference with cautious optimism and the hope that governments will recognize the common purpose that must bind us all—to bring to justice those responsible for genocide, crimes against humanity and war crimes, and, thereby, to help prevent them from occurring in the future.

Thank you.

Senator Ashcroft Confronts the ICC

SENATOR JOHN ASHCROFT

Mr. ASHCROFT. Mr. President, I rise today to express my profound concern for the International Criminal Court that was overwhelmingly approved in Rome late on Friday. I was pleased that the United States voted against final passage of this global criminal court. The Administration should be commended for rejecting this international folly, which would have been dead on arrival in the Senate.

Unfortunately, however, the danger from this Court has not passed. The Administration is already coming under pressure from proponents of the court to reconsider its opposition. Even more disturbing is the possibility that the Court would assert jurisdiction over American soldiers, despite the American refusal to join the court. The Administration should "just say no" to any efforts to get the United States to reconsider or to signal any informal compliance with the Court.

As both a Member of the Senate Foreign Relations Committee and as Chairman of the Subcommittee on the Constitution, Federalism and Property Rights, I find the International Criminal Court profoundly troubling. If there is one critical component of sovereignty it is the authority to define crimes and punishments. This Court strikes at the heart of sovereignty by taking this fundamental power away from individual countries and giving it to international bureaucrats.

There are other aspects of this Court that are equally troubling. As examples, the authorization of international independent prosecutors, the expense of such a permanent court, and the lack of any clear limits on the Court's jurisdiction are all alarming. But no aspect of this Court is more troubling than the fact that it has been framed without any apparent respect for—indeed, in direct contravention of—the United States Constitution.

As Chairman of the Constitution Subcommittee, I have a number of particular concerns about the Court. First and foremost, I remain concerned by the possibility that Americans could be dragged before this Court and denied the protections of the Bill of Rights.

Even more fundamentally, I am concerned that the Administration participated in these negotiations without making any effort to insist that the proposed International Criminal Court incorporate and honor the Bill of Rights. Even if one concedes that we need an International

John Ashcroft of Missouri (R) was elected to the United States Senate in 1994.

Criminal Court—which I emphatically do not—we should certainly insist on respect for the Bill of Rights as the price of American admission.

America's ideals and values are ascendant in the post–Cold War world. America's position as world leader is, in no small part, a product of a Constitution that is the envy of the world. The Administration should be justly proud of that Constitution and should have insisted that those principles form the cornerstone for any International Criminal Court. That unfortunately was not the official position of this Administration.

In the United States, there is a right to a jury of your peers. In the United States, there is a privilege against self-incrimination. In the United States, we have eliminated the prospect of criminal liability for ill-defined common law crimes. In the United States, the Constitution limits the authority of prosecutors. None of these protections will be guaranteed for defendants brought before this international star chamber.

The proposed Court negotiated in Rome neither reflects nor guarantees the protections of the Bill of Rights. The Administration was right to reject the Court and must remain steadfast in its refusal to join a court that stands as a rejection of American constitutional values. We must never trade away American sovereignty and the Bill of Rights so that international bureaucrats can sit in judgment of the United States military and our criminal justice system.

In today's *New York Times,* there is an opinion piece in which Anthony Lewis chastises the United States for missing a historic opportunity by failing to vote in favor of the International Criminal Court. The author states that the vote to form the International Criminal Court "will be seen as a turn in the road of history." That is perhaps the only point in the piece with which I agree. The approval of this Court was indeed "a turn in the road of history." By ceding the authority to define and punish crimes, many nations took an irrevocable step to the loss of national sovereignty and the reality of global government. I, for one, am heartened to see that the United States took the right turn on the road of history, and I will work hard to ensure that there is no backtracking.

(Senate—July 20, 1998)

PART II
National and International Security

Issue 4
Nuclear Weapons

INTRODUCTION

The development of nuclear weapons was judged by *Time* magazine to be the most significant event of the twentieth century. Born of world war and nurtured during the prolonged era of the Cold War, the presence of the atomic bomb altered the calculus by which nations look at and act towards one another. For those nations that came to possess them, nuclear weapons symbolized the high stakes game of international politics and the struggle for power and influence played out by its major protagonists.

Now that the end of the Cold War has considerably reduced the risk of nuclear conflict between the major nuclear weapon states, is there a need for the continued existence of such weapons? Or does their existence represent a risk, and a cost, no longer worth taking?

The first article in this section, the Goodpaster Committee report, which was sponsored by the Stimson Center Steering Committee for the Project on Eliminating Weapons of Mass Destruction, firmly concludes that, given the changed strategic context of the post–Cold War era, the continued presence of nuclear weapons is more a threat to national security than a protector of it. Citing the economic and political costs of maintaining a nuclear arsenal as well as the inherent risk of accidental or deliberate use, the committee concludes that nuclear weapons are of declining military and political utility and that the "assumed military and political value of nuclear weapons should be weighed against the dangers of continued nuclear reliance." While the report recognizes the continued deterrent function of nuclear weapons and thus does not advocate their unilateral elimination from the U.S. arsenal, it does state that "a world in which no state or group possessed nuclear weapons would be a safer place."

Robert G. Joseph and John F. Reichart counter the arguments of those whom they call the "New Eliminationists" by claiming that, although well intentioned, such theorists neglect to account adequately for the continued deterrent value of nuclear weapons in a world of new threats and new strategic challenges. They argue that, despite the fact that the strategic imperative of the Cold War no longer informs the nuclear dynamic, the deterrence of such new threats as the development of other weapons of mass destruction (that is, chemical and biological agents), the emergence of new nuclear weapon states, and the risk of proliferation of so-called rogue states warrants the maintenance of a "robust" nuclear capability. The need to maintain a hedge against the emergence or reemergence of a threat to national security is, for Joseph and Reichart, the "principal rationale for maintaining a credible and effective nuclear weapons posture."

As you read the articles, consider the following questions.

Discussion Questions

1. Is it possible to support the drastic reduction of the nuclear arsenal of the United States (to approximately five hundred weapons) and still maintain a credible nuclear deterrent?
2. Do the recommendations of Joseph and Reichart meet their own test for what a sound nuclear policy should look like?
3. Given the international community's stated goal of nonproliferation, does the continued existence of nuclear weapons undermine efforts to control their proliferation?
4. Considering the recent round of nuclear and missile tests by India and Pakistan, what conclusions are warranted concerning the utility of nuclear weapons in the post–Cold War international environment?

   For more information on this topic, visit the following websites:

   http://www.armscontrol.org
   The Arms Control Association

   http://www.csis.org
   Center for Strategic and International Studies

   http://www.ceip.org/programs/npp/nppbrief.htm
   Carnegie Endowment for International Peace: Non-Proliferation

The Declining Utility of Nuclear Weapons

THE GOODPASTER COMMITTEE

For over forty years, nuclear weapons have played a central role in U.S. foreign and defense policies. Throughout the Cold War, the United States relied on nuclear weapons to deter conventional and nuclear attacks by the Soviet Union and China on American territory, certain friendly states, and U.S. forces abroad. The extension of U.S. nuclear security assurances also dampened pressures for proliferation in Germany, Japan, South Korea, and other nations that otherwise might have chosen to seek to preserve their security through the independent possession of nuclear weapons. But the possession of nuclear weapons and reliance on nuclear deterrence also entailed significant costs and risks:

1. *Economic Costs.* The development and maintenance of large nuclear arsenals absorbed tremendous resources in the United States and the Soviet Union, and the final price tag for nuclear activities—especially environmental and safety costs—continues to rise. It is estimated that the United States will spend between $200 and $500 billion on environmental cleanup related to nuclear weapons facilities. The costs of cleaning up the monumentally worse contamination in the former Soviet Union is beyond calculation.[1] During a time of intense competition for budgetary resources, moreover, maintenance of the nuclear weapons infrastructure and currently planned force levels could divert scarce funds from other military programs of greater utility to U.S. national security.

2. *Political Costs.* Throughout the Cold War, the central role of nuclear weapons in U.S. and Soviet policies put the two states at odds with many non-nuclear states over nonproliferation policy and exposed them to increased dangers, particularly in crisis situations. If international support for nonproliferation continues to grow stronger, the United States's reliance on nuclear weapons is likely to be a source of renewed tension in relations with many non-nuclear states.

The Stimson Center Steering Committee for the Project on Eliminating Weapons of Mass Destruction included Andrew J. Goodpaster (chair), Howard Berman, Barry M. Blechman, William F. Burns, Charles A. Horner, James M. Jeffords, Michael Krepon, Robert S. McNamara, Will Marshall, Paul H. Nitze, Janne E. Nolan, Philip A. Odeen, Rozanne L. Ridgway, Scott D. Sagan, W. Y. Smith, John Steinbruner, and Victor Utgoff.

Reprinted by permission. *The Washington Quarterly*, Summer 1997. Vol. 20, No. 3, p. 91(5).

3. *Nuclear Accidents and Incidents.* Although the two nuclear superpowers devoted significant resources to the development of elaborate
security and safety systems, both countries suffered a number of near-
accidents and false alarms on several occasions. These incidents never
resulted in catastrophic consequences and were relatively few in number
compared to the total number of nuclear operations. Yet, even an advanced industrial power such as the United States with redundant safety
and security arrangements was unable to eliminate these risks entirely.
The risk of accident will persist so long as nuclear weapons exist. If an
accident ever occurred, the human, environmental, and economic costs
would be catastrophic.[2]

4. *Risk of Nuclear Use.* Most importantly, the very existence of
nuclear weapons entails a risk that these weapons will be used one day,
with devastating consequences for the United States and other nations.
The manipulation of nuclear risk in U.S.–Soviet relations, as during the
Cuban Missile Crisis and the 1973 Middle Eastern crisis, by its nature
implied a danger that a crisis could escalate and end in a cataclysmic nuclear exchange.[3] In the multipolar structure of international relations
that characterizes the post–Cold War period, the risks of nuclear use
could increase with every new nuclear power.

During the Cold War, the contributions of nuclear weapons to U.S.
national security and international stability were believed to outweigh the
dangers associated with their integration in foreign and defense policies
and, indeed, their very existence. There was no feasible alternative to reliance on nuclear deterrence, in any event. As long as the United States
faced a nuclear-armed and implacable foe in Moscow, there was little reason to reconsider the desirability of reliance on nuclear deterrence.

The strategic context that undergirded the Cold War calculus of nuclear risks and benefits has changed fundamentally, however. The dawn
of the nuclear age forced policymakers and military strategists to reex-
amine traditional assumptions about the uses and purposes of military
force in interstate relations. In a similar vein, the new strategic situation
demands a fundamental reassessment of the assumptions and theories
that have guided U.S. nuclear policy for four decades. What is the political and military utility of nuclear weapons in the post–Cold War era? Alternatively, what costs and dangers does continued reliance on nuclear
deterrence imply? In particular, what implications, if any, does the U.S.
nuclear posture have for international efforts to stem the spread of
weapons of mass destruction? These are the key questions that need to
be addressed.

In our view, U.S. nuclear weapons are of declining military and political utility in both addressing the residual threats of the Cold War and
in countering emerging threats to the security of the United States.

There is no need for the United States to use nuclear weapons against a non-nuclear opponent; sufficient U.S. conventional forces can and should be maintained to counter non-nuclear threats. In our view, the only military role of nuclear weapons should be to deter nuclear threats to the population and territory of the United States, to U.S. forces abroad, and to certain friendly states. Although the United States must be concerned about the proliferation of all weapons of mass destruction, a combination of defensive measures and strong conventional forces could neutralize the need for a nuclear retaliatory threat to deter chemical and biological attacks. Moreover, the nuclear deterrent function, the one necessary function in our view, can be preserved at much lower force levels, as long as other states move in tandem with the United States toward smaller nuclear forces. There is no military justification to maintain U.S. and Russian strategic nuclear stockpiles at their current or even planned START II [Strategic Arms Reduction Treaty] levels.

Current rationales for nuclear weapons are primarily political. Perceptions of the political and military utility of nuclear weapons, while changing, have been slow to catch up with the new strategic realities. Given the uncertainties surrounding the Russian reform movement, a certain reluctance to abandon traditional ways of thinking about nuclear weapons is understandable, and will necessarily constrain rapid movement to lower force levels.[4] However, the assumed military and political value of nuclear weapons should be weighed against the dangers of continuing nuclear reliance. In addition to the costs and risks already noted, political upheaval or the weakening of state authority in Russia or China could cripple existing systems for ensuring the safe handling and control of nuclear materials and weapons, increasing the odds of accidents, more widespread proliferation, or nuclear terrorism.

Indeed, the dispersion of nuclear weapons and nuclear weapons material is a major risk of continued nuclear reliance. Only nuclear weapons can destroy the United States as a society and a nation. States in the Middle East and Asia that are unfriendly to the United States already are seeking to acquire nuclear capabilities. While would-be proliferators may be motivated primarily by developments in their immediate regions, the actions and policies of the two largest nuclear powers could affect the health and durability of the nonproliferation regime more generally. A re-emphasis, or even continuing emphasis, on nuclear weapons in U.S. policy, for example, would undermine the United States's ability to persuade other states to cap, to reduce, or to eliminate their nuclear weapon capabilities. Indeed, a world in which no state or group possessed nuclear weapons would be a safer place for the United States.

In the long term, only a policy aimed at steadily curbing global reliance on nuclear weapons—including our own—is likely to progressively eliminate nuclear dangers. Under existing political conditions, the elimination of nuclear weapons is infeasible. But progress toward elimi-nation does not imply the creation of a world government. And much can be done in the current climate to reduce nuclear risks, while work-ing progressively to narrow the roles that nuclear weapons play in U.S. policy and in interstate relations.

NOTES

1. According to one estimate, the United States expended nearly $4 trillion on its nuclear forces over the past fifty years. The ultimate cost to the Soviet Union may be counted even higher, to the degree that the nuclear arms race contributed to Soviet economic stagnation and, eventually, to the dissolu-tion of the Soviet state. For an estimate of the total cost of the U.S. nuclear arsenal, see Stephen I. Schwartz, ed., *Atomic Audit: What the U.S. Nuclear Arsenal Really Cost* (Washington, D.C.: The U.S. Nuclear Weapons Cost Study Project, July 11, 1995), p. 3. For an estimate of the environmental clean-up costs, see Schwartz, p. 21. On the cost to the former Soviet Union, see Alexei G. Arbatov, ed., *Russian Arms Control Compliance and Imple-mentation* (Washington, D.C./Moscow: The Henry L. Stimson Center & The Center for Geopolitical and Military Forecasts, Spring 1994).
2. For examples of several incidents involving the nuclear weapons infra-structure in the United States during the Cold War, see Scott D. Sagan, *The Limits of Safety: Organizations, Accidents, and Nuclear Weapons* (Prince-ton, N.J.: Princeton University Press, 1993), Chapters 2–4. Recent reports from the former Soviet Union may indicate that the risks of a nuclear acci-dent are increasing due to the continued weakening of centralized control over nuclear facilities. See for example, Associated Press, "Russian Nu-clear Plant Fire Stirs Furor," *New York Times*, September 2, 1994, p. A8; Associated Press Wire Service, "Russia—Misguided Missile," March 13, 1995; "Unpaid bill triggers 15-minute power cut at Plesetsk ICBM test site," *Aerospace Daily*, September 18, 1995; and Oliver Wates, "Russian brass apoplectic over missiles power cut," Reuters News Service, Septem-ber 22, 1994.
3. In October 1962, the United States believed that there were neither strate-gic nor tactical nuclear warheads in Cuba. That belief influenced officials who were prepared to recommend to President Kennedy that he authorize an attack on the island. It is now known that at the height of the crisis, So-viet forces possessed approximately 60 strategic and 100 tactical warheads, and Khrushchev, anticipating a U.S. attack, had approved an order to move at least some of the warheads close to their delivery vehicles. Had the United States invaded Cuba, there was a high risk that the Soviets would have chosen to use their nuclear weapons.
4. Robert S. McNamara does not believe "uncertainties surrounding the Russian reform movement" should "necessarily constrain" balanced movement to lower force levels.

The Case for Nuclear Deterrence Today

ROBERT G. JOSEPH AND JOHN F. REICHART

The morality and utility of nuclear weapons have been debated passionately since their creation. Trinity, the first atomic detonation in 1945, vividly demonstrated the awesome destructive power of this technological leap. The explosion, which Manhattan Project's chief scientist Robert Oppenheimer described in apocalyptic terms, had an instant impact on the bomb's creators, several of whom would later question the wisdom of developing the weapon even though it had been designed and employed to end a conventional war that claimed the lives of tens of millions. At the time, no one disputed that the destruction of Hiroshima and Nagasaki had had a decisive impact on the Japanese leadership's decision to end the war, thereby saving a million or more American and Japanese lives. But neither did anyone relish a future in which the use of nuclear weapons would become an accepted condition of warfare.

In a well-intentioned effort to control, if not disinvent, nuclear weapons, therefore, the United States launched an urgent initiative within the new United Nations organization. The Baruch Plan would fail, however, because neither the United States nor the Soviet Union believed it could risk the consequences of not possessing these weapons in a Cold War climate of secrecy and mistrust. Given the failure to achieve international control and the Soviet subjugation of Eastern Europe, a consensus soon emerged that nuclear weapons were an essential component of the security posture of the West. In the preceding fifty years, conventional deterrence had twice failed to prevent world war, and in any case neither the United States nor the West Europeans had the will or means to match the Soviets' superior conventional forces. Hence, nuclear weapons seemed the only way to deter, even if based on a "balance of terror." Over the next four decades the names of deterrence

Robert G. Joseph and John F. Reichart are director and deputy director of the Center for Counterproliferation Research, National Defense University, and members of the National War College faculty. Ambassador Joseph is a former principal deputy assistant secretary of defense for international security policy. Dr. Reichart is a former member of the State Department policy planning staff. The opinions, conclusions, and recommendations expressed or implied in this article are solely those of the authors, and do not necessarily represent the views of the National Defense University, the Department of Defense, or any other government agency.

Reprinted by permission. *Orbis*, Winter 1998. Volume 42, Issue 1, p. 7, 13 pages.

doctrines would change with almost every administration, but the U.S. and NATO defense community consistently placed a reliance on nuclear weapons at the center of its strategy to deter Soviet bloc aggression.

Despite the sturdy public consensus in favor of nuclear weapons throughout the Cold War, some advocates continually called for abolition of these weapons. These political and religious groups ranged from ideological "peace" organizations cynically manipulated by Moscow, to dedicated pacifists, to mainline religious groups (epitomized by the work and guidance of both Catholic and Methodist bishops and others in the early and mid-1980s).[1] Despite their persistence, these movements had little influence on nuclear policy, force structure, or targeting largely because nuclear deterrence was seen by most observers, and almost all practitioners, as having worked to deter Soviet military forces from projecting force outward. The nuclear arsenal was thus a central ingredient in the broader strategy of containment and a critical tool of crisis stability during periodic bouts of brinkmanship.

While it is impossible to prove what would have happened had nuclear weapons not existed during the Cold War, the reality of what did not happen—World War III—would seem to vindicate those who advocated a strong nuclear deterrent. In the first half of the twentieth century tens of millions of combatants and civilians perished in war. In the second half of the century, millions more died in regional conflicts in which nuclear deterrence did not pertain. Yet, in Europe—arguably the most volatile Cold War battleground and potentially the deadliest because of the enormous concentration of armed forces there—war did not occur. The threat of escalation and nuclear annihilation made the prospect of war too horrific and reinforced caution in decision makers on both sides.

THE CASE OF THE "NEW ELIMINATIONISTS"

Today, noted groups and individuals advocating the abolition of nuclear weapons have revived the debate, again calling into question the role of these weapons in the contemporary security environment. This renewed debate should be welcomed and encouraged. It is essential that the role of nuclear weapons be understood, and policies about their employment subject to broad public support. Failure to achieve this understanding will undercut the support that is necessary both inside and outside the government for fashioning and maintaining a sound nuclear policy and a credible nuclear deterrent posture. Without a sound policy foundation, Western states could again become victims of their own fancy, such as occurred in the interwar period when attention was focused on outlawing war rather than deterring aggression.

What is the nature of the new nuclear debate? In the forefront are the "new eliminationists"—those advocating either complete abolition of nuclear weapons or drastic reductions as a first step to a nuclear-free world. They include various high-profile commissions, self-appointed committees, and distinguished individuals, including several retired four-star officers who held the highest "nuclear commands" during and after the Cold War. Representative of the arguments of these "new elim- inationists" are the Canberra Commission Report and the much publi- cized open letter from prominent generals and admirals concluding that nuclear weapons constitute "a peril to global peace and security," in light of which "the ultimate objective should be the complete and total elimination of nuclear weapons from all nations."[2]

Many, if not the majority of those who participated in the Canberra Commission and signed the open letter, as well as a large number of de- fense intellectuals who have since climbed on the bandwagon appear to support a two-step process. First, the major powers would quickly reduce their arsenals to a "few hundred" warheads. Secondly, they would pause for an assessment which, if conditions warrant, could then lead to total elimination. Often those taking this position explicitly disassociate them- selves from the "abolition now" camp, and criticize those who take the abolitionists to task for creating a straw man. Nevertheless, both camps rely on a similar rationale for their positions and recommendations which, although differing on timing and conditions, share the same goal.

The conclusions and recommendations of the "new elimination- ists" rest on four propositions:

1. The use of nuclear weapons against nonnuclear states is morally and politically indefensible, and the threat of nuclear use to deter these states is incredible. States such as Iraq, Iran, North Korea and the other so-called rogues can be deterred (even if armed with chemical and bio- logical weapons), and if necessary defeated by the West's vast technolog- ical superiority in conventional weaponry. The ability to hold at risk and destroy targets with nuclear weapons in these states provides no benefit. The United States would never—for ethical and political reasons—exer- cise such options.

2. The destructiveness of nuclear weapons is so great they have no military utility against another nuclear state except for deterrence. In this context, the justification for large deterrent stockpiles vanished with the demise of the Soviet Union. Russia, a new democracy strag- gling to reform, is now more a partner than competitor, and in any case cannot afford to maintain a modern nuclear arsenal.

3. The indefinite deployment of nuclear weapons, especially in light of the erosion of Russian control over its nuclear forces, carries a high risk of use through accident or inadvertence. Moreover, the prospect of "leak-

age" of sensitive materials and expertise from the former Soviet Union makes it imperative to improve security measures which can be enhanced by the reduction in overall force levels, and especially the dismantling of warheads.

4. The possession of nuclear weapons by some states stimulates others to acquire them, thereby reducing the security of all. The inherent double standard in the Non-Proliferation Treaty (NPT) regime must be overcome and its commitments to pursue complete nuclear disarmament must be fulfilled. Only in this manner will states such as India agree to become members. This strengthening of international norms will present further barriers to other states that clandestinely seek to acquire nuclear capabilities. The international community will thus come together to raise and enforce the barriers to acquisition of nuclear weapons.

RESPONDING TO THE CALL

A number of counter arguments have been made in response to the "new eliminationists." Perhaps the most direct is Sir Michael Quinlan's exposition of the dangers and fallacies of attempting to disinvent nuclear weapons.[3] Also, in well-argued testimony before Congress, Under Secretary of Defense Walter Slocombe has articulated the U.S. administration's case against abolishing nuclear weapons.[4] Neither, however, systematically addresses the core propositions of the new eliminationists which need to be examined one by one.

Morality and ethics. In terms of morality, the blanket charge that any use of nuclear weapons—and even reliance on the threat of nuclear retaliation for deterrence—would be immoral goes beyond past proclamations, such as those contained in the 1983 Catholic bishops' pastoral letter which, while calling for general disarmament and condemning the first use of nuclear weapons, left ambiguous the role of nuclear weapons for deterrence. If allowed to stand unchallenged, such a charge could carry substantial weight in the policy debate, especially in a democracy (and perhaps only in a democracy) built upon moral principles. But it does not take a trained ethicist to recognize that such blanket moral assertions are at best simplistic, and perhaps—in light of what we know about human nature and history—dangerous in themselves.

The use, or even threat of use, of any weapon may contain elements of moral ambiguity. And like other weapons—whether a club in Rwanda or artillery surrounding Sarajevo—nuclear weapons could be used in ways that are clearly immoral. Moreover, the scale of destruction that could result from the employment of even a few nuclear weapons makes imperative the need to consider carefully the full range of moral issues associated with the possession of these weapons. Perhaps for this reason, well-intentioned people have for decades debated where ethical lines should be drawn regarding the possession and use of nuclear weapons.

Yet, within this realm of considerable ambiguity, policymakers during the Cold War were forced to decide where the greater risk lay and make decisions with real consequences. Given the awful consequences of failure, the choice was not simple. On the one hand, nuclear deterrence could fail. In the aftermath of such failure, it was possible (but by no means certain, insofar as a conscious choice for use would have to be made by political authorities) that nuclear weapons would be unleashed on civilian populations with truly catastrophic consequences. On the other hand, in the absence of a credible nuclear deterrent, conventional deterrence could fail, as it had so often in the past, twice globally, resulting in another devastating war with casualties perhaps even greater than those in World War II.

Looking back, one might even argue that those who condemned nuclear weapons as immoral were simply wrong. The Western alliance's nuclear weapons were in fact the moral weapon of choice. They worked precisely as intended by deterring an immoral totalitarian state from attacking Western Europe and undermining the peace, values, and freedom which the democracies cherished. Indeed, given the tens of millions of innocent noncombatants killed in two world wars, one can argue that the possession of nuclear weapons to deter yet another outbreak of mass slaughter by conventional weapons, either in Europe or Asia, was squarely in the just war tradition.

The argument that the external environment has changed so much with the end of the Cold War that no ethical or moral basis for nuclear arms remains is likewise unconvincing. American lives and interests remain threatened. In fact, the proliferation of chemical and biological weapons have made the likelihood of conflict and the prospect of the use of weapons of mass destruction even greater than in the past in several key regions. But just as before, sound public and defense policy will emerge only from a prudent calculation of risks and benefits, not from sweeping generalizations about the morality or immorality of possession or use of nuclear weapons.

The "new eliminationists" who wrap themselves in the cloak of moral superiority and certainty should be asked to address the consequences of disarming the great democracies in a world in which advanced conventional, chemical, and biological weapons (and in some cases nuclear capabilities) continue to spread among states explicitly hostile to democratic values.

Utility. The primary purpose of nuclear weapons is and will remain the deterrence of the use of nuclear weapons by others. But this is not, nor has it ever been, the only rationale for these weapons. As noted, nuclear weapons were a key in NATO's planning to deter a Soviet conventional attack on Western Europe. Today, nuclear forces also contribute to the deterrence of states that possess the full spectrum of weapons of mass destruction, including biological and chemical weapons, such as Iraq in the Gulf War. Use of nuclear weapons against such states is not inconceivable, given sufficient provocation and threat. Conventional weapons may not be able to induce the shock and potential decisiveness of a nuclear weapon. A plausible hypothetical makes the point: Given clear intelligence that an adversary was making immediate preparations to launch biological agents against U.S. forces or population centers from a remote, deeply buried site, would not the president be prudent to explore a nuclear option, inasmuch as immediate, complete, and certain destruction of the target would be beyond the ability of even the most advanced conventional weapons?

Accidents, unauthorized use, and the "hair trigger." It is a truism that there is and always has been some level of risk of accidental or inadvertent use of nuclear weapons. But, just as there is a risk of a major dam breaking or an accident at a nuclear power plant, the real issue is how to manage and mitigate these risks. Current programs that make our stockpile and that of the former Soviet Union more secure are essential. But reducing the numbers of warheads does not in itself guarantee a reduction in risk. In any event, the risk of accidents or unauthorized use, though real, must be judged low, and this risk must be measured against the national security benefits gained from retaining nuclear weapons.

One increasingly popularized variant of the concerns stemming from inadvertent use is the growing alarm over the so-called "hair trigger" posture of currently deployed nuclear forces, especially Russian forces. In a recent commentary, former Senator Sam Nunn and Bruce Blair note that as a consequence of the "budget crunch facing the Russian military," Russia has declared "its readiness to launch on warning."[5] This crunch, according to the authors, has strained the Russian posture "to the point that Russian generals can no longer be confident of reliable retaliation after absorbing a systematic U.S. first strike" and "threatens to undermine the entire Russian system of command and control over its nuclear arsenal." The best near-term solution, they argue, is "de-alerting," which consists of measures such as placing heavy objects on the lids of missile silos, facing Russian mobile intercontinental ballistic missiles south, removing the tires from their launchers, and placing submarine forces on a "modified" alert status. In the longer term, "as confidence builds," all nuclear warheads might be separated from their delivery vehicles.

While Nunn and Blair do appear to have made a conceptual leap forward by arguing that the United States and Russia should renounce the logic of "mutual assured destruction"—a position earlier articulated by Presidents Reagan and Bush—their recommendations fall far short of achieving their goal of "mutual assured safety." The measures they propose are neither "adequately verifiable" nor "equitable" as they are described. In fact, very much like the "de-targeting" actions which the authors note "can be reversed in a matter of seconds," most of the "de-alerting" measures are easily and quickly reversible with little if any real time warning. As a result, such steps could actually be counterproductive—leading to greater instability and mistrust.

Real solutions, not arms control gimmicks, are required to address the problems of the Russian nuclear posture. We know from experience that dialogue and agreements must be governed by greater transparency, effective verification, and realistic expectations. We also know from experience that we must hedge against failure, which is why a missile defense system would be the best insurance against a Russian accidental or unauthorized launch. At various times in the past, Nunn promoted such a light missile defense. Now that he has called for the end of Mutual Assured Destruction (MAD), the central foundation upon which the Antiballistic Missile (ABM) Treaty was based, there should no longer be any doctrinal impediments to his support in procuring this insurance policy.

Possession by one stimulates acquisition by others. The international nonproliferation community has long held as a self-evident truth the belief that further proliferation can best be stemmed by the United States and the other nuclear states drastically reducing or eliminating their own nuclear stockpiles. But little evidence exists to support this article of faith.

In the past decade, the United States and Russia have already made radical reductions in their strategic and tactical nuclear arsenals, but proliferant states have shown little sign of restraint. To argue that these states will give up their nuclear ambitions if only the United States and other declared weapon states would go to zero is wishful thinking. As evident in the examples of the five declared nuclear powers, as well as the unacknowledged nuclear weapon states, motives for acquisition of nuclear weapons are complex and varied, ranging from security to prestige. The new proliferants—the Iraqs, Irans, and North Koreas—seek weapons of mass destruction as instruments of coercion and aggression and are not going to be persuaded to forego these tools as a consequence of others disarming. In fact, radical nuclear disarmament by the United States might promote proliferation by emboldening these states to seek relative parity with the United States (especially in a regional context).

Drastic reductions might also have a deleterious effect on the security calculations of U.S. allies who have long depended on the American nuclear umbrella. In an uncertain future, perhaps in the face of an aggressive China or resurgent Russia, the insecurities perceived by today's allies could compel them to develop their own nuclear deterrent capabilities or accommodate themselves to the threat in the absence of a credible American nuclear force.[6] The defection of even one major ally—Japan for instance—could have profoundly negative implications for global stability and U.S. security interests.

CONTINUING RATIONALE FOR NUCLEAR DETERRENCE

A principal rationale for maintaining a credible and effective nuclear weapon posture is based on the need to provide a hedge—an insurance policy—against a reversal in relations with Russia and China.[7] Over time, both of these nuclear states have demonstrated a tendency for radical shifts in their political orientation, as well as an enduring commitment to possess nuclear weapons both for the status they afford and as an essential part of their security strategy.

Neither Russia nor China would today seriously consider eliminating their nuclear arsenals, although they would both likely see real value in a unilaterally disarmed United States. Indeed, on the eve of the 1997 Helsinki Summit, while the United States was searching almost frantically to identify additional concessions to "broaden common ground" in the areas of a NATO–Russia charter and arms control, President Boris Yeltsin responded to a question involving a hypothesized NATO attack on Russia by emphasizing the importance of "nuclear means." This response was entirely consistent with an earlier remark by Russian defense minister Igor Rodionov, who stated: "We see the future of the Russian Armed Forces in using a rational composition of the Soviet Strategic Nuclear Forces to ensure guaranteed nuclear prevention of an all-out war and to prevent and localize armed conflicts in the vicinity of Russian borders."[8]

The contrast is stark. While Americans wring their hands over the pros and cons of dramatic reductions in U.S. nuclear forces, and even debate whether or not to go to zero nuclear weapons, the Russians and Chinese are modernizing their own nuclear forces. In the case of China, this entails building new missiles and warheads, recently tested. In the case of Russia, whose conventional forces are in desperate condition, nuclear modernization includes not only new missiles but elaborate and extraordinarily hardened command and control facilities. Russian doctrine today places more emphasis on nuclear weapons than did Soviet doctrine, as evidenced by Moscow's reversal of its long-standing no-first-use policy. The obvious point is that, given the inability to control or predict where these two states will be in five or ten years, it is essential to hedge against a reversal in relations. And the best hedge is to maintain a nuclear deterrent.

Turning to the contribution of nuclear weapons in a counterprolif-eration role, one can draw on the real world case of Desert Storm. Iraqi leaders attribute their decision not to use chemical weapons—and we now know biological agents as well—to the coalition's nuclear capabili-ties and warning of catastrophic consequences if Iraq were to use such weapons. General Wafic Al Sammarai, former head of Iraqi military in-telligence, has stated that Iraq did not arm its Scud missiles with chemi-cal weapons "because the warning was quite severe, and quite effective. The allied troops were certain to use nuclear arms and the price will be too dear and too high."[9] In retrospect, it appears that Saddam Hussein simply could not count on the United States (or perhaps Israel) refraining from responding with nuclear weapons, especially given his view of the world and demonstrated absence of constraints in the use of force to achieve his personal objectives.

Other factors may have weighed in the Iraqi decision, for example, practical operational considerations such as the perceived preparedness of U.S. forces to protect themselves—perhaps even more effectively than Iraqi forces—from the effects of chemical weapons on the battlefield. Citing interviews with Iraqi POWs, some analysts credit American pre-paredness for chemical warfare as the rationale for their non-use of chemicals in the Gulf War.

Whatever the mix of reasons for why deterrence of Iraqi biological and chemical weapons worked in the Gulf, however, most of the policy-level participants in that conflict consider the implied threat of a nuclear response to have been crucial. To be sure, senior Bush administration of-ficials have since testified that the United States would never have em-ployed nuclear weapons, but they make this statement not to deny the deterrent value of nuclear weapons, but simply to emphasize that there appeared to be no operational role for these weapons given the stun-ningly rapid victory of the coalition's conventional forces.[10]

Yet, what was important for deterrence was what Saddam Hussein believed. In this context, Secretary of Defense Richard Cheney's position is perhaps the most thoughtful. He states that nuclear weapons use was never seriously considered but that, had chemical or biological weapons been used against the United States, a nuclear response may have come under consideration. This is clearly the right message to send if the ob-jective is to strengthen deterrence.

Furthermore, as noted earlier, it has become popular to argue that radical reductions and even denuclearization might persuade regimes such as Iraq's to forego weapons of mass destruction entirely. This is simply astonishing. How can one believe that by drastically reducing or giving up its own nuclear weapons, one of the most important deterrent tools, the United States will strengthen deterrence? The opposite is surely the predictable outcome. For regimes such as those in Iraq, Iran,

Libya, and North Korea, weapons of mass destruction are their best counter to the West's conventional superiority. What is more, those governments say as much to the West and to their own people.

Why would these states grant the United States the overwhelming advantage of competing and conducting conflict on solely conventional terms? The answer is simple: they won't. As much as one would like to believe otherwise, all evidence is to the contrary. In the case of post–Desert Storm Iraq, Hussein has demonstrated his willingness to pay an enormous social and economic cost—estimated by some to approach $100 billion—to protect as much of his unconventional weapons infrastructure as possible.

Another argument of the nuclear abolitionists is that there are no "appropriate" targets for such weapons. Here, the premise of this argument is flawed. Deterrence suggests that the question of "appropriate targeting" resides, in large part, in the minds of the leaders one is seeking to deter—as was the case in Iraq. We also often hear that all relevant targets can be destroyed by advanced conventional weapons. Yet again, the evidence contradicts the assertion. In Desert Storm, the coalition was unsuccessful in its air strikes against underground targets which cannot in many cases be destroyed by conventional attack. The technology does not exist today—a fact recognized by states such as Libya which are placing their chemical and biological weapons facilities increasingly underground. In response to chemical attacks against American troops or biological attacks against U.S. population centers, the United States may want to destroy such targets promptly and with absolute certainty, rather than leave them operational even for a short time. It may also want to strike other military targets, perhaps even those that could be attacked with conventional forces, to cause shock and send a clear signal to all that any use of chemical and biological agents will be severely punished. What is essential is that the United States retain the option to respond and that this capability be known to potential adversaries. If one rules out these options, deterrence is undermined and the likelihood of conflict occurring increases, as well as the likelihood that chemical and biological weapons will be used against the United States and its allies.

THREE TESTS FOR A SOUND NUCLEAR POLICY

Policy decisions taken today regarding the U.S. nuclear stockpile will have real and long-standing consequences for peace and stability well into the next century. However one comes down on the core issues regarding nuclear weapons, policy recommendations derived from those convictions should be governed by three tests. First, the recommended policy prescriptions must be achievable in a real, not idealized, world. Secondly, understanding that unintended consequences can distort even the most well-intentioned policy, policy recommendations must be evaluated in light of all likely effects, with the risks and costs weighed carefully against the expected gains. Thirdly, the result of policy decisions must point us in the direction of a safer world and provide for greater security for the United States, its friends and allies.

Policy must be achievable. Even the "new eliminationists" argue that the move to abolish nuclear weapons, or even to go to very low numbers, should not be unilateral. But would all other nations with nuclear weapons or nuclear ambitions join the United States in this quest? Having led the world into the nuclear age, Americans in particular seem to possess a strong sense of responsibility to lead the world out of the nuclear age. While always quick to acknowledge that nuclear weapons can not be disinvented, the "new eliminationists" seek that very goal.

In fact, the optimism of these "new eliminationists"—some would say naivete—appears to be almost uniquely American. Looking at actions rather than words, the currency of nuclear weapons may actually be increasing in other countries. In Europe, France has been actively playing the nuclear card in the continental political context. In South Asia, India and Pakistan continue on a potentially deadly collision course, one that could involve nuclear confrontation. In the Middle East, one sees little evidence that Israel would even consider giving up the nuclear option. There, the call to disarmament is perceived at best as academically interesting, but of little relevance to a state whose existence is threatened by proliferation in its immediate neighborhood. In Iran, Iraq, and other states aggressively pursuing nuclear weapons, one can only wonder about the amusement that the American debate must invoke.

The elimination or reduction of nuclear weapons to very low levels would in any case pose currently insurmountable technical challenges. Monitoring, verification, and enforcement of a worldwide "zero option" regime would require levels of certainty that have not been achieved in any arms control regime to date. At low levels these critical aspects—which have been characterized alternatively as either central concerns by arms control skeptics or relegated to the realm of minor technical details by supporters of arms control—would assume enormous, undeniable importance. It is certainly unclear that sufficient safeguards can be invented, let alone implemented, and the monetary costs associated with that effort would likely be staggering. Russian resistance to suggestions for greater transparency in the current process of warhead dismantlement has revealed the barriers, both technical and psychological, that would frustrate complete nuclear disarmament. There is no realistic basis for confidence that these barriers can be surmounted.

Policy must take into account possible unintended consequences. The strategic consequences of drastic reductions in the U.S. nuclear force structure appear not to have been thought through by the "new eliminationists." What would be the effect on crisis stability in the event of a reversal in our relations with Russia? What would be the effect on potential regional adversaries who might then see parity with the United States as desirable and achievable? What would be the effect on our allies who have long relied on the U.S. nuclear guarantee? In sum, would a move to abolish nuclear weapons have the unintended consequence of encouraging conventional war and proliferation?

Policy must point us to a safer world. Those who promote the movement toward a nuclear-free world often see nuclear weapons as an evil in and of themselves. Some even argue that the elimination of these weapons is a precondition for a peaceful international order. The enduring lessons from World War II—particularly the need to avoid simplistic policy approaches which contributed to the most deadly conflict in our history—have again become blurred. For the United States and its allies, deterrence rather than disarmament through denuclearization remains the basis for sound policy, as deterrence has worked in the past to save countless lives by making the prospect of war horrific.

The prescriptions of the "new eliminationists" fail to satisfy these three tests for a sound policy. This is most dramatically, if unintentionally, revealed in the words of those generals and admirals who signed the open letter calling for nuclear disarmament, which states: "The exact circumstances and conditions that will make it possible to proceed, finally, to abolition cannot now be seen or prescribed."[11] One could hardly agree more. The prerequisites established by these and other eliminationists (such as near perfect inspection, surveillance and control of nuclear weapons infrastructures, and agreed procedures for forcible international intervention), when taken together, suggest that in a perfect world there may be no need for nuclear weapons. Here again, one could hardly agree more. The problem is the large and dangerous gap between wish and reality. In reaching across this wide gap in search of a better world—especially in light of this past century that had, until the atomic age, managed to achieve unprecedented levels of death in conventional wars—one ought not abandon too soon even those imperfect tools which have helped achieve an imperfect but nonetheless unprecedented stability.

In thinking about the role of nuclear weapons today and in the future, one must remember that, even at the height of the Cold War, no one possessed an exact understanding of how deterrence worked. In the end, it may have been the very uncertainty that surrounded the nuclear enterprise—the how, the when, and the where of our response up to and including strategic nuclear strikes—that imbued it with the greatest deterrent value. An adversary who knew, or thought he knew, what our exact response to a given provocation would be could work actively to undermine that course of action. This may be the case with deterrence today. We may not have a precisely drawn nuclear response to the use of chemical and biological weapons against us. We may not be able to tell our adversary—or even ourselves—what targets would be put at risk to nuclear response if he unleashed these weapons against us. It is, however, this very uncertainty—coupled with the certainty that we will respond decisively—that should prey on the minds of adversaries and that ultimately provides the rationale for nuclear weapons.

NOTES

1. See, for example, United States Catholic Conference, "The Challenge of Peace: God's Promise and Our Purpose," Washington, D.C., 1983.
2. "Statement on Nuclear Weapons," by International Generals and Admirals, Dec. 5, 1996, and George Lee Buffer, "The General's Bombshell: Phasing Out the U.S. Nuclear Arsenal," *Washington Post*, Jan. 12, 1997. Both are reprinted in the *Washington Quarterly*, Summer 1997, pp. 125, 131.
3. Sir Michael Quinlan, "The Future of Nuclear Weapons in World Affairs," *Bulletin of the Atlantic Council of the United States*, Nov. 20, 1996.
4. Statement of the Honorable Walter B. Slocombe, Under Secretary of Defense for Policy, before the Senate Governmental Affairs Subcommittee on International Security, Proliferation and Federal Services. Hearing on Nuclear Weapons and Deterrence, Feb. 12, 1997.
5. Sam Nunn and Bruce Blair, "From Nuclear Deterrence to Mutual Safety," *Washington Post*, June 22, 1997, sec. C, p. 1.
6. Germany and Japan are among the countries that are considered potential candidates for proliferation should the U.S. nuclear umbrella be removed. See Keith B. Payne, *Deterrence in the Second Nuclear Age* (Lexington, Ky.: University of Kentucky Press, 1996), pp. 21–22, for insights into Japanese views.
7. This section is taken from Robert Joseph, "Nuclear Deterrence and Regional Proliferators," *Washington Quarterly*, Summer 1997.
8. "Russia and Its Armed Forces in Changing Europe," *Military News Bulletin*, December 1996.
9. Quoted in Payne, *Deterrence*, p. 84. An extensive discussion of deterrence in the Gulf War appears on pages 81–87.
10. In the context of deterring the use of Iraqi chemical weapons, Secretary Baker writes: "I purposely left the impression that the use of chemical or biological agents by Iraq could invite tactical nuclear retaliation." James A. Baker, III, *The Politics of Diplomacy* (New York: G. P. Putnam's Sons, 1995), p. 359. See also, Colin Powell, *My American Journey* (New York: Random House, 1995). Powell looked at the operational utility of "small tactical nuclear weapons" only at the urging of Secretary Cheney and found them wanting.
11. See international generals' "Statement on Nuclear Weapons."

Issue 5
Nuclear Proliferation

INTRODUCTION

What difference does it make to America or to the world if yet another nation has nuclear arms? The two articles in this section illustrate different sides of the debate over India's recent demonstration of its nuclear capability. Whereas President Clinton denounces India's nuclear tests, the editors of *The Progressive* claim that if the United States is to have any credibility when it denounces other nations, it must first give up its own nuclear development program. How did the world arrive at this point in the debate? A brief summary will make clear where we stand and how we got there.

The development of nuclear weapons began in 1895 when German scientist Wilhelm Konrad Roentgen discovered X rays. Following his discovery, Marie and Pierre Curie discovered polonium in 1896 and radium in 1897. These discoveries gave rise to related theories, such as Albert Einstein's theory of relativity (1905). In 1921, American chemist H. D. Harkins announced the discovery of neutrons; and in 1933, Hungarian physicist Leo Szilard presented a theory about how a series of neutron collisions could produce a chain reaction that would release an enormous amount of energy. In 1934, Szilard received a patent for an atomic bomb. From 1942 to 1945, the first atomic bomb was developed by the secret Manhattan Project at Los Alamos, New Mexico. On August 6, 1945, an atomic bomb destroyed the Japanese city of Hiroshima. The destruction of Nagasaki by a second atomic bomb followed on August 9.

Today, the United States has 9,600 nuclear weapons, an amount that is considerably fewer than the 30,000 weapons it had at the height of the Cold War. About 2,600 of the current missiles are awaiting dismantlement. Other nations have thousands more. Although a series of ten major treaties, from the Limited Test Ban Treaty in 1963 to the START (Strategic Arms Reduction

Treaty) II in 1993, have been signed, the full arms reductions expected after the end of the Cold War have been stalled by a number of events, including the splintering of the former Soviet Union.

As you read the articles, consider the following questions.

Discussion Questions

1. On what rational basis can the United States argue that other countries should reject nuclear weapons when America maintains the largest nuclear force in the world?
2. Are nuclear weapons of any practical use?
3. What is the best strategy for minimizing the proliferation of nuclear weapons to countries around the world?

> For more information on this topic, visit the following websites:
>
> **http://www.atozindia.com/nuclear/index.htm**
> Indian Nuclear Testing
>
> **http://www.pbs.org/wgbh/pages/amex/bomb/**
> Nuclear Arms Race
>
> **http://infomanage.com/Nonproliferation/**
> Nonproliferation Web Directory

The President's Radio Address on Nuclear Tests by India, May 16,1998

PRESIDENT BILL CLINTON

The PRESIDENT: Good morning. This week I want to speak to you about a matter of grave concern to the United States and the international community: India's nuclear test explosions. These tests were unjustified and threaten to spark a dangerous nuclear arms race in Asia. As a result, and in accordance with our laws, I have imposed serious sanctions against India, including an end to our economic assistance, military financing, and credit or loan guarantees.

I'm at the G-8 summit of the major industrial powers in Birmingham, England, where the major nations here, along with friends and allies around the world, have joined us in condemning India's actions.

This is especially disappointing to me because I have long supported stronger ties between the United States and India. After all, India will soon be the world's most populous country. Already it has the world's largest middle class and 50 years of vibrant democracy to its credit. And America has been immeasurably enriched by the contributions of Indian Americans who work hard, believe in education, and have really been good citizens.

For all these reasons the United States and India should be close friends and partners for the 21st century. And they make it all the more unfortunate that India has pursued this course at a time when most nations are working hard to leave the terror of the nuclear age behind. So in this instance India is on the wrong side of history.

Over the past few years we've made remarkable progress in reducing nuclear arsenals around the world and combatting the spread of nuclear weapons. Building on the work of the Reagan and Bush administrations, we entered that START I treaty into force, lowering both Russian and American nuclear arsenals. And we ratified START II to go further. Now, when Russia's parliament approves START II, we'll be on course to cut American and Russian nuclear arsenals by two-thirds from their Cold War height. We also work with Ukraine, Belarus, and Kazakhstan to return to Russia the nuclear weapons left on their land when the Soviet Union broke apart. We extended indefinitely and unconditionally the Nonproliferation Treaty, which makes it harder for states that do not now possess nuclear weapons to acquire them. And just last month, working with the United Kingdom and the Republic of

Georgia, we helped to secure a small amount of bomb-grade uranium in the Republic of Georgia that could have posed a serious danger if it had fallen into the wrong hands. Two years ago I was proud to be the first national leader to sign the Comprehensive Test Ban Treaty, first proposed by President Eisenhower, advanced by President Kennedy, and brought to conclusion by my administration working with almost 60 other nations. This treaty, called the CTBT, bans all nuclear explosions, thus making it more difficult for the nuclear states to produce more advanced and dangerous weapons and much harder for non-nuclear states to develop them in the first place. Already, 149 other nations have signed on. The CTBT also strengthens our ability to detect and deter nuclear testing by other countries. That's a mission we must pursue, with or without this treaty, as India's actions so clearly remind us. The CTBT's global network of sensors and the short-notice on-site inspections it allows will improve our ability to monitor and discourage countries from cheating. I submitted the treaty to the Senate last fall. Now it's all the more important that the Senate act quickly, this year, so that we can increase the pressure on, and isolation of, other nations that may be considering their own nuclear test explosions. The Indian government has put itself at odds with the international community over these nuclear tests. I hope India will reverse course from the dangerous path it has chosen by signing the CTBT immediately and without conditions. And India's neighbors can set a strong example of responsibility for the world by not yielding to the pressure to follow India's example and conduct their own nuclear tests. I hope they won't do that. We have an opportunity to leave behind the darkest moments of the 20th century and embrace the most brilliant possibilities of the 21st. To do it we must walk away from nuclear weapons, not toward them. Let us renew our determination to end the era of nuclear testing once and for all. Thanks for listening.

The Return of Nuclear Terror

THE EDITORS OF *THE PROGRESSIVE*

By testing nuclear weapons, India and Pakistan have made a terrible mistake. And the United States—despite its pleas with both countries not to conduct nuclear tests—bears part of the blame.

On May 11 and May 13, India set off five explosions. One was a hydrogen bomb. Pakistan, a rival of India's since Britain split the countries apart in 1947, responded with what it claimed were six detonations. In both countries, most citizens responded with jubilation.

The United States denounced the tests, and President Clinton promised harsh economic sanctions. But who is our President to act all high and mighty about nuclear weapons? The United States maintains the world's largest nuclear arsenal and is still developing nuclear bombs at Lawrence Livermore Laboratory through the Stockpile Stewardship and Management Program. It manages to circumvent the Comprehensive Test Ban it signed in 1996 by conducting "subcritical" tests or simulating tests with sophisticated computers. President Clinton has threatened to use nuclear bombs against Iraq, Libya, and North Korea. And he has issued a directive that would allow for the use of U.S. atomic weapons against non-nuclear states, which breaks a promise the U.S. government made to these states during the negotiations of the Nuclear Non-Proliferation Treaty.

The other nuclear powers also have large arsenals—there are thousands of nuclear warheads in Russia, and hundreds each in China, France, and the United Kingdom. None of these nuclear powers has set up a schedule to get rid of them.

The nuclear powers have also been shamefully lax about controlling the proliferation of nuclear materials and technology.

But that is no excuse for India and Pakistan to test nuclear weapons of their own. There is a lot of foolish machismo surrounding these blasts. "Millions of Indians have viewed this occasion as the beginning of the rise of a strong and self-confident India," said India's prime minister, Atal Bihari Vajpayee, after the tests. "I fully share this assessment and this dream." Two weeks later, President Nawaz Sharif of Pakistan announced, "Today, we have evened the score with India."

The economic penalties will be severe for both countries. India's growth will be stunted, and Pakistan, already one of the ten poorest countries in the world, will wilt further.

Reprinted by permission. *The Progressive,* July 1998. Vol. 62, Issue 7, p. 8, 2/3p.

But above all, there is the horrible threat of nuclear war.

"It is absolutely critical that the world community stop the two countries before they blow each other up," says Pervez Hoodbhoy, a professor of nuclear physics at Islamabad University. "That's a real possibility. I am terrified."

Hoodbhoy is right. Every diplomatic effort needs to be made to lessen the likelihood of a nuclear war between India and Pakistan. It is an urgent situation.

But the old nuclear powers also need to change course. The U.S. government should take the lead. It should stop spreading nuclear material and technology. It should cease designing and testing new weapons. It should start obeying the letter and the spirit of the nuclear treaties it has signed. And it should get on the road to nuclear disarmament by setting and adhering to a schedule for destroying its nuclear stockpiles and for persuading the other powers to do likewise.

We must work not just for a nuclear-free India and Pakistan, but a nuclear-free world.

The alternative is disaster.

Issue 6
NATO Expansion

INTRODUCTION

Military alliances seldom outlive the purpose behind their formation. When the specter of increased communist influence in Europe loomed as a significant threat to Western democracies in the immediate post–World War II era, the response was the creation of a defensive collective security organization, the North Atlantic Treaty Organization, or NATO. Nowhere was the end of the Cold War of greater impact than to the security architecture of Europe. Indeed, one of the first topics to engage U.S. foreign and security policy-makers prior to the dissolution of the Soviet Union was the fate of NATO in the post–Cold War environment.

Arguments in support of both NATO continuation and its enlargement can be found in the article by John O'Sullivan. The main points of his defense of NATO enlargement are as follows:

1. Enlargement will consolidate the gains that the democratic world won in its victory in the Cold War.
2. Enlargement will act as a further hedge against political, social, and economic instability, as well as a boost to those forces that favor the expansion of democracy and free-market economies.

Perhaps the strongest argument in support of NATO and its expansion is to pose the question, If not NATO, then what? As nature abhors a vacuum, the world of realpolitik abhors a power vacuum. This question must be addressed in considering the likely consequences either of a Europe without a NATO or of a Europe standing pat in the security environment.

Alvin Z. Rubinstein interprets the decision to accelerate the expansion of NATO as "based neither on strategic logic nor military threat" but driven by domestic political reasons within the United States. While acknowledging the importance of such issues as "the costs; the effect on U.S.-Russian relations; and the strengthening of security and democratization in Europe," Rubinstein also points to "other neglected but equally important issues [involving] the strategic, political, and financial interests of the United States itself; the uncomfortable German factor; and the asymmetry between U.S. interests and those of Western Europe."

One thing is certain: The debate about the expansion of NATO has taken place in a political vacuum. Given that the question of enlargement represents a considerable expansion of U.S. foreign and security policy commitments, it is remarkable that this debate has taken place without more significant discussion. As you read these two articles, the developments in the Balkans as of April 1999 must not escape your attention. Try to assess the positions of the two authors, along with the questions at the end of this introduction, in light of what happened to the NATO mission in Kosovo.

Also, as you read the articles, consider the following questions.

Discussion Questions

1. Are the benefits of NATO expansion worth the risk of alienating Russia in the coming millennium?
2. What is NATO's new role, if it has to have a new role? Specifically, if "out-of-area" operations are its new function, how far out-of-area should NATO go?
3. Should the expansion of NATO go beyond the three new members admitted in March 1999? Why, or why not?
4. If not NATO, then what?
5. Does the United States need NATO to advance U.S. foreign and security policy objectives in the immediate future?

   For more information on this topic, visit the following websites:

   http://www.acus.org
   The Atlantic Council of the U.S.

   http://www.nato.int/
   The North Atlantic Treaty Organization

   http://www.igcc.ucsd.edu
   Institute on Global Conflict and Cooperation (IGCC)

Sold on NATO:

The Case for Expansion

JOHN O'SULLIVAN

The senate's vote to expand NATO will mean a stronger Atlantic alliance—and a more stable world in which the U.S. and the west will remain predominant.

The 80–19 vote by the U.S. Senate to endorse the admission of Poland, Hungary, and the Czech Republic to NATO took place in the same week as the European Union heads of government voted to launch Europe's single currency, the Euro. Both decisions were routinely described as "historic" by headline-writers and television anchor-persons. And, to be sure, both will have serious consequences in the short- and even medium-term. But only one of them is "historic," if that means likely to shape the long future. For the Euro points toward the chimera of a European superpower independent of (and perhaps rivaling) America, whereas NATO enlargement suggests that the future will continue to be a united Atlantic alliance under American leadership.

These opposing possibilities emerge in the extraordinary flux of post Cold War politics in which NATO has lost its traditional role as the main defense against Communism. We sometimes understate the revolutionary character of that change. In theory, NATO last month could have dissolved, expanded, or embarked on some other course entirely—and there are numerous ideas for "a new role for NATO" buzzing around in alliance bonnets and (covertly) in some anti-alliance bonnets.

Some of those ideas—notably, dissolution and "standing pat"—were never likely to be implemented. Quite apart from the sociological law that says organizations never go out of business even if their main aim has been achieved (the only exception being a slightly ominous one, the Committee for the Free World, which Midge Decter closed down after the dissolution of the Warsaw Pact), NATO's essential aim has not been permanently achieved. True, the Soviet threat is gone; but a nuclear-armed and potentially unstable Russia is still in the game; a major conflict has just been fought in the very Balkans which sparked the First World War; and there are a number of potential wars and civil wars lurking in such regions as the Tyrol, the Basque country, Northern Ireland (not yet finally settled),

John O'Sullivan is editor-at-large of *National Review,* and is founder and cochairman of the New Atlantic Initiative.
Reprinted by permission. *American Spectator,* June 1998, Vol. 31, Issue 6, p. 24, 5p, 1c.

Corsica, Belgium, Kosovo, and Eastern Europe and the Balkans generally where, it is said, "every England has its Ireland, and every Ireland its Ulster." If none of these seems to threaten the European peace very urgently at present, that is in part because the existence of NATO makes any such threat futile and even counter-productive. No nation or would-be nation wants to take NATO on.

And if not NATO, what? There are international bodies which could mediate some of the lesser conflicts: the Organization for Security Cooperation in Europe is explicitly given that responsibility, and the European Union is always itching to show it can play a Big Power role. But neither body has the military heft or the prestige to deter or repress serious strife. The OSCE is a collective security organization, and as Henry Kissinger said of a similar body: "When all participants agree, there is no need for it; when they split, it is useless." And the EU only made itself look ridiculous when it attempted to halt the Bosnian conflict in its relatively early stages when a decisive intervention might have succeeded.

As for dealing with a revived Russian threat, there is no military alliance in sight other than NATO that could do the job. In a sense, NATO today is Europe's defense. Except for the American forces, Western armies can no longer play an independent military role. They are wedded to NATO structures and dependent on NATO, especially American, technology. (As a French general admitted in the Gulf War: "The Americans are our eyes and ears.") If NATO were to dissolve—even if it were to be replaced by some European collective defense organization such as a beefed-up Western European Union—it would invite chaos as every irridentist faction sought to profit from the sudden absence of the main guarantor of European stability.

"Standing pat"—or military readiness to respond to an attack on an existing NATO member but no one else—has turned out to be similarly unrealistic. This approach would have turned Eastern Europe into a turbulent no-man's-land by forswearing any willingness to intervene if the region should erupt into war or civil war. Sound familiar? It is the policy NATO actually pursued for the first few years of the Bosnian conflict. To be sure, it was eventually abandoned, partly because of the "CNN factor" (i.e., Western public opinion cannot tolerate innocent people being raped, tortured, and murdered in full view if it seems that something could be done about it). But there was another reason too: the recognition among soldiers and politicians that NATO would eventually atrophy if people thought it could or would do nothing about the kinds of conflict most likely to occur in post Cold War Europe. As one British soldier memorably told a National Review correspondent: "Our governments have spent billions of pounds giving us the best equipment and the best training. People are going to start asking what it was all for, if we say we're incapable of knocking a few drunken Serbs off a hillside."

Other ideas for reforming NATO were more realistic, and indeed some are still on the agenda. The most canvassed item is that NATO should go "out of area" where, after all, most of the world's most dangerous conflicts now occur. This option probably had to wait until NATO enlargement had been agreed upon. For NATO would have been unlikely to leap over its next-door neighbors to intervene in Central Asia or North Africa or farther afield. The excluded countries would hardly have been willing to assist its military operations with free passage and logistical help. The most likely destinations for any NATO force are Eastern Europe and the Balkans. Indeed, NATO is already in Bosnia, and its operations there receive assistance from Hungary. If the other countries of the region were to be a permanent no-man's-land between the NATO powers and Russia—which is what exclusion from NATO would have meant—they would continue to be prey to economic backwardness, political instability, and ethnic-cum-national rivalries. Western investors would be less keen to direct capital to them. Extreme political movements would flourish. And some localities, if not entire countries, would succumb to civil wars and irridentist struggles such as have already disfigured many of the former Soviet republics. NATO would then expand eastwards anyway—not into countries made more stable and prosperous by NATO membership, but into nations made backward and unstable by the effects of exclusion.

And what of Russia in these circumstances? The Kremlin, let alone the Duma, would presumably be more concerned at NATO going into Eastern Europe than at Eastern Europe going into NATO. But how will the West allay the latter concern? If the Russians were asked to join in an intervention, as in Bosnia, then the former Soviet satellites would be horrified, perhaps to the point of resistance. If not, the Russians would face the considerable humiliation of non-local Western forces re-imposing order in what was recently their sphere of interest—and at a heightened moment of crisis. That would seem to be the worst scenario of all.

Which brings us to the policy of expanding NATO. The U.S. Senate has so far ratified only the admission of the first round of entrants. Other East European countries expect to be admitted over time as they meet the military and political criteria for entry. These are major changes in Western and U.S. policy, and they represent serious American military and diplomatic commitments. It is hardly surprising that they have aroused opposition from a heterogeneous yet influential coalition—America Firsters, notably Pat Buchanan himself, suspicious of foreign entanglements; old foreign policy liberals, including Thomas Friedman of the *New York Times*, nervous of alienating Russia's fledgling democracy; hard-headed "realists," such as Owen Harries of the *National Interest*, made dyspeptic by anything that smacks of over-extended Wilsonianism; and libertarians, such as the boys down at the Cato

Institute, who have tumbled to the fact that the U.S. Army is a federal agency.

Expansion opponents made some plausible arguments, appealing to isolationist instincts that are said to be rooted in American history. It is true that there is no "clear and present danger" to justify expansion. The dangers in question are future and hypothetical. But prudence—which is the virtue in foreign policy—suggests that we should prepare for eventualities we cannot entirely foresee. It is also true that our feckless European allies, far from increasing defense expenditure, are cutting it. But then so is America. The case for a modest defense build-up is independent of NATO expansion—and may even be strenghtened by it, if our allies are thus induced to hike defense spending even modestly. (This objection also ignores the fact that not merely the increase in—but the entirety of—the military spending of the new NATO members will be devoted to fighting alongside American troops rather than against them. By any standards, this is an increase in the defense spending of our NATO allies. Maybe we should even count it twice.) And finally, "Will Americans die for Danzig?" sounds a powerful rhetorical question. Yet they did last time, as *National Review* pointed out. Two world wars began because European powers made the miscalculation that America would not intervene. NATO enlargement will deter such miscalculations in the future, and because the alliance disposes of such overwhelming military force, it will deter them very effectively.

Still, these are seductive arguments. So it is remarkable, especially when isolationism is said to be growing, that such widespread and substantial opposition has been decisively defeated. Not only has NATO enlargment been endorsed by an overwhelming eighty senators, but it has continued to receive majority support in polls of both public and elite opinion. This suggests that fifty years experience of the Cold War shaped an American opinion that, however reluctantly, is prepared to shoulder the burdens of world and alliance leadership. Americans are isolationist in the abstract or when an intervention has plainly failed; they are rational and prudent interventionists when the matter is put to the test.

And on this occasion, they were confronted by a powerful short-term case for NATO expansion: namely, that it would extend the zone of prosperity and political stability in Europe. As Adrian Karatnycky of Freedom House points out, even the mere prospect of NATO membership has altered political behavior for the better in the applicant countries. They have been persuaded to make their economies freer, to entrench democratic practices, to extend constitutional protections for minorities and human rights, and in particular to settle their border and ethnic disputes. That in turn has made them more attractive venues for foreign investment. These countries are now better markets for American goods and capital and lesser threats to the regional peace, offering smaller anxieties for American diplomacy and fewer entangling invitations to intervene. All these important gains would have been put at risk if the U.S. Senate had rejected NATO enlargement.

Even if that list exhausted its gains, enlargement would still be a prudent and beneficial policy. But the larger and long-term argument is that NATO expansion is an important step toward consolidating the West under American leadership.

Just why the West needs to consolidate has been explained recently by such disparate voices as Margaret Thatcher and the *Economist* magazine. As the latter has described it, the geopolitical picture in the next century will contain no fewer than six superpowers, namely China, Russia, Japan, an Islamic bloc, "Europe," and the U.S. And in the second volume of her memoirs, Lady Thatcher added up a slightly different hypothetical list—the USA, Japan, the European Union, India, China, Brazil, and possibly Russia—to produce the following nightmare scenario:

> an unstable world in which there are more than half-a-dozen "great powers," all with their own clients, all vulnerable if they stand alone, all capable of increasing their power and influence if they form the right kind of alliance, and all engaged willy-nilly in perpetual diplomatic maneuvers to ensure that their relative positions might improve rather than deteriorate. In other words, 2095 might look like 1914 played on a somewhat larger stage.

Forecasting the crises that might occur in this hypothetical world is plainly a hazardous enterprise. But at the recent Congress of Istanbul held by the New Atlantic Initiative, Brian Beedham, in a brilliant exercise of the geopolitical imagination, suggested that the Atlantic democracies would face "in rising order of probability, a challenge to their present degree of military superiority; the growth of a powerful China whose foreign policy will reach much further into the world than that of today's China; and, partly because of that, a prolonged and dangerous multi-power contest for influence over a large segment of Asia," mainly because of its oil reserves.

What makes such challenges more threatening is that the U.S. will no longer hold the position of unique unipolar dominance that it enjoys today. It will certainly not wield the influence in international organizations and arrangements, ranging from the U.N. to the international trading system, that it does now. Although the U.S. will probably remain the single most powerful state, it will be less powerful than various possible anti-American combinations of two or more states—especially if one of those states is China which, in the *Economist*'s view, will be only marginally less potent than Uncle Sam.

Lady Thatcher, Mr. Beedham, and the *Economist* therefore reach exactly the same policy conclusion: The U.S. and "Europe" must remain united in the Atlantic alliance—indeed, that alliance must become a much deeper and more extensive relationship, what Mr. Beedham calls "a standing alliance." Such a superpower coalition would still be militarily head-and-shoulders above any potential rival or combination of rivals, and it would represent a share of world trade and productive capacity similar to that enjoyed by the U.S. after 1945.

Where would Russia fit into this picture? Fears that NATO expansion will humiliate the Russians and drive them into a foreign policy of permanent opposition to American interests are wildly overstated. We have it on the word of General Lebed (no softie) that NATO expansion causes him no nightmares. Nor should it. Judged in the proper long perspective, the induction of countries like Poland into an alliance in which the dominant member is the U.S. is a guarantee that they will be restrained rather than unleashed. Otherwise, attitudes in the Russian elite do not correspond to the simple "Russian humiliation" thesis, but fall instead into three broad schools.

There are those who want Russia to be treated as a "Great Power," best illustrated by the Russian general who on being asked whether his country would object if NATO intervened in Yugoslavia, replied: "You can drop an atom bomb on Belgrade if you like—as long as you consult us first!" They have been bought off (at too high a price) by the Founding Act relationship Russia now enjoys with NATO.

Second, there are the chauvinists and anti-Americans nostalgic for the Soviet empire, who would like to detach America from Europe altogether (the "Common European Home" strategy), or failing that, to construct a kind of "Jihad Central" in Moscow which would make trouble for the U.S. in the Third World. There is no point in seeking to appease such opponents; they are unappeasable. And insofar as they harbor ambitions to restore a Russian sphere of interest in Central and Eastern Europe, it is such ambitions that are a threat to peace and stability down the line. NATO expansion is a firm but implicit warning that this is unacceptable to the countries concerned and to the West.

Finally, there are the democratic reformers (a.k.a. "Westernizers") who opposed NATO expansion because it would not include Russia. They wish Russia to be one of the senior partners in a pan-Western alliance and feel rejected by the current limited NATO enlargement. The East Europeans, of course, want that enlargement precisely as a protection against Russia. This circle cannot be squared—for the moment; but fortunately the "Westernizers" are prepared to accept the halfway-house of the Partnership for Peace and the Founding Act—for the moment. What the West cannot do is close off the eventual possibility of Russian membership. That might humiliate a key group of friendly Russians, and it might not be consistent with U.S. and Western interests in fifty years time.

For it is far from fanciful to imagine that in a world in which China, either alone or in combination with Japan or other powers, poses the main challenge to the West, Russia itself would eventually join an enlarged NATO without objection from the East Europeans. After all, it was a very similar threat from the Soviet Union that persuaded the West Europeans and the U.S. to overcome much greater divisions and suspicions to forge NATO in the first place. The decision to enlarge NATO would then seem—in the retrospect of the future—to have been a large step toward such an expanded pan-Western bloc.

How is Mr. Beedham's "standing Atlantic alliance" to be achieved? The many aspects of this ambitious concept come down to a choice between two courses of action: Should the European Union develop a "defense identity"? Or should NATO grow an economic identity in the form of a free-trading Atlantic economic community? If the first course were adopted, a new series of developments would be set in motion.

The first is that it would gradually cease to be a unipolar alliance in which the U.S. is "first among equals," and become a bi-polar one in which the U.S. and the new structure embodying a "European defense identity" would share equal influence. Such ideas are very fashionable at present in the European Union, notably in Paris and Brussels, but they have certain obvious drawbacks. There is no military reason whatsoever for a European defense identity; it is entirely a political project designed to advance European federalism. As such, it would divert NATO's attention and resources from real problems in order to solve an imaginary one. And if a European collective defense body, within or without NATO, is intended to be capable of action independent of the U.S.—as self-respect and the statements of its partisans suggest—then it would require increases in defense spending far vaster than even the highest estimates of NATO expansion eastwards. Needless to say, no such spending hikes are on the agenda of any European politician.

A final drawback to a distinct European defense identity is its potential for damaging alliance cohesion. An organization in which one member occupies a position of undisputed leadership is naturally more harmonious than one in which leadership is a matter of doubt and thus a source of constant squabbling. And this is a vital consideration in an organization like NATO which may have to respond promptly and decisively to a military threat. Yet the concept of a "Twin Pillars" NATO is largely motivated by resentment of American leadership. Just recently, France decided not to re-establish full participation in the military structures of NATO precisely because the U.S. would not yield a naval leadership position in the Mediterranean to a European. It is only too likely that a NATO divided institutionally between "Europe" and the U.S. would be prey to an unending series of such controversies. And as we shall see below, the consequences of such division for the West's position in the wider world might well be disastrous.

For an independent superpower is bound to develop independent interests. That is how the world works. Eventually, the West would split as the European superpower—with its separate economy, independent military capability, and different diplomatic interests—inevitably became a rival to the U.S. The wider world would then become Lady Thatcher's "1914 played out on a somewhat larger stage." By contrast the second course would amount to the actual creation of a standing Atlantic alliance, and economic interdependence would give it a permanence that the present politico-military arrangements do not guarantee.

That is why such moderate opponents of NATO expansion as Brent Scowcroft and Sam Nunn were wrong to argue that the applicant countries should join the European Union before joining NATO. Given the EU's apparent reluctance to expand, that might have pushed back NATO membership, with its enhancing effect on stability, well into the future. It would have encouraged neo-isolationist opinion in the U.S. to believe that the EU should handle the defense not just of NATO's new members, but of Europe as a whole. And as Madeleine Albright pointed out at the time, it is not in America's interests to subordinate the critical security interests of NATO to the decisions of another institution of which the U.S. is not even a member.

But the most important argument against making EU membership a prerequisite of admission to NATO was that this would have led to a divided Atlantic alliance. Integrating the East Europeans into the EU but not NATO would have been to integrate them into only half the alliance. For the sake of a European "defense identity," it would have forced aspiring NATO members to pursue their security interests through European channels first. And during the interim period, there would have been strong institutional pressures on the East Europeans to identify their economic and trading interests with "Europe" rather than with an Atlantic bloc. The net result would have been the strengthening of those forces seeking a European entity militarily and economically independent of the U.S.

That is not what NATO's new members want, and it is not in the American interest. As advocates of expansion such as Poland's deputy foreign minister Radek Sikorski have argued, the new NATO members are more enthusiastic supporters of the Atlantic relationship than some of the chancelleries of Western Europe. The course of the Cold War, when the U.S. was a more reliable friend of "captive nations" than Western Europe, has led them to place a special value on American participation; their experience of socialist economics makes them suspicious of Brussels and its regulatory excesses; their geographical vulnerability persuades them to place a higher value on alliance cohesion; their recent history makes them more resistant than either Germany or France to Russian overtures favoring a "Common European Home" (without the U.S.); and they have a less parochial view of world politics than many West Europeans who have succumbed to a post-Maastricht gastro-intestinal obsession with their own internal affairs. While in Washington to argue for NATO enlargement, the foreign ministers of Hungary, Poland, and the Czech Republic endorsed U.S. policy towards Iraq at a time when West European reactions ranged from indifference to outright sabotage. This was a foretaste of how NATO expansion might work to strengthen the Atlantic elements in NATO: diplomatic support in return for military protection. That was always the underlying bargain in NATO, but Western Europe, in the grip of short-termism, now sees less need for protection. The East Europeans do not believe history has ended.

That has led some French observers to fear the rise of an Anglo-Polish-American bloc that would resist a "Twin Pillars" NATO and lobby for an alliance built firmly around American leadership. Such fears are (alas) almost certainly exaggerated. But in a saner world, that would indeed be American (and British) policy, and the Clinton administration would now be pushing strongly for an Atlantic free trade policy flexible enough to admit Eastern Europe and Turkey, despite their differences in economic structure. They would then be interjected into the full Western alliance from the first. For the logic of the French fears is wholly reasonable. An expanded NATO would be a less divided NATO. A less divided NATO would permanently entrench the Atlantic alliance. And a permanent Atlantic alliance would mean a safer world.

NATO Enlargement versus American Interests

ALVIN Z. RUBINSTEIN

The stage is set for the United States Senate to hold its first major foreign policy debate of the post–Cold War era. Following NATO's decision in Madrid in July 1997 to invite Poland, the Czech Republic, and Hungary to join its ranks, the Senate must signify its approval in accordance with the provisions of Article 10 of the North Atlantic Treaty (adopted in Washington D.C., on April 4, 1949), which stipulates that the admission of "any other European state" requires "unanimous agreement." With no other NATO government likely to act before the United States does, all eyes are on the Senate.

Whatever may be their public expressions of support for NATO enlargement, West European and Canadian leaders consider it an American policy initiative, and—in private—are far from unanimous about its alleged virtues. Indeed, most probably agree with the unguarded comments made by Canadian prime minister Jean Chrétien to his Belgian counterpart: "It's not for reasons of security; it's all done for short-term political reasons, to win elections."[1] However embarrassing this may be for Chrétien, for Americans it should be a wake-up call.

The decision to accelerate the timetable for NATO's expansion was based neither on strategic logic nor military threat, but was domestically driven. President Clinton's bid for votes among those with strong cultural, ethnic, and religious ties to Central and Eastern Europe led him to declare in Detroit on October 22, 1996, in the final two weeks of a bitterly contested election campaign, that he wanted the first group of Central and East European countries (CEEC) admitted in 1999 on "NATO's fiftieth anniversary and ten years after the fall of the Berlin wall." There was no prior consultation with congressional leaders, let alone with NATO leaders, and no explanation to the public. On December 10, 1996, a compliant NATO rubber-stamped Clinton's proposed schedule and brought the matter to the Madrid Summit for formal approval by the heads of government of the NATO countries.

Alvin Z. Rubinstein is a professor of political science at the University of Pennsylvania and a senior fellow at the Foreign Policy Research Institute. His published works include *Imperial Decline: Russia's Changing Role in Asia* (coedited with Stephen Blank; Duke University Press, 1997) and *Russian Foreign Policy: From Empire to Nation-State* (with Nicolai Petro; Longman, 1997).

Reprinted by permission. Orbis, Winter 98, Vol. 42 Issue 1, p. 37, 12p.

Yet, the pros and cons of strategic enlargement had still not been addressed, and most of the president's attention remained fixed on domestic matters. Testifying before the Senate Armed Forces Committee in late April 1997, Secretary of State Madeleine Albright encountered a deep vein of skepticism among members and later acknowledged, "there is no question that we have a very difficult job ahead of us."[2] On June 28, twenty senators, including Jesse Helms, chairman of the Foreign Affairs Committee, sent the president a letter expressing their reservations about enlargement and promising an "intense" debate.[3] If so, it could be a lengthy and difficult one. The issues are many, the choices stark, and the stakes involve nothing less than America's ability to ensure peace and stability on the European continent well into the next century. Ultimately, the Senate must decide, and as Secretary of State John Hay wrote in his diary on February 12, 1904, "A treaty entering the Senate is like a bull going into the arena: no one can say just how or when the final blow will fall—but one thing is certain—it will never leave the arena alive."[4] Far too many commentaries and official pronouncements consist more of boosterism than analysis. Several of the issues under which enlargement is discussed are familiar: the costs; the effect on U.S.-Russian relations; and the strengthening of security and democratization in Europe. Other neglected but equally important issues involve the strategic, political, and financial interests of the United States itself; the uncomfortable German factor; and the asymmetry between U.S. interests and those of Western Europe.

President Clinton has yet to make a speech to the country or Congress laying out in substantive and concrete fashion his reasons for believing that NATO enlargement is in the U.S. national interest. Whatever detailed case he may later make, he forced the alliance into accepting his Madrid initiative without prior justification or debate. His style is to wait until debate starts in the Senate before bringing his formidable powers and instruments of persuasion to bear. For the time being one must rely on sound bites at impromptu media opportunities or on snippets from speeches in which certain themes recur. His speech to the graduating class at West Point on May 31, 1997, is as good a point of departure as any. It raised the same points he has repeated time and again—always briefly, often verbatim.

THE FAMILIAR ISSUES

First there is the cost factor. Clinton said NATO enlargement was not "without cost" or risk, but gave no specifics. In a report to Congress on February 24, 1997, he held that the costs would be modest, averaging no more than $150 million to $200 million a year for the first ten years, basing his estimate on an in-house State Department study. But even staunch NATO-boosters are disinclined to agree with this minimalist figure. Several years ago, the highly respected Rand Corporation, known for its close ties to the Pentagon, calculated the cost at $3–5 billion per year over a ten-year period, with the U.S. share being $1–1.2 billion annually. The Congressional Budget Office posits costs greater than Rand's by a factor of two or three, depending upon the assumptions used.

Clearly, no one knows what enlargement will really cost, but the Clinton administration's estimates contravene experience. One need look no further than the Bosnian operation for evidence. In late November 1995, when the administration undertook to commit ground forces to Bosnia, it estimated the cost to the United States of helping to enforce the ceasefire at $1–1.2 billion for the year 1996. In fact, the cost was almost $4 billion; and as of mid-1997, about $7 billion. The Senate needs to evaluate the administration's estimates of the direct costs to the United States as well as its assumption that other NATO members will increase their defense outlays to help finance enlargement, especially since they have been steadily declining since the end of the Cold War.

An even tougher question involves the indirect costs of enlargement. If new members do increase defense spending to upgrade their military capabilities, it will come at the expense of economic and social investment, because none of their budgets could afford the large extra expenditures required. According to Professor Henryk Merzkowski of the Graduate Institute of International Studies in Geneva who has been studying the economic costs of NATO enlargement, Poland, the Czech Republic, and Hungary "spend well below the NATO average" for defense and for them to increase expenditures to the NATO level—much less to undertake the major modernization that would make their equipment compatible with NATO's—would mean that "productive investments will have to be curtailed" and higher taxes levied (a move apt to occasion strong domestic opposition); and they would have to accept "the inevitability of trade-offs between economic growth and strategic security interests."[5] Increased military spending would be at the expense of economic development. Notwithstanding Secretary of State Albright's assurance to a Senate committee that "NATO enlargement is not a scholarship program,"[6] that is precisely what it is likely to resemble: long-term government guaranteed loans to enable recipients to pay for costly goods and services with a promise of eventual repayment. Prospective members would thus be forced to purchase weapons they cannot afford and do not need, but which they must acquire as the entry fee for membership in the NATO club. The only winners would be U.S. arms merchants for which enlargement would be the boon of the decade.[7]

A second justification made by Clinton in his West Point speech is that the admission of new members will strengthen the alliance and that the "gains decisively outweigh the burdens." As evidence he cited only the assistance of Poland, the Czech Republic, and Hungary in NATO's operations in Bosnia. Yet historically, no alliance has strengthened itself by embracing weak, dependent, resource-poor, geographically vulnerable new members, none of whom is in immediate or foreseeable danger of attack by any power. In its present geographical and military position, the United States does not need the territory, know-how, or capability offered by the CEEC. Nor is the security of any other NATO country significantly enhanced by the three invitees whose defense only adds unnecessarily to every NATO country's burden. Rather, an enlarged NATO would benefit only the "Brussels-crats"—the generals and diplomats, staffers and office personnel, and mushrooming committees and conferences based at the headquarters. As Michael Mandelbaum and others have argued, at a time when Europe is at peace and secure, NATO seems bent, not on downsizing military establishments and building on the existing series of arms limitations agreements, but on upsetting the unparalleled strategic stability that it has enjoyed since the end of the Cold War.[8]

Clinton's third point is that NATO enlargement will foster democracy in the CEEC, encourage the peaceful resolution of disputes, and help build a peaceful, undivided Europe. He rejects the view that enlargement would create a new fault line in Europe closer to Russia's own borders. It may well be that its proponents hope that NATO enlargement will unify and heal Europe. But if so, then the Senate should ask why the West European members of NATO do not admit the CEEC to the European Union (EU) to facilitate their economic as well as military integration, and thereby deepen their political ties to the democracies of Western Europe. As matters stand, the EU has no immediate plans for the admission of new members, even though most CEEC members are more eager to join the EU than NATO.

President Clinton's laudable aims rest on the dubious assumption that NATO, a military alliance, can help further them. The diplomatic correspondent of the *New York Times*, R. W. Apple Jr., writes:

> What the allies must guard against, the Administration believes, are terrorism, illegal drugs, nationalist extremism and regional conflict fueled by ethnic, racial and religious hatreds. Yet Mr. Clinton has not spelled out what means would be used to do so. Warplanes are of little use against terrorism and drug smuggling, and naval power is of little help in fighting racism.[9]

As for the ability of the three newly invited members to satisfy NATO requirements and participate meaningfully, consider that in January 1994, when it adopted the Partnership for Peace (PFP) program, NATO laid down principles for aspiring members. These were specific, focused, modest steps to promote transparency in defense planning and budgeting, encourage civilian control of defense establishments, facilitate participation in joint NATO peacekeeping missions, and develop armed forces that could work effectively with NATO. The criteria for evaluating relative success or failure were clear and testable. Not one of the states invited to join comes anywhere near meeting PFP criteria, including such an obviously essential requirement as language competency in English so that their officers and troops can interact with NATO personnel and master the use of NATO equipment. But overnight, without waiting for a decent period of examination to pass, NATO has blithely leaped ahead, ignoring the institutional and operational standards it solemnly established three years ago. What we are witnessing is what Apple calls the primacy of President Clinton's "fervor" and "the ambition of his commitments" over well-considered steps to assure NATO's future.

In short, when the Senate considers NATO enlargement it should do so solely from the perspective of U.S. foreign policy: is the proposal in the U.S. national interest, or not? After all, our West European allies have their own national interests and priorities, as do the countries of Central and Eastern Europe, and they often differ from our own. Happily, the United States and its NATO allies usually have seen eye to eye on most vital matters relating to security and stability in Europe, but the era in which they all shared a perception of threat from the former Soviet Union is over. Today, Western European leaders see NATO enlargement in a different light than do most Americans. French president Jacques Chirac is not alone in cynically viewing the unilaterally accelerated process of enlargement as Clinton's payback to supportive domestic constituencies. And he, along with other West European leaders, has declared that new members "must pay their own way. France does not intend to raise its contributions to NATO because of the cost of enlargement. "[10] When asked why Italy supports enlargement, an Italian diplomat replied: "because, politically, we cannot afford not to back the United States."[11] The Senate needs to ensure that the bulk of the burden sharing does not fall on the United States in the decade ahead.

In the emerging strategic environment in Europe, economics counts for more than military capability, yet the enlargement promoted by President Clinton, with its emphasis on the military modernization of new members, is predicated on exactly the opposite rationale. For their part, the West Europeans consider the strengthening of the European Union far more important to their common future than an enlarged NATO based on a utopian vision of absolute security and ethno-nationalist harmony.

Indeed, a strong but minimalist NATO alliance offers manifold advantages. NATO's existing structure is in the best interests not only of U.S. security but of the entire European continent. First, NATO anchors

Germany in a U.S.-dominated security system, helps deepen the historic Franco-German reconciliation, and buys valuable time to advance European integration. The German question is rarely discussed to avoid stirring up unpleasant historical memories. For instance, when this author suggested at a conference on Euro-Atlantic security and NATO enlargement, held in Slovenia in April 1997, that enlargement clearly delivers Central and Eastern Europe into the German sphere and thus would destabilize Germany's intra-NATO relationships, the response was a storm of intense criticism from the European diplomats present. Germany remains a difficult, complex, emotionally charged issue. The longer it is housed in a viable, U.S.-managed NATO, the better.

Secondly, the NATO that exists today enjoys widespread support among the American people, thereby ensuring a U.S. military presence and a willingness to bear the cost of a long-term bargain-rate insurance policy for Western Europe. Moreover, a United States that spends upwards of $40 billion annually just to defend NATO can count on having its own way on most issues, further encouraging U.S. public support.

Thirdly, NATO as presently constituted can effectively engage an essentially nonhostile and Western-oriented Russia on a wide range of mutual concerns from nuclear downsizing to drug interdiction, from cooperation in the fight against terrorism to joint efforts on all-European ecological and environmental problems. But Russia's willingness to cooperate has already shown signs of diminishing and may erode further if Clinton's statement that "NATO's first members should not be its last" is borne out in the foreseeable future.

Finally, although freezing NATO membership would seemingly leave the CEEC to fend for themselves, it in fact would promote the aim of democratization and development in the CEEC by ensuring the peace of Europe and the stable, secure strategic environment in which these countries' scarce resources could be invested in the socioeconomic foundations of a democratic polity.

THE NEGLECTED ISSUES

As a global power, the United States has interests and commitments that transcend any one region of the world. Thus, while keeping in mind Western Europe's concerns as it discusses enlargement, the Senate should take a closer look at four heretofore largely ignored but interrelated issues: (1) enlargement and U.S. interests in East Asia; (2) Europe in the U.S. strategic perspective; (3) the German factor and alliance stability; and (4) out-of-area issues.

There is an essential connection between the increased commitments the United States would make towards Europe through NATO enlargement and its ability to act effectively in a variety of volatile situations in East Asia. Whereas in Europe political systems are stable, defense expenditures declining, territorial and ethnic irredentism marginalized and incapable of deranging the secure foundation of a long peace, and America's preeminence unchallenged, in East Asia very different trends prevail. Major threats to U.S. interests inhere in China's new assertiveness, Taiwan's sense of beleaguerment, the Sino-Russian entente, the succession struggle and unresolved nuclear problems in North Korea, and Japan's unpredictable responses to all the above. At the same time, the precise U.S. interests in need of defense in the Asia/Pacific, how much of America's resources should be committed there, how extensive a power projection capability is required, and what U.S. public sentiment will support over the long term are all critical unknowns. In light of these indeterminate variables in East Asia, prudence would suggest the unwisdom of the United States assuming unnecessary responsibilities in Europe.

From an American strategic perspective, the situation on the European continent could hardly be improved. Europe is at peace, and for the first time in the twentieth century no power threatens aggression or disruption of the territorial status quo. To be sure, we hear much about "ethnic and nationalistic tensions like those that tore Bosnia apart" and are told they constitute "the one immediate threat to European security today."[12] Eruptions of ethnic tensions may cause internal strife and may heighten tensions among small countries harboring irredentist ambitions, but none of the nations so afflicted possesses military power sufficient to threaten the peace of Europe. What is more, for the first time in European history that peace rests comfortably on a decisive commitment by a non-European power—the United States.

As matters now stand, America's vital national interest—preventing any hostile power from dominating the European landmass—is realized. Three times in this century the United States made enormous commitments of military and economic resources to defeat an aggressive power's attempt to dominate the European continent; Washington understood that U.S. security interests required maintaining a balance of power of sorts to prevent any European power from achieving hegemony. Twice the enemy was Germany; once the Soviet Union. Today the U.S.-led NATO alliance is the dominant military force on the European continent and securely binds a democratic Germany to the rest of Western Europe. To the east of the NATO community lies a vast borderland of twelve independent countries constituting a strategic buffer zone between Germany and Russia, the prime disrupters of Europe's peace since 1870. Farther still to the east lies Russia itself. Stripped of most of its former empire, severely weakened, increasingly ignored in key regional gatherings, and undergoing systemic decline, Russia has no prospects of regaining the commanding position it held in Central and Eastern Europe less than a decade ago—in sum, no threat to the structure of power that serves the NATO community exists, and it is difficult to imagine any strategic principle or concern so mighty as to justify jeopardizing the future of this irenic environment. As Senator John Warner of Virginia observed to Secretary of State Albright, "I come from the school that if it's not broken, why try and fix it?"[13] Why, indeed?

A secure strategic environment is predicated on stable relationships. In NATO this means maintaining a continuing equilibrium of forces among the interdependent actors. Any introduction of new elements into this discrete universe must affect the structure of power and the cohesion that have heretofore shaped the behavior of alliance members, and risks setting in motion unanticipated consequences detrimental to its future. Security and stability are mutually reinforcing phenomena in a condition of equilibrium, but not in a period of flux. Thus, although the admission of Poland, the Czech Republic, and Hungary is intended to enhance the security of all, it may inadvertently and paradoxically undermine security by disrupting the balance of power within NATO itself. Nowhere is such tinkering more apt to give rise to troublesome consequences than in its effects on the future behavior of Germany.

Germany is a member of NATO, a non-nuclear power, and a key EU partner in the forefront of West European integration. At present its power is contained and its capacity for independent initiatives limited. But with growing preeminence on the continent—it is already the most powerful country in Western Europe, the dominant member of the EU, and commercially and financially the most influential actor in the CEEC—Germany will naturally expect a political role commensurate with its economic-industrial power and responsibilities. A consensus spanning the German political spectrum currently supports Bonn's vigorous pursuit of its legitimate interests in the East. The military is especially enthusiastic about NATO enlargement and anticipates the establishment of a new command for Central and Eastern Europe, to be headed by a German.

Thus, NATO enlargement cannot help but transform Germany from a dependent marchland into the geopolitical lodestone of Europe. One result may be rekindled adversarial relationships between Germany and France on the one hand, and Germany and Russia on the other. A second result could be another setback for European integration as France and Britain assess the implications of Germany's new status. Finally, any perception by NATO members of an emerging "special relationship" between Germany and the United States would have a chilling effect on developments within the alliance and related security organizations such as the West European Union and the Organization for Security and Cooperation in Europe.

It is not too soon to consider Germany's future options in Europe and how current NATO decisions might affect them. Indications are already present suggesting that Bonn's foreign policy is becoming more "German" and less "European." Time will tell how the new members, all of whom are heavily dependent on Germany, will affect intra-NATO politicking and alignments. The German scholar Reinhardt Rummel believes enlargement may remove Germany's vulnerability to unwanted migration from Eastern Europe and the countries of the former Soviet Union, the psychological feeling that Germans have of continuing "to live at a front-line," and their fear that Germany may again be squeezed between two adversarial blocs. Rather, he imagines, NATO enlargement would allow Germany to recover "its natural geographical place, which is in the center of Europe, not at an artificial borderline of European sub-regions."[14] That seductive proposition that Germany should take its "natural place" at the center of Europe ought to sound alarm bells ringing in Washington. Any geopolitical development, however well intended, that transforms Germany from an ordinary nation-state into a strategic hub radiating political and military, as well as economic, influence across much of Europe will pose problems for America's presently unchallenged dominance. In the past, Germany's uneasiness over its eastern border contributed toward its collegiality as a NATO ally and reinforced the need for a continuing U.S. military presence. A change in that strategic situation could usher in a new era in which the United States loses its valuable leverage to Germany.

Fourth and finally, Clinton's diplomatic "triumph" at Madrid could prove as ephemeral as it is irrelevant to the panoply of out-of-area problems NATO is now wrestling with in the Mediterranean region, including terrorism, Islamic militancy, illegal immigration, and drug smuggling.

In the past, divergent national interests and ambitions around NATO's vast southern flank have caused serious intra-alliance tensions. In 1956, there was the Suez crisis; in the late 1960s, the Arab-Israeli conflict; in the 1970s and 1980s, the West Europeans' tilt toward Arab positions on peacemaking and the Palestinians, lax commercial and political relations with Libya, and accommodationist approach to Iran; and in April 1986, the refusal of France and Spain to grant U.S. bombers based in Britain overflight privileges to hit Libyan targets in retaliation for Muamar el-Qaddafi's terrorist action against American soldiers in Berlin. More recently, Bosnia precipitated acrimony and bitterness within NATO. At first, the West Europeans, seeking to nurture a common approach to security, felt confident in their ability to manage the collapse of Yugoslavia. However, as they realized their military limitations and dependence on the United States for logistical, intelligence, and combat support, their resentment at Clinton's equivocation grew.

That mood was aggravated, especially in Paris, by Washington's often high-handed behavior as illustrated by its lack of consultation on the timetable for NATO enlargement, surprise announcement by Secretary of Defense William Cohen that American troops would be withdrawn from Bosnia by June 30, 1998, and rejection of the majority's view at Madrid favoring NATO membership for Slovenia and Romania.

None of this augurs well for the most potentially disruptive issue to alliance cohesion to arise in the post–Cold War era, namely, how to deal with Libyan efforts to develop a chemical weapon capability. Showdown scenarios have been under consideration for several years, certainly since then CIA director John Deutch informed the Senate Select Committee on Intelligence on February 22, 1996, that Libya was building "the world's largest underground chemical weapons plant in a mountain near Tartunah," forty miles southeast of the capital, Tripoli. According to his estimates, the plant could become operational by late 1997–early 1998. Five weeks later, the normally low-key secretary of defense William J. Perry took the occasion of a visit to Egypt to warn Qaddafi that he "wouldn't rule anything out or anything in."[15] In August, German authorities charged three businessmen "with selling the Libyan government advanced equipment that can be used to manufacture nerve gas," the highly lethal gases Soman and Sarin.[16] In light of the dismaying past record of German companies in supplying Iraq with poison gas equipment, it is reasonable to assume that they continue to export such materiel to oil-rich Libya. One close observer believes that Qaddafi, after a brief halt, has resumed work on the plant.[17]

As a nonsignatory to the Chemical Weapons Convention that went into effect on April 30, 1997, Libya is not obligated to permit international inspection of suspect facilities. Should Qaddafi persist and his chemical weapons complex move toward completion, the United States will have to play all its cards. It could turn to the United Nations Security Council and request the imposition of stiff economic sanctions and, if need be, military action, but that would invite a possible Russian or Chinese veto and an ambivalent European and Arab reaction. Or it could take the matter to NATO and seek collective sanctions up to and including the use of force, but Western Europe's past unwillingness to get tough with Libya and resentment of U.S. steamroller tactics make its cooperation problematical. Or the United States could go at it alone, but the prospect of American casualties in the absence of allied support could well result in messy domestic fallout and a collapse in U.S. public support for NATO. Finally, the United States could preempt a Libyan chemical biological capability by using a "bunker buster" hydrogen bomb on Qaddafi's clandestine weapons plants. An improved version of such a weapon, developed during the Cold War to hit command and control centers, was unveiled by the Pentagon in late May 1997 as a weapon designed "to destroy underground factories or laboratories while causing relatively little surface damage."[18] But American use of a nuclear weapon, though militarily an attractive option against rogue states, would be a political nightmare and would surely destroy any prospects for nuclear downsizing and new arms control agreements.

CONCLUDING OBSERVATIONS

When all is said and done, and the Senate arrives at the penultimate hours before the momentous vote, the Clinton administration will doubtless make a last-ditch appeal based on three suppositions: that rejection of NATO enlargement would signal a return to the "isolationism" of the 1920s; that U.S. credibility as the leader of NATO and the free world would suffer; and that the honor of the United States requires that the Senate support the president's policy.

None of these assertions bears out. First, no one is challenging the long-standing U.S. commitment to NATO; only the enlargement of NATO is at issue. Secondly, how, in light of the expensive commitment the United States has made to the defense of Western Europe over the past five decades, could anyone invoke the hoary specter of isolationism? While the United States may have rejected the League of Nations after World War I and then disengaged to a great extent from European affairs, it was deeply involved in Latin America and East Asia. As one historian recently showed, "isolationism" has been less a real tradition in U.S. diplomacy than "a dirty word that interventionists, especially since Pearl Harbor, hurl at anyone who questions their policies."[19]

Thirdly, it is not America's credibility that is called into doubt, but President Clinton's judgment. No country is going to end its alliance with the United States as a consequence of the Senate's vote on enlargement. In fact, many in NATO would privately welcome a decision that accords with their own private views. Finally, the Senate is not bound to support a policy which the president cannot demonstrate is in the national interest. On the contrary, the honor and integrity of the democratic process require that senators vote, not for or against a president, but for whatever policy they judge to be in the best interests of the country.

The Senate would do well to recall the Gulf of Tonkin Resolution of August 1964, when an uncritical and emotional Congress voted almost unanimously to give a president with little experience in foreign policy a green light to commit the country to a war that proved costly, tragic, and ultimately irrelevant to America's vital interests. Now, more than thirty-three years after Lyndon Johnson struck all the right chords and received an overwhelming vote of confidence, it would be difficult to argue that rejection of the Tonkin Resolution would have rekindled "isolationism," undermined U.S. credibility among its allies, or tarnished the honor of the United States. On the contrary, our allies then— as now—longed for an America that knew how to say no to its own most destructive urges.

NOTES

1. "Chrétien rapped for remarks on US," *Boston Globe*, July 11, 1997, sec. A, p. 17.
2. As quoted in Thomas L. Friedman, "Expand NATO? The Senate Should Just Say No," *International Herald Tribune*, Apr. 29, 1997.
3. "Doubts From Senate on NATO Plans," *New York Times*, June 29, 1997.
4. As quoted in William Roscoe Thayer, John Hay, vol. 2 (Boston, Mass.: Houghton Mifflin Co., 1916; repub. AMS Press, New York, 1972), p. 393.
5. Henryk Kierzkowski, "Economic Costs of NATO Enlargement: A Central European Perspective," unpublished paper presented at the conference on "Central-Eastern Europe and Euro-Atlantic Security," Ljubljana-Bled, Slovenia, Apr. 24–26, 1997.
6. As quoted in Alison Mitchell, "Clinton Girding For Stiff Debate on NATO Issue," *New York Times*, June 29, 1997, sec. A, p. 6.
7. See Jeff Gerth and Tim Weiner, "Arms Makers See A Bonanza In Selling NATO Expansion," *New York Times*, June 29, 1997.
8. Michael Mandelbaum, *The Dawn of Peace in Europe* (New York: Twentieth Century Fund, 1996), passim.
9. R.W. Apple Jr., "Clinton's NATO: Keen on Growth, Murky on Mission," *New York Times*, July 13, 1997, Northeast edition.
10. Elizabeth Neuffer and Brian McGrory, "Leaders Sign 2 Security Agreements," *Boston Globe*, July 10, 1997, sec. A, p. 16.
11. Author's interview in Rome, May 1997.
12. For an example of such inexact use of the terminology, see Craig R. Whitney, "With Ethnic Strife, NATO Finds That The Enemy Is Within," *New York Times*, July 6, 1997, Northeast edition.
13. Quoted in R.W. Apple Jr., "Road To Approval is Rocky, and Gamble is Perilous," *New York Times*, May 15, 1997, sec. A, p. 18.
14. Reinhardt Rummel, "The German Debate in International Security Institutions," in Marco Carnovale, ed., *European Security and International Institutions After the Cold War* (New York: St. Martin's Press, 1995), pp. 187–88.
15. Phillip Shenon, "Perry, in Egypt, Warns Libya To Halt Chemical Weapons Plant," *New York Times*, Apr. 4, 1996.
16. Raymond Bonner, "Germany's Search for Libya Suspect Finds Ties To Its Own Spies," *New York Times*, Aug. 22, 1996, sec. A, p. 13.
17. Uzi Mahnaimi, "US Fury As Qaddafi Steps Up Work On Mustard Gas Factory," *Sunday Times*, Mar. 9, 1997. Mahnaimi is the newspaper's Middle East correspondent.
18. Matthew L. Wald, "U.S. Refits a Nuclear Bomb To Destroy Enemy Bunkers," *New York Times*, May 31, 1997.
19. Walter A. McDougall, *Promised Land, Crusader State: The American Encounter with the World Since 1776* (Boston: Houghton Mifflin Co., 1997), pp. 39–40.

Issue 7
Terrorism

INTRODUCTION

Terrorism, the indiscriminate use of violence to publicize a grievance, has always been a traditional instrument of the powerless or disenfranchised. Although terrorism seldom achieves its objectives, governments pay attention to it far out of proportion to the threat that it poses to the political and social order. Citizens demand action, and governments respond with tough talk and promises to eliminate both the perpetrators and those who lend support to them. Yet the scourge of terrorism continues to plague politics, both domestic and international. In fact, as access to chemical, biological, and even nuclear weapons seems to be increasing, concerns about the dangers and consequences of terrorism are heightened.

The article by David Tucker presents an overview of the approaches traditionally employed to combat terrorism. Discussing nine such strategies—ranging from offering no concessions to terrorist demands, to preempting terrorism by targeting its practitioners—Tucker's conclusion is that "patience, a willingness to accept partial and inconclusive results, an ability to absorb setbacks, and the determination to employ policies that take time" are the prerequisites of any successful counterterrorist strategy. Although perhaps not a satisfying answer, his conclusion is similar to that of the other author in this section, Steven L. Pomerantz, who acknowledges that it is not possible to acquire immunity from terrorist violence. Pomerantz does, however, advocate using force to combat the threat of terrorism emanating from foreign shores. Believing that "consistent firmness pays long-term dividends," Pomerantz equates terrorism with an act of war that requires the United States to use all means at its disposal to combat it.

As you read the articles, consider the following questions.

Discussion Questions

1. How likely is it that terrorist groups might possibly acquire weapons of mass destruction? Is the likelihood greater now than it was ten years ago?
2. Are there any weapons in the fight against terrorism that a free society should be leery of employing?
3. Is encouraging economic growth and democracy the one sure way of avoiding the emergence of terrorism?
4. Is state-sponsored terrorism as much of a problem as nonstate terrorism? Is it more of a problem?

   For more information on this topic, visit the following websites:

   `http://www.terrorism.com/`
   Terrorism Research Center

   `http://www.adl.org/`
   Anti-Defamation League

   `http://www.cdiss.org/terror.htm`
   Center for Defense and International Security Studies

Responding to Terrorism

DAVID TUCKER

Terrorism is back. Over the years, it has waxed and waned. Having reached high points in the early and late 1970s and again in the mid-1980s, and a low point in the late 1980s and early 1990s, it is now again on an upswing. Domestic terrorism—the bombings of the World Trade Center in New York and the Federal Building in Oklahoma City—caused a significant loss of life. Fear of international terrorism has shadowed our involvement in Bosnia, restricting our scope of activities. A poison gas attack in the Tokyo subway in 1995 highlighted what many fear is the growing willingness of terrorists to use weapons of mass destruction, while reminding us of our own vulnerability to such attacks. Two bombings at U.S. military facilities in Saudi Arabia in 1995 and 1996 took the lives of 24 Americans, strained our relations with the Saudis, called into question our ability to maintain our presence in this vital area, and, as we implemented additional security measures, added significantly to the cost of this presence. Terrorism has undermined, if not destroyed, a major U.S. foreign policy initiative, the Middle East peace process. Globally, U.S. casualties from terrorism have increased in the mid-1990s. The resurgence of terrorism and fears for the future recently led Secretary of Defense William Cohen to list terrorism as one of his principal concerns.[1]

As attacks on Americans and the attention paid them have increased, officials have reportedly conducted the same debates about how to respond to terrorism that their predecessors had 10 years ago, when terrorism was last at a high point. Once again, they have debated the relative merits of preemptive attacks, covert action, economic sanctions, military retaliation, and diplomacy, and whether to target the states that sponsor terrorist attacks or the organizations and individuals that carry them out—all of this, apparently, with little or no reference to our nearly 25-year experience combating terrorism.[2] But this experience should not be ignored. If we are to handle terrorism effectively in the future, at whatever level it threatens us, we should learn from what we have done before. Not only will doing this improve our ability to deal with terrorism, it will also tell us something about how we must operate in the post–Cold War world.

David Tucker is on the staff of the Assistant Secretary of Defense for Special Operations and Low-intensity Conflict in the U.S. Department of Defense and is the author most recently of *Skirmishes at the Edge of Empire: The United States and International Terrorism* (Praeger, 1997).

Reprinted by permission. *Washington Quarterly*, Winter 1998, Vol. 21, Issue 1, p. 103, 15p.

HOW THE UNITED STATES HAS RESPONDED TO TERRORISM

Over the years, the United States has combated terrorism in nine ways. It has negotiated international legal conventions, implemented defensive measures, addressed the causes of terrorism, followed a policy of making no concessions to terrorists' demands, imposed economic sanctions, retaliated militarily, prosecuted suspected terrorists (in some cases, following extradition or rendition from another country or seizure overseas), preempted terrorist attacks, and disrupted terrorist organizations. Today, "no concessions," prosecution, and economic sanctions remain the principal weapons we employ against terrorism, but all three present problem.[3] We will begin to develop wisdom in combating terrorism only when we can recognize these problems.

Option 1: The Policy of No Concessions

Policymakers use as their principal argument to support the policy of no concessions the belief that paying ransom or making other concessions only encourages more terrorism. Moreover, for fear of granting terrorists standing in the international community or among their peers, some analysts argue that a policy of no concessions should exclude even talking with terrorists. Former president Ronald Reagan, for example, announced that although his administration would honor the terms of the agreement Jimmy Carter's administration reached with Iran during the 1979 hostage crisis, it would not have negotiated with the Iranians in the first place. However strictly they interpret it, those who support a policy of no concessions do so for the same reason: If we make concessions, they say, the terrorists win and will only demand more, while other groups will follow their example and pick on the nationals of any government that gives in.

But terrorists do not necessarily make demands because they want them met, and terrorist groups do not necessarily have the same fundamental motivations and modus operandi; hence they may not respond to external stimuli in the same ways. Some terrorists benefit from violent acts even if their targets do not yield to their demands. Rather than immediate concessions, terrorists may seek publicity or the destruction of a society's sense of security and order. The Tupac Amaru seizure of the Japanese ambassador's residence in Lima appears to have been a case where the terrorists acted not only to force the government to meet demands but also to gain recognition and public standing following a period when they had lost both. That terrorists do not need to have demands met explains in part why we see terrorist acts like the World Trade Center bombing, in which demands do not play a central role.

In fact, conceding to terrorists may have no direct correlation with the level of violence. British firmness during the seizure of the Iranian embassy in London in 1980 and U.S. firmness following the kidnaping of Brig. Gen. James Dozier in Italy in 1981 did not prevent the subsequent kidnaping of Britons and Americans in Lebanon. Nor did publicity concerning Washington's effort to trade arms for hostages with Iran in the mid-1980s lead to an increase in terrorist attacks or hostage-taking. Again, when the Colombian government—which earlier had taken a hard line with terrorists and responded forcibly to terrorist attacks—made concessions to terrorists in the early 1980s, terrorism began to decrease. Indeed, studies have concluded that refusing to make concessions may not limit terrorism, despite what proponents of "no concessions" claim.[4]

Less effective in combating terrorism than its proponents claim, "no concessions" is also less relevant than it was when first articulated as a policy in the 1970s. Then, terrorism constituted part of struggles for so-called national liberation; Palestinian terrorism was the archetype. Negotiating with terrorists in these cases undermined the legitimacy of governments the United States wanted to protect. Therefore, we rightly resisted negotiating. Now, however, states sponsor terrorism directly. The United States works with or makes deals with these state sponsors, because we could not secure our regional or more general interests otherwise. Our relations with Iraq when we hoped to make it a counter to Iran or with Syria during the ongoing Middle East negotiations exemplify the degree to which we will deal with a state sponsor of terrorism if doing so serves our interests.

For several reasons, then, the United States should not adopt a rigid policy of no concessions. It may not work in every case and is less relevant in fighting modern-day terrorism. Besides, making concessions may even help us catch a terrorist: The *Washington Post* and *New York Times* conceded to the Unabomber's demand to publish his 35,000-word manifesto, because federal officials thought that doing so might lead to a suspect; according to media reports, it did. As a practical matter, therefore, policymakers will make exceptions—and concessions—when they have good reasons to do so. We should not worry that this will make us look weak. A flexible policy to which we can adhere consistently will work better and make us look stronger than a rigid policy we consistently violate.

Option 2: Prosecution

Washington has always used prosecution as the principal response to terrorist acts committed in the United States. For several reasons, it has come increasingly to rely on the same response in dealing with terrorist acts committed against Americans or their property outside the United States. Those who have worked to combat terrorism generally agree that apprehending terrorists outside the United States deters terrorism or makes it more difficult for terrorists to carry out their plans, primarily because it complicates their travel. They must be careful where they set foot and what kind of documentation they use—and as international terrorists require mobility to work, this significantly disrupts their activities.

Further, prosecuting specific acts, such as killing, hijacking, or hostage taking, rather than focusing on the contentious political issues that surround these acts, removes an impediment to interstate cooperation. In addition, Washington's counterterrorism actions have greater credibility when the government bases its claims about a terrorist act on the exacting standards of U.S. criminal procedure and on evidence that can be used in a public judicial process rather than on intelligence that we cannot make public without compromising sources and methods. Finally, we may have no other available response than to arrest individual terrorists and bring them to trial if the connection between the terrorists and their sponsors does not suffice to allow us to retaliate against the latter.

As an example of successful prosecution, one may note the case of Pan Am Flight 103, destroyed in a mid-air explosion over Lockerbie, Scotland, in 1988. After a three-year investigation, the U.S. and British governments indicted two Libyans for the bombing. The two governments, with the help of France—whose airliner, UTA 772, Libyans bombed over Niger in 1989—then persuaded the United Nations (UN) Security Council to endorse a series of demands on Libya based on the indictments. When Libya failed to meet these UN demands, the United States and Great Britain persuaded the Security Council to impose sanctions on Libya. Although this legal process has unfolded slowly, it has kept pressure on Libya since 1991. During this time, as far as we can tell and apparently in response to legal pressure and sanctions, Libya has ceased to sponsor international terrorist attacks. It continues to support terrorist groups, attacks Libyan dissidents, and retains its capacity to commit other terrorist acts, but the legal process so far has effectively countered Libyan terrorism directed at the United States and its allies.

The judicial approach has led to arrests and prosecutions in other cases as well. In 1996, after Pakistan turned over Ramzi Yousef to the United States, a federal court in New York City convicted him, as the man behind the 1993 bombing of the World Trade Center in New York, of a conspiracy to bomb U.S. passenger planes in East Asia. After the FBI seized Omar Mohammed Rezaq in Nigeria, a U.S. district court convicted him of air piracy in connection with the hijacking of an Egyptian airlines flight in 1985 that resulted in the death of a U.S. citizen and the injury of two others. An Asian country turned over Tsutomu Shirosaki to the United States for trial in connection with a mortar attack on a U.S. embassy in 1986. In 1997, the FBI arrested Mir Aimal Kansi in Pakistan on charges that he murdered two Central Intelligence Agency (CIA) employees outside the agency's headquarters in 1993.

Despite the general enthusiasm for prosecuting terrorists, supporters of the judicial response admit its limitations. The United States can conduct foreign criminal investigations only with the cooperation of the governments involved. Exercising extraterritorial legal authority without permission would likely damage our relations with other countries, and it could also weaken the international cooperation necessary to combat terrorism. Finally, in some cases our powerful forensic abilities may be useless. Had the bomb aboard Pan Am Flight 103 exploded while the plane was over deep ocean, authorities might have faced insuperable challenges to investigating the crime scene. The difficulties investigating the explosion aboard TWA flight 800 when its pieces fell into waters off Long Island, New York, highlight this problem.

Although proponents of the judicial approach present these political and practical restrictions as only minor limitations, this approach is less effective than its supporters tend to acknowledge. To avoid political disputes over what may or may not be legitimate uses of force for political reasons, prosecution focuses our attention on individual terrorists and thus does not affect the traditional core of the terrorist threat: state sponsorship. Moreover, the effectiveness of the sanctions against Libya in the Pan Am 103 case resulted not from a judicial process, but from a political process at the United Nations and in foreign capitals that got UN members to agree to act against Libya—a political process that has not always worked to U.S. advantage in other cases. Washington found it difficult to get international agreement to impose sanctions against Syria in 1986–1987, for example, and the administration faced constant pressure, even inside the government, to lift them. For similar reasons, the UN has hesitated to impose meaningful sanctions on Sudan for its support of terrorism.[5] The judicial process, then, provides limited leverage against terrorism and depends largely on an international political process that it does little to shape.

Furthermore, the judicial approach can prove misleading. First, by emphasizing the criminality of terrorism, it may make us less able to respond flexibly—some might say cynically—to the irreducible political core of terrorism. Second, in adopting the judicial approach, we set the burden of proof for overseas action as high as that for domestic action, an impractical standard that will hinder our counterterrorism activities abroad. Proponents of the judicial response claim that we can, in effect, pick and choose when and where to use the standard, but given our attachment to the rule of law, the domestic judicial standard may become the only standard. Where it cannot be applied—in cases where, for example, the forensic evidence is inconclusive—we may come to believe that we have no justification for action.

This problem has a long history. Even before the legal response became so important in our counterterrorism efforts, we faced political pressure to find a "smoking gun" before responding forcibly to a terrorist attack. The Reagan administration, for example, sought such evidence before U.S. forces launched the raid on Libya. With increasing reliance on the judicial approach, this attitude may become even more pronounced. For example, while the Clinton administration deliberated its response to the Iraqi assassination attempt on former President Bush, the *Washington Post* reported that

> intelligence analysis . . . [based on circumstantial evidence] had been considered adequate proof of complicity in previous U.S. policy deliberations, but officials said senior Clinton administration policymakers—a group dominated by lawyers—indicated from the outset they wanted to act only on the basis of evidence that would be sufficient to produce a courtroom conviction.[6]

According to another press account, President Clinton asked the Federal Bureau of Investigation (FBI) and the attorney general to take the lead in investigating the alleged assassination attempt, involving the State Department and the National Security Council (NSC) only in the very final stages of the decision-making process.[7] A similar attitude seems to prevail in the case of possible Iranian involvement in the bombings of U.S. military bases in Saudi Arabia. This makes the emphasis on prosecution a dangerous double-edged sword. If detailed forensic investigation gives credibility to U.S. government responses to terrorist acts, then the absence of such an investigation or its inconclusive results will detract from this credibility and may make officials hesitant to act, thus restricting our scope of international action.

The judicial approach is a double-edged sword for another reason: It establishes a precedent we may not want other nations to follow. The Iranian death sentence against novelist Salman Rushdie, for example, is an application of Iranian law outside its borders, similar to the application of our counterterrorism laws outside ours. Some will object that there is no moral equivalence between the United States applying the law to terrorists and Iran condemning Rushdie for exercising his right to free speech. Indeed, any right-thinking democrat rejects such an equivalence. But this only highlights the problem with applying a country's laws overseas: If we assert our right to do this, we can deny the right of other nations to do so only by arguing that their laws are inferior to ours—or even illegitimate. Inevitably, by making this case we will have to insist on moral and political distinctions between nations that, for the sake of diminishing the causes of war, have been excluded for the most part from legitimate international discourse for more than 300 years. This can hardly enhance our security.

Option 3: Economic Sanctions

"No concessions" and prosecution therefore prove problematic and less effective methods of responding to terrorism than the U.S. government claims. But economic sanctions—a government's decision deliberately to curtail or cease customary economic or financial relations so as to coerce another government—is less problematic and more effective as a response to terrorism than generally assumed.

In 1973, the United States used economic sanctions for the first time, to punish Libya for sponsoring international terrorism. Since then, in combination with Libya's own economic mismanagement and corruption, the array of U.S.- and UN-imposed sanctions has seriously weakened Muammar Qadaffi's regime, even though the sanctions have not touched the core of Libya's economy: its ability to export oil. The sanctions have produced this effect, moreover, at relatively little cost to the United States. Likewise, economic sanctions helped to change Syria's behavior. The United States last imposed economic sanctions on Syria in 1986 following a particularly vicious terrorist attempt. Since then, according to the State Department, Syria has not sponsored any terrorist attacks, although it continues to provide safe-haven and training facilities for terrorists.

Of course, economic sanctions alone cannot explain this change in Syria's behavior. The collapse of the Soviet Union and changes in Middle East politics have also played important roles. But for a country like Syria, with a weak economy and little in the way of valuable resources, sanctions—especially multilateral ones such as those imposed in 1986—can inflict serious economic damage. In the view of diplomats who have dealt with the Syrians, sanctions had a significant influence in stopping Syrian-sponsored attacks. And even in Iran, sanctions have had an effect, impairing Tehran's ability to get the long-term financing its oil and natural gas industry needs.[8]

Imposing economic sanctions places fewer moral, political, and, often, economic costs on the United States than using military force would, while producing better results than diplomatic demarches alone. But sanctions are far from an ideal policy tool. They are more effective if imposed multilaterally, but the time it takes to organize such a sanctions regime can allow the targeted country to adjust to the impending sanctions, weakening their effect. Unilateral U.S. sanctions will likely

become increasingly less effective as global economic integration increases and the U.S. economy becomes a smaller part of the world economy. Finally, sanctions are a blunt instrument; as we have seen in the
cases of Iraq and Haiti, they may hurt only the little people and not their
leaders, who are their real targets. This increases the difficulty of sustaining them over a long period of time.

RECONSIDERING OTHER METHODS

The limited effectiveness of the three methods the U.S. government currently considers most useful in fighting terrorism suggests that we look
at the six others we have used to see what help they might offer. I will
discuss the most oft-considered tactic, military force, at length, and then
consider more briefly each of the other five: treaties and conventions, addressing the causes of terrorism, defensive measures, preempting terrorist attacks, and disrupting terrorist groups.

Option 4: Military Force

On April 15, 1986, U.S. Air Force and Navy jets attacked targets in
Libya as retribution for both the bombing of a Berlin discotheque on
April 5 that killed 2 and injured 64 Americans, and other, earlier Libyan
actions. This was the first use of military force by the United States to
combat terrorism. Its primary purpose was to deter future acts of Libyan-
sponsored terrorism against the United States. It was also intended to indicate to the world the intensity of U.S. resolve to deal with this kind of
violence.

Generally speaking, the raid achieved its secondary more than its
primary purpose. As far as we know, after an initial outburst of revenge
attacks, Qadaffi did not sponsor an attack on Americans for roughly 12
months after the raid. Following this hiatus, and excluding a spate of anniversary attacks in 1988, five of which took place in April and one of
which allegedly was the bombing of Pan Am Flight 103 in December,
Libyan terrorist attacks against Americans returned to their typical level
of one or two a year. Sanctions and political pressure following the investigation into the bombing of the Pan Am flight probably explain, at
least in part, the absence of Libyan-sponsored attacks on Americans
since 1990. The most telling statistic concerning the raid, however, is
that Libyan-sponsored terrorist attacks killed and injured more Americans after the raid than before—not counting those killed in the Pan Am
bombing.[9] If the Reagan administration launched the raid primarily to
deter Qadaffi from killing Americans, it failed in that purpose.

The raid met more success in achieving its secondary purpose: proving U.S. resolve. According to diplomats in charge of our counterterrorism policy at the time, this proof of our seriousness got the attention of the Europeans and made them more willing to cooperate in efforts to combat terrorism by imposing sanctions on state sponsors (such as those imposed on Syria) and by expelling from European countries the "diplomats" from countries that supported terrorist activities, undoubtedly curtailing terrorist operations. According to records made public since the collapse of the Warsaw Pact, the raid also impressed the East Germans, who cited it in discussions with Palestinian terrorists when trying to persuade them to curtail their terrorist activities.[10] In these ways, the raid probably saved American lives and thus contributed indirectly to its primary purpose. Even so, the number of lives saved by the indirect effects of the raid do not likely outnumber those lost in the Pan Am bombing and other Libyan-sponsored terrorist operations launched after the raid.

On balance, then, our experience with Libya calls into question the utility of using military force to combat terrorism. Indeed, the economic and political pressure that Great Britain, the United States, and France could organize through the UN in response to the bombings of Pan Am Flight 103 and UTA Flight 772—rather than the U.S. military reprisal for the Berlin bombing—seems finally to have stopped Qadaffi's attacks on Americans.

Generally stated, using military force to combat terrorism will always involve an asymmetry of both force and opportunity between the United States and countries that sponsor terrorism. The activities of the United States and its citizens around the world present many more lucrative targets to terrorists than they or their sponsors present to us. More important, terrorists and their sponsors accept the killing of innocents, making them much less restrained than we are in the use of violence. Our military activity may kill innocents, as it did in the raid on Libya, but we do not deliberately target them.

Moreover, we place other constraints on our use of force. A raid on Libya's oil production capabilities would have been a devastating blow to Qadaffi, but the Reagan administration ruled out such an option in favor of attacks on targets associated with terrorism, since this would fit within the international legal understanding of self-defense. Finally, coercing good behavior—our objective when we combat terrorism—may require applying the coercion again and again, which the United States has difficulty doing, given our official and public attitudes toward the use of force. When Qadaffi launched his attacks on the second anniversary of the raid, for example, we did not respond with military force. In any violent confrontation outside of a conventional military engagement, then, we are likely to be at a disadvantage.

Option 5: Negotiating Treaties and Conventions

Establishing international norms for dealing with terrorism helps to focus attention on terrorism and encourages like-minded countries to work together. It does not necessarily overcome political differences or the self-interest that guides national decision-making, however, which limits the utility of the resulting treaties and conventions. For example, in January 1994, the French prime minister cited his country's national interests while ignoring the Swiss government's request to extradite two suspected terrorists. Whenever the United States criticizes continued German contacts with Iran, which have included discussions between intelligence officials, the Germans defend these contacts by referring to Germany's economic interest.[11]

Option 6: Addressing Terrorism's Causes

The U.S. government has sought to combat terrorism by addressing its socioeconomic and political roots. But no one has clearly proven what specifically causes terrorism. Both poverty and the unequal distribution of wealth, for example, often thought to cause terrorism, exist in areas free from political violence. Where poverty and terrorism coexist, economic growth might remove this cause of violence, but economic growth can also threaten traditional ways of life and thus generate terrorism; much of the fundamentalist religious rebellion around the world exemplifies this dynamic. Moreover, encouraging the establishment of democracy so that grievances may find peaceful expression does not necessarily decrease terrorism. The Soviet Union did not have a problem with terrorism, but Russia does, and Spain's terrorist problem also worsened as it democratized. Encouraging economic growth and democracy may help resolve some conflicts only to generate new ones or create new opportunities for the violent expression of old ones.

Option 7: Defending Against Terrorism

For more than 25 years, the U.S. government has taken steps to make its personnel and facilities overseas harder targets for terrorists to hit. These defensive measures have had notable effects. By following proper procedures with appropriate seriousness, U.S. personnel overseas have made themselves and the facilities in which they work demonstrably more secure than they were before these programs began. In 1980, terrorists launched 177 attacks on U.S. diplomats, military personnel, and other U.S. government officials; in 1995, 10. Terrorists have not stopped targeting Americans, of course, and greater security measures for U.S. officials overseas has probably only deflected some attacks to easier targets, such as American businesspeople or other civilians, or compelled terrorists to devise more sophisticated or lethal means of attack. Still, it is a positive development that America now conducts its official business overseas with more security from terrorist attack than it once did. This success has come at a price, of course, in dollars and personnel resources, costs that will increase in response to the Saudi bombings, and the imposition of these costs constitutes some degree of success for terrorists and their sponsors.

Option 8: Preempting Terrorism

Whereas addressing the causes of terrorism works, if at all, only in the long term, a country can take short-term steps to stop, or preempt, a specific terrorist act. Americans often think of preemption in terms of lethal force or believe it to be a euphemism for assassination. But preempting a terrorist attack might require nothing more than warning another country that a terrorist group is planning to use its territory, or organizing a police raid that arrests suspects before they can carry out a terrorist attack.

More than any other method of combating terrorism, preemption requires specific, accurate, and timely intelligence. A warning to the wrong country or the arrest of the wrong suspects will not stop a terrorist attack. Accurate intelligence is even more important if a situation requires lethal force. We can apologize to another country for a false warning and free mistakenly arrested suspects, but we cannot raise the dead.

Option 9: Disrupting Terrorists

Whereas addressing terrorism's causes has only limited effectiveness and preemption has only limited application, disruption offers a middle ground. Disrupting terrorist activity means targeting a terrorist organization and taking measures not to stop a particular operation but to render all its activities more difficult and, eventually, to make the organization ineffective. Unlike addressing causes, disruption allows us to focus our resources on targeting a specific group. Unlike preemption, disruption does not require that we act before a specific attack takes place, and it thus allows for the gradual build-up of intelligence that permits accurate targeting. In the mid-1980s, the United States conducted a successful campaign to disrupt the Abu Nidal Organization (ANO), one of the most deadly terrorist groups. As reported in a series of newspaper articles, this campaign combined public diplomacy with diplomatic and intelligence initiatives to shut down ANO operations.

As with all the methods we have examined, disruption has its weaknesses. Like preemption, disruption depends critically on intelligence. And it tends to work best against well-developed organizations, like the ANO, that have a significant infrastructure. Groups that do not present such a target prove more immune to disruption.

HOW THE UNITED STATES SHOULD RESPOND

As this survey suggests, we should not single out any one—or even three—of the methods we have used to combat terrorism as the most important. To some degree, all suffer from limited effectiveness and applicability, or both. For this reason, success has come when we have combined them and taken advantage of circumstances. Libya's current restraint, for example, is the result of relentless diplomatic pressure, sanctions, public diplomacy, disrupting its terrorist operations, and direct and indirect military action (such as the raid in 1986 and support to Qadaffi's opponents in Chad). This campaign took advantage of such circumstances as falling oil prices (Qadaffi kept supporting terrorism as oil revenues declined but his support became more circumscribed and deprived him of money for other purposes), the disappearance of a powerful ally (the pre-Gorbachev Soviet Union), and the inefficiencies of Libya's domestic arrangements, which have prevented it from adapting well to external pressures.

Our success combining counterterrorism methods suggests in turn that we find additional ways to combine these methods. Carefully targeted sanctions combined with the discreet use of military force may prove more effective than our current tactic of using sanctions and force successively. If the trend toward more independent groups backed by wealthy individuals or religious sects continues, finding and prosecuting individuals will remain an important way to combat terrorism. But, under certain circumstances, we might usefully supplement this approach with disruptive techniques including sabotage, legal proceedings, and information warfare, to attack the assets of the individuals and sects that support terrorism. If the likelihood of terrorist use of weapons of mass destruction increases, we may become willing to accept measures currently deemed too risky.

Combining methods will not by itself increase our effectiveness against terrorism. We must employ these methods in a strategy that counters terrorism slowly but relentlessly. The horror and shock at a terrorist attack may encourage calls for immediate violent revenge, but this will seldom be an effective response: The asymmetry between the terrorists and their victims will always place us at a disadvantage in the use of violence. As a result, the United States should use conventional military force sparingly in combating terrorism, emphasizing instead public diplomacy, diplomatic and economic pressure, the discreet use of force, and, when possible, prosecution. Such an approach will prevent us getting involved in a tit-for-tat exchange that we will likely lose.

More generally still, our efforts against terrorism will be no more successful than our overall foreign policy and national security strategy. Those devoted to fighting terrorism sometimes forget that the purpose of combating terrorism is to enhance our security and that combating terrorism is only part of this broader effort, because terrorism is not the greatest threat we face. We should remember, especially as calls for stronger action against terrorism mount, that imposing sanctions, using military force, or snatching a terrorist from the streets of a foreign capital—any effort we make to combat terrorism—should be undertaken only if in striking a blow against terrorism it does not undermine our overall well-being.[12] In particular we must recall, as we contemplate how to respond to terrorism, that without the cooperation of our allies and other nations, we would have a much more difficult time combating terrorism, and preserving our security. Integrating counterterrorist efforts into our overall foreign policy and security strategy should also allow us to moderate our attachment both to the policy of no concessions and to an overly legalistic approach to combating terrorism.

Finally, this survey should encourage us. The different methods we use to combat terrorism did not develop all at once or arbitrarily. We have developed and adapted our methods as terrorism has changed. We should be able to do so as terrorism changes in the future.

This record should encourage us not only about our ability to combat terrorism in the post–Cold War world but also about our more general prospects in this world. We must now accommodate ourselves to a geopolitical situation that does not play to our strengths. For the time being, we have no grand reasons to go to war, and we confront few if any threats that the arsenal of democracy can overwhelm with decisive force—the two traditional U.S. ways of responding to threats. Nor as time passes will we have the economic or military weight to tip the balance of power in our favor singlehandedly. The threats and problems we confront with military resources diminishing and our weight in the world declining will likely be smaller and more difficult to assess and counter.

To prevent the slow but sure erosion of our security in this world, we will need patience, a willingness to accept partial and inconclusive results, an ability to absorb setbacks, and the determination to employ policies that take time. Maintaining favorable balances of power will require allies and thus an ability to accept compromise and ambiguity and a willingness to act for something less than the establishment of worldwide democracy. Because these new attitudes so starkly contrast with our past behavior, several authoritative commentators have suggested that the United States will have difficulty adapting and may not be able to do so.[13] Our campaign against international terrorism is at least somewhat reassuring in this regard, however, because for the past 25 years, under administrations of both parties, with only occasional lapses, we have fought terrorists and their sponsors using the modern equivalent of Roman methods of siege warfare, which one of these commentators argues we should emulate.[14] We have been patient, accepted inconclusive results, suffered setbacks, but struggled on. We have worked with allies, applied sanctions, practiced other economic forms of statecraft, undertaken slow but steady criminal investigations, engaged in diplomatic cajolery, gathered intelligence, and operated clandestinely. We have, in the case of terrorism, pursued our goals with the persistent application of diplomacy and force that the United States was supposed to be incapable of achieving. To the extent that the problems we now confront resemble terrorism—in its indirect, slow, but persistent method of attack—we can learn and draw some consolation from our history of combating it.

The views expressed here are the author's and not those of the Department of Defense or the U.S. government.

NOTES

1. Patrick Pexton, "Cohen Focuses Sights on Terrorism," *Navy Times,* September 22, 1991, p. 4.
2. David B. Ottaway, "U.S. Considers Slugging It Out With International Terrorism," *Washington Post,* October 17, 1996, p. A25.
3. *Patterns of Global Terrorism: 1996* (Washington, D.C.: Department of State, 1997), p. iv.
4. Richard Clutterbuck, "Negotiating with Terrorists," *Terrorism and Political Violence* 4 (Winter 1990), p. 285; *The Impact of Government Behavior on Frequency, Type, and Targets of Terrorist Group Activity* (McLean, Va.: Defense Systems, Inc., December 15, 1982), pp. 6–55, 56; Martha Crenshaw, "How Terrorism Declines," *Terrorism and Political Violence* 3 (Spring 1991), pp. 74, 79.
5. John M. Goshko, "UN Remains Reluctant to Impose Tough Sanctions on Sudan for Terrorist Links," *Washington Post,* November 24, 1996, p. A32.
6. R. Jeffrey Smith, "Iraqi Officer Recruited Suspects in Plot Against Bush, U.S. Says," *Washington Post,* July 1, 1993, p. A18.
7. "Commander for a Day," *Economist,* July 3, 1993, p. 25.
8. Thomas W. Lippman, "U.S. Economic Offensive Against Iran's Energy Industry Is Bearing Fruit," *Washington Post,* March 3, 1997, p. A8.
9. David Tucker, *Skirmishes at the Edge of Empire: The United States and International Terrorism* (Westport, Conn.: Praeger, 1997), p. 97.
10. "Stasi Assistance for PLO 'terrorists' alleged," *Die Welt,* April 16, 1991, p. 3; in Foreign Broadcast Information Service, West Europe, June 27, 1991, p. 29.
11. Sharon Waxman, "France's Release of Iranians Triggers Swiss Complaint," *Washington Post,* January 1, 1994, p. A15; Steve Vogel, "Allies Oppose

Bonn's Iran Links," *Washington Post*, November 6, 1993, p. A18; "EU Nations' Envoys Going Back to Iran," *Washington Post*, April 30, 1997, p. 15.

12. As an example of increasing calls for a stronger response to terrorism, see David Morgan, "Gingrich Backs Preemptive Acts on Terror," *Philadelphia Inquirer*, August 21, 1966, p. 11.

13. Henry Kissinger, "We Live in an Age of Transition," *Daedalus* 124 (Summer 1995), p. 103; Samuel P. Huntington, "America's Changing Strategic Interests," *Survival* 33 (January–February 1991), p. 16; Edward Luttwak, "Toward Post-Heroic Warfare," *Foreign Affairs* 74 (May/June 1995), pp. 109–122.

14. Edward Luttwak, "Toward Post-Heroic Warfare," pp. 116–118.

The Best Defense

STEVEN L. POMERANTZ

After the bombings of U.S. embassies in Africa last week, Secretary of State Madeleine Albright went out of her way to tell the world what the United States would not do in response: "We are not a nation that retaliates just in order to get vengeance," she said, "[nor do we] forget our own legal system while searching for those who have harmed us." Nobody, of course, wants U.S. warplanes going off half-cocked, raining missiles on every state that could plausibly have sponsored the terrorist attacks. Nevertheless, Albright's statement, which other Clinton officials have echoed, is emblematic of our government's familiar and often futile approach to international terrorism—one that fails to take advantage of the most powerful tools at our disposal.

To be sure, when it comes to terrorism at home, law enforcement and the criminal justice system—our only available options—have been effective. The FBI has an outstanding record in this area of its jurisdiction: over the years, the bureau has prevented many potentially devastating acts of terrorism. When incidents have occurred, federal law enforcement has brought the perpetrators to the bar of justice—the convictions in the Oklahoma City blast being only the most recent

Steven L. Pomerantz is executive vice president of the Washington, D.C.–based Institute for the Study of Terrorism and Political Violence. A retired FBI assistant director, he served as chief of counterterrorism for that organization.

Reprinted by permission. *New Republic*, July 31, 1998. Issue 4363, page 14, 2p.

example. Today, thanks largely to the work of federal investigators and prosecutors, most of the domestic terrorist organizations that have operated in this country, from the Order on the far right to the United Freedom Front on the far left, are crippled or altogether dismantled.

When it comes to terrorism abroad, however, the government has been far less successful at prevention and punishment—for reasons that, in large part, are beyond the control of the law enforcement officials dispatched to investigate incidents. Although both Kenya and Tanzania seem to be cooperating with the FBI, such unequivocal support from foreign governments is unusual. In recent years, even nominal allies like Saudi Arabia and Greece have been less than helpful when terrorists have struck at U.S. citizens on their soil, often because bringing the terrorists to justice would have caused political trouble for those governments. The Saudis, for example, have successfully stonewalled U.S. officials trying to investigate the bombing of U.S. military barracks there two years ago. And one commonly heard explanation is that the trail would lead to militant elements of the Saudi opposition party, which is backed by Iran.

And finding the terrorists is sometimes the easy part. Most terrorists operate with the quiet (and sometimes not-so-quiet) assistance of states hostile to the United States; when pursued, the terrorists frequently take shelter there, and it's nearly impossible to get them out. The most egregious example of this is the status of the two Libyans accused of bombing Pan Am Flight 103 in the skies over Scotland in December 1988. A U.S. grand jury has indicted the two men—both Libyan government intelligence agents. But Libya has refused to grant extradition to either the United States or Britain—and even economic sanctions have not forced a change of behavior.

There's no reason to expect a different outcome now, at least if the Clinton White House remains on the traditional course of U.S. administrations. It could take months or years for the FBI to sift through all the rubble in Kenya and Tanzania and then identify and track down the myriad suspects. By the time the United States could get its hands on the suspects—or, more likely, try to get some generally unfriendly nation to give up the suspects—more years would surely have passed. And that's assuming extradition was even possible. The message to new potential terrorists will be clear: Acting against the United States abroad is a low-risk proposition.

The fundamental problem here is that international terrorism is not only a crime. It is also, for all intents and purposes, an act of war, and the United States needs to treat it as such. That means, for starters, a significantly more aggressive diplomatic posture. There's no reason to tolerate Saudi obstruction over the 1996 Khobar Towers bombing. Yes, Saudi goodwill is valuable, but it's hardly worth allowing the killers of

U.S. soldiers to go unpunished. There's also no reason the administration can't be firmer with nations known to be backing anti-U.S. terrorists—such as Iran, Sudan, and North Korea. Of course, diplomacy is less effective when it's not backed by the credible threat of force. And so the United States must be prepared to use covert action or overt means against terrorists and the nations that back them.

The United States has done so before, with at least some success. In 1986, the Reagan administration sent Navy bombers into Libya. The idea was to punish Muammar Qaddafi for backing and orchestrating the bombing of a disco in Berlin, Germany, frequented by U.S. soldiers stationed there. Although Qaddafi survived the attack (the administration denied targeting him, but his barracks were hit by the U.S. bombers), the strike had its desired effect. By most accounts, Libya grew more cautious in the following years. A message had been sent, and received.

To be sure, using force is not without risk. Military operations endanger the lives of U.S. soldiers and can create diplomatic problems with other nations. In addition, it may not be possible to finger individual suspects with complete certainty, making the selection of targets all the more difficult. Don't forget, too, that military action often claims innocent civilian casualties. And, while covert action can seem like a more appealing solution, we have enacted laws and established policies that ostensibly limit or forbid many of the actions we'd often like to contemplate—such as the assassination of terrorists and their leaders.

These are all compelling questions—the kind a democracy should ask. But faced with a foreign threat against U.S. citizens—that is, a war—even a democracy must base its decisions on different imperatives and standards of proof. The issue is not vengeance. The issue is exacting a price for terrorism so as to make it less likely that terrorists will want to strike again. A nation's paramount obligation is the protection of its citizens—countries, like individuals, must have core values over which they do not compromise or negotiate. The short-term costs, in lives, effort, and money, may be high, but consistent firmness pays long-term dividends.

We can never be immune from terrorist violence. We can, however, raise the price for those who attack us and the nations that sponsor and support them. In so doing, we can expect that, eventually, we will make the cost high enough to significantly reduce the number of international terrorist incidents directed at American interests. In Africa last week, bombs exploded. Shrapnel filled the air, followed by prolonged wails of suffering. No one who saw this horror on the nightly news can doubt the morality or justification for toughening our position on international terrorism. These were the sights and sounds of war, as well as of crime. The Clinton administration must start actively seeking new and more appropriate ways to respond.

Issue 8
Mercenaries

INTRODUCTION

Mercenaries are soldiers for hire from countries other than those in which they operate. The patriotism that motivates most soldiers to defend their homeland is not what motivates mercenaries. They practice their trade for the money it provides—thus the term *mercenary.*

Soldiers for hire are nothing new, dating back to ancient times. In the 1300s, even the Pope hired a mercenary group to fight to save the church's papal lands in Italy. In modern times, mercenaries have been most active in developing countries. In one strangely convoluted case in the 1960s, mercenaries even fought United Nations forces in a civil war in Congo. More recently, in the West African country of Angola, the Marxist government hired a mercenary force to fight rebels backed by the U.S. Central Intelligence Agency. In Latin America, U.S. Senate investigators in 1991 documented the activities of British and Israeli mercenaries in drug-related conflicts in Colombia.

Who are these mercenaries? A review of *Soldier of Fortune* magazine reveals stories about macho free spirits who crave adventure and exotic weapons. Probably most readers of such publications only fantasize about mercenary activity, but some of these modern-day Paladins are currently in the gun-for-hire business.

In addition, a new quasi-mercenary phenomenon is emerging: private military organizations that are professionally run. Often led by retired senior military officers from major countries, these organizations tend to deal exclusively with national governments. For a fee, they provide advice on defense strategy, train units in the national armed forces, help governments procure arms, or fight the government's battles.

Are mercenaries' activities ethical or legitimate? Can a distinction in this regard be made between freewheeling gunslingers and professional private military companies? The United Nations' answer appears to be "no." The General Assembly has adopted a convention against mercenary organizations, which is presented here as the second reading selection. Even the newer, professionally run private military organizations raise the ire of UN Secretary General Kofi Annan, who in the first selection is quoted as saying that there is no "distinction between respectable mercenaries and non-respectable mercenaries." Elsewhere in the first selection, written by David Shearer, appears a further description of the currently active professional military companies and some of their activities.

As you read the articles, consider the following questions.

Discussion Questions

1. Do you see any ethical problems for American military officers, trained by the US government for the defense of the US, selling their military knowledge and skills to foreign governments as advisers? Would your answer differ if the US government opposed the foreign government benefiting from this American expertise?
2. Why do developing countries, more than industrialized countries, seem especially concerned about the use of mercenaries?
3. Under what circumstances—if any—do you believe that the use of mercenaries is acceptable?

   For more information on this topic, visit the following websites:

   http://www.unchr.ch/html/menu2/7/b/mercenary/a_main.htm
   (home page of the U.N.'s Special Rapporteur on mercenaries in developing countries; has U.N. resolutions, reports, etc.)

   http://www.sandline.com
   (web site of Sandline International, a British firm which bills itself on this site as a "private military company")

   http://www.mpri.com
   (web site of MPRI [originally known as Military Professional Resources Incorporated] an American firm of retired military personnel, which provides assistance to other governments)

Outsourcing War

DAVID SHEARER

For nearly three centuries, the accepted international norm has been that only nation-states should be permitted to fight wars. Not surprisingly, the rise of private military companies in the 1990s—and the possibility that they may view conflict as a legitimate business activity—has provoked outrage and prompted calls for them to be outlawed. The popular press has labeled these companies "mercenaries" and "dogs of war," conjuring up images of freebooting and rampaging Rambos overthrowing weak—usually African—governments. At a press conference convened in June 1997 to discuss the ongoing civil war in Sierra Leone, Secretary General Kofi Annan bristled at the suggestion that the United Nations would ever consider working with "respectable" mercenary organizations, arguing that there is no "distinction between respectable mercenaries and non-respectable mercenaries."

But is this depiction fair? Certainly these soldiers might meet the three most widely accepted criteria defining a mercenary: They are foreign to a conflict; they are motivated chiefly by financial gain; and, in some cases, they have participated directly in combat. They differ significantly, however, from infamous characters such as Irishman "Mad" Mike Hoare and Frenchman Bob Denard, who fought in the Congo and elsewhere in the 1960s. What most sets today's military companies apart is their approach. They have a distinct corporate character, have openly defended their usefulness and professionalism, have used internationally accepted legal and financial instruments to secure their deals, and so far have supported only recognized governments and avoided regimes unpalatable to the international community. As Enrique Bernales Ballesteros, the UN's special rapporteur on the use of mercenaries, has noted, personnel working for these companies, "even when they have a military background and are highly paid" cannot be considered as "coming within the legal scope of mercenary status."

Dismissing private-sector military personnel as little more than modern-day soldiers of fortune would not only be simplistic but would obscure the broader issues that these military companies raise. Why have they emerged in the 1990s? What role might they play in the future? Can

David Shearer is a research associate at the International Institute for Strategic Studies in London. He was a senior adviser to the UN Department of Humanitarian Affairs in Liberia and Rwanda in 1995 and 1996.
Reprinted by permission. *Foreign Policy*, Fall 1998. Issue 112, p. 68, 14p.

they be regulated? Practitioners and academics who specialize in conflict resolution typically argue that private military companies hinder efforts to end wars and broker peace. Yet, the evidence suggests that coercion is often essential to breaking deadlocks and bringing opposing parties to the negotiating table. In this context, military companies can be seen not as part of the problem but as part of the solution—especially for struggling but legitimate governments that lack the resources to field effective fighting forces. As the political and economic costs of peacekeeping continue to escalate, it may increasingly make sense for multilateral organizations and Western governments to consider outsourcing some aspects of these interventions to the private sector.

THESE GUNS FOR HIRE

Private military forces are as old as warfare itself. The ancient Chinese, Greek, and Roman armies employed large numbers of mercenaries, and mercenaries comprised about half of William the Conqueror's army in the eleventh century. During the fourteenth century, Italian city-states contracted private military forces, known as condottieri, to protect themselves—an early acknowledgement that hiring mercenaries can often prove more cost-effective than maintaining standing armies. Private forces have also served states' immediate strategic interests. The United Kingdom, for example, hired 30,000 Hessian soldiers to fight in the American War of Independence to avoid conscripting its own citizens. In the late eighteenth century, foreigners comprised half of the armed forces of Prussia and a third of the armies of France and the United Kingdom. Mercantile companies were licensed by the state to wage war to serve their countries' economic interests. In 1815, the East India Company, which colonized India on behalf of the British government, boasted an army of 150,000 soldiers.

But with the rise of nationalism in the nineteenth century, the idea of fighting for one's country rather than for commercial interests gained currency. Governments came to command a monopoly over violence and became increasingly keen on limiting the risks to their neutrality that arose when their citizens fought other peoples' wars. Conscripted armies under the control of the state became the norm—apart from the activities of a few individuals that capitalized on the upheavals caused by African independence throughout the 1960s and 1970s.

In the past decade, however, the increasing inability of weak governments to counter internal violence has created a ready market for private military forces. This demand has also been fueled by a shift in Western priorities. The strategic interests of major powers in countries such as Mozambique, Rwanda, and Sierra Leone have declined with the end of the

Cold War. As a result, Western countries are more reluctant to intervene militarily in weak states, and their politicians are disinclined to explain casualties to their electorates. Furthermore, Western armies, designed primarily to fight the sophisticated international conflicts envisaged by Cold War strategists, are ill equipped to tackle low-intensity civil wars, with their complicated ethnic agendas, blurred boundaries between combatants and civilians, and loose military hierarchies. The failed U.S.-led involvement in Somalia in 1993 reinforced American resolve never to enter a conflict unless vital domestic interests were at stake.

Meanwhile, UN peacekeeping efforts have fallen victim to Western governments' fears of sustaining casualties, becoming entangled in expanding conflicts, and incurring escalating costs. The number of personnel in UN operations has fallen from a peak of 76,000 in 1994 to around 15,000 today. Multilateral interventions appear increasingly likely to be limited to situations where the UN gains the consent of the warring parties rather than—as allowed under Chapter VII of the UN Charter—to be designed to enforce a peace on reluctant belligerents. Bilateral, as well as multilateral, commitments have also been trimmed. France's long-standing deployment of troops in its former African colonies, for example, has declined: French troops will be cut by 40 percent to about 5,000 by 2000. Paris has stated that it will no longer engage in unilateral military interventions in Africa, effectively creating a strategic vacuum.

Into this gap have stepped today's private military companies. Most such enterprises hail from South Africa, the United Kingdom, the United States, and occasionally France and Israel. They all share essentially the same goals to improve their client's military capability, thereby allowing that client to function better in war or deter conflict more effectively. This process might involve military assessments, training, or occasionally weapons procurement. Direct involvement in combat is less common, although two companies, Executive Outcomes (EO) of South Africa and Sandline International of Great Britain, advertise their skills in this area. EO has provided training and strategic advice to the armed forces of Angola and Sierra Leone; its apartheid-era soldiers have fought in both countries.

Other companies, such as Military Professional Resources Incorporated (MPRI), a Virginia-based firm headed by retired U.S. army generals, has limited its services to training and has hired former U.S. military personnel to develop the military forces of Bosnia-Herzegovina and Croatia. Some organizations engage in more passive activities, such as protecting premises and people. The British company Defence Systems Limited, for example, guards embassies and protects the interests of corporations working in unstable areas. Other outfits provide businesses with risk analyses, and several have developed specialist expertise in resolving the kidnapping incidents that plague firms operating in Latin America.

Military companies are unfettered by political constraints. They view conflict as a business opportunity and have taken advantage of the pervasive influence of economic liberalism in the late twentieth century. They have also been quick to adapt to the complex agendas of civil wars. Their ability to operate has been enhanced by an expanded pool of military expertise made available by reductions in Western forces. Many recruits come from highly disciplined military units, such as the British Special Air Service and the South African and American special forces. Likewise, cheap and accessible Soviet-made weaponry has helped strengthen the companies' capabilities.

When help from other quarters was unavailable, Sir Julius Chan, prime minister of Papua New Guinea, claimed in 1997 that he was forced to "go to the private sector" to counter Bougainville Revolutionary Army (BRA) insurgents. After negotiations with the BRA collapsed, Chan signed a $36 million contract with Sandline International to train his national forces and plan an offensive against the separatists. The government was particularly anxious to reopen Bougainville's Panguna Copper Mine, once the source of 30 percent of the country's export earnings.

Western mining corporations also stand to benefit when a private military company restores order, thereby raising questions as to whether these business entities share any formal ties. In April 1997, the *London Independent* reported that Anthony Buckingham, a director of Heritage Oil and Gas and Branch Energy, introduced EO to the governments of Angola and Sierra Leone. But Buckingham has emphatically stated that "there is no corporate link between Executive Outcomes and the Branch Heritage group." EO officials likewise strongly deny any financial or operational/business links with mining companies. While critics decry even this nebulous relationship as neocolonialist behavior in the worst tradition of Cecil Rhodes, Buckingham observes that "If there is no stability there is no investment and no one benefits." The lure of rich resources and the risks of exploiting them in unstable areas are powerful incentives for companies to maintain stability in weak states. This motivation can also chime with a government's own wishes. A mining company depends on security to protect its investments; a beleaguered government buys increased security to shore up its rule, while the prospect of mining revenues can supplement its coffers. Furthermore, a military company, while strengthening its client government's military performance, protects a mining company's operations because revenues from these sources guarantee its payment. In the developing world, minerals and hardwoods may soon emerge as the currency of stability. The source of payment is a crucial difference between the intervention of a military company and that of the UN, which is funded by donors, not by the state in question. Coupling multinational companies with an external security force potentially gives foreigners powerful leverage over a government and its affairs—a risk that some governments appear willing to take.

Another trend, reminiscent of the privateers of earlier centuries, is the willingness of private military companies to act as proxies for Western governments. MPRI has specialized exclusively in military services, originally for the privatization-minded U.S. Department of Defense. MPRI's first two major international contracts were with the Croatian government in 1994 to update its Warsaw Pact–oriented military. When the sophisticated Croatian offensive, Operation Storm, took the Serb-held Krajina enclave in August 1995, there was inevitable suspicion that MPRI was involved. The operation played an important role in reversing the tide of war against the Serbs and—consistent with American policy—in bringing both sides to the negotiating table. MPRI, although denying that it had played a role, has benefited from these rumors. In 1995, the company was contracted, in the aftermath of the Dayton accord, to strengthen the Muslim-Croat Federation's army in order to deter Bosnian Serb aggression. Since it is funded by the contracting government, MPRI has delivered a cheaper service and done so at less political risk than would have been possible had U.S. troops been used. The scenario serves as an example of how the private military sector can allow policymakers to achieve their foreign-policy goals free from the need to secure public approval and safe in the knowledge that should the situation deteriorate, official participation can be fudged.

Other American companies have also worked to further administration policy. Corporate giants such as Science Applications International Corporation and Braddock, Dunn & McDonald, Inc. and its subsidiary Vinnell Corporation are primarily high-technology suppliers to the military-industrial market but have also diversified into military training. They are contracted by the Saudi government to upgrade and train its armed forces in the use of mainly U.S. weaponry. Some British companies have also supported government interests: The London-based Saladin Security, for example, trains Omani government forces working alongside British Army officers who are seconded there. But on the whole, British companies are smaller and less diversified than their U.S. counterparts and have tended to focus on protecting commercial interests. Nonetheless, they maintain close contacts with Britain's Ministry of Defence and are an important source of intelligence.

THE FUTURE OF PEACEKEEPING?

Some private military companies, such as EO, possess sufficient coercive capability to break a stalemate in a conflict. Unlike multinational forces, they do not act impartially but are hired to win a conflict (or deter it) on the client's terms. EO and Sandline International have argued that military force has an underutilized potential to bring conflicts to a close. However, bludgeoning the other side into accepting a peace agreement runs in diametric opposition to most academic studies of conflict resolution. These studies center on consent bringing warring sides together with the implicit assumption that each wants to negotiate an end to the war. To a large degree, the international community has responded to civil wars in this manner, especially those of limited strategic interest. Ceasefires act as holding positions; mediation seeks to bring combatants to an agreement. Peacekeepers, acting under mandates to be evenhanded and to use minimal force, are deployed to support this process.

The flaw in this approach is that according to recent empirical studies, outright victories, rather than negotiated peace settlements, have ended the greater part of the twentieth century's internal conflicts. Combatants in Angola, Bosnia, and Sierra Leone consistently resisted a negotiated, consent-based settlement. There appeared to be little chance of a breakthrough until more coercive measures were applied. So why has the international community continued to persist with negotiated settlements and even-handedness in cases where one side was clearly at fault? The reason, for the most part, is self-interest. Such an approach avoids direct intervention and the subsequent political risks.

Yet when it suits them, Western states have also been proponents of "battlefield diplomacy" to resolve conflicts. This approach was favored throughout the Cold War when the object was to limit Soviet expansionism. More recently, the United States tacitly supported the aims of Laurent Kabila's military campaign to oust President Mobutu Sese Seku in the former Zaire. France allegedly backed former military ruler Denis Sassou Nguesso's overthrow of Congolese president Pascal Lissouba in September 1997. And by condoning the Croatian capture of Serb-held Krajina, Washington was implicitly recognizing the value of resolution through force.

However, the likelihood that a military solution can bring durable peace to a country depends on the nature of the peace agreement, as well as on how effectively follow-up measures such as demobilization, cantonment of fighters, and rehabilitation are implemented. Despite EO's involvement in Angola, for example, peace is still not finally secure. Nevertheless, its military involvement was instrumental in turning the tables of war in favor of the government's side, a development that coerced the National Union for the Total Independence of Angola (UNITA) to negotiate and eventually sign the 1994 Lusaka Accords. Similarly, in Sierra Leone, EO battered the Revolutionary United Front (RUF) faction into submission, creating sufficient stability to hold the first elections in 27 years. Later military offensives compelled the RUF to return to the negotiating table and sign a peace accord in November 1997. But just three months after EO left, the government was overthrown by disgruntled members of the armed forces, highlighting the importance of implementing postconflict measures.

These shortcomings are often seized upon as proof that the efforts of military companies have failed. But EO has always acknowledged its limitations. The UN did not engage members of EO in Sierra Leone, possibly because it chose to label them as mercenaries and therefore as untouchable. The entire episode illustrates that it is better to acknowledge the existence of military companies and engage them politically than to ignore them and hope that somehow a peace agreement will stay intact.

REGULATING THE MARKET

Since the demand for military force is unlikely to end anytime soon, military companies, in their various guises, appear here to stay. Should there be some attempt to regulate them, or is it the right of sovereign states—as with the purchase of weaponry—to employ who they wish as long as they ensure that their employees behave within acceptable bounds? There is widespread discomfort with a laissez-faire approach, most of it caused by military companies' lack of accountability. Although most military companies have only worked for legitimate governments, there is little to stop them from working for rebel movements in the future.

To make matters even more complicated, deciding which is the "legitimate" side in a civil conflict is not always straightforward. Many modern governments were once classified as "insurgents" or "terrorists" while in opposition, among them South Africa's African National Congress and Ugandan president Yoweri Museveni's National Resistance Army. The governments that grew out of these movements are now internationally recognized.

Military companies are motivated first and foremost by profit and are responsible primarily to their shareholders. Consequently, financial losses, in spite of any strategic or political considerations, may prompt a company to pull out. There are also few checks on their adherence to human-rights conventions. The problem is not a lack of human-rights law. During times of war, the employees of military companies fall under the auspices of Common Article 3 of the Geneva Conventions, which is binding on all combatants. They are also bound by a state's obligations to UN human-rights conventions as "agents" of the government that employs them. What is absent is adequate independent observation of their activities—a feature common to all parties in a conflict but especially characteristic of military companies that have no permanent attachments to national governments.

Efforts at controlling mercenaries through international law in the 1960s and 1970s were led by African states that faced a skeptical reception from the United States and major European powers. The most accepted definition of a mercenary, found in Article 47 of the 1977 Additional Protocols to the Geneva Conventions, is so riddled with loopholes that few international-law scholars believe it could withstand the rigors of the courtroom. International apathy is palpable. France and the United States have not signed the Additional Protocols, and the UN's 1989 International Convention against the Recruitment, Use, Financing, and Training of Mercenaries has attracted only 12 signatories. Three of these signatories, Angola, the former Yugoslavia, and the former Zaire, have gone on to employ mercenaries. Most states have domestic laws that ban mercenaries but few, if any, have acted on them. Britain's Foreign Enlistment Act, for example, was introduced in 1870, and there has yet to be a prosecution.

The drive to regulate military companies has been most passionate when home governments—not those who contract them—are affected. The British government is currently investigating regulation after Sandline International, claiming it had clearance from the Foreign and Commonwealth Office, appeared to violate UN sanctions by supplying arms and military expertise to the ousted Sierra Leonean government. Sandline executives, portrayed in the media as "mercenaries," embarrassed Britain's new Labour Party government, which had entered office touting its platform of an "ethical" foreign policy.

South Africa too has come under both domestic and international pressure to control the increasing number of companies based there. Its parliament passed the Regulation of Foreign Military Assistance Bill in May 1998. Privately, however, most commentators in South Africa believe that while the legislation provides a framework for government policy and satisfies its critics, its real impact will be limited. Military companies are mostly registered offshore and can easily relocate to other countries, making it difficult to pin them down under specific jurisdictions. A growing trend is for international companies to form joint ventures with local companies, avoiding the effects of the legislation in any one country. Angola, for example, has over 80 security firms, many of them in joint ownership. Companies can also easily disguise their activities by purporting to be security companies performing protection services while actually engaging in more coercive military operations.

The principal obstacle to regulating private military companies has been the tendency to brand them as "mercenaries' of the kind witnessed in Africa 30 years ago, rather than to recognize them as multinational entrepreneurs eager to solidify their legitimacy. Consequently, regulation can be best achieved through constructive engagement. This process would likely expose governments and international institutions to accusations of sanctioning the use of "soldiers of fortune" to shore up the international system. Yet, this tack offers the international community greater leverage to influence the activities of companies that believe legitimacy is the key to their future growth and prosperity. In an effort to broaden their appeal, for instance, military companies have offered greater transparency. Sandline International maintains that it is prepared to place itself under the scrutiny of international monitors and accept an international regulatory framework. This pledge is a necessary step; a careful audit would establish corporate links that might affect the company's operations.

Engagement could well begin with dialogue between key multilateral institutions and the private military sector. Liaison at senior levels of the UN, for example, is needed, and the Department of Peacekeeping is an obvious starting point. UN field personnel should be permitted to contact military companies and plan strategies for conflict resolution where appropriate. Had there been a structured transition between EO's departure and the planned deployment of UN observers, the military coup in Sierra Leone might have been averted. EO could have maintained a threat of enforcement that would have bought time for the UN to fully implement postconflict programs, allowing RUF combatants to become confident enough about their future that they might demobilize. Direct engagement could also provide an opportunity to lay out a code of conduct that might incorporate more specific operational issues rising from the work of military companies. Observation of companies such as EO to ensure that they adhere to basic principles of warfare is needed, something in which the International Committee of the Red Cross could take a lead.

The prospect that private military companies might gain some degree of legitimacy within the international community begs the question as to whether these firms could take on UN peacekeeping functions and improve on UN efforts. Military companies see this as an area of potential growth and are quick to point out the advantages they offer. There is no denying that they are cheaper than UN operations. EO cost Sierra Leone's government $35 million for the 22 months it was there, versus a planned UN operation budgeted at $47 million for eight months. Likewise, its annual cost in Angola was a fraction of that of the UN's operation—for example, in 1996–97, UNAVEM III cost $135 million. Admittedly, EO and other such firms provide military support, not peacekeeping, but there is no doubt that they can mobilize more quickly and appear less sensitive to casualties. However, accepting a UN mandate or conditions may also undermine a company's effectiveness. As any soldier who has served in a UN operation will attest, a peacekeeping mission is only as effective as the operation's mandate.

GIVE WAR A CHANCE

Policymakers and multilateral organizations have paid little attention to private-sector involvement in wars. Yet low-intensity conflicts—the type that military companies have specialized in up to now—will be the wars that prevail in the first part of the twenty-first century. Their virulence and random nature could undermine the viability of many nation-states. These wars defy orthodox means of resolution, thus creating the circumstances that have contributed to the expansion of military companies into this area.

Conflict resolution theory needs to look more closely at the impact of coercion, not dismiss it. Military companies may in fact offer new possibilities for building peace that, while not universal in applicability, can hasten the end to a war and limit loss of life. Moreover, there is no evidence that private-sector intervention will erode the state. Despite the commercial motives of military companies, their interventions, if anything, have strengthened the ability of governments to control their territory. Yet, military companies are unlikely to resolve conflicts in the long term. Political intervention and postconflict peacebuilding efforts are still necessary. Although the UN's special rapporteur on the use of mercenaries has acknowledged the difficulties in equating military companies with mercenaries, the debate has not moved beyond that point. Admittedly, the UN is in a sticky position. Although some member states have condemned the use of military companies, others have employed their services or condoned their operations. Meanwhile, the future of private military interests looks bright. "Now entering its eleventh year, MPRI has over 400 employees," declares the company's Web site, noting that in 1997 the volume of business exceeded $48 million. Even with a mercenary label and its associated moral stain, EO and Sandline continue to tout their services to beleaguered governments. Other companies are likely to emerge that offer EO's services, particularly in terms of low-key military training and advising for governments. The most rapid expansion is likely to be linked to the protection of commercial interests, although these can act as a springboard for more aggressive, military actions alongside local companies and power brokers. Mainstream companies, from the United States in particular, are also likely to encroach into low-intensity conflict areas. With backing from a cautious administration not wanting to forego strategic influence, the temptation to use military companies might prove irresistible.

Regulation of military companies will be problematic, given the diversity of their services and the breadth of their market niche. Yet, in many respects, the private military industry is no different from any other sector in the global economy that is required to conform to codes of practice—except that in the former's case, the risk of political instability and social mayhem is amplified if more unscrupulous actors become involved. There is good reason to glance back in history to a time when private military forces operated more or less freely. Historian Anthony Mockler notes that one hundred years after the first condottieri entered Italy: "The lines had become crossed and tangled: mercenaries had become rulers and rulers had become mercenaries."

WANT TO KNOW MORE?

Mercenaries have been around for as long as warfare itself. For detailed accounts of their history, see Anthony Mockler's *Mercenaries* (London: MacDonald, 1969) and Janice Thomson's *Mercenaries, Pirates & Sovereigns: State Building and Extraterritorial Violence in Early Modern Europe* (New Jersey: Princeton University Press, 1996).

Several recent articles and studies scrutinize private military companies and their activities worldwide: David Shearer's *Private Armies and Military Intervention*, Adelphi Paper 316 (New York: International Institute for Strategic Studies, February 1998); William Shawcross' "In Praise of Sandline" (*The Spectator*, August 1, 1998); Al J. Venter's "Market Forces: How Hired Guns Succeeded Where the United Nations Failed" (Jane's *International Defense Review*, March 1, 1998); Ken Silverstein's "Privatizing War" (*The Nation*, July 28, 1997); and David Isenberg's *Soldiers of Fortune Ltd.: A Profile of Today's Private Sector Corporate Mercenary Firms* (Washington: Center for Defense Information, November 1997).

The legal status of mercenaries is addressed in Francoise Hampson's "Mercenaries: Diagnosis Before Prescription" (Netherlands' *Yearbook of International Law*, No. 3, 1991) and Edward Kwakwa's "The Current Status of Mercenaries in the Law of Armed Conflict" (*Hastings International and Comparative Law Review*, vol. 14, 1990).

Martin van Crevald examines the changing dynamics of conflict in *The Transformation of War* (New York: The Free Press, 1991). Two studies provide empirical evidence that outright victory, rather than negotiated peace, has ended the greater part of the twentieth century's internal conflicts: Stephen John Stedman's *Peacemaking in Civil Wars: International Mediation in Zimbabwe 1974–1980* (Boulder: Lynne Rienner, 1991) and Roy Licklider's "The Consequences of Negotiated Settlements in Civil Wars 1954–1993" (*American Political Science Review*, September 1995).

On human rights, see a series of reports by the UN's special rapporteur on mercenaries that are available online: *Report on the Question of the Use of Mercenaries as a Means of Violating Human Rights and Impeding the Exercise of the Right of Peoples to Self-Determination.*

PORTRAIT OF A PRIVATE ARMY

In its promotional literature, Executive Outcomes (EO) describes itself as a company with a "solid history of success," thanks to the efforts of its "highly effective work force." This work force is essentially a demobilized army for hire. Based in South Africa, the company was established in 1989 by Eeben Barlow and is staffed almost exclusively by veterans from the former South African Defence Force. EO claims to be able to draw on over 2,000 personnel and forces, all of whom are assembled on a contract-by-contract basis and recruited chiefly by word-of-mouth. This policy has not only ensured quality control but a preexisting military hierarchy of highly experienced troops. EO personnel have distinguished themselves from other companies by entering into combat, claiming that accompanying the clients' troops increases their effectiveness and confidence.

EO's first major contract was in Angola in May 1993 to rescue the Soyo oil fields in the north from the rebel National Union for the Total Independence of Angola (UNIT). The Angolan government then hired over 500 personnel from September 1993 to January 1996 for an estimated $40 million a year (including weaponry) to train nearly 5,000 soldiers. EO's arrival, coinciding with the lifting of the arms embargo on Angola, helped reverse the course of the war, and UNIT suffered significant defeats. EO's second contract, this time with the Sierra Leonean government in May 1995, lasted 22 months and cost $35 million—about one-third of the country's defense budget. EO, working with local civilian militia, battered the Revolutionary United Front into submission. In February 1997, EO was subcontracted to the British military company, Sandline International, to train and plan military operations against the Bougainville Resistance Army in Papua New Guinea.

EO's military effectiveness testifies to its expertise in low-intensity conflict. It has planned its operations closely with government officials and uses government equipment, although it has arranged the purchase of weaponry. Its hallmark has been its highly mobile operations using MI-17 helicopter troop carriers, on occasion supported by MI-24 helicopter gun-ships and Soviet-made ground attack aircraft. But EO's biggest strength has been its use of intelligence capabilities, particularly through the cultivation of local populations, augmented with night-sighting and radio intercept devices. Casualties have remained relatively light. EO acknowledges that 11 of its personnel died in Angola, with seven still missing, and four killed in Sierra Leone. Two others died from accident and sickness.

United Nations General Assembly Resolution 52/112 of 12 December 1997

The General Assembly,

Recalling its resolutions 49/150 of 23 December 1994, 50/138 of 21 December 1995 and 51/83 of 12 December 1996,

Recalling also all of its relevant resolutions in which, inter alia, it condemned any State that permitted or tolerated the recruitment, financing, training, assembly, transit and use of mercenaries with the objective of overthrowing the Governments of States Members of the United Nations, especially those of developing countries, or of fighting against national liberation movements, and recalling further the relevant resolutions of the Security Council, the Economic and Social Council and the Organization of African Unity,

Reaffirming the purposes and principles enshrined in the Charter of the United Nations concerning the strict observance of the principles of sovereign equality, political independence, territorial integrity of States, the non-use of force or threat of use of force in international relations and self-determination of peoples,

Alarmed and concerned about the danger which the activities of mercenaries constitute to peace and security in developing countries, particularly in Africa and in small States, where democratically elected Governments have been overthrown by mercenaries or through mercenary international criminal activities,

Deeply concerned about the loss of life, the substantial damage to property and the negative effects on the polity and economies of affected countries resulting from mercenary aggression and criminal activities,

Convinced that it is necessary for Member States to ratify the International Convention against the Recruitment, Use, Financing and Training of Mercenaries, adopted by the General Assembly in 1989, and to develop and maintain international cooperation among States for the prevention, prosecution and punishment of mercenary activities,

Further convinced that, notwithstanding the way in which mercenaries or mercenary-related activities are used or the form they take to acquire some semblance of legitimacy, they are a threat to peace, security and the self-determination of peoples and an obstacle to the enjoyment of human rights by peoples,

1. Takes note of the report of the Special Rapporteur of the Commission on Human Rights on the use of mercenaries as a means of

impeding the exercise of the right of peoples to self-determination concerning the use of mercenaries and mercenary-related activities to topple sovereign Governments and to violate the human rights of peoples and impede the exercise of self-determination despite its resolution 51/83;

2. Reaffirms that the use of mercenaries and their recruitment, financing and training are causes for grave concern to all States and violate the purposes and principles enshrined in the Charter of the United Nations;

3. Urges all States to take the necessary steps and to exercise the utmost vigilance against the menace posed by the activities of mercenaries and to take appropriate legislative measures to ensure that their territories and other territories under their control, as well as their nationals, are not used for the recruitment, assembly, financing, training and transit of mercenaries for the planning of activities designed to destabilize or overthrow the Government or threaten the territorial integrity and political unity of sovereign States or to promote secession or fight the national liberation movements struggling against colonial or other forms of alien domination or occupation;

4. Calls upon all States that have not yet done so to consider taking the necessary action to sign or to ratify the International Convention against the Recruitment, Use, Financing and Training of Mercenaries;

5. Urges all States to cooperate fully with the Special Rapporteur in the fulfilment of his mandate;

6. Requests the Office of the United Nations High Commissioner for Human Rights, as a matter of priority, to publicize the adverse effects of mercenary activities on the right to self-determination and, when requested and where necessary, to render advisory services to States that are affected by the activities of mercenaries;

7. Further requests the Secretary-General to invite Governments to make proposals towards a clearer legal definition of mercenaries;

8. Requests the Special Rapporteur to report, with specific recommendations, his findings on the use of mercenaries to undermine the right of peoples to self-determination to the General Assembly at its fifty-third session;

9. Decides to consider at its fifty-third session the question of the use of mercenaries as a means of violating human rights and impeding the exercise of the right of peoples to self-determination under the agenda item entitled "Rights of peoples to self-determination."

PART III
International Political Economy

Issue 9
Protectionism

INTRODUCTION

A few miles east of San Diego, California, near the Otay Mesa border crossing to Mexico, is a peculiar sight. On the American side of the border, there are large buildings on which familiar corporate names, mainly those of electronics companies, are prominently displayed. A short distance away—just beyond the border fence—inside Mexico, there are other buildings on which the names of those same companies appear.

Strange? Not really. The buildings on the U.S. side are warehouses from which parts are trucked a few blocks away to the companies' buildings in Mexico. In Mexico the parts are assembled, and the finished products then are trucked back into the United States for distribution and sale. Why do these companies not assemble the parts in the United States? The reason, of course, is labor costs. The wage rate for this type of skilled labor in California is about $12.00 an hour. In Mexico these companies pay less than $2.00 per hour— one-sixth the U.S. rate. Under provisions of NAFTA (North American Free Trade Agreement) these assembled products enter the United States tariff free. No wonder American companies like this procedure!

But what about workers in San Diego and elsewhere in the United States who otherwise could have had these jobs but are now unemployed? To them the phrase "free trade" may have a hollow ring. On the other hand, consumers in San Diego and elsewhere likely will be able to buy these Mexican-assembled products at lower prices than if they had been assembled in the United States. Free trade may threaten jobs, but it also may benefit the consumer. Which concern should be paramount?

In the first article, Robert J. Samuelson, columnist for *Newsweek* magazine, argues strongly in favor of free trade. In his review of a book by Patrick Buchanan, the conservative television commentator and presidential candidate, Samuelson attacks Buchanan's arguments point by point.

In the second article, Pat Buchanan argues passionately against free trade. In his view, the government is obligated to give top priority to protecting American workers and companies and thus should use barriers to imports, such as tariffs and quantitative limits on imports, to achieve this end.

As you read the articles, consider the following questions.

Discussion Questions

1. Why do proponents of free trade say that unrestricted imports are good for the U.S. economy, even when American workers are being put out of work by imports?
2. The value of products that the U.S. buys from other countries is a lot greater than the value of products that the U.S. sells abroad. How would Pat Buchanan's position on trade affect this trade deficit?
3. What restrictions, if any, would you favor on American defense companies selling equipment with military applications to other countries?

    For more information on this topic, visit the following websites:

    http://www.wto.org/
    (web site of the World Trade Organization; especially click on "dispute settlement")

    http://www.uschamber.org/policy/index.html
    (web site of U.S. Chamber of Commerce, which favors free trade)

    http://www.cbea.org/
    (web site of the Caribbean Banana Exporters Association, banana producers in the Caribbean which are hurt by U.S. policy supporting Latin American banana exporters)

Trade Free or Die:
Pat Buchanan and the Illusions of Protectionism

ROBERT J. SAMUELSON

[A Review of *The Great Betrayal: How American Sovereignty and Social Justice Are Being Sacrificed to the Gods of the Global Economy*, by Patrick J. Buchanan (Little, Brown)]

I. In many ways, the timing of Pat Buchanan's plea for more protectionism could not be worse. The American economy is humming along, with unemployment around 5 percent since late 1996. If more than two decades of trade deficits have crippled us, the consequences are not immediately obvious. Not only is the economy of the United States now the strongest among advanced societies, but American companies still remain formidable, if not always dominant, competitors in many critical industries: computers and software; aerospace; biotechnology; communications and entertainment; banking and finance; business consulting; and medicine. The auto and steel industries—once given up for dead—have recovered from fierce foreign competition.

The coexistence of extraordinary prosperity and constant trade deficits is a paradox to be explained, but Buchanan ignores it. Reading him, you would not know that the United States is in a mighty boom. The temptation, then, is to dismiss his book as irrelevant. That is not a good idea. An all-but-announced Republican presidential candidate in 2000, Buchanan is a born-again protectionist, who sees his conversion as a harbinger of a broader shift among the public. "The Young Turks of the New Conservatism who would capture the Republican Party for Barry Goldwater in 1964 and Ronald Reagan in 1980 [were] free traders," he writes. "I know, because I was one of them." His hopes of a protectionist revival are not preposterous, regardless of the fate of his own candidacy. In a weakening economy, the message could play. Fears of an overseas job drain can be exploited; and working-class Democrats (Reagan Democrats) can be wooed with promises of greater job security. A populist majority might one day rally to economic nationalism.

Until now, of course, protectionism has been a political flop. Every politician who has tried to ride it to the White House has failed: John

Robert J. Samuelson writes a column for *Newsweek* and *The Washington Post* Writers Group. He is the author of *The Good Life and Its Discontents: The American Dream in the Age of Entitlement* (Vintage).

Reprinted by permission. *New Republic*, June 22, 1998. Vol. 218, Issue 25, p. 27.

Connally in 1980, Richard Gephardt in 1988, Ross Perot in 1992, Pat Buchanan in 1996. It's worth trying to understand why. A common theory is that protectionism does not have much of a constituency. It is good rhetoric, but in the end it does not attract many voters, because not many Americans would benefit from import restrictions, especially if they resulted in retaliation against American exports. The raw numbers seem to confirm this. In 1997, for example, imports equaled only 13 percent of the economy's output, or Gross Domestic Product, and this was nearly offset by exports, 12 percent of GDP. Such figures suggest that protectionism has only a tiny constituency.

Buchanan, by contrast, argues quite plausibly that trade politics must be seen in a broader context, and that the free-trade consensus that arose after World War II has been crumbling for decades. It rested on three pillars, he says, each of them now weakened. The first pillar was a general sense that American industry was invincible; but that confidence shattered in the late 1970s and early 1980s, when many venerable American companies (Ford, Caterpillar, U.S. Steel, Xerox, Intel) came under siege from foreign competition. The second pillar of the postwar period was the cold war: greater trade with our allies promoted their prosperity (it was said), and this inoculated them against communism. The end of the cold war obviously dispensed with this argument. And the third pillar was the once-common belief that protectionism (and the Smoot-Hawley tariff) had been a major cause of the Great Depression. But memories fade, and much modern scholarship discounts protectionism as a major cause of the Depression.

The correct implication is that protectionism could again find a large following. The present optimism of Americans masks a deep uneasiness about the global economy that, once today's boom ends (as it will), could reemerge. We face a collision between an instinctive nationalism and the relentless expansion of global markets. Just because protectionism is not a desirable response does not mean that every protectionist grievance is bogus. Many of its complaints are clearly true: burgeoning global trade and investment do erode national sovereignty and self-sufficiency; and they do threaten some industries and workers; and they do create divided loyalties for American companies between enhancing profits and preserving American jobs.

It would be unnatural if Americans did not worry about these developments. Moreover, the economy's exposure to global competition is greater than the raw trade statistics indicate. In 1997, for example, imports accounted for only about 13 percent of American car and truck sales. But the entire auto industry faces global competition, because imports could capture almost any individual sale; and foreign car firms now produce here. The same is true of many industries. Global competition doesn't yet affect a majority of workers, but its impact—real and psychological—extends beyond an isolated minority.

Polls also find Americans to be ambivalent about trade. A CBS survey in late 1996 asked whether trade was good or bad for the country. The response was that 69 percent said it was good and 17 percent said it was bad. But a *Los Angeles Times* poll a few months earlier asked whether imports should be restricted to "protect American industry and jobs" or freely admitted "to permit the widest choices and lowest prices." The response: 63 percent favored restrictions, only 28 percent didn't.

It is easy to imagine a recession and a huge trade deficit fueling protectionism. Or a general isolationist drift could infect trade policies. One sign of how weak the free-trade consensus has grown is that the hostility is not confined to one party. Both Democrats and Republicans have protectionist wings. Three decades ago, this was unthinkable. Buchanan's audience is not economists or academics. It is the political class, and the editorial boards, and the opinion-makers. Despite its poor logic, his case has a glib allure. Protectionism has been so disreputable for so long that its opponents have grown complacent. They have not candidly acknowledged possible conflicts between free trade and foreign policy goals. And if they don't wake up, they could lose the argument by default.

II. One thing is certain: the case for free trade cannot honestly be made on the basis of heritage. The greatest virtue of Buchanan's book is to remind us that America has mostly been a protectionist nation.

The political culture is certainly receptive. The godfather of protectionism was Alexander Hamilton, whose "Report on Manufactures," written in 1791, urged a protective tariff to nurture industry. To Hamilton, American "wealth . . . independence and security" depended on "the prosperity" of manufacturing. "Every nation," he argued, "ought to endeavor to possess within itself all the essentials of national supply." The Tariff Act of 1789, which imposed duties of 5 percent on many imports, was the second law passed by Congress. Later tariffs went higher, and they stayed high for most of the nineteenth century. With the exception of slavery, they were the largest source of conflict between North and South.

The Tariff Act of 1828—the Tariff of Abominations—almost triggered secession. It imposed an average duty of 62 percent on 92 percent of the country's imports. The South Carolina legislature subsequently declared it and a revised tariff "null, void." A secessionist crisis was avoided in 1833 only because Congress agreed to reduce the tariff to 20 percent over ten years. In general, the South, a big exporter of cotton and a big importer of manufactured products, detested high tariffs. The North, with a larger manufacturing base, adored them.

One reason that tariffs stayed high was their role as the federal government's main source of revenue for most of the century. (The Civil War was the major exception.) But they were also kept high to protect industry. In the 1830s and 1840s, the Whig Party—headed by Henry

Clay—urged national economic development through internal improvements (roads, harbors, bridges) and high tariffs. Lincoln, an early Whig, generally supported high tariffs.

Protectionism was often equated with patriotism. Listen to Justin Morrill, a Republican senator from Vermont who entered Congress as a Whig in 1855, and was among the most steadfast guardians of high tariffs until his death in 1898: "Free trade abjures patriotism and boasts of cosmopolitism. It regards the labor of our own people with no more favor than that of the barbarian on the Danube or the cooly on the Ganges." Buchanan enthuses over such flag-waving. He argues that high tariffs enabled America to become the world's great industrial power in the nineteenth century.

During the last half of the century, many individual tariff rates hovered around 50 percent, and the average tariff (on dutiable and non-dutiable items alike) was about 30 percent. They stayed high partly to repay the huge national debt run up during the Civil War. (The federal debt rose from $65 million in 1860 to $2.8 billion in 1866.) But there were other reasons for the persistence of the tariffs. They were blatant protectionism and fervent nationalism.

A historic reversal was accomplished by Cordell Hull, Roosevelt's secretary of state, who shepherded the Reciprocal Trade Agreements Act of 1934 through Congress. This law transferred much of Congress's power to set tariffs to the president, who could negotiate mutual tariff cuts with other countries. A former senator from Tennessee, Hull had long believed that trade fostered goodwill among nations. And the Depression produced a backlash against protectionism. The backlash continued after World War II. In the 1940s, the United States helped to create new global institutions to prevent the return of '30s protectionism and deflation. These included the International Monetary Fund, which would make short-term loans of foreign exchange, generally dollars, to countries with big trade deficits (the idea was to preempt competitive currency devaluations or protectionism); and the General Agreement on Tariffs and Trade, which would negotiate and police tariff cuts and international trade rules.

Trade also quickly emerged as a central weapon against communism. The Japanese needed to trade to buy basic raw materials (food, fuel, minerals). "Japan cannot remain in the free world unless something is done to allow her to make a living," President Eisenhower said. Otherwise, "it is going to the Communists." For Europe, trade succeeded the Marshall Plan as a recovery strategy from war. In trade negotiations, American officials often made more concessions than they received. In 1954, the State Department proposed unilateral concessions on roughly half of all Japanese imports, from glassware to optical goods to cars. Hardly anyone—the textile, apparel, and shoe industries were major exceptions—felt threatened, because American industry and technology were so dominant.

In 1962, Congress passed John F. Kennedy's Trade Expansion Act, authorizing new trade talks, by huge margins (78–8 in the Senate and 299–125 in the House). As a 23-year-old editorial writer for the *St. Louis Globe-Democrat*, Buchanan was caught up in the fervor. Passage of the Trade Expansion Act, he wrote, was a "thumping administration triumph" that could "become the most potent cold war weapon in the free Western arsenal. . . ." Although he thinks expanded trade was then justified, he says that Americans went overboard. Free trade is not just an idea, Buchanan argues; it is a false religion that "holds out the promise that if we follow the gospel of free trade, paradise can be created on earth." Buchanan contemptuously quotes the nineteenth-century French economist Frederic Bastiat: "Free trade means harmony of interests and peace between nations. . . . We place this indirect and social effect a thousand times above the direct or purely economic effect."

On this, Buchanan is more clear-eyed than many free-trade enthusiasts. It is true that trade cemented America's cold war alliances, but this does not mean that trade can take us the next step—to universal peace and goodwill. What held the cold war alliance together was the cold war. It is dangerous to generalize from this experience; and a lot of history warns against viewing trade as a shield against war. Before World War I, Germany and Britain were major trading partners. Germany also traded heavily with Russia, Holland, and Belgium—and attacked them all.

Trade does not just bind countries together; it also arouses suspicions. In the 1980s, many Americans wrongly feared that the country would be taken over by the Japanese. Canadians feel constantly assaulted by American trade and culture, and so (to a lesser extent) do Europeans. Nationalism endures and endures; and although the tensions and conflicts rarely end in war, trade is not an automatic pacifier.

III. What trade has going for it, of course, is economics. The most astonishing thing about Buchanan's book is that, although it is ostensibly about economics, it almost never engages in genuinely economic thinking. For Buchanan, the decision to expand or to restrict trade is mainly a political choice. Thus he ignores lower communications and transportation costs (container ships, transoceanic telephone cables, jets, satellites, and, now, the Internet) as driving forces; and as the cost of doing business across borders goes down, the demand to do business— including political pressures to permit it—goes up.

Neither Buchanan nor anyone else can repeal this relationship. Certainly countries can prevent trade by shutting themselves off from the world (as China did until the late 1970s), but it is harder and harder to do with surgical precision. With trade comes travel, and modern communications, and global finance. Controlling the process has proven arduous even for the countries (such as Japan) most determined to do so.

This is one reason why more and more countries have embraced the global economy across a broad range of industries and activities. The other reason is that the potential economic gains of doing so have become self-evident. Buchanan treats the process mainly as a zero-sum game: one country's gain is another country's loss. If this were true, there would not be much global trade and investment. When losers recognized their losses, they would withdraw. Trade would occur mainly as a consequence of sheer economic necessity—countries importing essential raw materials (fuel, food, minerals) or goods produced only in a few countries (commercial jets, for example); or as a consequence of coercion—the strong compelling the weak to trade on disadvantageous terms, an informal neocolonialism. Otherwise trade would wither.

What is true, of course, is that individual companies or individual workers can lose in trade. General Motors can lose to Toyota; Hitachi can lose to IBM. But what is bad for a company or an industry is not necessarily bad for a country. Moreover, domestic competition causes more job losses than trade. Consider, for example, the job losses counted by the consulting firm Challenger, Gray & Christmas. Between 1993 and 1997, it found almost 2.5 million job cuts by American companies. The top five industries were: aerospace and defense, 270,166; retailing, 256,834; telecommunications, 213,675; computers, 212,033; financial services (banking, brokerage houses), 166,672; and transportation (airlines, trucking companies), 136,008. None of these cuts involved global trade. The causes ranged from defense cutbacks (aerospace) to new technology (computers). But Buchanan wishes to leave the false impression that, but for trade, the economy would be far less turbulent and harsh.

Given Buchanan's ignorance of economics, it is no surprise that his history, too, is badly warped. To suggest that the vast industrialization of the late nineteenth century, and America's rise as the world's most powerful economy, owes a great deal to protectionism is absurd. In the last half of the nineteenth century, the American economy benefited from a virtuous circle. Railroads expanded dramatically. Between 1860 and 1900, the miles of track rose from roughly 30,000 to more than 200,000. Lower transportation costs expanded markets. In turn, this encouraged investment in new manufacturing technologies that lowered costs through economies of scale. Industrial output soared for all manner of consumer goods (clothes, shoes, furniture), for farm implements, for machinery. Larger markets and lower costs fostered new methods of retailing and wholesaling: the mail-order house Sears, Roebuck was founded in 1891.

None of this depended on protectionism. Some basic technologies (steelmaking, railroads) originated in Europe. And the United States also imported another vital ingredient of growth: people. In each of the century's last four decades, immigration averaged more than 5 percent of the nation's population. As for trade, it grew as the American economy grew. Between 1870 and 1890, both imports and exports almost doubled. The decisive limit on imports was the ability to export (as it is for most countries), not high tariffs.

Tariffs may have protected some American industries, but any effect on the overall economy is exaggerated. Suppose there were no tariffs; some companies might then have faced cheaper imports. To survive, American companies would have had to cut prices; and they could have done so by reducing wages. In this era, wages were what economists call "flexible": employers cut them when they thought that they must or they could. Between 1866 and 1880, annual wages for nonfarm workers actually declined 21 percent. But this did not mean lower living standards, because prices dropped even more. Over the same period, purchasing power for average workers rose 23 percent.

The point is that a country's capacity to achieve economic growth lies mainly in its own people, values, resources, and institutions. Trade supplements this in many ways. The simplest is comparative advantage, as it was classically conceived by David Ricardo. Countries specialize in what they do best, even if one country could produce everything more efficiently than another. Suppose the United States makes both shoes and supercomputers more efficiently than Spain. We need 100 workers to produce either one supercomputer or 1,000 pairs of shoes annually; and Spain needs 1,000 workers to make a supercomputer and 200 workers to make 1,000 pairs of shoes. Total production of computers and shoes will still be greatest if each country concentrates on its strength (shoes for Spain, computers for us) and trades with the other to satisfy its needs: America will have more supercomputers and shoes, and so will Spain.

Much trade of this type occurs. The United States imports shoes, toys, and sporting goods; it exports bulldozers, computers, and corn. Trade's greatest benefits, though, may transcend comparative advantage. Not everyone has to reinvent the wheel or the computer chip. Technologies, products, and management practices that have been developed abroad can be deployed at home. In theory, these gains can occur without a country opening itself to trade. Information can be stolen; products and processes can be imitated. In practice, however, it is much easier if a country is open.

For commercial or technological insight does not derive from a single dazzling flash. It consists in thousands upon thousands of small details. It encompasses how things are made, distributed, sold, financed, repaired, and replaced. The more isolated a country, the harder it is to come by all the details. Whatever its tariff rates, the United States in the nineteenth century was open in this critical sense. Its people traveled freely abroad; immigration was large; merchants were eager traders; and industrialists borrowed ideas from wherever they could.

These same processes also operated after World War II. All countries could (in theory) tap the same international reservoir of technologies, products, and management systems. Yet some countries did better than others, which was a reflection of their practices and policies. Despite mercantilist tendencies, Japan enthusiastically embraced trade; it systematically imported (via licensing agreements) foreign technology; and it routinely studied American management. The combination of high saving and proven investment opportunities propelled great economic growth, averaging about 10 percent a year in the 1960s. Countries that were more shut off (China, the former Soviet bloc, India) fared less well. And only when other Asian societies began imitating Japan did their economic growth accelerate.

This explains why poorer countries should now like trade. It has helped lift millions of people in Europe and Asia from abject poverty. But what's in it for us? Trade can help to erode a country's relative economic superiority, and for the United States it has contributed to such an erosion. As other countries advanced rapidly, our dominance of the early postwar decades was lost. But this history cannot be undone. To preserve our position, we would have needed to be ruthlessly protectionist in the 1950s and 1960s: a policy that deliberately aimed to restrain the economic progress of Europe and Japan. But this would have been unwise, and even Buchanan does not contend otherwise. To long for our superiority of the 1940s is an exercise in nostalgia. Still, what is not true, then or now, is that trade impoverishes us. It is not depressing our living standards. It is elevating them. Trade may enable poorer nations to catch up, or to grow faster than we do; but this does not cause us to slow down. It is not a zero-sum game. We gain, too.

Competition is one way. Many countries now make and trade the same things, so comparative advantage doesn't really apply. Japan makes and trades cars, computer chips, and telephone switching centers; and so do the United States and Germany. The result is bigger markets that enable efficient producers to achieve greater economies of scale by spreading costs across more buyers. Prices to consumers drop. Boeing, Microsoft, and Caterpillar all have lower unit costs because they are selling to a world market. Domestic competition also intensifies. Imports compel domestic rivals to improve. Chevrolets and Chryslers are now better and more efficiently made because Americans can buy Toyotas and Hondas. In many industries—cars, copying machines, and machine tools, to name a few—American firms and workers have had to adapt to the best foreign practices and technologies.

What haunts free trade is the specter that all production will flow to low-wage countries. Yet this does not happen, for two reasons. First, low-wage workers in poor countries are usually less productive than well-paid workers in rich countries. In 1995, Malaysian wages were almost 10 percent of American wages; but the productivity of Malaysian workers (output per hour worked) was also about 10 percent of American levels, according to Stephen Golub of Swarthmore College. Companies shift production abroad, Golub maintains, only when relative productivity exceeds relative wages. If Malaysians earn and produce 90 percent less, there is no advantage in moving to Malaysia.

Second, when developing countries export, they earn foreign exchange (mostly dollars) to import—and do so. The global market for pharmaceuticals and software could not exist without the global market for shoes and shirts. In practice, developing countries' trade with advanced countries is fairly balanced, whether in deficit or surplus, as the table below shows. It gives developing countries' manufacturing trade with advanced countries as a share of their GDP. (The data is from Golub.)

Trade With Advanced Countries 1995 Percent of GDP

	Exports	Imports	Balance
Brazil	1.7	3.1	−1.4
China	8.8	7.7	+1.1
India	3.8	3.3	+0.5
Indonesia	6.4	8.7	−2.2
Korea	12.3	13.9	−1.6
Mexico	19.3	16.8	+2.5

On economic grounds, then, the case against trade is puny. Gains dwarf losses. Still, the puzzle remains: If trade is good for us, why do we run massive trade deficits? We must (it seems) be doing something wrong if we regularly import more than we export. Well, we aren't. The explanation is that our trade accounts are incomplete. They omit a major American export which—if it were included in the reckoning—would bring our trade flows closer to balance. That American export is money.

The dollar serves as the world's major money: a means of exchange, a store of value. It is used to conduct trade and to make investments. In 1996, countries kept 59 percent of their official foreign exchange reserve in dollars; the next largest reserve currency was the German mark at 14 percent. Multinational companies keep accounts in dollars. So do wealthy individuals. In some countries, where people distrust the local money, dollars circulate as a parallel currency to conduct everyday business. Indeed, the Federal Reserve estimates that more paper dollars (the folding stuff) exist outside the United States than inside.

The United States provides the world a service, in the form of a fairly stable currency. To pay for this service, the world sends us imports. It is a good deal for us: every year Americans buy 1 or 2 percent more than we produce. This is the size of our current account deficit, a measure of trade and other current overseas flows (such as tourism and freight).

The concept here is the old idea of seigniorage: the profit that a government earns when it can produce money at a cost less than its face value. If a government can print a dollar for 5 cents, it reaps a 95 cent windfall when it spends that dollar. Similarly, the United States reaps a windfall when the world uses our money. The transfer occurs through the exchange rate; the world's demand for dollars holds the dollar's exchange rate high enough so that we do not balance our visible trade. (A high exchange rate makes imports cheaper and exports more expensive.) But for many reasons—intellectual laziness, theoretical messiness—most economists have not applied seigniorage to the world economy.

That is too bad. If they did, we would see that the trade debate's main symbol—the nagging trade deficit—does not symbolize what it is supposed to symbolize. It does not show that we are becoming "uncompetitive," or that we are "deindustrializing," or that we are "losing jobs" abroad. In any single year, shifts in the trade balance may reflect temporary factors. Stronger or weaker growth abroad will affect demand for our exports; stronger or weaker growth here will affect our demand for imports. Changes in technology or exchange rates may alter trade flows in particular industries and products. Yet the continuous trade deficits of the United States do not reflect any of these things. They reflect the world's demand for dollars. Perhaps that demand will someday abate (Europe's single currency, the euro, may provide an alternative global money); and if it does, the American trade account will swing closer to balance. For now, though, it is virtually condemned to deficit.

If we acknowledged this, much of the present trade debate would disappear, because the presumed goal of a "good" trade policy—a trade balance or a trade surplus—would be seen as unrealistic and probably undesirable. Instead, the debate over the economics of trade is simplistic and distorted. The supporters of free trade claim that it creates jobs; the opponents of free trade claim that it destroys jobs. Although both are true for individual workers and industries, they are usually not true for the economy as a whole. We could have "full employment" if we didn't trade at all; and in a workforce of nearly 140 million people, the number of net jobs affected by trade (jobs created by exports minus jobs lost to imports) is tiny. Trade's true advantage is that it raises living standards.

IV. The trouble is that the trade debate should concern more than wages or jobs. Buchanan's political appeal lies in his unabashed nationalism, and he is correct that we do not trade for the benefit of the British or the Brazilians or the Chinese. Trade needs to be connected to larger national purposes, and free-traders have grown lax about making such a connection. They are too eager to reduce the debate to a technical dispute over economic gain and loss. Although Buchanan engages in the same exercise—and reaches the wrong conclusion—he is much more willing to cast trade in terms of advancing broader American interests, preserving our national identity, and maintaining our moral values. A lot of this patriotic chest-thumping is nothing more than rhetorical flourish. And yet Buchanan is actually onto something.

Since World War II, American trade policy has made two central assumptions. The first, inherited from the Depression, is that protectionism destabilizes the world economy and that free trade stabilizes it. The second is that free trade enhances American security interests. Both notions were once right, but times have changed. Matters are now more ambiguous. A big outbreak of protectionism would still harm the world economy. Too much economic activity depends on trade for it to be cut painlessly. Yet deepening economic ties among countries—"globalization"—may also create instability. As for trade and security, they were fused by the cold war. Our main trading partners were military allies, and they generally embraced democratic values. Now trade has spread to some countries that do not share our values and to some countries that one day might be adversaries (China and Russia, most obviously).

What has gradually disintegrated is the postwar convergence among economic, strategic, and moral interests. Global economics has raced well ahead of global politics, creating potentially dangerous instabilities that are only barely perceived and may not be easily subdued. Commercial interests may increasingly conflict with security interests or moral values. If we decide, for whatever reason, not to trade with India or China, other countries will probably fill the void. The possibility is hardly theoretical. After India's recent nuclear tests, the United States immediately imposed sanctions; but most other countries—Japan was an exception—did not. There are other examples, involving Iran, Libya, and Cuba. Commercial rivalries can undermine security alliances: If our "allies" aid our "adversaries," are they truly our allies?

The very expansion of global commerce has also raised economic interdependence to a new level. Until now, the "world economy" has been viewed less as an organic whole than as the sum of its parts. It is the collective consequence of individual economies whose performance (though affected by trade) mainly reflects their own strengths and weaknesses. This may still be true, but it is less so. The growing connections among nations—through trade, financial markets, computer systems, people flows—may be creating an independent beast whose behavior affects everyone and is not easily controlled by anyone. Asia's economic crisis is surely testing the notion that growing "globalization" can boomerang. South Korea, Thailand, and Indonesia all borrowed too much abroad; Japanese, European, and American banks lent too much. Excesses went unchecked by either local or international governmental supervision. Economic growth in all these countries has now plunged. There are spillover effects, and this could portend future crises.

Protectionism's best case is that it might insulate us against potential global instability. We would sacrifice somewhat higher living standards for somewhat greater tranquility. But this is not what protectionists have in mind; and if it were, it would be hard—maybe impossible—to achieve.

Consider Buchanan's program. He would impose sliding tariffs on countries reflecting his likes and dislikes. Europe would be hit with a 15 percent tariff; Canada would be spared if it adopted our tariffs (otherwise foreign goods would pour into the United States via Canada). Aside from a 15 percent tariff, Japan would have to end its trade surplus or face tariffs that would do so. Poorer countries would face an "equalization" tariff to offset their lower wages (such tariffs could go to 90 or 95 percent).

The result, Buchanan says, would be "millions of high-paying manufacturing jobs for all our workers—immigrant and native-born, black and white, Hispanic and Asian— . . . and trade and budget surpluses as American workers find higher-paying jobs and contribute more to Social Security and Medicare, deficit reduction and tax reduction." Well, not exactly. If the program worked as planned, it would repatriate low-wage jobs making toys and textiles and eliminate high-wage jobs making planes and bulldozers. Overseas markets for American exports would shrink, because countries that could not sell to us could not buy from us. And it is extremely doubtful that Buchanan's program would work as planned. He ignores floating exchange rates: if we raise tariffs by 15 percent, other countries' currencies may fall by 15 percent, leaving import prices unchanged.

Moreover, anything like Buchanan's plan might also create so much uncertainty that it would depress global economic growth. Companies might not invest in the United States—to make toys or textiles—because they could not be sure that high tariffs would not be repealed or neutralized by exchange rates. Yet companies might not invest elsewhere, because they could not know whether the tariffs might work or, if they did not work, whether they might inspire higher tariffs. All countries would suffer from lower investment and growth.

The point is that global commerce has become so widespread that it cannot be wrenched apart, short of some calamity. It is increasingly hard to find major American companies (trucking firms, railroads, or electric utilities, perhaps) that do not have major overseas stakes, either through trade or investment. Coca-Cola sells 70 percent of its beverages outside North America; McDonald's has almost half its 23,000 outlets in foreign countries; Intel derives 56 percent of its revenues abroad. The quest for global markets is one of the economic hallmarks of our times. The recent announcement of the Chrysler/Daimler-Benz merger emphasizes the point. To the extent that people like Buchanan try to frustrate it, they will simply inspire more ingenious—and probably more inefficient—ways for companies and investors to try to evade new barriers.

Even more daunting is the inclusion in the global trading system of countries that do not qualify as either allies or adversaries. We are, in effect, taking a colossal gamble that our commitment to greater trade will turn out for the best. This gamble rests on two pious hopes. The first is that trade, by tying countries closer to each other, diminishes or eliminates the prospect of war among them. Countries that trade are too interdependent to take up arms against each other. Again, Buchanan is properly skeptical of this; what he might also have said is that we could be far more threatened by a modernized China or Russia than by countries that exist in self-imposed economic isolation. One obvious aim of Chinese trade is to transform its military into a world-class force. In theory, American policy prohibits the export of potentially defense-related technology. In practice, controlling "dual use" technologies (those that have both civilian and military applications) was difficult even in the cold war. It is much more so now.

The other (related) pious hope is that greater trade abets prosperity, and that the entire process builds a new middle class, which in turn leads to the triumph of democracy and respect for individual liberties. As nations become more like us, the dogma says, they will be less antagonistic. In some countries, this has happened. Yet surely there is no logical or mechanical connection between growing trade and the creation of genuine democracies. Political progress does not automatically follow economic progress. A less inviting possibility is that rapid economic growth will subvert traditional political and social systems without immediately creating viable, open alternatives. Nor is it inevitable that all democracies will be friendly with each other. Americans too easily think—this erroneous assumption has characterized all recent administrations, from Reagan to Clinton—that we can find a formula for cloning our beliefs and our institutions in foreign cultures.

None of this seems to matter much now. The world is generally at peace. America is prosperous. People easily overlook the contradictions and the inconsistencies. Yet these abound and, in more stressful times, they could bubble to the surface. The more countries blend economically, the more their values and their political systems collide. What we consider normal and desirable, other countries often consider abnormal and undesirable. To some extent, differences will persist: if McDonald's wants to do business in Russia, it will have to conform to Russia's laws and customs. But to some extent, differences will erode: if Russia wants McDonald's, it will have to accommodate that company's needs and demands. How are these conflicts to be mediated? And, if the world economy is becoming an organic whole, how are collective problems or crises to be prevented or mitigated?

The answers are not obvious. Except in the crudest sense, a market is not just the meeting place of buyer and seller. It is a framework to conduct ongoing business. It is a political, social, and cultural phenomenon, as well as an economic one. It requires laws, customs, and understandings to foster the certainty that is needed for investors and enterprises to risk capital and to make forward commitments. A market is a system to deal with common conflicts. All nations build market frameworks, for better or worse. A global economy requires its counterpart. Not surprisingly, then, more global commerce has meant more global rules. These now apply, in some form, to banking, insurance, communications, air travel, government procurement, copyright protection (for everything from CDs to software), the environment, and health and safety.

These rules go well beyond the standard stuff of trade policy: tariffs and quotas. Not surprisingly, Buchanan attaches an inflammatory label to this process. He calls it world government. But the label is accurate. We are haphazardly building a crude world government, in a fragmented and piecemeal fashion. To flourish, the world economy probably needs more of it. There are many ideas. One recent proposal would create global accounting standards so that investors can more easily compare companies across borders. Much of this makes economic sense, and the United States has led the process. We have urged global rules to "open up markets," curb industrial subsidies (which might hurt our companies), and make government procedures more "transparent" (to limit discrimination against our firms).

Not surprisingly, many countries resent these rules as intrusions, as violations of their sovereignty. We are (it is said) trying to Americanize the world, to foist our values and our institutions on others. Interestingly, many Americans also deplore the process, because even though we have taken the lead in crafting these new global conventions, we don't run them unilaterally. We are (it is said) surrendering our sovereignty to global bureaucrats.

And indeed we are. Here is the nub of the matter. The ultimate promise of ever-greater global commerce is a universal contentment based on a spreading addiction to material well-being. Prosperity has a tranquilizing effect. It dulls the dangers of undiluted nationalism. People increasingly lead the same lifestyles: drinking Coke, driving Toyotas, conversing on the Internet. All this numbs national differences and permits a growing overlay of international agencies and authorities needed to regulate the global economy. Countries see that they have a common stake in cooperation. There are disagreements and conflicts, to be sure, but they are small-time, and they substitute for larger human tragedies of war and poverty.

This is the underlying moral logic that justifies the commercialization of the world, though hardly anyone puts it quite so forthrightly. It is a seductive vision that can draw much inspiration from the experience of the last halfcentury. Over this period, the world economy has been a spectacular success. It has helped power an enormous advance in human well-being. Free trade has triumphed to an extent that hardly anyone could have foreseen at the end of World War II.

In the end, however, the vision is almost certainly false. Just because people watch the same movies and eat at the same fast-food outlets does not mean that they have been homogenized. National identities are not so easily retired. For good and ill, ethnic and religious differences show a remarkable ability to survive the march of material progress. National affections and animosities endure; and combined with the terrible and unpredictable potential of modern technology, they preserve humankind's capacity for ordinary trouble and unimaginable tragedy.

The world is fusing economically more than it is fusing (or will ever fuse) politically. We have created a system that requires ever-greater amounts of global cooperation, because it generates new and unfamiliar forms of international conflicts. One day, perhaps, the irresistible force of world markets may meet the immovable object of nationalism. Protectionism and isolationism are not so much agendas as moods, and countries—including the United States—might react to domestic disruption and international disorder by blaming foreigners and trying to withdraw from a global system on which most nations now increasingly depend. Buchanan has inadvertently identified the dilemma, but he has done exactly nothing to resolve it.

Chinese Rockets' Red Glare Is as Blinding as Free-Trade Fanaticism

PATRICK BUCHANAN

"A strict interpretation of patriotism [is] injurious to business," wrote famed artillery-maker Alfred Krupp. True to his word, Krupp sold to both sides in the Franco-Prussian war.

On the eve of World War I, Krupp's firm was filling "Russian orders for the latest artillery pieces and French orders for specially designed anti-Zeppelin guns while soliciting British orders for warships. In the 1880s, Hiram Maxim sold the 'Maxim gun,' the first modern machine gun, to his adopted homeland of Britain and to its future enemies, the Boers of South Africa and the German Reich."

So observes defense writer Andrew Moravcsik, making a point familiar to Americans who recall that arms peddlers sold the Plains Indians the Winchester rifles they used on the U.S. 7th Cavalry.

The irreconcilable conflict between free trade and national security is exposed anew by today's blazing controversy about Loral Space & Communications' alleged transfer of missile technology to China.

Defending the use of China's rockets to launch its satellites, Hughes Electronics Corp. argues the waiver it received from President Clinton to do so was endorsed by 15 Republican members of Congress from California. Moreover, Hughes says, if U.S. satellite builders are not allowed to use low-cost Chinese rockets, European builders, which demand fewer protections for technology secrets, will do so and take satellite supremacy away from the United States.

Thus, the corporate interests of Hughes required that China achieve successful launches of Long March rockets—which just happen to be the twin brothers of the rockets China is fitting with nuclear warheads.

Hughes claims it never transferred technology to Beijing. Yet, it is undeniable that China's military acquired invaluable experience in perfecting rockets by launching U.S. satellites. And, according to *The Washington Times*, 13 of China's 18 operational ICBMs are targeted on the United States.

Not only is free-trade fanaticism imperiling national security, but, if it is not abandoned, it eventually will kill the Republican Party.

Patrick Buchanan, a candidate for President, is a journalist, former television commentator and White House official during the Nixon Administration.
Reprinted by permission. *Insight on the News*, June 22, 1998. Vol. 14, No. 23, p. 30(1).

Americans may prattle on about a "strategic partnership," but Beijing looks at the United States as the last impediment to seizing Taiwan and achieving hegemony in Asia. How can our free-trade zealots not see this? In China, we are dealing with a nation that never has embraced the nonsense of a global economy where the world is one huge and happy suburban mall.

Beijing does not practice free trade; it conducts "strategic trade" to strengthen itself for the coming clash. In China, there is no distinction between the private and the state. Thousands of Chinese companies—from hotels to toy factories—are run by the People's Liberation Army, or PLA. The PLA exploits its unrestricted access to the huge U.S. market to earn hard currency for the aggrandizement of state power. China's civilian sector buys what strategic interests dictate, such as those 46 supercomputers recently sold by the United States, the precise whereabouts of which we cannot confirm.

U.S. companies are lured into China by offers of access to the "world's greatest market" and a low-wage labor force. Once there, the U.S. firms find that access to China's consumers is restricted and the hidden price of low-wage Chinese labor is mandatory transfer of technology to Chinese "partners," who copy the U.S. machines and begin replicating our factories.

As the profits of many U.S. companies now depend on Chinese workers who produce for export to America, these firms become apologists for Beijing and ferocious opponents of sanctions. When Congress considered sanctions against China in 1996 for persecuting dissidents, bullying Taiwan and selling missiles to Iran, our major defense contractors—Allied Signal, Boeing, General Electric, Hewlett-Packard, Honeywell, Lockheed-Martin, McDonnell Douglas, TRW, Rockwell International and United Technologies—lobbied against sanctions.

The Business Roundtable has been hooked on the China trade, and its interests no longer are compatible with the national security.

As U.S. purchases of Chinese goods account for 7 percent of its gross domestic product, or GDP, while China's purchases of U.S. goods account for one-tenth of 1 percent of our GDP, we could snap China's spine in six months.

How? Impose on Chinese goods the same 40 percent taxes and tariffs China imposes on U.S.-made goods. Instantly, China either would forfeit its U.S. market to free Asia or begin subsidizing, with tariff payments, our 7th Fleet.

The profits of U.S. companies in the China trade would shrink and the Dow take a hit, but the dragon would be on its keister.

Query: If China had the leverage over the United States that we have over China, would Beijing use it to force us to conform U.S. policy to its strategic objectives—or would it embrace free trade?

Issue 10
EMU

INTRODUCTION

It was September 19, 1946, and Winston Churchill, the legendary Prime Minister of Great Britain during World War II, was now out of office. Speaking in Zurich, Churchill said: "We must build a kind of united states of Europe. . . . I am now going to say something that will astonish you. The first step in the recreation of the European family must be a partnership between France and Germany." Really? France and Germany, longtime adversaries, cooperating in a European governmental structure? Churchill's statement seemed outlandish at the time, but now, more than fifty years later, France, Germany, and other European countries are well down the road toward creating a central European government through the European Union.

It all began with Churchill, Jean Monnet, Robert Schuman, and other European leaders who dreamed of bringing an end to war among European powers. Monnet and Schuman, in particular, believed that this goal could best be achieved by fostering economic interdependence among these countries, particularly through free trade within a common market. They recognized that it is difficult for countries that are dependent on one another for essential products to fight each other. As the European institutions that were created to administer the common market became stronger and as cooperation increased, leading eventually to open borders among most members, the way was paved for further unification.

The latest and most significant joint effort has been the creation of a monetary union by France, Germany, and nine other members of the fifteen-member European Union. In this European Monetary Union (EMU), these governments have established a European central bank that will play a significant role in determining interest rates for all eleven countries. Likewise, they have created a European currency, the euro, which has existed for some purposes since January 1999 and which will appear as a tangible currency in 2002. For a national government to give up both its currency and control over its monetary policy is a major relinquishment of sovereignty. Why would these governments do this?

The first article, by the American economist Martin Feldstein, was written before the EMU's creation. Feldstein sees problems ahead: Instead of increased cooperation among EMU members, he believes that conflict among them will increase. Moreover, Feldstein contends that conflicts with the United States may emerge as a more unified Europe seeks to disengage from the United States.

The second article, by Pierre Jacquet, was written as some members of the European Union were contemplating their future in the monetary union. This noted student of the European scene summarizes the main benefits that member-governments believed they could expect from this venture: less political conflict and more economic efficiencies.

As you read the articles, consider the following questions.

Discussion Questions

1. Why are the nations in the EMU willing to give up control of policy over something as important as interest rates to a European-wide organization? What do they have to gain?
2. Will centralized control of monetary policy in the EMU likely promote greater cooperation among EMU members, or greater conflict?
3. The EMU seems to be an important benchmark on the road to political unification of Europe. What would the likely consequences of a United States of Europe be for America?

    For more information on this topic, visit the following websites:

    http://www.econ.yale.edu/~corsetti/euro/
    (extensive sources of information on the Euro; web page by Prof. Giancarlo Corsetti of Yale University)

    http://amue.lf.net/
    (web site of the Association for the Monetary Union of Europe, a European business group favoring the EMU)

    http://www.ecb.int/
    (web page of the EMU's new European Central Bank)

EMU and International Conflict

MARTIN FELDSTEIN

Monnet was mistaken.

To most Americans, European economic and monetary union seems like an obscure financial undertaking of no relevance to the United States. That perception is far from correct. If EMU does come into existence, as now seems increasingly likely, it will change the political character of Europe in ways that could lead to conflicts in Europe and confrontations with the United States.

The immediate effects of EMU would be to replace the individual national currencies of the participating countries in 2002 with a single currency, the euro, and to shift responsibility for monetary policy from the national central banks to a new European Central Bank (ECB). But the more fundamental long-term effect of adopting a single currency would be the creation of a political union, a European federal state with responsibility for a Europe-wide foreign and security policy as well as for what are now domestic economic and social policies. While the individual governments and key political figures differ in their reasons for wanting a political union, there is no doubt that the real rationale for EMU is political and not economic. Indeed, the adverse economic effects of a single currency on unemployment and inflation would outweigh any gains from facilitating trade and capital flows among the EMU members.[1]

The 1992 Maastricht Treaty that created the EMU calls explicitly for the evolution to a future political union. But even without that specific treaty language, the shift to a single currency would be a dramatic and irreversible step toward that goal. There is no sizable country anywhere in the world that does not have its own currency. A national currency is both a symbol of sovereignty and the key to the pursuit of an independent monetary and budget policy. The tentative decision of the 15 European Union (EU) member states (with the exceptions of Denmark and the United Kingdom), embodied in the Maastricht Treaty, to abandon their national currencies for the euro is therefore a decision of fundamental political significance.

For many Europeans, reaching back to Jean Monnet and his contemporaries immediately after World War II, a political union of European nations is conceived of as a way of reducing the risk of another

Martin Feldstein is Professor of Economics at Harvard University and is also president of the National Bureau of Economic Research.

Reprinted by permission. *Foreign Affairs*, Nov.–Dec. 1997. Vol. 76, Issue 6, p. 60.

intra-European war among the individual nation-states. But the attempt to manage a monetary union and the subsequent development of a political union are more likely to have the opposite effect. Instead of increasing intra-European harmony and global peace, the shift to EMU and the political integration that would follow it would be more likely to lead to increased conflicts within Europe and between Europe and the United States.

What are the reasons for such conflicts? In the beginning there would be important disagreements among the EMU member countries about the goals and methods of monetary policy. These would be exacerbated whenever the business cycle raised unemployment in a particular country or group of countries. These economic disagreements could contribute to a more general distrust among the European nations. As the political union developed, new conflicts would reflect incompatible expectations about the sharing of power and substantive disagreements over domestic and international policies. Since not all European nations would be part of the monetary and political union, there would be conflicts between the members and nonmembers within Europe, including the states of Eastern Europe and the former Soviet Union.

Conflicts would also develop between the European political union and non-European nations, including the United States, over issues of foreign policy and international trade. While disagreements among the European countries might weaken any European consensus on foreign affairs, the dominant countries of the EU would be able to determine the foreign and military policies for the European community as a whole. A political union of the scale and affluence of Europe and the ability to project military power would be a formidable force in global politics.

Although 50 years of European peace since the end of World War II may augur well for the future, it must be remembered that there were also more than 50 years of peace between the Congress of Vienna and the Franco-Prussian War. Moreover, contrary to the hopes and assumptions of Monnet and other advocates of European integration, the devastating American Civil War shows that a formal political union is no guarantee against an intra-European war. Although it is impossible to know for certain whether these conflicts would lead to war, it is too real a possibility to ignore in weighing the potential effects of EMU and the European political integration that would follow.

THE POLITICS AND ECONOMICS OF MONETARY POLICY

The most direct link between EMU and intra-European conflicts would be disagreement about the goals and methods of monetary policy. The Maastricht Treaty established the ECB and transfers all responsibility for monetary policy after the start of EMU from individual national central banks to the ECB. The ECB alone would control the supply of euros and set the short-term euro interest rate.

Maastricht makes price stability the primary objective of European monetary policy, paralleling the charter of Germany's Bundesbank. The treaty also provides that the ECB would be independent of all political control by the member states and by European-level political institutions. (Although the treaty states that the ECB will report to the European Parliament, this was intended to follow the Bundesbank tradition of an information report rather than any political oversight.) These conditions are very much what Germany wants for the ECB and for monetary policy. Because of its historical experience, the German public is hypersensitive on inflation and fears any monetary arrangement that does not give primacy to price stability and insulate monetary policy from political influence.

But German opinion differs sharply from the opinions about monetary policy in France and other European countries. The notion of a politically independent central bank is contrary to European traditions. Until recently, when Maastricht required all prospective EMU countries to give their central banks independence, most of the central banks of Europe reported to their ministries of finance, and the finance ministers were at least partially responsible for setting interest rates.

The French have been particularly vocal in calling for political control over monetary policy. In a televised speech just before the 1992 French referendum on the Maastricht Treaty, then-President François Mitterrand assured the French public that, contrary to the explicit language of the treaty, European monetary policy would not be under the direction of European central bankers but would be subject to political oversight that, by implication, would be less concerned with inflation and more concerned with unemployment. Mitterrand's statement was a political forecast; France recognizes that the institutions of the EMU would evolve, and continually presses for some form of political body to exert control over the ECB. It has already made considerable progress toward that end.

The December 1996 meeting of the EU Council of Ministers in Dublin emphasized that growth as well as price stability would be an explicit goal of future EMU monetary policy. It also established a new ministerial level "stability council" described as a "complement" or a "counterweight" to the ECB. Although this body falls short of one that could exercise political control over the ECB, it marked a first French success in establishing that monetary policy should be subject to some counterweight and that growth (that is, short-run macroeconomic expansion) as well as price stability should be a goal of EMU policy. At the

European summit in Amsterdam in June 1997, the newly elected French government of Lionel Jospin made further progress. The summit added an employment chapter to the Maastricht Treaty, emphasizing that employment is a parallel goal to price stability. More important, statements by politicians at the Amsterdam summit appear to have redefined the role of the political authorities in making exchange rate policy and, therefore, in managing monetary policy.

More specifically, the Maastricht Treaty divided responsibility for exchange rate policy between the ECB and the EU Economics and Finance Council, which consists of cabinet ministers of member governments, in an ambiguous way. The drafters of that part of the treaty (the German participants in particular) intended to limit ECOFIN's role to fundamental aspects of the exchange rate system and to leave to the ECB policies that cause short-run changes in the value of the euro. For example, a decision to fix the exchange rate between the euro and the Japanese yen permanently would be a decision for ECOFIN. In contrast, raising or lowering euro interest rates to increase or decrease the exchange value of the euro would be left to the ECB. Although this distinction was the German view, the French expected that ECOFIN would eventually get to give orders about short-run variations in the desired level of the euro exchange rate. The formal rules remain ambiguous, but the government leaders at the Amsterdam summit appear to have accepted a shift of responsibility for short-run exchange rate policy to ECOFIN. Since discretionary changes in nominal exchange rates can be achieved only by changes in monetary policy, this shift would establish a much more fundamental role for ECOFIN, a political body, in the making of monetary policy.

One further recent development relating to the independence of the ECB is noteworthy. Members of the key monetary policy committee of the European Parliament have called for a role for the parliament in supervising the ECB, including its interest rate policies. They have specifically pointed to congressional oversight of the U.S. Federal Reserve as a possible model for such supervision. Although this arrangement may strike a reasonable balance between independence and accountability, parliamentary oversight would clearly be a major shift from the complete independence called for in the Maastricht Treaty, and consequently an area for contention.

At present, individual European governments (especially in France and Germany) are suppressing their disagreement about the control of monetary policy to minimize the risk of political disapproval of EMU in their respective countries. But if EMU proceeds, the independence of the ECB and the goals of monetary policy will become a source of serious conflict among member countries.

INFLATION VERSUS UNEMPLOYMENT

The issue of who controls monetary policy is closely related to the question of the proper goal of monetary policy. In recent years, because of the Maastricht Treaty's requirements for entering EMU, most countries have resisted the temptation to use monetary policy to reduce unemployment and have followed the Bundesbank in keeping inflation rates below three percent. But once the disciplining example of the Bundesbank is eliminated and monetary policy is made by an ECB in which all member countries vote equally, there is a strong risk that the prevailing sentiment will be for higher inflation. Over the past 12 months, international financial markets have anticipated that outcome by depressing the value of the deutsche mark, the French franc, and the other European currencies that move with them by 25 percent relative to the dollar and the yen.

If the German public sees the inflation rate rise under EMU, it will become increasingly antagonistic toward the EMU arrangement and toward the countries that vote for inflationary monetary policy. Moreover, since an inflationary monetary policy would lower unemployment only temporarily (while leaving the inflation rate permanently higher), the persistence of high unemployment would lead to political pressure for recurring rounds of expansionary monetary policy, causing continuing dissatisfaction among the anti-inflationary countries.

Countries that are more concerned about unemployment than inflation might nevertheless be critical of the ECB for not pursuing an even more aggressive expansionary policy. Although countries have been properly reluctant to attempt such policies in recent years, they can regard their decisions not to do so as decisions they made themselves. But with a single currency, such governments would suffer the frustration of not being able to decide for themselves and of being forced to accept the common monetary policy created by the ECB.

This general conflict about the governance and character of monetary policy would be exacerbated whenever a country experienced a decline in exports or other type of decline in aggregate demand that led to a cyclical increase in unemployment. The shift to a single currency would mean that the fall in demand in a country could not be offset, as it could be with an individual national currency, by an automatic decline in the exchange value of the currency (making its exports more competitive) and a decline in its interest rates (increasing domestic interest-sensitive spending by households and businesses) or by using its own monetary policy to shift interest rates and exchange rates. The ECB would have to make monetary policy with a view to the conditions in all of Europe, not just a particular country or region. The result would be a conflict between the country with rising unemployment and the rest of the EU.

TAXES AND TRANSFERS

Without the automatic countercyclical response of financial markets and the ability to use monetary policy to offset a decline in demand, European governments would want to use tax cuts and increases in government outlays to stimulate demand and reverse cyclical increases in unemployment. But the "stability pact" that was adopted under pressure from Germany tells governments that they cannot run fiscal deficits above three percent of GDP after the start of EMU. This restriction creates an important source of tension between countries with cyclical unemployment increases and the other members of the monetary union. The decision at the 1997 Amsterdam summit to weaken the application of financial penalties for violating this deficit ceiling would undoubtedly encourage more violations and, therefore, more quarrels about "irresponsible" fiscal policies.

Since national monetary and fiscal policies would be precluded, the most likely outcome of the shift to a single monetary policy would be the growth of substantial transfers from the EU to countries that experience cyclical increases in unemployment. Financing those transfers would require a significant increase in tax revenues collected by the EU.

The debates about how large such transfers should be and how the taxes to finance them should be collected would exacerbate the more general disagreement that will inevitably arise as the union seeks to restrict the level and structure of the taxes that individual countries may levy. The European Commission is already trying to get countries to move toward more coordination of their domestic tax policies on the grounds that existing differences in tax rates and rules create competitive advantages for some countries. The shift to a single currency would increase the pressure for tax harmonization. As general responsibility for economic policy shifts from national capitals to the European Commission, the European tradition of focusing taxing authority at a single level would be likely to lead to a shift of the exclusive taxing power from the national to the European level. The EU will therefore be disregarding national preferences about redistribution, the size of government, and the structure of taxes. While the pressures for such coordination might be overwhelming once a single currency has been adopted, the loss of national control over taxes and transfers would be another serious source of irritation within the EU.

LONG-TERM UNEMPLOYMENT

As the decisions shift away from national governments, it will become harder to reach agreement on policy changes to deal with the high unemployment due to excessive regulation and social welfare payments.

The shift of policy decisions from national governments to the European level would eliminate the ability to learn from the experiences of individual countries that try different policies and to benefit from the competitive pressures to adopt national policies that succeed. Moreover, the changes in labor market rules and social benefits that have been proposed by certain national governments are now being opposed not only by labor unions within the individual countries but also by other European governments that fear the resulting gains in competitiveness. Thus we hear of opposition to "social dumping" when an inefficient enterprise is closed and witness the imposition of a Europe-wide limit on the number of hours that employees can work. A politically more unified Europe would make it easier to enforce policies that prevent changes in national labor laws or national transfer payments that would reduce structural unemployment and increase national competitiveness.

If EU legislation succeeds in preventing member countries from competing with each other, they will collectively become less able to compete with the rest of the world. The result would undoubtedly be pressure for increased EU trade barriers, justified by reference to differences in social policy between Europe and other countries. European imposition of such protectionist policies would undermine the entire global trading system and create serious conflicts with the United States and other trading partners.

INCOMPATIBLE EXPECTATIONS

As the monetary union evolves into a more general political union, conflicts would arise from incompatible expectations about the sharing of power. France sees EMU and the resulting political union as a way of becoming a comanager of Europe and an equal of Germany, which has nearly 50 percent more people. In the economic sphere, the current domination of European monetary policy by the Bundesbank would be replaced by that of the ECB, in which France and Germany would sit and vote as equals. As the French contemplate the eventual membership of the economic and political union, they may also hope that their natural Mediterranean allies, Italy and Spain, will give France a decisive influence on European policies. And the skillful French civil servants might come to dominate the administration of the European government.

Germany's expectations and aspirations are more difficult to interpret. Some German leaders no doubt believe, as Chancellor Helmut Kohl frequently says, that joining a political union improves the prospects for peace by "containing a potentially dangerous Germany within Europe." Other Germans are no doubt less self-sacrificing and simply disagree with the French assessment of the consequences of greater economic and political integration. They see Germany as the natural leader within the EU because of its economic weight, military capability, and central location in an EU that will soon include Poland, the Czech Republic, and Hungary. As Kohl has said, not without ambiguity, "Germany is our fatherland, but Europe is our future."

What is clear is that a French aspiration for equality and a German expectation of hegemony are not consistent. Both visions drive their countrymen to support the pursuit of EMU, and both would lead to disagreements and conflicts when they could not be fulfilled.

The aspirations of the smaller countries to have a seat at the table may be frustrated. As the EU expands from 15 current members to include at least 6 more countries of Eastern Europe, the role that smaller countries will be allowed to play will become more and more limited. Current EU voting rules will give way to weighted voting arrangements in which the larger countries have a predominant share of the votes. This change will frustrate countries that recognize that they have sacrificed the ability to control their own domestic policies and their own foreign relations without having received in exchange an effective say in Europe's policies.

This loss of sovereignty would affect not just monetary and tax policies but a wide range of current domestic policies that will gradually come under the jurisdiction of the European Commission or European Parliament. Rule-making by the European Commission reached a crescendo in 1994 with edicts about such things as the quality of beer and the permissible shape of imported bananas. A fear that complaints about bureaucratic meddling could jeopardize approval of the Maastricht Treaty in national referendums led to a reduction in rule-making by the Brussels bureaucracy and a rhetorical emphasis on Maastricht's principle of "subsidiarity," which asserts that activities will be assigned to whatever level of government is most appropriate—European, national, or local. There is, however, little reason to believe that this vague principle will do much to restrain the substitution of Brussels rules or Strasbourg legislation for what are now domestic policies. Even the Tenth Amendment to the U.S. Constitution, which reserves to the states (or to the people) any powers not delegated to the national government, has not prevented the shift of power to the national government over an enormous range of local issues, such as speed limits on local roads and the age at which individuals may consume alcohol.

A EUROPEAN MILITARY AND FOREIGN POLICY

The collapse of the Soviet Union has changed the basis for European foreign policy and military collaboration. Although the United States and the countries of Western Europe have had an extremely close alliance since the end of World War II and continue to coordinate military efforts within the NATO structure, many Europeans in positions of responsibility see their economic interests and foreign policy goals differing from those of the United States with respect to many parts of the world, including Eastern Europe, the Middle East, Africa, and even Latin America. The French and German governments also want to develop an independent military capability that can operate without U.S. participation or consent.

Although the European nations could now more readily pursue an independent foreign policy and military strategy, they are clearly hampered in doing so effectively by the decentralized political structure of Europe. Chancellor Konrad Adenauer summarized the situation in stark terms for French Foreign Minister Christian Pineau on the day in 1956 when England and France gave in to American pressure to abandon their attack on the Suez Canal: "France and England will never be powers comparable to the United States and the Soviet Union. Nor Germany, either. There remains to them only one way of playing a decisive role in the world; that is to unite to make Europe. England is not ripe for it but the affair of Suez will help to prepare her spirits for it. We have no time to waste: Europe will be your revenge."[2] That was a year before the Treaty of Rome launched the Common Market.

The creation of a political union based on the EMU with explicit authority to develop a common foreign and defense policy would accelerate the development of an independent European military structure capable of projecting force outside Western Europe. Steps in that direction are already occurring in anticipation of the stronger political union that will follow the start of EMU. In March 1997, on the 40th anniversary of the Treaty of Rome, France and Germany announced their desire to see a merger of the EU with the existing European military alliance, the Western European Union, so as to strengthen the military coordination of European nations outside the NATO framework. An explicit agreement was reached with the United States that will allow the European members of NATO to use European NATO forces and equipment under European control without U.S. participation.

The attempt to forge a common military and foreign policy for Europe would be an additional source of conflict among the member nations (as well as with those outside the group). European countries differ in their national ambitions and in their attitudes about projecting force and influencing foreign affairs. An attempt to require countries like Portugal and Ireland to participate in an unwanted war in the Middle East or Eastern Europe could create powerful conflicts among the European nations.

THE RISK OF WAR

There is no doubt that a Europe of nearly 300 million people with an economy approximately equal in size to that of the United States could create a formidable military force. Whether that would be good or bad in the long run for world peace cannot be foretold with any certainty. A politically unified Europe with an independent military and foreign policy would accelerate the reduction of the U.S. military presence in Europe, weaken the role of NATO, and, to that extent, make Europe more vulnerable to attack. The weakening of America's current global hegemony would undoubtedly complicate international military relationships more generally.

Although Russia is now focusing on industrial restructuring, it remains a major nuclear power. Relations between Russia and Western Europe are important but unpredictable. Might a stronger Russia at some time in the future try to regain control over the currently independent Ukraine? Would a stronger, unified EU seek to discourage such action by force? Could that lead to war between Russia and the EU? How would a strong and unified Europe relate to other nations in the vicinity, including those of North Africa and the Middle East, and the Muslim states of the former Soviet Union, which are important or potential sources of energy for Western Europe?

War within Europe itself would be abhorrent but not impossible. The conflicts over economic policies and interference with national sovereignty could reinforce long-standing animosities based on history, nationality, and religion. Germany's assertion that it needs to be contained in a larger European political entity is itself a warning. Would such a structure contain Germany, or tempt it to exercise hegemonic leadership?

A critical feature of the EU in general and EMU in particular is that there is no legitimate way for a member to withdraw. This is a marriage made in heaven that must last forever. But if countries discover that the shift to a single currency is hurting their economies and that the new political arrangements also are not to their liking, some of them will want to leave. The majority may not look kindly on secession, either out of economic self-interest or a more general concern about the stability of the entire union. The American experience with the secession of the South may contain some lessons about the danger of a treaty or constitution that has no exits.

IMPLICATIONS FOR THE UNITED STATES

If, as seems most likely, EMU does occur and does lead to a political union with an independent military and foreign policy, the United States must rethink its own foreign policy with respect to Europe. First, the United States would have an opportunity to play a new, useful role within Europe, helping to balance national pressures and prevent the inevitable conflicts from developing into more serious confrontations. The United States should therefore emphasize that it wants its relations with the individual nations of Europe to remain as strong as they are today and should not allow Brussels to intervene between Washington and the national capitals of Europe.

Second, the United States must be aware that an economically and politically unified Europe would seek a different relationship with the United States. French officials in particular have been outspoken in emphasizing that a primary reason for a European monetary and political union is as a counterweight to the influence of the United States, both within European and in international affairs more generally. For the French, American influence is an old issue that frustrated de Gaulle and recurs in attacks on American "cultural imperialism" and U.S. attempts to influence Europe's policies toward countries like Libya, Iraq, and Iran. Such issues would become more widespread in a powerful, independent Europe.

Finally, the United States must recognize that it would no longer be able to count on Europe as an ally in all its relations with third countries. It was safe to assume such support when conflict with the Soviet Union dominated international relations and Europe's interest in containing the Soviet Union coincided with America's. But the global configuration of relations is now more complex. And the Europeans, guided by a combination of economic self-interest, historical traditions, and national pride, may seek alliances and pursue policies that are contrary to the interests of the United States. Although this divergence may tend to happen in any case because of the apparent end of the Soviet threat, the creation of a monetary union that led to a strong political union would accelerate it. If EMU occurs and leads to such a political union in Europe, the world will be a very different and not necessarily safer place.

NOTES

1. I have discussed the economic costs and benefits of EMU for Europeans in "The Case Against EMU," *The Economist*, June 13, 1992, pp. 12–19, and in "The Political Economy of the European Economic and Monetary Union:

Political Sources of an Economic Liability," *Journal of Economic Perspectives*, Fall 1997, forthcoming.
2. Quoted in Henry Kissinger, *Diplomacy*, New York: Simon & Schuster, 1994, p. 547.

EMU: A Worthwhile Gamble

PIERRE JACQUET

At the beginning of 1998, the odds are that the European monetary union (EMU) will start on time by 1 January 1999 and will include a large number of countries, possibly eleven out of the fifteen current member states.[1] This will undoubtedly be a major step in the European integration process, one whose implications are mind-boggling and cannot be inferred from any convincing analogy. The creation of EMU will take place in a context characterized by high and persistent unemployment in all countries of continental Europe. As EMU has become the major political and economic manifestation of European cooperation, the risk is that it might be expected to solve or at least alleviate European economic difficulties, and that acute disappointment might result if it does not.

Notwithstanding its deep political significance, however, EMU is first and foremost another way of organizing monetary policy in Europe, replacing individual, national policies by a single, centralized one. As such, it cannot deliver more than monetary policy can. An important question, therefore, is to ask whether EMU will lead to a better monetary policy and policy mix for Europe. This will have a significant impact on European unemployment; but it is not plausible to attribute all European unemployment to monetary policy mistakes that EMU could solve. There remain fundamental issues that nation-states, individually but also collectively in Europe, need to address irrespective of EMU, or even more urgently within EMU. These include all aspects of structural reform, from the tax system to the labour market and the welfare state. EMU cannot and should not be thought of as a substitute for such reform. In fact, structural reform may well be the necessary complement to EMU, to help compensate for the loss of national monetary policy autonomy.

Reprinted by permission. *International Affairs* 74:1, 1998.

This article argues that EMU is a worthwhile gamble. The very fact that a large number of countries have been willing to take the gamble is striking testimony to the political dynamism of the European Union. It is simply misleading to focus on and lament the difficulties experienced along the way and the relatively slow pace of innovation in other dimensions of European integration, such as institutional reform or the common defence policy. EMU is a unique experience in sharing a major attribute of sovereignty, and for that very reason is an admirable venture. But it does represent a gamble, requiring constant attention and cooperation.

After a brief discussion of the reasons why there was widespread support to create a monetary union in Europe, the second section elaborates on the making of the policy mix within EMU and on the current debate about economic policy coordination. The third section concludes.

WHY EMU?

Three different approaches have converged to produce support for monetary union in Europe. The first aimed at promoting tighter political integration and saw monetary union as a catalyst. The second focused on the economic benefits to be expected from a single currency. The third emphasized the political economy costs of keeping separate currencies within a wide, unified market for goods and services. Each of these approaches leads to different prescriptions as to EMU membership and the institutional and political measures that should accompany monetary union. While the three jointly produced the support that was needed for the project to get through, the failure to converge on one single rationale now spells disagreement and misunderstanding.

The Political Motive

There is no question that the political motive has been a central force behind European integration. Economic *rapprochement* and cooperation were not undertaken only for their own merits, but also, and often mainly, because they were thought instrumental in promoting reconciliation and peace after the disastrous outcomes of the first half of this century. As is well known, this was a central tenet of Jean Monnet's visionary approach. As a central attribute of sovereignty, money provided an attractive vehicle for furthering political integration. The creation of a single currency would signal the decision by member states to melt individual monetary sovereignty into collective management; moreover, its circulation would carry a strong symbolic overtone of the existence of a united Europe.

Beyond these uncontroversial assertions, however, confusion reigns. The concept of political integration or union is too wide and encompasses too many dimensions to provide an operational objective. While all member states will undoubtedly agree on the ultimate goal of preserving peace and prosperity and on the virtues of economic cooperation in pursuit of that goal, there is no unanimity on the specifics it implies with respect to political organization, to the proper mix of centralization and local autonomy, to the broad issue of subsidiarity and to the institutional arrangements through which joint decision-making should be organized—let alone the pace at which specific steps should be taken and implemented. The quest for power through integration also constitutes a bone of contention, as it may conflict with individual foreign policy options in the field of transatlantic relations and beyond. Part of the relationship between European monetary union and political integration hinges precisely on the conception and use of money as an instrument of power and on the idea that the euro could and should emerge as a competitor to the US dollar. It may indeed become a world currency;[2] but that evolution in itself will not create the political will to use it as an instrument of power, which would first require agreement exactly on what this means.[3]

Logically, therefore, the quest for political integration will not elicit broad support for monetary union. On the contrary, the feeling that EMU is but a Trojan horse for the introduction of an uncontrollable momentum towards political union may well explain in part the latent opposition to the project, both within member states and among them. At the same time, however, the end of the Cold War and German unification have brought the political question to the fore, as the collapse of the former international political system and the war in Yugoslavia further highlighted the lack of a coherent European political response, presence and role. The political integration of Europe, as well as its enlargement to the east, are important objectives—in particular for the reunited Germany. For the keenest supporters of further political integration through monetary union, however, the idea of a core group of countries proceeding faster than the others looks promising, is even perhaps the key to success. For them, the overriding goal is to deepen European integration, and this might involve, at least temporarily, a narrowing of the participants in integration.

Failure to achieve monetary union—now unlikely—would be a major political setback for European integration, because it has become the most important objective of that project. But the reverse is not necessarily true: the success of monetary union does not automatically imply that other aspects of European integration will progress smoothly thereafter. Sharing monetary policy sovereignty is a strong act of political cooperation; but the presumption that this, in itself, will generate a natural dynamic in respect of other dimensions of political integration, such as institutions and defence, is not fully convincing.

The Economic Rationale

The main reason why Jean Monnet's approach delivered results was because there were benefits to be gained from economic integration *per se*, as distinct from its contribution to political *rapprochment*. Does EMU also meet this test? Supporters highlight benefits to accrue from the planned single currency of both a microeconomic and a macroeconomic nature.

On the microeconomic side, the major benefit is one of reduced uncertainty, as monetary union implies the irrevocable locking—even the disappearance—of exchange rates. Thus an important, remaining barrier to trade integration goes away. Monetary union will lead to increased price transparency, better information and heightened competition. Economic agents, including businesses, will benefit directly from lower uncertainty, and indirectly from the further benefits to be expected from a more integrated market in goods and services as well as greater capital mobility. As emphasized by a report from the Commission,[4] the single currency augments the benefits to be expected from the single market, because it furthers the degree of market integration from which such benefits are derived. Similarly, the more integrated the market, the greater the microeconomic benefits to be expected from a single currency.

At the macroeconomic level, the disappearance of intra-European exchange rates implies that no resources will have to be spent to defend exchange rates any longer. Experience in the exchange rate mechanism (ERM) of the European Monetary System (EMS) suggests that stabilizing exchange rates can be very costly if it goes against speculators' expectations; monetary union provides exchange rate stability at a lesser cost. Moreover, keeping different currencies while pursuing exchange rate stability poses a moral hazard problem: as long as there exist currencies and exchange rates, there also exists a presumption that the exchange rates could change. This feeds speculation, but it also implies that economic agents take into account the possibility of devaluing or revaluing exchange rates in choosing how to act. Central banks therefore face a twofold credibility challenge: first, convincing speculators that they are serious about maintaining exchange rate stability; and second, convincing domestic agents that they will not use the option of devaluing should domestic costs increase faster than costs abroad. The way in which the domestic challenge unfolds in turn shapes potential speculators' expectations. Monetary union implies that the recourse to a short-term monetary fix is no longer available. It may therefore help to focus economic policies on structural aspects and mobilize domestic support in favour of structural action.

It should be clear, however, that a focus on the benefits offered by monetary union misses half the story. There are indeed benefits, but there are also costs. These stem precisely from the loss of the exchange rate as an instrument of adjustment. Should all prices and wages be fully flexible, the exchange rate would be superfluous. Relative prices would adjust automatically to maintain full employment and external balance. In the presence of price and wage rigidities, however, this adjustment does not take place easily, and does not happen immediately. In such conditions the exchange rate provides an easy and relatively less costly way to change a country's prices and wage costs respective to those of other countries. This is useful when the economic problem facing that country has to do with a departure of domestic price and wage levels from those existing abroad, a situation which occurs in the face of idiosyncratic shocks (economists also call these shocks 'asymmetric'). For example, the devaluation of the French franc in August 1969 was a successful response to the wage increase that took place across the board in France in the spring of that year in the wake of the Grenelle agreements.

A branch of the economic literature has researched these costs and the qualitative features that may tilt the cost–benefit analysis of monetary union towards the benefits. This is the so-called 'optimum currency area' (OCA) literature.[5] Its initiator, Robert Mundell, asked the following question in 1963: what is the optimum domain within which a single currency, whose exchange rate *vis-à-vis* the rest of the world would be flexible, should circulate? Later, his followers approached the question of creating a monetary union on the basis of a qualitative comparison between costs and benefits. What emerges naturally from this literature is confirmation that a central problem within a monetary union is how to respond to asymmetric shocks. The response will be less costly the higher the price and wage flexibility; the greater the mobility of factors of production, namely capital and labour; and the more generous the availability of fiscal transfers from other parts of the union. These features together determine the vulnerability of regions within a monetary union to asymmetric shocks. This analysis suggests that the success of EMU depends on two related questions:

1. Will the EU be the theatre of major asymmetric shocks in the future?
2. Does it exhibit enough of the features of an OCA?

The response to both questions is a matter of judgement. One cannot rule out the emergence of asymmetric shocks. The most recent one, of course, was the unification of the two parts of Germany. Many economists agree that keeping exchange rates stable in spite of such a shock carried very significant macroeconomic costs. A standard response would have been to let the Deutschmark appreciate temporarily as monetary conditions were tightened in Germany to deal with the heightened risk of inflation. Instead, other countries decided to maintain a fixed exchange rate with Germany and had to import an unnecessary monetary tightness that resulted in high real interest rates and prevented recovery from taking place. The situation also inspired speculators' defiance and resulted in the crisis and disruption of the ERM in 1992–3. Validating the OCA approach, the countries that left the ERM, Britain and Italy, subsequently enjoyed a higher rate of economic growth. While both the nature and the size of such a shock were unique, it would be a mistake to rule out the emergence of country asymmetries in the future. Economic structures and social compacts still differ widely across countries in Europe. Hence, even if the environment is common to all countries, individual responses are still likely to exhibit strong national characteristics and lead to asymmetries. It might, for example, be complacent to rule out a period of social upheaval like that of May 1968, leading to across-the-board wage increases in a particular country. Over time, one could expect trades unions to join forces across the EU. So far, however, conflict mitigation takes almost exclusively domestic routes. There seems to be no real basis for ruling out the presence of asymmetric shocks in the future. Most of the sectoral shocks, however, would be asymmetric within countries (for example, the steel industry crisis hit the region of Lorraine asymmetrically within the monetary union constituted by France), but not asymmetric within Europe, as most European trade is intra-industry trade and sectoral specialization does not take place along national lines.

As for the second question, namely whether the EU exhibits the characteristics of an OCA, the answer would appear to be unambiguously negative. Labour mobility, in particular, is very poor. It has become customary to compare the EU with the United States, where interstate labour mobility is a central adjustment mechanism. In addition, the United States is a political union, and as such allows interstate transfers to play a central role in adjustment to asymmetric shocks among states. Europe looks poorly equipped in comparison. Its central budget is hopelessly insufficient to play a stabilizing role. International solidarity within Europe is still unconvincing and underdeveloped.

The cost–benefit analysis of monetary union therefore suggests that it is a major gamble. While the OCA approach helps in forming a judgement, it does not give precise clues about whether it is worth taking that gamble or not; but it does imply that some countries would prefer not to join now, and to wait for more structural convergence to take place. In particular, the OCA view has a lot to say for a core approach to monetary union: a smaller monetary union among countries exhibiting a higher degree of convergence might be closer to the OCA benchmark and therefore prove less costly and more sustainable.

The OCA approach also takes us back to political union. A first observation is that many existing monetary unions—nation-states— would fail the OCA test, notably with respect to labour mobility. A logical conclusion is that political union may be a valid substitute for the OCA criteria in terms of making monetary union sustainable. Second, many American economists have emphasized the role of transfers of resources to regions hit by an asymmetric shock. On this view, once monetary union has been introduced in Europe there will be powerful pressures towards transferring at least some tax authority to a European body in charge of administering a sufficiently large fund that could be used for stabilization purposes in regions adversely hit within the union. For those concerned about the gradual loss of sovereignty implied by European integration, this makes monetary union even less desirable, by creating the feeling that countries that sign up for monetary union in fact sign up for much more.

It is important to point out some of the pitfalls of the OCA approach. First of all, it rests on features that are endogenous rather than exogenous: labour mobility, for example, is not a given; it can evolve over time depending on the perception of its necessity. Monetary union can help to develop the incentive for increasing labour mobility in Europe. Second, the discussion on OCAs has emphasized that, in the short term at least, exchange rate flexibility can act as a substitute for factor (capital and labour) mobility and market flexibility. Hence, countries entering monetary union and losing the exchange rate instrument need to develop these characteristics. On closer scrutiny, however, it becomes apparent that nominal exchange rate changes are poor substitutes as their real effects can only be transient.[6] The flexibility of goods, labour and capital markets should therefore be improved whether or not monetary union takes place. Monetary union may, however, act as a catalyst both towards the perception of a lack of flexibility and in creating further incentives to undertake reform. Third, transfers of resources themselves do not always foster adjustment; they simply diminish the local costs of an adverse shock. In fact, in some instances, they may create a disincentive to adjust, by hiding the size and relevance of the initial shock or the need for reform. Fourth and finally, local fiscal autonomy can be an effective substitute for resource transfers from other parts of the union, as it allows adversely hit regions to use the fiscal policy stabilizers to mitigate the impact of the shock. This suggests that a successful monetary union should involve decentralized fiscal policy, at least within limits. This point will be further discussed in the section on economic policy coordination below.

Political Economy Considerations

The third approach to monetary union consists in comparing it with alternative monetary arrangements for Europe. Surprisingly, this approach has been less often pursued than those consisting simply of pointing out the benefits of monetary union or its pitfalls. From a pragmatic standpoint, however, the real question should not be whether EMU is intrinsically a good, desirable arrangement, but rather whether it is to be preferred to alternative solutions to the European monetary poblem.[7]

A useful way to consider Europe's monetary dilemma is in terms of the so-called 'inconsistent' triangle:[8] free capital mobility, stable exchange rates, and autonomous, national monetary policies are mutually inconsistent. In a context of perfectly mobile capital, arbitrage will equate the domestic return with the foreign return, and therefore the domestic interest rate with the foreign rate augmented by the expected rate of depreciation of the domestic currency (which is the expected capital gain from investing abroad in an instrument denominated in the foreign currency). This is the so-called 'interest rate parity condition.' It implies that, in a context of free capital mobility, two countries can maintain fixed exchange rates only if they adopt a single monetary policy. Alternatively, if they decide to keep their national autonomy and choose their own course for monetary policy, the exchange rate will have to move with changes in expectations.

Capital mobility in Europe has made considerable progress, as a result of technological and institutional change and in the context of the achievement of the single European market. There has been some legitimate debate as to whether some 'sand' should not be thrown 'in the wheels,' with the reintroduction of limited controls aiming at preventing excessive short-term, speculative capital movements. Beyond the technical difficulties, such a solution would require much broader political agreement than currently exists, notably because it would be costly unless applied by all major countries, both within Europe and beyond Europe. If one takes full capital mobility for granted, the choice for Europe would therefore seem to be either exchange rate flexibility, or monetary union, the latter being defined by the loss of national monetary autonomy to a single European central bank.

Of course, it is always possible to muddle through inconsistencies. The experience of the EMS, however, shows that this can be costly at times, when recurrent speculative crises require action to defend existing exchange rates, and can result in systemic disruptions. True enough, the ERM exhibited lasting stability between 1987 and 1992, thus defying the inconsistent triangle; but in fact, all central banks were *de facto* shadowing the Bundesbank's monetary policy, which solved the inconsistency. As long as this deliberate choice was judged to be credible, market expectations obliged. Credibility was based on the determination to discuss and prepare for monetary union, on the intergovernmental conference leading to the Maastricht treaty, and on signing and ratifying the treaty. As soon as difficulties became apparent, in the 'no' vote of the first Danish referendum and the narrow 'yes' vote of the French referendum, the underlying inconsistency became obvious. The costs of shadowing the Bundesbank's choices in the wake of the German asymmetric shock led to speculators expecting monetary policy changes in various countries. The system thus became unsustainable. On 2 August 1993 the margins of fluctuations were enlarged from plus or minus 2.25 per cent to plus or minus 15 per cent. A wide potential for flexibility had been introduced into a system aiming at stability.

Short of reintroducing capital controls, which would imply a departure from one of the objectives of the single market, the current system of stable but adjustable exchange rates is therefore not satisfactory. The benefits from stability can be achieved only by limiting monetary sovereignty; but an informal limitation is not likely to be credible in all circumstances; should any doubt appear, speculation will take place and disrupt stability. In short, such a system exhibits all the costs of fixed exchange rates (the loss of the exchange rate instrument plus the need to defend the parities) without the benefits (reduced uncertainty). This is why the European monetary dilemma amounts to choosing either floating exchange rates or monetary union. The only policy difference between the two systems has to do with the domain of monetary policy: in the former case, monetary policy remains a prerogative of the nationstates; in the latter, it is exercised jointly among them by a common central bank.

The alternative to monetary union, therefore, is not the maintenance of the current system, which can be sustained only through the recurrent cost of fighting speculation. It is, rather, a system of floating exchange rates. We know from both theory and experience that floating exchange rates are very volatile and may overshoot their equilibrium values for sustained periods of time. Under flexible exchange rates, the European single market would be the theatre of exchange rate overvaluations and undervaluations. As an arrangement among sovereign states, the working of the single market relies on a continuing commitment by these states to accept the discipline of competition. Some producer groups, however, might complain about unfair competition from undervalued currencies and ask for protection. In the absence of political union, such interest groups would express their concern at a national level. The major risk of floating exchange rates, therefore, would be a weakening of the political commitment to the single market in some member states. The large depreciation of sterling and of the Italian lira in September 1992 provides a case in point. Several sectors suffered from British and Italian competition and asked for trade protection. Interestingly, it is precisely because Europe is not a political union that the move to monetary union appears particularly valuable as a way to strengthen the single market.

Unlike the two other perspectives, this approach to monetary union suggests that its geographical scope should be that of the single market. In particular, major countries should become members of the EMU, if not initially, very soon after its creation. For the sake of the single market, countries that stay outside EMU, including the UK, would need to accept some form of exchange rate discipline even if they do not want to participate in an ERM type of arrangement. They could not therefore count on keeping monetary sovereignty unscathed without alienating their trade partners within the single market. The inconsistent triangle, however, makes any exchange rate discipline short of monetary union fragile and potentially costly.

Monetary union thus appears to be a necessary condition for the single market to be politically sustainable in a context of free capital mobility. But it may not be a sufficient condition. In particular, international frictions will still exist within the EMU. Instead of focusing on exchange rates, they will stem from social and economic (especially fiscal) discrepancies that may be perceived to tilt competition unfairly. In particular, one might expect EMU to heighten the tension already perceptible on social conditions in the labour markets. A central task will be to manage these tensions, through a mix of minimum standards and mutual recognition. This brings us back again to political union, as monetary union will generate pressures to work on sharing sovereignty in other areas. But the end result is still unknown. Full harmonization of social policies, in particular, will not happen until competition among social systems has led to a convergence of views on the way to provide adequate social treatment in modern, open economies. This is the same process that led to the harmonization of monetary policies towards the demanding German standard. The EMS was a minimum framework of understanding, aiming at preserving exchange rate stability among highly open trade partners; competition among monetary policies prevailed under the system, finally leading to full convergence and monetary union.

EMU AND ECONOMIC POLICY COORDINATION

As argued above, monetary union is the alternative to be preferred if the objective is to buttress the single market and make it less vulnerable to potential centrifugal protectionist pressures. But, as also discussed, it remains a gamble, and while it is now well under way, attention must shift to measures that are necessary to transform the gamble into unambiguous success. The bottom line is that one should not expect monetary union to solve all Europe's problems. It amounts simply to replacing national monetary policies by joint monetary policy undertaken at the European level. What national monetary policies could not do, it would be foolish to expect a common monetary policy to do. But monetary union may well further expose structural weaknesses, as individual countries will no longer be able to resort to the short-term monetary fix.

Structural reform is therefore as urgent as ever. It requires deliberate action at the national level in the first place; but this should not preclude a joint European approach on some issues. On the capital markets, for example, joint decisions will have to be made with respect to taxation, to regulation and supervision, and to lender-of-last-resort facilities. These questions are not directly linked to monetary union. But by deepening the integration of financial markets and competition, monetary union does make them more immediate. On labour markets, as already mentioned, pressure will mount for minimal harmonization and mutual recognition. The mutual recognition of welfare rights may also surface as labour mobility is pushed upwards. All these difficult questions illustrate that there is ample room for a European coordination of structural policies.

This article focuses on macroeconomic policy coordination. While it is no substitute for structural change, it plays an important cyclical and structural role. It interferes with structural aspects in two ways: first, structural reform will be easier to conduct during the upward phase of the economic cycle; second, in the spirit of the hysteresis explanation of lasting unemployment, one can expect lasting cyclical unemployment to become structural, because a long-term unemployed person loses his or her qualification to work. The costs of macroeconomic policy mistakes can therefore be particularly important.

Policy-Mix and Coordination: The Limits of Rules

The Maastricht treaty makes explicit room for macroeconomic policy coordination (beyond monetary policy). Article 2 lists common objectives, to be met by 'the adoption of an economic policy which is based on the close coordination of Member States' economic policies' (art. 3A: I). Article 103 specifies that member states' economic policies are a matter of common concern to be coordinated within the Council. The Council (art. 103, para. 2) 'shall, acting by a qualified majority on a recommendation from the Commission, formulate a draft for the broad guidelines of the economic policies of the Member States and of the Community.' The European Council, acting by a qualified majority, then adopts a recommendation setting out these broad guidelines and informs the European Parliament of its recommendation. Article 103, para. 3, also gives the Council the responsibility to monitor economic developments in each of the member states and the consistency of economic policies with the broad guidelines referred to above. In the case of a departure from these guidelines, 'the Council may, acting by a qualified majority on a recommendation from the Commission, make the necessary recommendation to the Member State concerned' (art. 103: 4). It may also, with the same procedure, make its recommendations public.

Clearly the treaty thus installs a framework for coordinating policies. This does not guarantee actual, close coordination. Significant discretion remains as to implementation. A parallel can be drawn with article 104c, concerned with fiscal discipline. At the pressing suggestion of the German finance minister, Theo Waigel, member governments signed a stability pact signalling in a solemn way their joint determination to abide strictly by the article's provisions. In effect, the stability pact is nothing more than a clear reaffirmation of article 104c, including its provisions about sanctions. It is interesting to note that, under German pressure, the priority was given to fiscal discipline rather than to the joint definition of broad economic guidelines. The French concern at Amsterdam in June 1997 was precisely to balance this approach with a similar undertaking with respect to coordination and article 103, giving rise to the resolution on growth and employment then adopted by the European Council. This episode illustrates two very different approaches to coordination,[9] which echo the theoretical debate of rules versus discretion. A first approach sees coordination as a response to international interdependence, and illustrates the benefits for interdependent countries from taking full account of interdependencies in determining the use of economic policy instruments. It involves a discretionary, evolving adaptation of economic policy choices towards joint welfare maximization. A general result is that policy coordination leads to superior outcome and maximizes joint welfare. A second approach sees coordination as the necessary way to produce valuable international public goods, such as free trade, stable exchange rates and regime preservation. For example, preserving a stable, non-inflationary monetary union requires collective fiscal disciple. One may interpret the stability pact (or article 104c of the treaty) as a coordinated approach designed to produce the public good of fiscal discipline. Such an approach usually relies on a system of rules of behavior.

Given the difficulty of implementing discretionary coordination of economic policies, a system of rules has sometimes also been devised in order to limit the costs of non-cooperative discretion. In the field of exchange rate management, for example, the absence of cooperation can lead to competitive depreciation. The fear that this could happen has been a major force driving European monetary cooperation since the late 1960s, when the Bretton Woods system of fixed exchange rates began to crumble and the Werner plan was devised to create a monetary union in Europe. The first, significant success was the creation of EMS in 1979. But this is often misinterpreted as a cooperative agreement: in fact, it amounts rather to a system of rules that constrain exchange rate management, but within which individual monetary policies compete with each other. Such competition led to a *de facto* harmonization on the German monetary policy standard, to become full, formal harmonization within a monetary union.

Monetary union itself rigidly ties national policies into a single policy for Europe. It is, therefore, the ultimate rule that can be imposed, and cannot be interpreted as an exercise of coordination of monetary policies in which each country would choose its own policy to maximize joint welfare. As the previous discussion illustrated, one can think of monetary union as a regime-preserving measure, strengthening the single market in a political economy sense.

Understandably, most European integration efforts to date have focused on devising rules rather than on pursuing cooperative discretion. Adopting common rules is time-consuming and difficult; it requires an impressive dose of political cooperation; but it is yet politically more feasible and, most importantly, more credible than maintaining effective discretionary cooperation, a process that requires a continuing willingness to defer to the common good by opposition to pursuing the narrower national objectives. While the tendency to rule cooperation is therefore understandable, it may also have undesirable consequences.

Rules typically are sub-optimal. They can also be counterproductive. For example, Europe has suffered from an ill-adapted policy mix in the early 1990s, based on too tight a monetary policy, for the sake of maintaining fixed exchange rates with the Deutschmark.[10] This self-imposed rule, interpreted as the vibrant expression of European monetary cooperation, deprived European countries of a much-needed margin of manoeuvre on the domestic front. While monetary policy could therefore not be used for economic stabilization purposes, fiscal policy had to bear the brunt of the slowdown in economic growth. Hence, some of the fiscal problems experienced by European countries find their origin in part in the rigidity of the exchange rate commitment, responsible for higher real interest rates and slower growth. A proper coordination of economic policies after the shock of German reunification would typically have involved a willingness to let the Deutschmark temporarily appreciate against other currencies. An early recognition of the problem would also have allowed a readjustment of exchange rates well before it had to be imposed by markets, thus largely avoiding the September 1992 crisis and the turmoil that followed. In the absence of monetary union, therefore, the appropriate response should have been to let exchange rates move. If monetary union had been in place, the problem would have been very different, because the common European monetary policy would have been designed on the basis of the average inflationary pressures across Europe, unlike the Bundesbank's policy, which was exclusively focused on the inflationary risk in Germany. This example also serves to illustrate that monetary union is fundamentally different from a fixed exchange rate system: both imply a single monetary policy (in the presence of mobile capital flows), but under monetary union that monetary policy is jointly determined.

However, it is misleading to consider monetary policy in a vacuum. A central macroeconomic question is the determination of the policy mix, namely the combination of fiscal and monetary policies. A key ingredient of the success of American economic policy since the late 1980s has been the policy mix based on aggressive monetary expansion (with short-term real interest rates at zero) together with fiscal restriction. Fiscal policy aimed at restoring public finance sustainability while monetary policy aimed not only at price stability but also at maintaining growth (and additionally helping the banking sector absorb its bad loans). Low real interest rates in turn contributed to facilitate the fiscal adjustment task. Continental Europe has followed the opposite course: monetary policy was kept too tight, because it aimed at managing the inflationary costs of German unification domestically, and at maintaining exchange rates fixed to the Deutschmark in other countries; and fiscal policy was allowed to drift simply to avoid deepening the recession. The result is eloquent: full employment, balanced budget and a buoyant economy in the United States; high unemployment, large fiscal deficits and dismal growth results in continental Europe. It is hard to avoid the conclusion that part of the European problem has to do with a damaging policy-mix error.

With the dramatic decline in interest rates over the last two years, a more appropriate policy mix has emerged in Europe. It is possible to argue that, given the duration of the slump and the slack in the economy, and given the very low level of the inflationary risk, real interest rates are still too high and monetary policy should be much more expansionary. This makes the recent move by the Bundesbank, followed by other central banks, to raise short-term interest rates incomprehensible, unless one considers that European economies, including Germany, are running at full employment. The policy mix, however, has clearly improved. But the size of the necessary fiscal adjustment calls for much more of the same policy mix. A key question therefore hinges on the nature of the policy mix that will emerge under EMU.

There is a significant risk that monetary policy will be too tight under EMU. The European central bank may be willing to flex its muscles in order to establish early its anti-inflationary credibility. More fundamentally, the policy mix between one single central bank and a large number of decentralized fiscal policies may resemble what is known in game theory as a 'prisoner's dilemma': while the desired outcome should be monetary ease together with fiscal restriction, the likely outcome is rather one in which the central bank will not trust the commitment of member states to adjust their deficits seriously enough, will see itself as the guardian of the temple and will resist expansion by fear of inflation; fiscal adjustment, however, will prove more difficult if monetary expansion is not forthcoming. A major test of macroeconomic policy coordination thus rests with proper communication between the central bank and fiscal authorities. The 'Euro Council,' currently under debate, while fully acknowledging the independence of the European central bank, envisages holding joint sessions between fiscal authorities and representatives of the central bank. This seems a move in the right direction.

The stability pact also provides a partial solution to this coordination dilemma. By signalling the commitment of all member states to adhere strictly to the norm, it may ease some of the fears on the part of the central bank. But, as argued above, it is important that member governments keep one instrument, namely fiscal policy, available to respond to asymmetric shocks. Clearly, in order to restore the necessary margin of manoeuvre given the stability pact commitment, budget deficits must be kept well below the upper limit. We know that this will require some time. During this transition period, economies will be particularly vulnerable to asymmetric shocks, as their hands will be tied both on fiscal and on monetary policy.

A distinct problem that at times may call for coordination concerns the exchange rate of the euro with respect to other currencies, such as the dollar and the yen. In principle, Europe as a whole will be a much closer economy than its individual members, and can therefore contemplate its exchange rate with some benign neglect. But there is an important risk for European competitiveness in the early years of the single currency. Some observers have commented that EMU uncertainties could lead to a weak euro. The odds, however, are that the euro will look an attractive asset and a better substitute for the dollar than any of the existing currencies; initially, it may benefit from a vote of confidence as EMU happens on schedule and as it becomes clear that the European central bank is indeed independent, has a single objective of price stability, and is protected by a treaty that does not even envision a change of statutes (short of a new treaty). The chances are, therefore, that the euro could be overvalued, thus creating a major problem of competitiveness at a time when Europe is still trying to recover after years of slow growth. Nor is it only a problem originating in Europe: the US current account is expected to show ever larger deficits, and the Asian crisis of

1997 promises to contribute to it. The long-term dependence of the United States on foreign capital inflows may well push the dollar downwards in the medium term, compounding the overvaluation of the euro. If this scenario were to take place, benign neglect in Europe would be a mistake. The response of macroeconomic policies, and in particular monetary policy, in Europe would become even more crucial. For the time being, the responsibility for exchange rate management seems to be divided between the central bank and the Council of Finance Ministers. The way in which they cooperate will be particularly crucial.

The initial years within EMU, therefore, will test the willingness of member states to solve difficulties through a discretionary approach rather than through strict obedience to arbitrary rules. It is important that the stability pact be interpreted in a dynamic way rather than on a strict year-to-year basis, and that the deficit limit over time be conceived as a collective limit rather than a sum of individual ones. Such a sense of solidarity, however, may take time to develop, even though it would be in the collective interest. Finally, the stability pact, as a system of rules, exhibits serious weaknesses. Not only does it infringe the necessary flexibility, at least initially while deficits are still too close to, or above, the upper limit; it also oversimplifies the fiscal sustainability problem in Europe, by creating the impression that meeting a deficit target does the job. Most of the public debt predicament, in Europe, is due to structural problems linked to transfer spending and the welfare state in the context of rising health costs and an ageing population.[11] Neither EMU nor the stability pact can act as substitutes for the willingness, at the level of each government, to undertake seriously reform to restore control over public spending.

CONCLUDING REMARKS

Those American economists who are among the most influential, are often sceptical of the merits of EMU. Both Martin Feldstein and Milton Friedman,[12] for example, have recently predicted sombre prospects for Europe under monetary union. Both claim that EMU is essentially politically driven: as argued above, this is only partly true, and certainly insufficient to explain the project. Both also concur in forecasting that instead of promoting peace and harmony, EMU might do just the reverse. Unfortunately, neither of them justifies this political judgement by analysing convincing alternatives to EMU. Moreover, they seem to forget that European countries are bound to manage an ever growing interdependence and cannot individually afford the spoiled perception of national autonomy of a large country that remains by all existing standards the only superpower in the world. Feldstein and Friedman point at substantial risks, however. But then, again, reform and change are always risky.

With or without EMU, interdependence among European countries is inescapable, and is deeper within Europe than between European and non-European countries. The single market has added an additional twist to regionalization in that sense. Yet most of the fears, and also most of the expectations, about EMU are derived from visions that misinterpret interdependence. The fear that EMU is taking us too far in terms of European integration ignores the inescapable need to cooperate in most economic and social dimensions. Money is no exception, and it has been argued here that exchange rate stabilization, in the context of full capital mobility, was best achieved through monetary union. But the expectation that EMU will lead to deeper political union ignores the breadth of interdependence, which extends well beyond monetary matters and does not always call for centralized solutions. National sovereignty, even deprived of money, still has a long life.

EMU should be considered above all as a better way to organize monetary relations in Europe than any of the alternatives. It is nonetheless a political and an economic gamble. The gamble will be a collective one, as it is important for Europe to conduct macroeconomic policies friendly to growth and employment. But it will be first and foremost, an individual, national gamble for all member countries, as it will expose the need for overdue structural reform. If countries are not ready to undertake reform, not taking part in EMU will not solve their problems. If they are, then they will more easily adapt to EMU, and it is hard to see the benefits from staying outside. The focus should now be on making the gamble a success.

NOTES

1. Among the four 'outs,' three countries are unwilling to join (Britain, Denmark, and Sweden); Greece is not close to meeting the criteria yet.
2. See e.g. Fred Bergsten, 'The dollar and the euro,' *Foreign Affairs* 76: 4, July–August 1997, pp. 83–95; George Alogoskoufis, Richard Portes and Hélène Rey, *The emergence of the euro as an international currency.* Discussion Paper Series no. 1741 (London: Centre for Economic Policy Research, 1997). A dissenting view can be found in Benjamin J. Cohen, 'Who challenges whom? The euro vs the dollar,' *Politique Etrangère* (forthcoming, 1998).
3. For a critical discussion of the concept of economic power, see e.e. Richard N. Cooper, 'Le pourvoir économique après la guerre froide,' *Politique Etrangère* 2, summer 1997.
4. Commission of the European Communities, 'One market, one money: an evaluation of the potential benefits and costs of forming an economic and monetary union,' *European Economy* 44, October 1990.

5. See esp. Robert A. Mundell, 'A theory of optimum currency areas,' *American Economic Review* 51, September 1961, pp. 657–65; Ronald I. McKinnon, 'Optimum currency areas,' *American Economic Review* 53, September 1963, pp. 717–25; Peter Kenen, 'The theory of optimum currency areas: an eclectic view,' R. A. Mundell and A. K. Swoboda, eds, *Monetary problems of the international economy* (Chicago, IL: University of Chicago Press, 1969); E. Tower and Thomas D. Willet, *The theory of optimum currency areas and exchange-rate flexibility*. Special Studies in International Economies no. 11 (Princeton, NJ: Princeton International Finance Section 1976).

6. For a discussion see William H. Buiter, 'Politique macroéconomique dans la période de transition vers l'union monétaire' (Macroeconomic policy in the transition to monetary union), *Revue d'économie politique* 105: 5, September–October 1995).

7. This section partially draws on Pierre Jacquet and Jean Pisani-Ferry, 'The exchange rate issue in Europe', in P. Jacquet and J. Pisani-Ferry, eds, *L'Europe entre marché unique et monnaie unique. Perspectives françaises et britanniques*, Les cahiers de l'ifri 20, 1997.

8. See Tommaso Padoa-Schioppa, 'The European monetary system: a long-term view,' in F. Giavazzi, S. Micossi and M. Miller, eds, *The European monetary system* (Cambridge: Cambridge University Press, 1988). Padoa-Schioppa in face describes an 'inconsistent quarter' between free trade, free capital mobility, stable exchange rates and autonomous national monetary policies. Since free trade has been achieved in Europe, the quartet reduces to a triangle. Taking full capital mobility for granted still reduces it to a dilemma between flexible exchange rates or monetary union.

9. Niels Thygesen, 'Coordination of national policies,' in the *New Palgrave dictionary of monetary and finance, vol. 1* (Basingstoke: Macmillan, 1992), pp. 458–61.

10. See the discussion in Pierre-Alain Muet, 'Déficit de croissance et chômage: let coût de la non-coopération,' Etudes et recherches no. I (Paris: Groupement d'Etudes et de Recherches Notre Europe, 1997); and Heiner Flassbeck, Pierre Jacquet, Brian Henry and Robert Levine, *Unemployment in the United States, Germany, France and the United Kingdom: first ideas about common features, differences and coherent explanation*, mimeo (Bonn: Friedrich Ebert Stiftung, 1997).

11. For a discussion of the European fiscal problem, see e.g. Claude Bismut and Pierre Jacquet, *Fiscal consolidation in Europe*, Les cahiers de l'ifri 19, 1997.

12. Martin Feldstein, 'EMU and international conflict, *Foreign Affairs* 76: 6, November–December 1997; Milton Friedman, 'Why Europe can't afford the euro. The danger of a common currency,' *The Times*, 19 November 1997 (see also in *Deutsche Bundesbank Auszüge aus Presseartikeln* 68, 20 November 1997).

Issue 11
IMF

INTRODUCTION

Three blocks west of the White House, there is a structure that looks like any other federal office building in Washington. But it is not like any other. Occupying half a city block, the big complex is the headquarters of a worldwide organization, the International Monetary Fund, and its twin, the World Bank.

Though little known among the public, the IMF has become a major player in international financial circles—and extraordinarily controversial. Today, with more than 180 governments as members, the IMF is over fifty years old. Its origins date back to the period following World War II, when a conference of allied governments to address postwar economic issues was held at the venerable Mount Washington Hotel in the White Mountains near Bretton Woods, New Hampshire.

In the beginning, the IMF's primary role was to monitor a system of fixed currency exchange rates. With the end of the fixed rate regime in the 1970s, however, the IMF turned greater attention to its other role: lender of last resort to governments in financial distress. Particularly when developing countries have had problems repaying foreign debts, the IMF has been available to lend them money when commercial lenders have found the risk to be too great.

But here is the rub: IMF loans come with demanding conditions to which borrower-governments must strictly adhere if loan disbursements are to continue. Often these conditions are difficult for governments to accept politically because of their unpopularity with the masses—measures such as reducing government spending, ending subsidies, and raising taxes, which are risky actions for a government. The IMF's medicine may be good economics, but bad politics.

The two selections in this section relate to the IMF's role in assisting countries in Southeast Asia that recently have encountered severe financial problems. The first article, by Harvard economist Jeffrey Sachs, provides a cutting critique of the IMF's role in Southeast Asia and in other countries where Sachs has been a consultant to governments. He sees the IMF as an instrument of U. S. foreign policy, which does more harm than good. The second selection is a defense by the IMF of its actions in Southeast Asia. The IMF counters that it is increasingly sensitive to the political consequences of its actions but that government must make significant reforms if there are to be long-term solutions to these countries' economic problems.

As you read the articles, consider the following questions.

Discussion Questions

1. The IMF is an international organization comprised of many different countries, but is viewed by some devloping countries—especially former colonies—as a tool of the richest countries, many of which are former colonial powers. Is the IMF merely a modern-day expression of colonialism?
2. Suppose that there were no IMF, as some of its most severe critics wish. What would be the likely outcome of financial crises in developing countries then? Would the lack of the IMF force them to be more self-reliant and financially responsible? Or would they sink further into financial disaster?
3. Looking at both the positive and negative consequences of its actions, on balance how useful do you believe the IMF is?

    For more information on this topic, visit the following websites:

    `http://www.imf.org/`
    (web site of the International Monetary Fund)

    `http://www.oxanalytica.com/asiapg.htm`
    ("Asia [financial] Crisis Analysis" by Oxford Analytica, prominent British research and consulting group)

    `http://www.stern.nyu.edu/~nroubini/asia/AsiaHomepage.html`
    (extensive sources and links on the Asian currency crisis; by Prof. Nouriel Roubini of New York University)

The IMF and the Asian Flu   ⚖

JEFFREY SACHS

The International Monetary Fund has displayed its awesome power in recent months in assuming the central role in the unfolding Asian financial crisis. Since July, the IMF has organized financial bailouts totaling more than $100 billion of public funds in Indonesia, South Korea, and Thailand. Yet the IMF is almost unknown to the American people. Its vague public image—carefully tended by the institution itself—is something like the cartoon in a recent *Time* magazine profile: The IMF, garbed as Superman, sweeps low over the earth, extinguishing financial blazes. But a careful examination of the actual record shows that the IMF, loyal to financial orthodoxy and mindful of creditors to the neglect of debtor countries, often pours oil on the flames.

Consider the IMF's recent actions in Asia. Asia's current crisis has all the ingredients of a financial panic made in the private sector. Asian banks are large debtors to foreign banks, and a large part of the debt is very short-term. Despite sound "fundamentals" in Asia—such as budget surpluses, high saving rates, low inflation, and export-oriented industries—foreign creditors began to withdraw money from Asia last spring because of growing concerns about currency overvaluation, bank scandals, and weak real estate markets.

These concerns multiplied in midyear when Thailand devalued the baht. Suddenly, international banks became wary of extending new loans in Asia as the old loans fell due. The banks were becoming a bit worried about Asia's long-term prospects, which still looked rather good, but were much more worried about what the other investors were doing. Each investor understood that Thailand, Indonesia, and Korea would be pushed into outright default if enough creditors pulled the plug on new loans. In the end, each creditor started to rush for the doors precisely because the other creditors were doing the same thing.

In this kind of shaky situation, the role of public policy is to help the markets escape a self-fulfilling stampede. Six months ago, the appropriate steps for senior finance officials in the United States, Japan, and Europe would have been to try to slow the flight of the creditors. The major banks should have been brought together in mid-1997 to underscore their collective interest in avoiding a self-defeating panic (such

Jeffrey Sachs is director of the Harvard Institute for International Development and Galen L. Stone Professor of International Trade at Harvard University.

Reprinted by permission. *The American Prospect*, March–April 1998. No. 37, p. 16.

discussions in fact began only at the end of December 1997, once the panic was already in full swing). At the same time, the key central banks led by the Federal Reserve might have extended some credit lines to their Asian counterparts, without great public fanfare and without adding to the market anxieties.

Instead, the IMF arrived in Thailand in July filled with ostentatious declarations that all was wrong and that fundamental and immediate surgery was needed. (Ironically, the ink was not even dry on the IMF's 1997 annual report, which gave Thailand and its neighbors high marks on economic management!) The IMF deepened the sense of panic not only because of its dire public pronouncements but also because its proposed medicine—high interest rates, budget cuts, and immediate bank closures—convinced the markets that Asia indeed was about to enter a severe contraction (as had happened earlier in Argentina, Bulgaria, and Mexico). Instead of dousing the fire, the IMF in effect screamed fire in the theater. The scene was repeated in Indonesia in November and Korea in December. By then, the panic had spread to virtually all of East Asia.

Even though the original fire could well have been contained, the ensuing panic has proved devastating. In Indonesia, Korea, and Thailand, stock and currency markets plummeted after the IMF entered the scene, and this despite the enormous bailout loans to these countries. Asia's own banks have stopped making loans in response to the IMF's insistence on closing "weak" banks. The local banks could read the warnings. They started to call in their own loans to build up cash reserves, since otherwise the IMF might insist on their own closure. In the end, the IMF programs could well cause Asia much more harm than benefit. Asian governments will borrow tens of billions of dollars to enable their banks to pay off foreign creditors, but the internal economies may well collapse. The Asian governments will get stuck with debts owed to the IMF and foreign governments, and the economies will contract sharply, while the foreign creditors will escape unscathed.

The IMF has provided a benchmark for judging its effectiveness in Asia. In the August program for Thailand, the IMF projected Thai growth of 3.5 percent for 1998. In the November Indonesia program, the IMF projected 1998 growth of 3 percent. And most recently in Korea, the IMF is targeting growth of 2.5 percent. These projections almost surely will fail just as the IMFs projections failed in Argentina, Bulgaria, and Mexico (more on this below). All three Asian countries are likely to suffer extreme contractions next year at the hands of the IMF's policy-induced credit crunch. Industrial production in Thailand was down 8 percent in November compared with a year earlier. A wave of bankruptcies is sweeping Korea, and a massive rise in unemployment seems set to hit all three of the economies. Most private forecasters are projecting outright declines in gross domestic product (GDP) next year, a sharp change indeed for economies that have grown at more than 6 percent per year for a decade or more. If history is a guide, the IMF will simply ignore its own faulty forecasts for the Asian program, rather than asking what went wrong.

WHAT IS THE IMF?

The Asian story is hardly unique. In most of the developing world, the IMF is not a figure that swoops in for a quick rescue. On the contrary, for perhaps half of the developing world outside of China and India, the IMF is an all-too-constant presence, almost a surrogate government in financial matters. Not unlike the days when the British Empire placed senior officials directly into the Egyptian and Ottoman finance ministries, the IMF is insinuated into the inner sanctums of nearly 75 developing-country governments around the world—countries with a combined population of some 1.4 billion. These governments rarely move without consulting the IMF staff, and when they do, they risk their lifelines to capital markets, foreign aid, and international respectability. Newspaper headlines in these countries herald the comings and goings of IMF staff.

The IMF's power rests on three bases. Most importantly, the IMF is the instrument by which the U.S. Treasury intervenes in developing countries. When the United States took the initiative in bailing out Mexico in 1994 and Korea in 1997, it turned to the IMF as the institution that could provide the cover, the staff, and the bucks to do the job. Second, many developing countries genuinely welcome the chance to sign a "contract" with the world community, represented by the IMF, in which good economic policies are rewarded with emergency loans. Third, and much more dangerous, IMF power also flows from the institution's carefully constructed image of infallibility. The IMF gets its way in the developing world because to disagree publicly with the IMF is viewed in the international community as rejecting financial rectitude itself.

In dozens of cases each year in which developing-country governments manifestly do not agree with IMF prescriptions, they are terrified to murmur any opposition. To do so immediately brands the government as "lacking seriousness" in economic management. The new President elect of Korea spent the first day following his election victory genuflecting to the IMF. Already the international financial press is judging Korea on whether or not it adheres to the IMF "medicine," without even asking whether the medicine is sensibly prescribed. From the point of view of the U.S. government, the IMF's aura of infallibility is obviously a convenient myth. Pesky developing countries are kept in line with little effort, and U.S. policymakers are confident that the IMF will do their bidding in any event. In fact, since the IMF has economic programs in some 75 countries, and since the U.S. Treasury carefully tracks a mere handful of these at any one time, the IMF staff is really running the show in most of the developing world with almost no supervision from the United States or anyone else. RVT autonomy is especially real in the poorest countries of the world, for which the Treasury and U.S. financial community have little time or interest.

No doubt the IMF is a convenient instrument of U.S. financial diplomacy in the high-profile cases. For a small amount of U.S. appropriations every few years, the United States gains effective control (shared to some extent with the European Union and Japan) over a large pool of money that can be lent to developing countries without congressional meddling. Since the IMF pools resources from all the member countries, the United States's own contribution is multiplied several fold, and the U.S. influence inside the organization is all out of proportion to the U.S. contribution. Moreover, when the IMF loans money to governments, the loans are nearly risk free, since most governments recognize that their entire international standing rests on a timely repayment of those loans even if that means default to other creditors, extreme internal recession, or sales of valuable domestic assets.

The immense authority of a secretive international institution may be cozy for senior U.S. policymakers, but it can be deeply troubling for developing countries that live under IMF programs. The IMF claims that these fears are overblown: After all, its economic programs are voluntary—the IMF cannot impose a program on an unwilling government. This voluntarism is a matter of semantics, however. When the most powerful governments of the world inform a poor developing country that it must agree with the IMF or else lose access to foreign aid, the goodwill of major governments, the chances for debt restructuring, and the confidence of private markets (which are encouraged by the G-7 to use IMF agreements as focal points for their own bargaining), the notion of voluntarism is a bit stretched.

The IMF also argues that it is a true international organization, jointly governed by developing and developed countries. True, the IMF is a voluntary association of member governments, now 182 in number. And true, it is governed by an executive board that represents the finance ministries of all of the member countries. But in fact, the executive board is largely a rubber-stamp institution of the U.S. Treasury and the major finance ministries of Europe and Japan, and the IMF senior staff itself. Voting is weighted by financial contribution (the so-called quota), so that the United States, the European Union, and Japan combined have a comfortable majority. Moreover, the quota allocations are set to preserve the voting clout of the developed countries. India and China have smaller votes than the Netherlands, for example, despite economies that are roughly four and ten times larger in purchasing-power terms (and populations, of course, that are more than 60 times larger). The board is also extremely weak in its operational oversight of the IMF staff: It almost never looks beyond IMF staff reports, and almost never seeks independent information or independent follow-up evaluations. Moreover, since IMF program documents are automatically confidential, the public has almost no ability to weigh in on IMF decisions.

AN IMF PRONE TO MISTAKES

The great power of a secretive international bureaucracy would be troubling enough to believers in limited government and public accountability. The problem is worse. The IMF's mask of infallibility hides a record of mediocrity punctuated by some truly costly blunders. Of course, these blunders almost never come to public light. When an internal IMF review criticized the IMF's role in Mexico in 1993 and 1994, it was quickly hushed up and never made public. In most cases, critical reviews are never put to paper. When anything goes wrong in an IMF-country program, it is easy enough to blame the government of that country for failing to abide by the (secret) words of wisdom of IMF staff.

As an economic advisor to many developing-country governments, I have had a rare opportunity to witness IMF operations at close range. Let me mention a few cases.

In 1985, Bolivia faced a 24,000 percent hyperinflation, a 30 percent drop in living standards, and a catastrophic rise in poverty, reflecting a generation of mismanagement by dictatorships, over-indebtedness, and the collapse of tin exports. When a new democratically elected government came into office in 1985 and bravely carried out a dramatic stabilization program, the IMF nearly torpedoed the government's successful efforts by demanding a resumption of payments on a mountain of bad debts inherited from past military governments. Luckily, Bolivia fought this one—in this case it had almost nothing to lose. The United States backed the Bolivians, in part as a reward for Bolivia's economic reforms and its cooperation with U.S. antidrug policy. As a result, Bolivia pioneered debt relief two years before it became official IMF policy. And though the IMF had initially opposed the whole approach, Bolivia's success was later trumpeted as an IMF success story.

In 1989, postcommunist Poland desperately needed a fund to stabilize the exchange rate. A stabilization fund is a pool of money that allows the central bank to intervene in currency markets to prevent damaging speculative swings in its exchange rate. The idea of a stabilization fund was a novelty; the IMF didn't warm up to the idea until six years later when such funds finally became part of IMF policies. The IMF mission to Poland dismissed the idea of a stabilization fund.

Fortunately, the Poles were able to lobby the United States directly (thank goodness for Chicago voters), the zloty stabilization fund was established without the IMF's initiative, and Poland succeeded in breaking the hyperinflation. Again, Poland's success was later championed as an IMF success story.

In 1992, Estonia wanted to break out of the disastrous hyperinflation that gripped the 15 successor states of the Soviet Union. The IMF's brief was both ludicrous and explicit: Try to keep all of the successor states joined in a common ruble currency, which would be managed from 15 capitals, with 15 coordinated IMF programs. The vision was preposterous: Any introductory economics student would have figured out that with 15 independent central banks all issuing credit in a shared currency, the outcome would be continuing hyperinflation. The Estonians told the IMF that they would introduce their own currency with or without the IMF support. The IMF relented in Estonia, and the Estonians became the first stable post-Soviet economy. Not only was Estonia paraded as an IMF success story, but the hapless other 14 successor states—which experienced a full year more of hyperinflation under the IMF's flawed policy—were castigated by the fund for their errant ways.

In Bulgaria in 1996, the IMF praised the government for its continuing reforms, and signed a new agreement with the Bulgarian government for a one-year loan. The program forecast a zero growth rate in 1996 and 2.5 percent for 1997. The IMF recognized that there was a budding banking crisis but neither the IMF nor the Bulgarian government really knew how to handle it. In a ham-handed way, the IMF and the government decided to take "tough" action, including the announcement of sudden bank closures. Depositors panicked; the rest of the banks collapsed, and the flight from the currency produced a hyperinflation. Defying IMF predictions, in 1996 GDP collapsed by 10.9 percent (in fact, this represents a staggering fall of around 20 percent in the second half of 1996). Of course, the IMF blamed the entire mishap on the government. Ironically, the IMF has entered Asia with the same ill-prepared calls for immediate bank closures.

Bulgaria is one of three recent IMF cases that resemble the Asian financial crisis. The other two are Mexico and Argentina in 1995. These second two IMF interventions are often viewed as great IMF success stories, but a closer look is disquieting. In Mexico in 1994, as in East Asia in 1997, foreign creditors turned abruptly from euphoria to flight. The outflow of funds started moderately in April 1994; it became a stampede in December 1994, following the devaluation of the Mexican peso. Like Asia, Mexico was basically a solvent, creditworthy country hit by a panicked withdrawal of foreign funds. And like today's crisis countries in Asia, Mexico had so much short-term debt that the sudden withdrawal of confidence threatened to push Mexico into default.

The United States and the IMF led a bailout operation in early 1995. The IMF was assigned the task of designing the "macroeconomic framework"—the set of monetary, interest rate, exchange rate, and fiscal policy targets—to accompany the bailout loan to Mexico. The IMF didn't really understand the Mexican crisis, and treated it incorrectly as a typical case of a profligate government rather than crisis in the private capital markets. The IMF called for a lot of monetary and fiscal stringency that unnecessarily added to the contractionary effects of the creditor panic. In setting up the program, the IMF forecast a Mexican growth rate of 1.5 percent in 1995. The actual outcome was –6.1 percent. This whopping prediction error of 7.6 percentage points within the year was never explained, and apparently did not lead the IMF to reconsider its strategy in Mexico or in similar countries.

Three months after the Mexico shock, Argentina felt the tidal wave of investor panic. Once again, the IMF was thrust into a case of banking crisis made in the private sector rather than the government sector. Once again, the IMF resorted to its tried-and-true tactics: budget cuts, interest rate increases, a credit squeeze. And once again, the IMF left a benchmark for judging its own work. As of April 1995, the IMF projected Argentine GDP growth of 2 percent to 3 percent in 1995. The actual outcome was –4.6 percent, again a miss of around 7 percent of GDP within the very year of the program.

The list of questionable judgments can be extended into many other areas. Just to name a few:

- The IMF rejected the idea of debt relief for seven years after the outbreak of the developing-country debt crisis in 1982. Official IMF policy insisted that no relief was needed. When the U.S. Treasury finally shifted position in April 1989, the IMF suddenly swung around. There was, apparently, no follow-up review of why the decision on debt relief had been so long delayed, and at what cost.
- While many high-profile countries have received debt relief after 1989, many of the poorest of the poor have continued to languish. The recent IMF-World Bank initiative on debt relief for Highly Indebted Poor Countries (HIPC) was long delayed, and is exceedingly limited in scope and lacking in urgency.
- The IMF has missed the boat in the former Soviet Union, failing to help countries to institute separate national currencies until after they had been ravaged by hyperinflation, and generally failing to address the linkages between corruption, disastrous tax systems, poor public management, and ongoing macroeconomic turmoil.
- The IMF rejected stabilization funds for Russia and other transition

economies when they could have been useful. It finally adopted the policy of supporting such funds in 1995. Again, there was no external review of past decisions.

AN ACCOUNTABLE IMF

It is high time that we take the IMF seriously—seriously enough to hold it accountable for its actions, its failed forecasts, and the details of the "advice" that it imposes on the developing world. The IMF will be with us for the foreseeable future. The name of the game is reform, not elimination of the institution. Public bureaucracies need to be tamed by transparency, disclosure, oversight, and where possible, competition. Before Congress delivers more money to the institution, the IMF should be held accountable to the same standards of good governance that it sanctimoniously preaches for others.

First, all IMF program documents should be made public, and thereby open to public debate and critical scrutiny. Even with $100 billion of taxpayers' money on the line, the programs in Asia were not made public by the IMF (in fact, Korea made the main loan agreement public a couple of weeks after signing, while the Thailand and Indonesia documents remain confidential). In some cases, a delay of a few weeks or even months might be understandable, when market-sensitive information must be withheld. The current system of a 30-year embargo of program documents is preposterous. In addition, the IMF archives should be opened so that scholars and market participants can better understand what the IMF has done and failed to do in the past. What really happened in Russia, Mexico, and Argentina? How did the IMF decide on its strategy for the developing-country debt crises?

Second, the executive board should start doing its job of overseeing the staff, rather than simply rubber-stamping the staff's programs. A properly functioning executive board, perhaps with voting weights adjusted to reflect economic realities, would realize that there is more information, informed opinion, and ideas around than are found within the fund itself. With issues as complex and challenging as the debt crisis, postcommunist market transition, the Asian currency crisis, or the failures of economic growth in Africa, the executive board should take the lead in canvassing outside opinion and testing the IMF staff's recommendations and approaches. The executive board should also take the minimal step of formalizing a process of external review and evaluation of past programs. The World Bank introduced external evaluations as a result of strong pressures from environmental groups aghast at the environmental mismanagement of World Bank projects. By many accounts, the process has added integrity and discipline to World Bank programs.

Finally, and most importantly, it is time to end the IMF's artificial monopoly on policymaking in the developing world. The IMF complains frequently that member governments don't feel proper "ownership" of the programs that they sign with the IMF, and therefore that these governments fail to implement them adequately. The subtext is clear: "Ownership" is simply a buzzword meaning happier compliance with the directives from Washington. It is time for real ownership in the developing world. This will come when programs are designed by member governments, with the help rather than the command of the IMF, thereby making it far more likely that programs will be tailored to the specific and complex circumstances of the particular countries. Some of the favorite nostrums of the IMF and the U.S. government—such as insisting that countries open their capital markets to global markets even before adequate banking supervision is in place—will fall by the wayside as the realities of local circumstances are brought to the fore. Better advice from the start will save us the headaches—and the tens of billions of dollars—that expensive bailout operations cost.

As democracies gain strength in Latin America, Africa, postcommunist Europe, and developing Asia, we should expect and rejoice in the moral authority and political legitimacy of elected leaders to chart the economic course for their nations. The G-7 and the IMF itself should give these new democracies the space to act. The IMF's advice might prove useful—even welcome—if it becomes part of a true collaboration between rich and poor nations in search of common global goals.

The IMF's Response to the Asian Crisis

INTERNATIONAL MONETARY FUND

JANUARY 17, 1999

The financial crisis that erupted in Asia in mid-1997 led to sharp declines in the currencies, stock markets, and other asset prices of a number of Asian countries ... threatened these countries' financial systems; and disrupted their real economies, with large contractions in activity that created a human crisis alongside the financial one. In addition to its severe effects in Asia, the crisis has put pressure on emerging markets outside the region; contributed to virulent contagion and volatility in international financial markets; and is expected to halve the rate of world growth in both 1998 and 1999, from the rates of some 4 percent that were projected precrisis for both years, to an estimated outcome of about 2 percent.

ORIGINS OF THE CRISIS

The crisis unfolded against the backdrop of several decades of outstanding economic performance in Asia, and the difficulties that the East Asian countries face are not primarily the result of macroeconomic imbalances. Rather, they stemmed from weaknesses in financial systems and, to a lesser extent, governance. A combination of inadequate financial sector supervision, poor assessment and management of financial risk, and the maintenance of relatively fixed exchange rates led banks and corporations to borrow large amounts of international capital, much of it short-term, denominated in foreign currency, and unhedged. As time went on, this inflow of foreign capital tended to be used to finance poorer-quality investments.

Although private sector expenditure and financing decisions led to the crisis, it was made worse by governance issues, notably government involvement in the private sector and lack of transparency in corporate and fiscal accounting and the provision of financial and economic data. Developments in the advanced economies, such as weak growth in

Europe and Japan that left a shortage of attractive investment opportunities and kept interest rates low in those economies, also contributed to the buildup of the crisis.

After the crisis erupted in Thailand with a series of speculative attacks on the baht, contagion spread rapidly to other economies in the region that seemed vulnerable to an erosion of competitiveness after the devaluation of the baht or were perceived by investors to have similar financial or macroeconomic problems. As the contagion spread to Korea, the world's eleventh largest economy, the possibility of a default by Korea raised a potential threat to the international monetary system.

THE IMF'S ROLE IN THE INTERNATIONAL MONETARY SYSTEM AND IN FINANCIAL CRISES

The IMF is charged with safeguarding the stability of the international monetary system. Thus, a central role for the IMF in resolving the Asian financial crisis was clear, and has been reaffirmed by the international community in various multilateral fora. The IMF's priority was also clear: to help restore confidence to the economies affected by the crisis.

THE IMF'S IMMEDIATE RESPONSE TO THE CRISIS

In pursuit of its immediate goal of restoring confidence in the region, the IMF responded quickly by:

Helping the three countries most affected by the crisis—Indonesia, Korea, and Thailand—arrange programs of economic stabilization and reform that could restore confidence and be supported by the IMF;[1]

Approving in 1997 some SDR 26 billion or about US$35 billion of IMF financial support[2] for reform programs in Indonesia, Korea, and Thailand, and spearheading the mobilization of some US$77 billion of additional financing from multilateral and bilateral sources in support of these reform programs. . . . In July 1998, committed assistance for Indonesia was augmented by an additional US$1.3 billion from the IMF and an estimated US$5 billion from multilateral and bilateral sources; and

Intensifying its consultations with other members both within and outside the region that were affected by the crisis and needed to take policy steps to ward off the contagion effects, although not necessarily requiring IMF financial support.

The IMF's immediate effort to reestablish confidence in the affected countries entailed:

A temporary tightening of monetary policy to stem exchange rate depreciation;

Concerted action to correct the weaknesses in the financial system, which contributed significantly to the crisis;

Structural reforms to remove features of the economy that had become impediments to growth (such as monopolies, trade barriers, and nontransparent corporate practices) and to improve the efficiency of financial intermediation and the future soundness of financial systems;

Efforts to assist in reopening or maintaining lines of external financing; and

The maintenance of a sound fiscal policy, including providing for rising budgetary costs of financial sector restructuring, while protecting social spending. Once the severity of the economic downturn in the affected countries became clear, fiscal policy was oriented toward supporting economic activity and expanding the social sector safety net.

Forceful, far-reaching structural reforms are at the heart of all the programs, marking an evolution in emphasis from many of the programs that the IMF has supported in the past, where the underlying country problem was imbalances reflecting inappropriate macroeconomic policies.

Because financial sector problems were a major cause of the crisis, the centerpiece of the Asian programs has been the comprehensive reform of financial systems. While tailored to the needs of individual countries, in all cases the programs have arranged for:

The closure of unviable financial institutions, with the associated write down of shareholders' capital;

The recapitalization of undercapitalized institutions;

Close supervision of weak institutions; and

Increased potential for foreign participation in domestic financial systems.

To address the governance issues that also contributed to the crisis, the reform of the financial systems is being buttressed by measures designed to improve the efficiency of markets, break the close links between business and governments, and ensure that the integration of the national economy with international financial markets is properly segmented. Transparency is being increased, both as regards economic (on external reserves and liabilities in particular) and fiscal data, and in the financial and corporate sectors.

The reform efforts have been invaluably aided by the World Bank, with its focus on the structural and sectoral issues that underpin the macroeconomy, and the Asian Development Bank (ADB), with its regional specialization. The IMF's Interim Committee reviewed and endorsed the overall strategy adopted by the international community in dealing with the Asian crisis at the 1998 Bank-Fund Annual Meetings in October.

Details on the programs of economic reform, chronological highlights, and economic indicators for Thailand, Indonesia, and Korea, respectively indicate that for all three countries, the programs have been adapted, reinforced, or accelerated, as economic developments have unfolded and as economic and financial conditions have warranted.

ADDITIONAL MEASURES TAKEN BY THE IMF IN RESPONSE TO THE CRISIS

In addition to the IMF's first line of response—assisting in the design of the programs and providing financial resources for their support—the following steps have also been taken:

The Executive Board made use of the accelerated procedures established under the emergency financing mechanism and the exceptional circumstances clause[3] to meet the exceptional needs of the member countries in terms of approval time and access.

The Supplemental Reserve Facility (SRF) was created, for the special circumstances of members experiencing exceptional balance of payments difficulties owing to a large short-term financing need resulting from a sudden loss of market confidence.

The coordination of the IMF with the other international financial institutions, notably the World Bank and the Asian Development Bank, and with bilateral donors was intensified, to muster truly international support for the affected countries' economic reform programs.

A strengthened level of dialogue between the IMF and a variety of constituencies in the program countries was initiated, including consultations with labor groups and extensive contacts with the press and the public.

The IMF programs have been associated with coordinated efforts between international creditor banks and debtors in the affected countries to resolve the severe private sector financing problems at the heart of the crisis, and the IMF has provided support to this process as appropriate. Thailand reached an early understanding on debt roll-over with key Japanese creditor banks in August 1997. Talks between Korea and a group of foreign creditor banks on the voluntary restructuring of short-term debt began in late December 1997 and were finalized in March 1998. In June 1998, Indonesia and a steering committee of its foreign bank creditors agreed on a framework for the voluntary restructuring of interbank debt, trade credit, and corporate debt.

IMF member countries have attained new levels of transparency through the release to the public of the letters of intent describing their programs of economic reform. With the permission of the respective authorities of Indonesia, Korea, and Thailand, the IMF has posted the letters of intent on the IMF website so that details of the programs are readily available to all interested parties. Korea and Thailand have also issued Public Information Notices (PINs), a relatively new means for countries to make known to the public the views of the IMF Executive Board on national economic policies. All three countries are subscribers to the IMF Special Data Dissemination Standard (SDDS), and Indonesia and Thailand have established hyperlinks from the IMF Dissemination Standards Bulletin Board (DSBB) to their respective national economic and financial data.

Ad hoc measures have been taken as necessary, including the appointment of former IMF Deputy Managing Director Prabhakar Narvekar as a Special Advisor to the Indonesian authorities; the establishment of resident representative posts in Korea and Thailand (and the expansion of the existing post in Indonesia); and various activities through the IMF's newly opened Asia and Pacific Regional Office.

The IMF has been responding to the requests it has received from its members, from its own Interim Committee and from multilateral fora such as the Group of Seven and the Group of Twenty-Four nations, to investigate aspects related to the financial crisis, from the role of hedge funds, to promoting financial sector soundness and strengthening the architecture of the international monetary system.[4]

Amid the urgent need for a concerted international response to the crisis situation, the great uncertainty in Asia, and the unexpectedly virulent financial contagion, the IMF-supported programs have, as would be expected, come under scrutiny from a wide range of commentators, and a healthy debate is taking place. The IMF has undertaken and made public a rigorous, albeit preliminary, internal review of the design and early experiences with IMF-supported programs in Indonesia, Korea, and Thailand, in part to contribute to this debate.[5] However, some criticisms of the programs are based on fundamental misunderstandings about the IMF's response to events in Asia.

EARLY RESULTS AND THE OUTLOOK

The crisis in Asia is still unfolding and further disturbances cannot be ruled out, especially in light of significant, unanticipated setbacks. The magnitude of the recessions in the affected Asian countries has exceeded all initial expectations. Political instability and the related social and economic disturbances in Indonesia in May 1998 hindered progress there. The further weakening of the Japanese economy has had a particularly large, negative impact on demand in the region and on international financial market sentiment. Following the several waves of pressure on emerging markets since 1997 that had emanated mainly from Asia, Russia became a new source of contagion during August 1998, causing confidence to deteriorate further globally. Brazil, which has taken steps to address its chronic fiscal imbalances and obtain large-scale financial support for its program of economic reform from the international community, has been susceptible to market contagion and volatility. It is a real risk that market confidence may not recover for some time, which could imply significant net outflows of foreign capital from many economies, as witnessed in the Asian crisis countries, with prolonged depressive effects on trade and activity. However, this risk can be contained, as long as the Asian crisis countries and other affected economies continue to implement the right stabilization and reform policies that will help to generate recovery.

Despite the significant setbacks that have occurred in the resolution of the Asian crisis, there has also been notable progress in some countries in the implementation of corrective policies and the stabilization of exchange rates:

The exchange rates of the Asian crisis economies have strengthened from their lows, which were reached in the first part of 1998. While the Indonesian rupiah remains deeply depreciated, it too has recovered significantly.

In Korea and Thailand, interest rates have declined markedly since January as currency pressures have eased. In fact, in both countries, interest rates have fallen to pre-crisis levels.

Korea and Thailand, in particular, have made significant progress in macroeconomic stabilization and have begun to implement structural reforms. In Indonesia, the modified policy program in effect since late June 1998 has been implemented broadly as planned, with some positive results.

The turnarounds in current account positions, from deficit to surplus, have been rapid and large for all three countries.

Equity prices rose significantly from their lows in Korea and Thailand in 1998.

Reserves have strengthened substantially in Korea and Thailand, and Korea made repurchases to the IMF under the Supplemental Reserve Facility totalling US$2.8 billion in December 1998, indicating the progress made in the country's emergence from its foreign exchange crisis one year earlier.

Amid these signs of progress, the IMF remains acutely concerned about the greater-than-anticipated contractions in economy activity in the affected countries, and is well aware that much hard work remains to be done in terms of economic restructuring and the temporary adverse effects that it can have on output and employment. It is focusing efforts on its intermediate goal of shortening and easing the adjustment period in the program countries, including:

The alleviation of the social costs of adjustment, including through strengthening and expanding the social safety net and encouraging a social dialogue among employers, employees, and government; and

The easing of the effect of credit tightness and reductions in trade financing on exporters and small and medium enterprises, and other measures to support domestic demand.

Targeted fiscal positions have been eased over time to allow for greater social spending in all three affected countries. In Indonesia, for example, the overall budgetary cost of social safety net programs has been targeted at about 8 percent of GDP per annum, with a projected fiscal deficit to accommodate the social spending. The social spending includes funding to help increase the availability of food, fuel, and medicine to those in need; employment-generating programs targeted to poor and vulnerable regions and households; health expenditure, including on village health centers and immunization programs; and student aid to minimize the decline in school enrollment.

Amid the sharp recessions and heavy social costs of the crisis, there are nonetheless indications that if countries persist in implementing programs of economic stabilization and reform, and if financial market confidence gradually returns—which depends on, among other things, Japan implementing its planned fiscal stimulus and bank restructuring— the affected Asian economies could begin to recover in the course of 1999.[6] Small declines in output or modest recoveries are in prospect, except for Indonesia, where the reform process is less advanced and political uncertainties have complicated economic difficulties. While the situation in all the countries is tenuous, there have been some signs of bottoming out in Korea and Thailand. The rate of decline in industrial production has begun to moderate in recent months; recently, the unemployment rate in Korea has declined slightly, and the sale of new vehicles in Thailand, an indicator of consumer confidence and of the strength of the nonbank financial sector, rose on a 12-month basis for the first time since the beginning of the crisis.

LESSONS FROM THE CRISIS AND THE WAY FORWARD

While the Asian financial crisis is still unfolding, the IMF has already begun to draw lessons from the crisis on how to strengthen the architecture of the international financial system to lessen the frequency and severity of future disturbances. The Asian crisis has once again high-lighted the importance of a sound macroeconomic policy framework, and the dangers of unsustainably large current account deficits. Beyond this, the IMF has identified six major areas where initiatives already under way should be strengthened:

One, more effective surveillance over countries' economic policies and practices, facilitated by fuller disclosure of all relevant economic and financial data. The IMF has established, and will further improve, data standards to guide members in releasing reliable and timely data to the public. The Fund is presently engaging in a consultative process with all interested parties concerning the reporting of data on monetary authorities' foreign reserves, amid the growing recognition after the developments in Asian financial markets of the importance of gross reserve and related data;

Two, financial sector reform, including better prudential regulation and supervision. Working with the Basle Committee on Banking Supervision and the World Bank, the Fund has helped develop and disseminate a set of "best practices" in the banking area;

Three, ensuring that the integration of international financial markets is orderly and properly sequenced (supported by, among other things, a sound financial sector and appropriate macroeconomic and exchange rate policies) in order to maximize the benefits from and minimize the risks of international capital movements;

Four, promoting regional surveillance;

Five, a worldwide effort to promote good governance and fight against corruption, including the adoption by the Interim Committee of the Board of Governors of the IMF on April 16, 1998 of the "Code of Good Practices on Fiscal Transparency—Declaration on Principles" to serve as a guide for members, and to enhance the accountability and credibility of fiscal policy as a key feature of good governance; and

Six, more effective structures for orderly debt workouts, including better bankruptcy laws at the national level and better ways at the international level of associating private sector creditors and investors with official efforts to help resolve sovereign and private debt problems.

These efforts need to be supported by adequate financial resources for the IMF, supplemented in case of need by other bilateral and multilateral resources, that can be deployed in support of strong adjustment programs. Progress toward implementation of the IMF quota increase and the New Arrangements to Borrow (NAB) have improved the international community's ability to assist countries in the resolution of financial crises.

All of the above steps support the long-term objective of the IMF's response to the Asian financial crisis, which is to enable the affected Asian economies to emerge more strongly to resume development and to help strengthen the international monetary system to meet the challenges of the next century.

NOTES

1. The Philippines extended and augmented its existing IMF-supported program in 1997, and arranged a stand-by facility in 1998.
2. Amounts denominated in the IMF unit of account, the Special Drawing Right (SDR), have been converted to dollar amounts at an exchange rate of 1SDR = US$1.35.
3. The emergency financing mechanism strengthens the IMF's ability to respond swiftly in support of a member country facing an external financial crisis and seeking financial assistance from the IMF in support of a strong economic adjustment program. The exceptional circumstances clause allows the IMF to grant a member access to its resources in excess of the usual limits.
4. See, "The Report of the Managing Director to the Interim Committee on Strengthening the Architecture of the International Monetary System," October 1998.
5. See, "IMF-Supported Programs in Indonesia, Korea, and Thailand: A Preliminary Assessment," January 1999.
6. See the December 1998 IMF World Economic Outlook.

PART IV
Democracy at Risk

Issue 12
The Future of Democracy

INTRODUCTION

What is the greatest danger facing democracy in the world today? The authors of the articles in this section offer similar yet distinct answers. Both agree that technology and globalization are transforming the international political landscape. For Benjamin R. Barber, democracy may die from apathy. Although Americans claim to champion democracy, Barber charges, hunger for the profits to be gained from our dominance of global technology leads us to ignore challenges to democracy whenever they conflict with our desire to gain wealth. For Arthur M. Schlesinger, Jr., however, democracy has always been threatened by a wide array of political, social, and economic forces, some of which, like Nazism and communism, nearly threatened the continuation of democracy in the twentieth century.

Part of the problem is that there is still no general agreement on precisely what democracy is. The common formula requires a balance of majority rule and minority rights. Around the world, however, elected leaders sometimes exercise nearly dictatorial power while claiming to observe all rights. Can democracy long retain its cogency under such conditions?

Schlesinger maintains that religious, racial, and ethnic differences continuously undermine democratic states. The dissolution of the former Soviet Union and the wars in and among the new states of the former Yugoslavia indeed pose some of the most serious challenges to the stability of the international community at the end of the twentieth century. But are these conflicts challenges to democracy or to certain types of nationalism? If we examine Schlesinger's argument more carefully, perhaps we shall conclude that democracy is defective. It simply does not solve all the problems it was meant to solve. After all, when James Madison wrote his defense of the U.S. Constitution in *Federalist Papers* 10 and 51, he claimed that democracy alone could not resolve the number one threat to stability in society: "the violence of faction." According to Madison, the division of rich and poor in society leads everywhere and always to a division of interests that normally results in violence. In order to avoid the violence of faction, a nation must have a republic with a government with divided powers among competing groups. Only checks and balances could assure freedom. It is not the participation inherent in democracy, therefore, but the limitations on power imposed by a republican framework that guarantees order and freedom. If we agree with Madison, we must look to republican representational forms of government to secure democratic freedoms, and it is precisely these republican forms that governments across the world have such difficulty in instituting.

But Benjamin Barber also has a problem, which may be a Marxist critique in disguise. By 1850, the writings of Karl Marx and Friedrich Engels announced that economics dominates politics. By World War I, Lenin had published his analysis of imperialism, in which he said that the monopolistic power of world capitalist institutions was creating a new international regime that respected neither national identity nor ethnic pride.

Do either Barber or Schlesinger offer anything new to our understanding of the challenges facing democracy?

As you read the articles, consider the following questions.

Discussion Questions

1. What is democracy?
2. To what extent do Americans truly value democracy?
3. Do challenges to democracy exist that neither Barber nor Schlesinger have identified?

> For more information on this topic, visit the following websites:
>
> http://www.democracy.net/
> Democratic participation
>
> http://www.worldpolicy.org/americas/democracy/democracy,html
> Electoral Systems of the World
>
> http://info.acm.org/crossroads/xrds1-4/democracy.html
> Direct Democracy

Democracy at Risk:
American Culture in a Global Culture

BENJAMIN R. BARBER

Is American culture global? Internationalists often insist that it is, but it comes closer to the truth to say that global culture is American—increasingly trapped within American culture in its technologically facilitated, free market supported, globalizing form. While it is fashionable to try to tame the idea of the Americanizing of global culture by referring to dialectical interactions and two-way interfaces that make America global even as the globe becomes American, to me this is either wishful thinking on the part of those subjected to the depredations of what I have called "McWorld,"[1] or diplomatic rationalization by the corporate beneficiaries of globalization who want to disguise their new soft hegemony in a still softer ideological cloak.

This cloak deploys the metaphors of reciprocity and mutual assimilation, which suggest that dominant cultures are themselves modified by the cultures they affect to modify. But this is a peculiar reciprocity—the reciprocity of the python who swallows the hare: "Oh look!" cry fans of the hare, "the python has not swallowed the hare, the hare has swallowed the python! For see how like a hare the python looks!" But of course after a week or two of active digestion, the hare is gone and only the python remains.

McWorld does take on the colors of the cultures it swallows up—for a while: thus the pop music accented with Reggae and Latino rhythms in the Los Angeles barrio, Big Macs served with French wine in Paris or made from Bulgarian beef in Eastern Europe, Mickey speaking French at Euro-Disney. But, in the end, MTV and McDonald's and Disneyland are American cultural icons, seemingly innocent Trojan-American horses nosing their way into other nations' cultures.

McWorld represents an American push into the future animated by onrushing economic, technological, and ecological forces that demand integration and uniformity and that mesmerize people everywhere with fast music, fast computers, and fast food, MTV, Macintosh, and McDonald's—pressing nations into one homogeneous global culture, one

Benjamin R. Barber is the director of the Walt Whitman Center for the Culture and Politics of Democracy at Rutgers University, as well as the author of numerous books, including *Strong Democracy, Jihad vs. McWorld*, and, most recently, *A Place for Us: How to Make Society Civil and Democracy Strong*.
Reprinted by permission. *World Policy Journal*, Summer 1998. Vol. 15, No. 2, p. 29.

McWorld tied together by communications, information, entertainment, and commerce.

Even where McWorld is opposed by forces of reactionary tribalism and traditional religion, it trumps its opponents. Iranian zealots may keep one ear tuned to the mullahs urging holy war, but the other is cocked to Rupert Murdoch's Star Television, which beams in *Dynasty* reruns or *The Simpsons* from hovering satellites. Underneath their chadors, Iran's women wear Western high-fashion outfits, which, the moment they leave the transparency of public space and enter the opaque safety of the private, they flaunt as if they were in Paris or Rome. The Russian Orthodox Church may remain a bastion of faith in Russia's privatizing world, but it has nonetheless managed to enter into a joint venture with California businessmen to bottle and sell natural waters from the Saint Springs. Brooding neo-Nazis in America's far-right "militias" are comfortable recruiting on the Internet, and both the far left and the far right have turned to rock music to get their traditional messages out to the new generation.

DEMOCRACY AT RISK

This new globalizing culture is likely to displace not only its reactionary critics but its democratic rivals, who dream of a genuinely internationalized civil society made up of free citizens from many different cultures. For America's global culture is not so much hostile as indifferent to democracy: its goal is a global consumer society comprised neither of tribesmen (too commercially challenged to shop) nor of citizens (too civically engaged to shop), both of whom make lousy clients, but of consumers. Consumers are a new breed of women and men who are equal (potential customers all) without being just; and who are peaceful (placid and reactive rather than active) without being democratic.

In Europe, Asia, and the Americas, markets have already eroded national sovereignty and given birth to a new global culture of international banks, trade associations, transnational lobbies like OPEC, world news services like CNN and the BBC, and multinational corporations, the new sovereigns of a world where nation-states scarcely know how to regulate their own economies, let alone control runaway global markets. While mills and factories sit on sovereign territory under the eye and potential regulation of nation-states, currency markets and the Internet exist everywhere, but nowhere in particular. And although they produce neither common interests nor common law, common markets do demand, along with a common currency, a common language (English, which Japanese teenagers now prefer to use whenever possible and which is an official, if not the official, language of every international conference held today).

Moreover, common markets produce common behaviors of the kind bred by cosmopolitan city life everywhere. Commercial pilots, computer programmers, film directors, international bankers, media specialists, oil riggers, entertainment celebrities, ecology experts, movie producers, demographers, accountants, professors, lawyers, athletes—these comprise a new breed of men and women for whom religion, culture, and ethnic nationality are marginal elements in a working identity. It is shopping that has a common signature today around the world. Cynics might even suggest that some of the recent revolutions in Eastern Europe had as their true goal not liberty and the right to vote but well-paying jobs and the right to shop. It is perhaps no surprise that as the Communists and nationalists return to power in Russia and Hungary and elsewhere, it is not shopping but only democracy that is put at risk.

Shopping means consumption and consumption depends on the fabrication of needs as well as goods. As I argued in *Jihad vs. McWorld,* the new global culture is a product of American popular culture driven by expansionist commerce. Its template is American, its form is style. Its goods are as much images as material, an aesthetic as well as a product line. It is about culture as commodity, where what you think is defined by what you wear and apparel becomes a species of ideology. Think about those Harley-Davidson motorcycles and Cadillac motorcars that have been hoisted from the roadways to the marquees of global-market cafes like the Harley-Davidson and the Hard Rock. They are not about transportation anymore. You no longer drive them, their iconographic messages drive you. They conjure up synthetic behavior from old movies and new celebrities, whose personal appearances are the key to such popular international cafe chains as Planet Hollywood.

The new churches of this global commercial civilization are shopping malls, the privatized "public" squares and neighborless "neighborhoods" of suburbia. The new products are not so much goods as image exports that help create a common world taste around common logos, advertising slogans, celebrities, songs, brand names, jingles, and trademarks. Hard power here yields to soft, while ideology is transmuted into what I have called a kind of videology that works through sound bites and film clips. Videology is fuzzier and less dogmatic than traditional political ideology; as a consequence it may be far more successful in instilling the novel values required for global markets to succeed.

These values are not imposed by coercive governments or authoritative schools, but bleed into the culture from such pseudocultural products as films and advertising, which feel neither coercive nor intrusive but are often linked to a world of material goods, fast food, fashion accessories, and entertainment. *The Lion King* and *Jurassic Park* are not just films; they are global merchandising machines that sell food, music, clothes, and toys. *Titanic* is a billion-dollar movie, which makes it much more than just a movie.

America's global culture is nearly irresistible. Japan has, for example, become more culturally insistent on its own traditions in recent years, even as its people seek an ever greater purchase on McWorld. Burgers and fries now dominate noodles and sushi, and Japanese teens struggle with English phrases they hardly understand to project a sense of global cool. In France, another country that prided itself on resistance to McWorld, and where less than a decade ago cultural purists complained bitterly of a looming Sixieme Republique ("la Republique Americaine") and assailed the corruptions of franglais, economic health is today measured in part by the success of EuroDisney just outside of Paris. And though the Socialist government of Lionel Jospin struggles to preserve some sense of France's commitment to social welfare against the tide of privatistic market thinking that is sweeping across the Western world, France becomes more and more commercial in a manner that is more and more American. The sudden appearance of "Aloween" as a holiday to alleviate the shopping doldrums of the pre-pre-Christmas season is only the most appealing (and appalling) example of this tendency.

MACRO-PEACE

Homogenization is not the whole story, of course. In light of the continuing existence of tribal bloodshed, terrorism, religious extremism, right-wing fanaticism, and civil war throughout the world, prophecies about the end of history look terminally dumb. But if microwars persist, McWorld's pacifying markets are likely to establish a macropeace that favors the triumph of commerce and consumerism and gives to those who control information, communications, and entertainment ultimate (if inadvertent) control over global culture—and over human destiny. This suggests that the historian Paul Kennedy's worry about the decline of America,[2] predicated largely on the decline of its traditional "hard goods" economy, is misplaced and that a renewed American hegemony is far more likely—although it will be a hegemony rooted in information and technology, not in GNP or the potential of the manufacturing sector.

Unless we can offer an alternative, the triumph of globalization is increasingly likely to mean not a global multiculture or a framework for co-operation in the context of difference, but the sacrifice of both variety and democracy to a totalizing consumerism that, without coercion, will rob us of our freedom and our character. The first casualty of McWorld is citizenship. The second is democracy. For a world of the ubiquitous consumer is a world of choice without power, of democracy without citizens, and in a world without citizens—although private economic choice may be maximized—there can be little real freedom and no democracy.

The mantra of free markets is globalism's siren call. Is there any activity more intrinsically globalizing than trade, any ideology less interested in nations than capitalism, any challenge to frontiers more audacious than the market? In a number of ways, corporations are today more the central players in global affairs than either nations or tribes. We say these global corporations are multinational, but they are more appropriately termed postnational, or even anti-national. They abjure the very idea of national boundaries or any other parochialism that limits them in time or space.

On "Planet Reebok," boasts the familiar athletic shoe campaign, "there are no boundaries." The ads for Ralph Lauren's designer perfume collections also reject boundaries, while a Coca-Cola campaign for the 1996 summer Olympics in Atlanta featured a blimp circumnavigating the globe trying to foment a "global" cola party among obviously distinct cultures, with each quickly succumbing to the lure of assimilationist cola consumerism.

A popular protectionist bumper sticker in the United States (one that predates the North American Free Trade Agreement) reads, "Real Americans Buy American," and many Americans believe that, in backing NAFTA, Washington sold out the country's labor interests. The trouble is that it is hard to know which car is really more American: The Chevy built in Mexico primarily from non-American imported parts and then shipped to the United States so American consumers can "buy American." The Ford built in Germany by Turkish workers for export to the Nigerian market. Or the Toyota Camry thought up at Toyota's Newport Beach (California) Design Center, built by American workers at the Georgetown, Kentucky, Toyota plant from parts that, other than the engine and drive train, are almost exclusively American, and test-driven at Toyota's 12,000-acre Arizona proving grounds.

To combat this creeping "foreignization" of American products, the government has instituted a system of automobile labels by which consumers are supposed to be informed of content percentages, foreign or American, but no one really knows how to do the calculations.

No wonder so many corporations refuse to define themselves in terms of their labor force. In the global economy, the determining factors are neither capital nor work nor material but rather how these three are manipulated by information, communications, and administration—the true levers of the new economics.

These levers are virtual rather than material, and they resist the kinds of physical and territorial regulation typical of traditional governmental monitoring (which itself has been hobbled by deregulatory ideology and the concept of the minimal state). The phrase "virtual corporation," which when Robert Kuttner, the economist and coeditor of *The American Prospect*, first used it a few years ago seemed novel, is now widely accepted.[3] In Kuttner's thinking, the corporation as a physical entity with a stable mission or location was likely to give way to a shifting set of temporary relationships connected by computer networks, telephone, and fax.

INVISIBLE BONDS

Can globalization defined in these ways support traditional understandings of democratic national sovereignty—the authority people supposedly exercise over the shaping of their communities and their lives? On the contrary, it would seem to be a calamity not just for nations but for their citizens. We talk about democratic markets and market democracy, but in truth markets decisively constrain democracy. The new bonds of the market are, however, invisible, even comfortable, accompanied as they are by a pleasant rhetoric of private choice and personal consumer freedom. "We give you liberty" proclaims an advertisement for a Midwestern baked potato chain, "because we give you the choice of toppings!" Global liberty looks more and more like the choice of toppings in a world where chain store spuds are the only available fare.

In the 1960s, the critical theorist Herbert Marcuse prophesied a conformitarian world brought to heel by technology rather than terror, in which civilized humanity would be reduced to "One Dimensional Man." But in the sixties, the other side of Marcuse's dialectic—the power of protest prevailed, and his prophecy seemed hyperbolic, even to him. For though he foresaw totalizing, even "totalitarian" tendencies in industrial culture, he also foresaw forces that might break the containment (he had celebrated the radical moment of resistance in Hegel's dialectic in his earlier *Reason and Revolution*).

Today, the potential of the market for assimilation of all distinctions and rebelliousness and the blurring of all ideological opposition (abetted by the fuzziness of borders between news and entertainment, information and amusement) give Marcuse's fears renewed currency. Global consumerism threatens a totalizing society in which consuming becomes the defining human essence. One-dimensionality achieves a palpable political geography in the controlled (and controlling) architecture of the shopping mall, where public squares have been supplanted by private spaces designed to maximize commerce. Malls are the privatized public squares of the new fringe city "privatopia" that secedes from the larger common society (vulgar, multiracial, and dangerous) to a gated world of placid safety.

MARKET PANACEAS

Supporters of free market ideology continue to dismiss this line of criticism as a stale rehearsal of Marcuse's overheated prophecies. Many argue that consumer society, though it may debase taste, nevertheless enhances choice and thus entails a kind of democracy: the sovereignty of consumers. But however "sovereign" consumers may feel, voting dollars or yen or euros is not the same as voting a common political will. Market relations are not a surrogate for social relations. The problem is not with capitalism per se, but with the notion that capitalism alone can respond to every human need and provide solutions to all of our problems.

Just as statist progressives may once have thought that a paternalistic government could solve every human problem, antistatist conservatives today are convinced not only that the state can solve no human problem, but that the market can now do everything that the state has failed to do. Where statist panaceas once were sovereign, market panaceas now seem to reign—with calamitous consequences. For privatization annihilates the very idea of the public and removes from under us the ground of our commonality.

Much of my earlier analysis of McWorld turned on my analysis of market mania: the disastrous modern confusion between the moderate and mostly well-founded claim that flexibly regulated markets remain the most efficient instruments of economic productivity and wealth accumulation, and the zany, overblown claim that naked, wholly unregulated markets are the sole means by which we can produce and distribute everything we care about—from durable goods to spiritual values, from capital development to social justice, from profitability today to sustainable environments into the next century, from Disneyland kiddie-play to serious culture, from private wealth to the essential commonweal.

This second claim has moved people who fear government to insist that goods as diverse and obviously public as education, culture, penology, full employment, social welfare, and ecological survival be handed over to the profit sector for arbitration and disposal. Having privatized prisons (nearly one out of every six inmates in the United States is now incarcerated in a privatized for-profit facility), will we next "outsource" the electric chair, turning over to the private sector the sovereign state's defining power over capital punishment? Crime pays, after all!

The disappointment with bureaucratic interventionalism in the name of well-meaning paternalistic welfare states has led to governmental downsizing, which has probably been a good thing for individual liberty and for civil society. But the effects of democratization via devolution are quite different from the effects of privatization.

Partnership between government and citizens of the kind being promoted by moderates on both sides of the political divide today is one thing; a modest devolution of power to state and municipal governments may improve the efficiency of the public sector even as it empowers civil society to take on greater responsibility. But wholesale privatization—which has become the magic potion of those who would restore the antique notion of the market's "invisible hand"—is a recipe for the destruction of our communities and our commonality, our sovereignty and our power to shape our common lives.

THE END OF DEMOCRACY

Privatization is not to be confused with decentralization, which involves the devolution of power to municipal and local governments and to the citizens who make them work. Privatization is not about the limitation of government; it is about the termination of democracy. For the "government" dismantled in our name is actually the only common power we possess to protect our common liberties and advance our common interest. Its destruction does less to emancipate us than to secure our servitude to global corporatism and consumer materialism.

American conservatives like William Bennett and Pat Buchanan have recognized as much, and the radical right in Europe is capitalizing on anxiety arising in the face of globalization (the export of jobs, the import of redundant labor) by engendering a new politics of fear. If the end of big government leaves big business with a monopoly over our needs and desires, the prospects for individual liberty and a robust civil society will diminish.

Markets, which permit us private rather than public modes of discourse, are simply not designed to do the things democratic communities can do. They allow us as consumers to tell producers what we want (or allow producers by means of advertising and cultural persuasion to tell us what we want), but prevent us from speaking as citizens to one another about the social consequences of our private consumer choices. As a consumer, I may want a car that goes 130 miles an hour, but as a citizen I can still vote for a reasonable speed limit that will conserve gasoline and secure safe streets. As a consumer, I prefer inexpensive goods, but that is not to say that as a citizen I will be unwilling to pay a surcharge to guarantee that what I buy is not manufactured by child labor.

There is no contradiction here: just the difference between the consumer and the citizen. The consumer in me and the citizen in me. Hence, as a private consumer, I may say, "I want a pair of expensive running shoes." But as a citizen I may say, "How about better athletic facilities in our public schools?" As a consumer I may pay to see violence-saturated

Hollywood thrillers and listen to woman-hating rap lyrics, but as a citizen I may support rating systems and warning labels that help us and our children make prudent moral judgments. The point is that markets preclude "we" thinking and "we" actions, trusting in the power of aggregated individual choices (the famous invisible hand) to somehow secure the common good. Only it does not work that way. The quest by consumers for private satisfaction and of producers for private profit simply does not add up to the satisfaction for citizens of their public interests.

Markets are contractual rather than communitarian: they stroke our solitary egos, offering durable goods and fleeting dreams, but not a common identity or collective membership, thus opening the way to more savage and undemocratic forms of identity such as tribalism. One of the twentieth century's most poignant lessons, taught by the sad history of the Weimar Republic as well as by the modern story of urban gangs, is simply this: if we cannot secure democratic communities to express our need for belonging, undemocratic communities will quickly offer themselves to us. From them we will get the warm fraternity and membership we look for in community, but at the expense of liberty and equality. Gangs instead of neighborhood associations, blood tribes instead of voluntary associations, misogynist fraternities instead of communities of common interest, an "Aryan Nation" instead of a democratic nation.

GLOBAL MARKETS

At the global level, the failure of institutions to provide meaningful forms of democratic membership (which is precisely global consumerism's failure) is likely to spawn new forms of global tribalism. Much of the opposition to "Europe" in democratic countries like Denmark and Switzerland arose out of a conviction that Europe was insufficiently democratic: too technocratic and bureaucratic and legalistic, good for corporate entities but less obviously beneficial to citizens. Markets give us the goods but not the lives we want; they provide prosperity for some but lead to despair for many and dignity for none. The world's 26,000 or more international nongovernmental organizations (NGOs) are no match for the Fortune 500 multinational corporations of McWorld. The institutions that are our nation's most formidable expression of sovereignty may no longer be able to rival McWorld's power.

The questions I raised five years ago in writing *Jihad vs. McWorld* are more relevant than ever. What, I asked then, is the Pentagon compared to Disneyland? Today, the Pentagon is reluctant to risk a single soldier's life in pursuit of American interests abroad, while Disney has taken over a major network, bought a baseball team, founded a sovereign synthetic living community in Celebration, Florida, salvaged (but sanitized) Times square, and made an attempt to "re-create" a battlefield of the Civil War on the "useless" turf where the war was actually contested. What then is G. I. Joe compared to the Mouse?

Can the U.S. Information Agency pretend to project America's image more cannily than Hollywood? What is the United Nations or—in the face of the Asian currency crisis—the International Monetary Fund, compared to the trillion-dollar-a-day global currency market? Such global institutions do not even have an address: you can call your broker to sell a declining stock, but who can Indonesia call when its currency goes down the drain (not George Soros, though it tried). Similarly, you can write to someone on the World Wide Web, but you cannot write to the Web itself, which is a virtual abstraction lost in the very cyberspace it defines, with neither a fax number nor a Web address.

Markets do not even know how to regulate themselves to survive, let alone to nurture democratic civic communities. They are unable to produce the kinds of regulatory antibodies they need in order to protect themselves from the self-generating viruses of monopoly and infectious greed: left to their own devices, corporations downsize until they have in effect fired not only their employees but their customers as well since, as Henry Ford understood, their employees turn out to be one and the same as their customers.

That is the paradox of McWorld. It cannot survive the conditions it inevitably tends to create unless it is checked and regulated by civic and democratic forces it inevitably tends to destroy. It destroys the financial base of the consumers it needs on the way to selling them products at more efficient prices. It overproduces goods and underproduces employment, unable to see the connection between them. It needs democracy more than democracy needs it, yet while democracy cultivates free markets, markets often fail to cultivate democracy. It is not an accident that China, the world's last great communist political system, without abdicating its totalitarian control, has become the world's fastest-growing market economy, even in these years of the Asian slowdown.

In spring 1996, Pepsi-Cola's director of East European operations allowed, "We think we can survive and prosper, whatever regime is going to be here [in Russia]." Governments may turn the clock back on democracy, but "whatever happens" they will not "turn back the clock on consumers and deny them modern, Western brands." Inundating frustrated peoples in transitional democracies with consumer goods they have identified with life in the "democratic West" has become a favorite ploy of governments wanting to retain dictatorial control. Consumerism may turn out to be to the new converts of free-market ideology what bread and circuses were during the Roman Empire: seductive diversions that give the appearance of freedom (shopping) without granting its real substance (self-government). That is certainly one of the lessons from China.

Advocates of privatization and markets have of course insisted that markets not only reinforce democracy but are themselves inherently and deeply democratic. This is again to confuse private choices made by consumers with civic choices made by citizens. It is to be deluded to think that the liberty to choose between 27 varieties of aspirin and the liberty to choose an affordable health system to which everyone will have full and equal access are the same.

The pretended autonomy of consumers permits producers to talk like populists: If we dislike the homogeneity of McWorld, don't blame its purveyors, indict its consumers. If popular taste is plastic, popular standards meretricious, and popular consumption homogenizing, impeach the populace whose choices are determinative, not the corporations whose profits depend solely on their faithfully serving that populace. The public is two-faced, conclude populist merchandisers: people say they detest television scandal mongering, but they watch it avidly. Exhausted by the Monica Lewinsky–Clinton coverage, news anchor Peter Jennings confesses that he does "not know how to account for the fact that the public is clearly fed up but continues to watch."

As if the quarter of a trillion dollar annual advertising expenditures of these same corporations were but window dressing; as if consumer tastes are established in a vacuum; as if the desires and wants on the basis of which markets prosper are not themselves engendered and shaped by those very same markets. As if consumer tastes were established in a vacuum rather than through what a recent *New Yorker* essay calls the "science of shopping," which has become a big business among consumer industry consultants who tell retailers where to strategically place goods and how to orchestrate store atmospherics. As if, finally, human beings were not complex and divided, often loathing what they "like," often finding it hard to live up to what they believe in.

"Save us from what we want!" has become the plaintive motto of unhappy moderns inundated with products they neither approve of nor feel able to resist. Living in a world where the puerile, the ignorant, the tawdry, and the base are everywhere privileged and rewarded, how can they honor the promise of their better selves? It may be that consumers want what they are proffered, but what they are proffered has a great deal to do with what they want.

SOFT POWER

The manipulation of wants has been accelerated by the interactive character of buying and selling in McWorld's ever softer markets. Hard consumer goods are becoming linked to soft technologies rooted in information, entertainment, and life style, and products are emerging that blur the line between goods and services. With the saturation of traditional markets and what the socio-economic commentator William Greider has described in his recent critique of global markets as a vast surfeit of goods, capitalism can no longer afford to serve only real needs and wants.[4] In the traditional economy, products were manufactured and sold for profit to meet the demand of consumers who made their needs known through the market. In the new postmodern capitalist economy, needs are manufactured to meet the supply of producers who market products through promotion, spin, packaging, advertising, and cultural persuasion.

Whereas the old economy, mirroring hard power, dealt in hard goods aimed at the body, the new economy, mirroring soft power, depends on soft services aimed at the mind and spirit. "I don't want customers to think that they are walking into a clothing store," says designer Donna Karan (DKNY). "I want them to think that they are walking into an environment, that I am transforming them out of their lives and into an experience, that it's not about clothes, it's about who they are as people."

Where once the body more or less spoke up for its natural needs, today the mind and spirit must be manipulated into wanting and needing all kinds of things of which neither the body could have demanded nor the autonomous mind dreamed. Why should millions of music lovers replace perfectly good vinyl LP collections for a marginal, indeed a quite controversial improvement in sound or size in the forms of CDs? And now the industry has announced that we have a new "need"—for DVD-RAM digital technology that will make the recent CD and videotape innovations obsolete. This compulsory obsolescence of what appear to be perfectly adequate technologies may pay tribute to human ingenuity, but more often than not it is a recognition of market greed.

The targeting of mind and spirit by corporations seeking to transform how humans think about "need" leads material markets into strange territory. As it assimilates and transforms so many other ideologies, postmodern capitalism has not shied away from assimilating and transforming religion. If Madonna can play erotic games with a crucifix, why shouldn't Mazda and American Express work to acquire some commercial purchase on the Holy Spirit? "Trucks," intones a gravelly voiced pitchman in a 1993 Mazda television ad, "are a spiritual thing for me." The new Mazda pickup is "like a friend . . . with a new V-6 and a soul to match."

To create a global demand for such American products as cigarettes, soft drinks, and running shoes—for which there can be said to be no natural "need"—need must be globally manufactured. For Coca-Cola, Marlboro, Nike, Hershey, Levi's, Pepsi, Wrigley, or McDonald's, selling American products means selling America, its popular culture, its putative prosperity, its ubiquitous imagery and software—and thus its very soul. Merchandizing is as much about symbols as about goods, about selling not life's necessities but life styles. The style being marketed is uniquely American yet potentially global. It is an incoherent and contradictory yet seductive style that is less "democratic" than physical-culture youthful, rich urban, austere cowboy, Hollywood glamorous, Garden of Eden unbounded, good-willed to a fault, socially aware, politically correct, mall-pervaded, and ironically often dominated by images of black ghetto life—black, however, as in Michael Jordan hip and rapper cool, rather than as in welfare-poor miserable and prison-bound squalid.

MANIPULATING HABITS

Because sales depend less on autonomous choices by independent buyers than on the manipulated habits and shaped behavior of media-immersed consumers, those who control markets cannot help but address behavior and attitude. Tea drinkers are improbable prospects for Coca-Cola sales, so when it entered the Asian market, the Coca-Cola company quite literally found it necessary to declare war on Indian tea culture. Long-lunch, eat-at-home traditions obstruct the development of fast food franchises. However, successful fast food franchises have inevitably undermined Mediterranean long-lunch, eat-at-home rituals, inadvertently corrupting "family values" as thoroughly as Hollywood action movies have done. For fast food is about accommodating a culture in which work is central and social relationships are secondary, in which fast trumps slow and simple beats complex. Highly developed public transportation systems attenuate automobile sales and depress steel, cement, rubber, and petroleum profits. Agricultural life styles (rise at daybreak, work all day, go to bed at dusk) may be inhospitable to television watching. People uninterested in spectator sports buy fewer athletic shoes. The moral logic of austerity that might appeal to serious Muslims or Christians or secular ascetics gets in the way of the economic logic of consumption. Tobacco companies have to target the young since use of their products tends to erode their consumer base.

Notice how so many of the new technological gadgets marketed as innovative ways of "liberating" us from the office and the workplace actually imprison us in an expanding zone of work. Do fax machines, cellular telephones, and home computer modems free us up or tie us down with electronic tentacles that make work ubiquitous? Even the Sony Walkman, that invitation to bring music to our leisure and work worlds, is in truth a device that artificially enhances the need to buy cassettes for 24-hour-a-day listening, even as it turns listening to music from a social into a solitary occupation and links it to other consumption-enhancing activities like jogging. Walkmen sell not just music but cassettes, and not only cassettes but athletic shoes as well—just as athletic shoes sell Walkmen and cassettes. You can take a walk in the woods (if you can find some woods) in a comfortable pair of old shoes and tune into nature's music for free; jogging to the music of a Whitney Houston movie sound track, on the other hand, means big profits for McWorld, as shoes, tapes, electronics, and a film are all sold at once.

Can responsible corporate managers then be anything other than irresponsible citizens in McWorld's new era of sovereign consumer markets? There is no conspiracy here, only an inadvertent triumph of the logic of private profits over the logic of public goods. To sell all that McWorld has to sell, sometime citizens must be made over into full-time consumers. That's why in place of our old town squares and multi-use urban downtowns we now have enclosed malls that offer nothing but commerce. These malls are not totalitarian in the same way that fascist and communist states once were, but they are in a similar fashion focused on monobehavioral activity, constructing a "new man" around activities suited to the obsessive preoccupation with profit. To this degree, we may call them "totalizing," if not totalitarian.

Malls are the capital cities and theme parks of McWorld's expanding nation: no community theater, no childcare center, no Hyde Park Speakers' Corner, no church or synagogue, no town hall, no grange, no schoolhouse—just one store after another and the demand that we shed every other identity except that of consumer, that we shed our sociability and our citizenship for the solitary pleasures of shopping. Nowadays, malls do not even pretend to sell "necessities" (no dry cleaners, no hardware store, no grocery store). Theme boutiques and gadget outlets—the Disney Store, the Sharper Image, Brookstone, and the Nature Store—predominate, and sell you nothing that you want until you get inside and realize you "need" everything they sell. To date, only in the pure suburbs like those on Long Island and in New Jersey do we find spaces with no public squares or sidewalks or multi-use centers of sociability. But imagine all the world as New Jersey.

THE ILLUSION OF COMPETITION

The autonomy of consumers is an illusion—the market's most democratic illusion. But there is another illusion, more basic and antique, in the arguments of those who insist that markets are democratic: this is that the market in which consumers shop is any freer than the shoppers themselves. Ironically, approximately egalitarian capitalist competition only began to exist under the watchful eye of interventionist, Keynesian democratic governments that used regulation and law to assure a competitive evenhandedness that markets were incapable of on their own. In this era of deregulation and government downsizing, the competitive vitality of markets has never been in greater jeopardy. Particularly in the newly sovereign market domain defined by information, entertainment, and telecommunications (the "infotainment telesector," as I have called it elsewhere), conglomeration and monopoly are becoming the rule.

Take Disney for example. Having domesticated the Lion King and the Beast, and having successfully annexed and tranquilized New York City's tenderloin district in Times Square, it also acquired Capital Cities/ABC for $19 billion, and now owns the Anaheim Angels baseball team. Likewise, Rupert Murdoch's News Corporation has bought the Los Angeles Dodgers in order to broadcast their games on its Fox television network and thus compete with Ted Turner's Atlanta Braves and Wayne Huizinga's (Blockbuster Video) winning World Series team, the Florida Marlins. "Content" is the key to the new technology, and there is no point in owning broadcast networks or cable systems if you have nothing to put on them.

The fashionable word for all this vertical corporate integration is synergy, but synergy turns out to be just another word for monopoly. Like so many of the new conglomerates of McWorld, Disney owns not just film studios, theme parks, and sports teams, but trademark tie-ins, publishing houses, television stations, newspapers, and entire new towns. One manager gushed that, in taking over ABC, Disney had become not just a world-class but a "universe class" operation. Disney has simply followed the modern corporate imperative, which is to own deep and own wide. And so Paramount acquired Simon and Schuster, which owned Madison Square Garden and the Knicks basketball and Rangers hockey teams, only to be acquired itself by Viacom, the cable company—a big fish eaten by a bigger fish. If you own hardware, the rule goes, buy software; thus Japan's Sony swallowed up Columbia Pictures and took a big (apparently indigestible) bite of Hollywood. If you own television stations, buy film libraries; thus Ted Turner bought and "colorized" the MGM film library; thus Bill Gates of Microsoft bought the rights to reproduce the works of art in museum collections on CD-ROM—after also having bought into the new production company started by ex-Disney executive Jeffrey Katzenberg, record producer mogul David Geffen, and megahit film director Steven Spielberg. Dream Works itself is helping to corrupt the boundary between news and entertainment. Its first film, *The Peacemaker*, a disappointing action drama about stolen ex-Soviet nuclear weapons, had an earlier incarnation as a television news special.

Entrepreneurship and capitalist competition suffer at the hands of these new post-capitalist monopolists. Bill Gates has been including his Web browser free on all computers delivered with his Microsoft Windows software in order to put Netscape, a competitor, out of business. The U.S. Justice Department finally arose from its slumber to take antitrust action. Rupert Murdoch's News Corporation uses his Harper Collins publishing firm to help market the Murdoch empire in China, most recently by voiding a book contract with Christopher Patten, the former governor of Hong Kong, who is highly critical of the Chinese government. If pluralism and the enhancement of choice are rationales for McWorld's global activities, the theory is flatly contradicted by the practices.

Poised on the edge of the twenty-first century, Disney's and McWorld's other telecommunication conglomerates seem to yearn to return to the nineteenth-century world of monopoly in which there were no antitrust laws. Michael Eisner is no John D. Rockefeller, Bill Gates is no Cornelius Vanderbilt, and Steven Spielberg is no Andrew Carnegie. But that is only because Eisner, Gates, and Spielberg are far more powerful than these robber barons ever were. Are they really the harbingers of new realms of liberty, these titans who exercise an inadvertent sovereignty not over oil, steel, and railroads, the muscles of our postindustrial world's body, but over the pictures, information, and ideas that are the sinews of the postmodern soul?

REILLUMINATING PUBLIC SPACE

McWorld thus does little for consumer autonomy, less for competition, and nothing at all for the kinds of liberty and pluralism essential to political freedom. But perhaps still more dangerous to liberty, McWorld has encroached upon and helped push aside public space. Its greatest victory—and here it has been mightily assisted by the antigovernmental privatizing ideology that has dominated politics in recent years—has been its contribution to the eradication of civic space.

Yet, once upon a time, between the oppositional poles of government and market, there was a vital middle choice. Though in eclipse today, the powerful imagery of civil society held the key to America's early democratic energy and civic activism (just as it helped Eastern Europeans break away from the Soviet Empire). For it was the great virtue of civil society in days past that it shared with government a sense of things public and a regard for the general good, yet (unlike government) made no claims to exercise a monopoly over legitimate coercion. Rather, it was a voluntary "private" realm devoted to public goods.

Civil society is the domain that can potentially mediate between the state and the private sector, between the rabid identity of an exclusive tribe and the exhausting identity of the solitary consumer, between Jihad and McWorld. Civil society offers women and men a space for activity that is simultaneously voluntary and public; a space that unites the virtue of the private sector liberty—with the virtue of the public sector—concern for the general good.

Civil society is thus a dwelling place that is neither a tribal fireside nor a shopping mall; it asks us to vote neither our political opinions nor our consumer desires but only to interact with one another around common concerns. It shares with the private sector the blessing of liberty; it is voluntary and made up of freely associated individuals and groups. But unlike the private sector, it aims at common ground and cooperative action. Civil society is thus public without being coercive, voluntary without being private.

My model for a genuinely democratic global culture would be a global civil society, hooped together by the many bands of civic associations represented by NGOs, churches, foundations, citizen organizations, and other civic groups. International organizations like Civicus and Civitas, which bring together civic associations from many nations to explore transnational agendas, represent the seedlings of a new global society. It is precisely here, where markets thrive even as subnational tribes make war on them, that civil society and a space for citizens is most needed. And it is here that Civicus does its most important work— not just as a club for like-minded NGOs but as an association that develops countervailing power in the face of a totalizing global consumerism, countervailing power that may one day carve out civic and social space for citizens and for some meaningful form of transnational democracy.

The task today in theory, no less than in practice, is to reilluminate public space for a civil society in eclipse. Unless a third way can be found between private markets and coercive government, between McWorld's anarchistic individualism and Jihad's dogmatic communitarianism, we may survive as consumers and clansmen, but we will cease to exist as democratic citizens.

NOTES

This essay was adapted from a paper given at a conference, "American Culture in a Global Culture," held at Bard College, November 1997.

1. See my *Jihad vs. McWorld* (New York: Times Books, 1995).
2. Paul Kennedy, *The Rise and Fall of the Great Powers: Economic Change and Military Conflict from 1500 to 2000* (New York: Random House, 1987).
3. Robert Kuttner, "Brave New Corporate 'Workplace of the Future,'" *Berkshire Eagle*, August 1, 1993.
4. William Greider, *One World, Ready or Not: The Manic Logic of Global Capitalism* (New York: Simon & Schuster, 1996).

Has Democracy a Future?

ARTHUR M. SCHLESINGER JR.

Through a glass darkly.

The twentieth century has no doubt been, as Isaiah Berlin has said, "the most terrible century in Western history." But this terrible century has—or appears to be having—a happy ending. As in melodramas of old, the maiden democracy, bound by villains to the railroad track, is rescued in the nick of time from the onrushing train. As the century draws to a close, both major villains have perished, fascism with a bang, communism with a whimper.

A season of triumphalism has followed. Two centuries ago Kant argued in his *Idea for a Universal History* that the republican form of government was destined to supersede all others. At last the prophecy seemed on the way to fulfillment. Savants hailed "the end of history." "For the first time in all history," President Clinton declared in his second inaugural address, "more people on this planet live under democracy than dictatorship." The *New York Times*, after careful checking, approved: 3.1 billion people live in democracies, 2.66 billion do not. According to end-of-history doctrine as expounded by its prophet, the minority can look forward to "the universalization of Western liberal democracy as the final form of human government."

For historians, this euphoria rang a bell of memory. Did not the same radiant hope accompany the transition from the nineteenth to the twentieth century? This most terrible hundred years in Western history started out in an atmosphere of optimism and high expectations. People of good will in 1900 believed in the inevitability of democracy, the invincibility of progress, the decency of human nature, and the coming reign of reason and peace. David Starr Jordan, the president of Stanford University, expressed the mood in his turn-of-the-century book *The Call of the Twentieth Century*. "The man of the Twentieth Century," Jordan predicted, "will be a hopeful man. He will love the world and the world will love him."

Looking back, we recall a century marked a good deal less by love than by hate, irrationality, and atrocity, one that for a long dark passage inspired the gravest forebodings about the very survival of the human race. Democracy, striding confidently into the 1900s, found itself almost at once on the defensive. The Great War, exposing the pretension that democracy would guarantee peace, shattered old structures of security and order and

Arthur Schlesinger Jr. is an award winning historian, writer and former special assistant to President John F. Kennedy.

Reprinted by permission. *Foreign Affairs*, Sept.–Oct. 1997. Vol. 76, No. 5, p. 2.

unleashed angry energies of revolution—revolution not for democracy but against it. Bolshevism in Russia, Fascism in Italy, Nazism in Germany, militarism in Japan all despised, denounced, and, wherever they could, destroyed individual rights and the processes of self-government.

In another decade the Great Depression came along to expose the pretension that democracy would guarantee prosperity. A third of the way into the century, democracy seemed a helpless thing, spiritless, paralyzed, doomed. Contempt for democracy spread among elites and masses alike: contempt for parliamentary dithering, for "talking-shops," for liberties of expression and opposition, for bourgeois civility and cowardice, for pragmatic muddling through.

In another decade the Second World War threatened to administer the coup de grâce. Liberal society, its back to the wall, fought for its life. There was considerable defeatism in the West. The title of Anne Morrow Lindbergh's 1940 bestseller proclaimed totalitarianism *The Wave of the Future*. It was, she wrote, a "new, and perhaps even ultimately good, conception of humanity trying to come to birth." Hitlerism and Stalinism were merely "scum on the wave of the future . . . The wave of the future is coming and there is no fighting it." By 1941 only about a dozen democracies were left on the planet.

The political, economic, and moral failures of democracy had handed the initiative to totalitarianism. Something like this could happen again. If liberal democracy fails in the 21st century, as it failed in the twentieth, to construct a humane, prosperous, and peaceful world, it will invite the rise of alternative creeds apt to be based, like fascism and communism, on flight from freedom and surrender to authority.

After all, democracy in its modern version—representative government, party competition, the secret ballot, all founded on guarantees of individual rights and freedoms—is at most 200 years old. A majority of the world's inhabitants may be living under democracy in 1997, but democratic hegemony is a mere flash in the long vistas of recorded history. One wonders how deeply democracy has sunk roots in previously democratic countries in the years since the collapse of the totalitarian challenges. Now the democratic adventure must confront tremendous pent-up energies that threaten to blow it off course and even drive it onto the rocks.

THE LAW OF ACCELERATION

Much of this energy is pent up within democracy itself. The most fateful source in the United States is race. "The problem of the twentieth century," W. E. B. Du Bois observed in 1900, "is the problem of the color line." His prediction will come to full flower in the 21st century. Minorities seek full membership in the larger American society. Doors slammed in their faces drive them to protest. The revolt against racism has taken time to gather strength. White America belatedly awakens to the cruelties long practiced against nonwhite peoples, and the revolt intensifies. As Tocqueville explained long ago, "Patiently endured so long as it seemed beyond redress, a grievance comes to appear intolerable once the possibility of removing it crosses men's minds. For the mere fact that certain abuses have been remedied draws attention to others, and they now appear more galling; people may suffer less, but their sensibility is exacerbated."

There are other pent-up energies. Modern democracy itself is the political offspring of technology and capitalism, the two most dynamic—that is to say, destabilizing—forces loose in the world today. Both are driven ever onward by self-generated momentum that strains the bonds of social control and of political sovereignty.

Technology created the clock, the printing press, the compass, the steam engine, the power loom, and the other innovations that laid the foundation for capitalism and that in time generated rationalism, individualism, and democracy. At first technological advance was unsystematic and intermittent. Soon it was institutionalized. "The greatest invention of the nineteenth century," said Alfred North Whitehead, "was the invention of the method of invention."

In the twentieth century, scientific and technological innovation increased at an exponential rate. Henry Adams, the most brilliant of American historians, meditated on the acceleration of history. "The world did not double or treble its movement between 1800 and 1900," Adams wrote in 1909, "but, measured by any standard . . . the tension and vibration and volume and so-called progression of society were fully a thousand times greater in 1900 than in 1800;—the force had doubled ten times over, and the speed, when measured by electrical standards as in telegraphy, approached infinity, and had annihilated both space and time." Nothing, Adams thought, could slow this process, for "the law of acceleration . . . cannot be supposed to relax its energy to suit the convenience of man."

The law of acceleration now hurtles us into a new age. The shift from a factory-based to a computer-based economy is more traumatic even than our great-grandparents' shift from a farm-based to a factory-based economy. The Industrial Revolution extended over generations and allowed time for human and institutional adjustment. The Computer Revolution is far swifter, more concentrated, and more drastic in its impact.

HYPERINTERACTIVE STATE

The computerized world poses problems for democracy. Where the Industrial Revolution created more jobs than it destroyed, the Computer Revolution threatens to destroy more jobs than it creates. It also threatens to erect new and rigid class barriers, especially between the well-educated and the ill-educated. Economic inequality has already grown in the United States to the point where disparities are greater in egalitarian America than in the class-ridden societies of Europe. Felix Rohatyn, the investment banker and rescuer of a bankrupt New York City, speaks of the "huge transfers of wealth from lower-skilled middle-class workers to the owners of capital assets and to a new technological aristocracy." Those who skip or flunk the computer will fall into the Blade Runner proletariat, a snarling, embittered, violent underclass.

The computer will also affect the procedures of democratic politics. James Madison in The *Federalist Papers* distinguished between "pure democracy," by which he meant a system in which citizens assemble and administer the government in person, and a republic, by which he meant a system in which the majority expresses its will through "a scheme of representation." For most of American history, "pure democracy" was necessarily limited to town meetings in small villages. Now the interactivity introduced by the Computer Revolution makes "pure democracy," technically feasible on a national scale.

Brian Beedham in an article in the December 21, 1996, *Economist* applauds this development, claiming representative democracy is "a half-finished thing." Every citizen, Beedham argues, is entitled to an equal say in the conduct of public affairs. The rise of public opinion polls, focus groups, and referendums suggests popular demand for a finished democracy. With a nation of computers plugged into information and communication networks, "full democracy" is just around the corner. Full democracy, pure democracy, plebiscitary democracy, direct democracy, cyberdemocracy, the electronic town hall: under whatever name, is this a desirable prospect?

Perhaps not. Interactivity encourages instant responses, discourages second thoughts, and offers outlets for demagoguery, egomania, insult, and hate. Listen to talk radio! In too interactive a polity, a "common passion," as Madison thought, could sweep through a people and lead to emotional and ill-judged actions. Remembering the explosion of popular indignation when President Truman fired General Douglas MacArthur, one is grateful that the electronic town hall was not running the country in 1951. The Internet has done little thus far to foster the reasoned exchanges that in Madison's words "refine and enlarge the public views."

UNBRIDLED CAPITALISM

While the onrush of technology creates new substantive problems and promises to revise the political system through which we deal with them, the onrush of capitalism may have even more disruptive consequences. Let us understand the relationship between capitalism and democracy. Democracy is impossible without private ownership because private property—resources beyond the arbitrary reach of the state—provides the only secure basis for political opposition and intellectual freedom. But the capitalist market is no guarantee of democracy, as Deng Xiaoping, Lee Kuan Yew, Pinochet, and Franco, not to mention Hitler and Mussolini, have amply demonstrated. Democracy requires capitalism, but capitalism does not require democracy, at least in the short run.

Capitalism has proved itself the supreme engine of innovation, production, and distribution. But its method, as it careens ahead, heedless of little beyond its own profits, is what Joseph Schumpeter called "creative destruction." In its economic theory, capitalism rests on the concept of equilibrium. In practice, its very virtues drive it toward disequilibrium. This is the dilemma of contemporary conservatism. The unfettered market that conservatives worship undermines the values—stability, morality, family, community, work, discipline, delayed gratification—that conservatives avow. The glitter of the marketplace, the greed, the short-termism, the exploitation of prurient appetites, the ease of fraud, the devil-take-the-hindmost ethos—all these are at war with purported conservative ideals. "Stationary capitalism," as Schumpeter said, "is a contradiction in terms."

Even premier capitalists are appalled by what runaway capitalism has wrought. If understanding of capitalism can be measured by success in making money out of it, no one understands contemporary capitalism better than the financier and philanthropist George Soros. "Although I have made a fortune in the financial markets," Soros writes, "I now fear that the untrammeled intensification of laissez-faire capitalism and the spread of market values into all areas of life is endangering our open and democratic society." The "uninhibited pursuit of self-interest," Soros continues, results in "intolerable inequities and instability."

The Computer Revolution offers wondrous, new possibilities for creative destruction. One goal of capitalist creativity is the globalized economy. One—unplanned—candidate for capitalist destruction is the nation-state, the traditional site of democracy. The computer turns the untrammeled market into a global juggernaut crashing across frontiers, enfeebling national powers of taxation and regulation, undercutting national management of interest rates and exchange rates, widening disparities of wealth both within and between nations, dragging down labor standards, degrading the environment, denying nations the shaping of their own economic destiny, accountable to no one, creating a world economy without a world polity. Cyberspace is beyond national control. No authorities exist to provide international control. Where is democracy now?

THE ASIAN SHIFT

The end of the Eurocentric era raises further problems for democracy. Self-government, individual rights, equality before the law are European inventions. Now the age of the Pacific is upon us. The breakthrough of Japan in the century coming to an end heralds the breakthrough of China and India in the century ahead. The economic magnetism of Asia is already altering the contours of the global economy, and foreshadows historic shifts in the planetary balance of power.

I am not greatly concerned about the "clash of civilizations" that worries some thoughtful analysts. Civilizations are rarely unified. Countries within the same civilization are more likely to fight with each other than to join in monolithic assaults on other civilizations. But the impact of the rise of Asia on the future of democracy is worth consideration. The Asian tradition, we are told, values the group more than the individual, order more than argument, authority more than liberty, solidarity more than freedom. Some Asian leaders, notably Lee Kuan Yew of Singapore and Mahathir bin Mohamad of Malaysia, love to contrast Asian discipline and stability with the disorder and decadence they impute to the individualistic West. They denounce the attempt to hold Asian countries to Western democratic standards as the new form of Western imperialism.

Nevertheless, both India and Japan are functioning democracies. If the claim that human rights are universal is proof of Western arrogance, the restriction of those rights to Europe and the Americas brands non-Western peoples as lesser breeds incapable of appreciating personal liberty and self-government, and that is surely Western arrogance too. In fact, many Asians fight for human rights, and at the risk of their freedom and their lives. "Why do we assume," asks Christopher Patten, the last British governor of Hong Kong, "that Lee Kuan Yew is the embodiment of Asian values rather than Daw Aung San Suu Kyi," the courageous opposition leader under prolonged house arrest in Burma? A pre-Tiananmen Square wall poster in Beijing proclaimed: "We cannot tolerate that human rights and democracy are only slogans of the Western bourgeoisie and the Eastern proletariat only needs dictatorship." In the words of the Indian economist Amartya Sen, "The so-called Asian values that are invoked to justify authoritarianism are not especially Asian in any significant sense." Chris Patten concludes, "I think the Asian value debate is piffle. What are these Asian values? When you home in on what one or two Asian leaders mean by them, what they actually mean is that anyone who disagrees with me should shut up."

Still, the new salience of Asia on the world scene, the absence of historical predilections for democracy, and the self-interest of rulers who see democracy as a threat to their power suggest a period of Asian resistance to the spread of the democratic idea.

CULTURE LASHES BACK

That resistance will be reinforced by the defensive reaction around the planet to relentless globalization—a reaction that takes the form of withdrawal from modernity. The world today is torn in opposite directions. Globalization is in the saddle and rides mankind, but at the same time drives people to seek refuge from its powerful forces beyond their control and comprehension. They retreat into familiar, intelligible, protective units. They crave the politics of identity. The faster the world integrates, the more people will huddle in their religious or ethnic or tribal enclaves. Integration and disintegration feed on each other.

A militant expression of what Samuel Huntington calls cultural backlash is the upsurge of religious fundamentalism. Islamic fundamentalism seems especially hostile to freedom of expression, to women's rights, and, contrary to historical Islam, to other religions. Nor is the fundamentalist revival confined to the Third World. Many people living lives of quiet desperation in modern societies hunger for transcendent meaning and turn to inerrant faith for solace and support.

According to a 1995 Gallup poll, more than a third of American adults claim that God speaks to them directly. One hopes it is the God of love rather than the God of wrath on the other end of the line. Fundamentalism, carried too far, has ominous implications for democracy. Those who believe they are executing the will of the Almighty are notably harsh on nonbelievers. A fanatic, as the Irish-American wit Finley Peter Dunne's Mr. Dooley once observed, "does what he thinks th' Lord wud do if He only knew th' facts in th' case." Fanaticism is the mortal enemy of democracy.

Back to the question: Has democracy a future? Yes, Virginia, it does, but not the glorious future predicted in the triumphalist moment. Democracy has survived the twentieth century by the skin of its teeth. It will not enjoy a free ride through the century to come.

In America, democracy must run a gauntlet of challenges. The most crucial is still Du Bois' color line. Much depends on the availability of jobs, especially in the inner city. If employment remains high, political action will mitigate racial tensions, particularly when minorities understand that in the longer run, ethnic gerrymandering will reduce, not increase, their influence. Tension will be mitigated even more by intermarriage. Sex—and love—between people of different creeds and colors can probably be counted on to arrest the disuniting of America.

The national capacity to absorb and assimilate newcomers will remain powerful. The call of the mainstream will appeal far more than linguistic or ethnic ghettos, above all to the young. English will continue as the dominant language. Indeed, in essentials the national character will be recognizably much as it has been for a couple of centuries. People seeking clues to the American mystery will still read, and quote, Tocqueville.

Technology will rush on according to Adams' law of acceleration. But for all the temptations of interactivity and all the unpopularity of elected officials, I doubt that Americans will sanction the degradation of representative democracy into a system of plebiscites. Capitalism too will careen on, through downs as well as ups, but laissez-faire ideology will probably wane as capitalists discover the range of troubles the unfettered market cannot solve, or makes worse. Unbridled capitalism, with low wages, long hours, and exploited workers, excites social resentment, revives class warfare, and infuses Marxism with new life. To move along constructive lines, capitalism must subordinate short-term plans and profits to such long-term social necessities as investment in education, research and development, environmental protection, the extension of health care, the rehabilitation of infrastructure, the redemption of the city. Capitalists are not likely to do this by themselves. Long-term perspectives demand public leadership and affirmative government.

In the world at large, can capitalism, once loose from national moorings, be held to social accountability? Will international institutions acquire the authority to impose, for example, a global SEC? This won't happen next week, but continuing abuse of power will build a constituency for reform. Wars will still disturb the tenor of life, but where in the past they generally arose from aggression across national frontiers, the wars of the 21st century will more likely be between ethnic, religious, ideological, or tribal factions within the same country. Such wars are harder to define and to control. Let us pray that no factional zealot gets hold of an atomic bomb.

Nation-states will continue to decline as effective power units: too small for the big problems, as the sociologist Daniel Bell has said, and too big for the small problems. Despite this decline, nationalism will persist as the most potent of political emotions. Whether democracy, a Western creation, can be transplanted to parts of the world with different cultures and traditions is far from certain. Yet I would expect a gradual expansion of democratic institutions and ideals. It is hard to believe that the instinct for political and intellectual freedom is limited to a happy few around the North Atlantic littoral.

Democracy in the 21st century must manage the pressures of race, of technology, and of capitalism, and it must cope with the spiritual frustrations and yearnings generated in the vast anonymity of global society. The great strength of democracy is its capacity for self-correction.

Intelligent diagnosis and guidance are essential. "Perhaps no form of government," said the historian and diplomat Lord Bryce, "needs great leaders so much as democracy." Yet even the greatest of democratic leaders lack the talent to cajole violent, retrograde, and intractable humankind into utopia. Still, with the failures of democracy in the twentieth century at the back of their minds, leaders in the century to come may do a better job than we have done of making the world safe for democracy.

Issue 13
Russian Democracy

INTRODUCTION

Grigory Yavlinsky, author of the second article in this section, is surely correct in his argument that Russia will be a vitally important country in the coming millennium. The fate of Russia is too important to be placed on the back burner of the world's major political and economic powers. Unquestionably, Russia will rise again. The concern, as posed by Yavlinsky, is whether Russia will become a quasi-democratic corporatist state, or a Western-style, democratic market economy.

Both of our authors recognize the difficult and uncertain path that Russia has ahead. Plagued by economic oligarchs, Russia faces the challenge of channeling its economic growth towards building an economy to benefit all of its citizens, rather than the top-of-the-heap nomenklatura* capitalists who now dominate the economy.

On the democratic front, there are more reasons for optimism, as noted by Yavlinsky. "Russians are freer than at any time in their history." With this freedom, however, comes the challenge of constructing a civil society, upon whose foundations the structures of a democratic society can be built. Perhaps the most important objective is establishing respect for the rule of law to counter the popular perception that contacts and corruption count for more than entrepreneurship and hard work.

As you read the articles, consider the following questions.

*Nomenklatura—A term used to describe Soviet era government officials. Given their inside knowledge and positions within the state run economy, they tended to profit from the privitization of the Russian economy after the collapse of the Soviet Union.

Discussion Questions

1. What stake does the United States and the world have in Russia's future? Should we be content to settle for a stable, corporatist Russia?
2. Can Europe and the United States play an important role in promoting the democratization and economic development process in Russia?
3. Was the rapid privitization of the Soviet economy a mistake, inviting the oligarchic, corporatist turn taken in recent years?

    For more information on this topic, visit the following websites:

    `http://www.online.ru/sp/iet/index.html`
    Institute for the Economy in Transition

    `http://www.hhs.se/site/ret/ret.htm`
    Russian Economic Trends

    `http://www.foreignpolicy-infocus.org`
    Foreign Policy in Focus

Russia, Land of Enterprise

NORMAN LAMONT

Six years ago in Washington it fell to me as chancellor of the exchequer to introduce Yegor Gaidar, then Russia's finance minister, to a packed meeting of the IMF. It was rather like introducing a new member of the House of Commons. We walked together up the aisle, but instead of being greeted by the Speaker the newly admitted member shook hands with Michel Camdessus, then, as now, the IMF's managing director.

It was a historic moment. It was the acknowledgment of Russia's wish to enter the global economy. I vainly attempted to interest the British media. None were interested. I was even taken to task by *The Spectator*'s City columnist for spending too much time on Russia.

It had all started when Gorbachev invited himself to attend the G7 meeting at Lancaster House in 1991. Somewhat portentously he had announced that Russia was attending not as a supplicant, but as a partner. After that meeting, I, as chairman of the G7 group of finance ministers, went to Moscow. Boris Yeltsin, the coming man, made it clear to me that reform would happen in Russia, even if it didn't in Gorbachev's Soviet Union.

It was then that I first met young economic reformers like Yavlinsky, Fyodorov and Shokhin. They could have come straight from the pages of Turgenev's *Fathers and Sons*. They had all the passion of 19th-century Russian liberals for foreign ideas. I was impressed by their courage and understanding of market economics.

I particularly wanted to help improve the efficiency of Russia's primitive banking system. I arranged technical assistance from the Bank of England. With Yeltsin's approval I devised a scheme for British banks, with government assistance, to take young Russians for training. I wrote to hundreds of UK firms and, as a result, over 1,000 young Russians were trained in British financial institutions.

Two weeks ago I found myself again reflecting on these matters in St Petersburg at the time of Yeltsin's double whammy of default and devaluation. At that point there was little sense of crisis. Admittedly there were a few queues outside banks, and in shops new price tags were being placed on top of old.

But at the Grand Hotel, the mobsters' molls, dressed head to toe from Prada, continued to slip through the metal detector to the caviar

Norman Lamont is a former Conservative Member of Parliament and Chancellor of the Exchequer.

Reprinted by permission. *Spectator*, Sept. 5, 1998. Vol. 281, No. 8874, p. 11.

hall, followed by squat men with crew cuts and open-necked check shirts. On the streets I noticed many fourwheel-drive vehicles with dark windows, and one Rolls Royce, though most cars were old. The shop windows seemed full of goods compared with the empty shelves in Moscow during my last visit.

However, away from the centre and up Moskovsky Prospekt you find a different city. The buildings are crumbling, the streets full of rubble and the shops much drabber. I wondered what life must be like in Gorky or Volgograd. Millions of Russians today survive outside the formal economy and have not seen money for years.

Commentators have eagerly written off Yeltsin's presidency as an abject failure. One wonders what they imagined success could possibly have looked like. The holding and winning of the first direct election for a Russian president was a historic achievement. On the economic front, it was Yeltsin's lifting of price controls that brought many more goods into the shops. Russia has the beginnings of a new service economy.

In recent days it has been suggested that attempts at full-scale reform of Russia's economy were naive and always doomed to failure. It is ironic to recall that the original IMF programmes for Russia were criticised by economists like Jeffrey Sachs for being insufficiently radical.

It was always clear that economic reform was a more difficult task in Russia than in Eastern Europe. The difference between 45 and 70 years of communism is huge. In Hungary, Poland and Yugoslavia the market economy was never entirely extinguished. Stalin's legacy was many giant, unprivatisable, singleproduct factories, frequently the sole employer in a city. It is unsurprising that the "oligarchs" have ended up controlling large parts of the new, emerging economy. That was the only way in which large parts of the economy could be privatised. One of Gorbachev's fears was that privatisation would mean that state assets would be handed over to a few billionaires. At the time I put that down to his lack of understanding of privatisation. I still think he misunderstood privatisation, but he was proved right.

Whatever government emerges from the present crisis is likely to try to "get the economy moving" by printing money and breathing fresh life into the giant business enterprises with their banking affiliates. It is argued that this takes more account of the social realities of Russia. Sadly it will also prove a complete dead end.

Whoever is head of the Russian government, Chernomyrdin, Lushkov or Lebed, is unlikely to be able to call a complete halt to reform. The process may slow for a while, but then it will start again.

Millions of Russians have glimpsed the possibility of a better life. As the Iranians have discovered, it is impossible to close an economy off from the consumerist culture of the rest of the world. Many Russians have taken to capitalism. I once asked Grigor Yavlinsky—then an adviser to

Gorbachev—whether communism had extinguished the spirit of enterprise. "You do not realise," he replied, "what enterprise ordinary people have to have merely to survive." There are plenty of enterprising Russians.

The crucial issues will not go away. A stable currency must be the top priority. Two pressing problems are tax collection and intercompany debts. Many Russian firms continue to produce goods and spare parts for other firms regardless of whether they are paid or not. But this adds to the problem of tax collection. At the moment Russian tax revenues are below 20 per cent of GDP, which means the state cannot provide basic services or pay its employees.

Another key failure has been the absence of a proper framework of law. A modern market economy needs a stable framework. The Duma has passed a continually changing and bewildering array of laws.

The immediate future of Russia looks immensely bleak and frightening. But Adam Smith once observed that there is a deal of ruin in a nation. Many Russians have been living near to subsistence for years. They have shown great patience and stoicism.

Russia by itself will not cause a slump in the West. If there is a global slow-down or recession it will be for other reasons. But Russia matters for itself. What happens there will affect us all politically. Russia is a challenge to the West.

Nine years ago Francis Fukuyama wrote a bold and brilliant essay. Writing before Gorbachev's reforms had reached their climax, he predicted the 20th century would close by seeing the universalisation of Western liberal democracy as the final form of human government. The consequences would be the end of conflict between large states caught in the grip of history. He called this The End of History.

If Russia goes badly wrong, what we may see is history starting all over again.

Russia's Phony Capitalism

GRIGORY YAVLINSKY

Oligarchy or democracy?

Russia faces a watershed decision. The vital question for Russia is whether it will become a quasi-democratic oligarchy with corporatist, criminal characteristics or take the more difficult, painful road to becoming a normal, Western-style democracy with a market economy. Communism is no longer an option. That was settled in the 1996 presidential election.

Russians will make this fateful choice and be its principal victims or beneficiaries. But its consequences to Americans, Europeans, and others who share this shrinking globe should not be underestimated. Contrary to the widespread view in the United States that Russia is essentially irrelevant or of secondary concern, our continental country, stretching from Eastern Europe to upper Asia, will be important in the next century because of its location between east and west, its possession of weapons of mass destruction, its natural resources, and its potential as a consumer market.

Unlike previous choices in recent Russian history, the decision will not be made on a single day by a coup or an election. Rather, it will evolve through the many decisions made by Russia's millions of people, leaders and ordinary citizens alike, over the coming years. Even President Boris Yeltsin's sacking of much of his cabinet in March, while deeply disturbing, was one more bump along the road, not the end of the journey. Nevertheless, the route chosen will be no less important than the choices made earlier in the decade in its effect on the society in which our children and grandchildren live.

Corporatist states, marked by high-level criminality but bearing the trappings of democracy, differ more than is sometimes recognized from Western-style market democracies. Their markets are driven by oligarchs whose highest goal is increasing their personal wealth. Freedom of the press and other civil liberties are suppressed. Laws are frequently ignored or suspended and constitutions obeyed only when convenient. Corruption is rife from the streets to the halls of power. Personalities, contacts, and clans count for more than institutions and laws. For examples, one need only reflect on the unhappy experiences of many Latin American countries in the 1970s and 1980s.

Grigory Yavlinsky is a Russian economist and the leader of Yabloko, a democratic, reformist political party currently in opposition to the major party.
Reprinted by permission. *Foreign Affairs*, May–June 1998. Vol. 77, Issue 3, p. 67, 13p.

Alternatively, in Western-style democracies, markets are driven by the consumer. Government economic policies are intended to serve the nation, not those in power. Through hard work, citizens can succeed. Personal freedom is universally respected, including the right to express opinions that differ from those of the government. Civilian rule is unchallenged. Corruption is normally minimal and its spread swiftly checked. Laws and constitutions are respected by both government leaders and citizens. The contrast with oligarchy is stark. Over the past year, increasing numbers of Russians have come to appreciate that their country stands at a fork in the road.

RUSSIA'S ROBBER BARONS

The Russian economy today shows signs of evolution toward Western-style capitalism on the one hand and the consolidation of corporatist, criminal-style capitalism on the other. Western conventional wisdom emphasizes the former and thus sees a Russia moving steadily toward a market economy. Indeed, Russia has managed to lower inflation and, within reasonable limits, stabilize its currency. Moscow is a boomtown. Some of the newly established and privatized corporations that operate with international mentalities and ambitions are making their way to the top. Certain regions of the country have received favorable international credit ratings, and a handful of Russian companies have held successful international bond issues. Young people are now ready to adapt to the new market system and steer clear of crime as the country develops new rules. The International Monetary Fund, while occasionally delaying tranches of its $10 billion loan because of poor tax collection, always seems to reinstate them after promises by senior Russian officials to do better. All this seemingly points toward the path of a normalized Western market economy.

But while Russia has its economic success stories, many aspects of the economy suggest that it is moving toward a corporatist market in which corruption is rampant. The most important of these trends is the rise of the Russian oligarchs, who have created a form of robber-baron capitalism. Far from creating an open market, Russia has consolidated a semi-criminal oligarchy that was already largely in place under the old Soviet system. After communism's collapse, it merely changed its appearance, just as a snake sheds its skin.

The new ruling elite is neither democratic nor communist, neither conservative nor liberal—merely rapaciously greedy. In an interview published in the *Financial Times* in November 1996, one Russian tycoon claimed that the country's seven largest bankers, who became the core of Yeltsin's reelection campaign, controlled more than half the Russian economy. No one doubts that these nomenklatura capitalists have had a profound impact on the Russian economy, but their market of insider deals and political connections stands in the way of an open economy that would benefit all Russian citizens. The robber-baron market cannot tackle important social and economic questions. It is primarily concerned with issues that affect its masters' short-term power and prosperity.

At recent debates at Harvard University's U.S.-Russian Investment Symposium and at the Davos World Economic Forum, Western investors sharply criticized the robber-baron mentality of many Russian business leaders and the process of privatization under former Deputy Premier Anatoly Chubais. As George Soros put it, first "the assets of the state were stolen, and then when the state itself became valuable as a source of legitimacy, it too was stolen."

Last summer's auction by the state of the Svyazinvest telecommunications giant is an example of how these tycoons operate. This auction was to be the first where competitive bids were held for a privatizing company. Unlike earlier auctions, where the tycoons collaborated to gain huge shares of industry for a fraction of their actual worth, during the Svyazinvest auction the leaders of the rival industrial syndicates could not agree on who would get the company and were therefore forced to bid against each other. The "bankers' war" that ensued was fought not with bullets but through allegations of graft aired by their media outlets. As a result, some of these tycoons were removed from their government posts and corruption charges were leveled against Chubais and his privatization team. Such a fiasco hardly suggests a healthy capitalist system. Worse, as of this writing, the same players are positioning themselves for a second round in the war—the auction of the Rosneft oil company.

There are many reasons why a country with nuclear, chemical, and biological weapons should not be allowed to slip into the chaos of rule by semi-criminal, corporate, oligarchic robber barons. Unfortunately, those who believe that the capitalism of the robber barons will eventually give way to a market economy that benefits all in society, as occurred in the United States at the turn of the century, are mistaken. America had an established middle class with a work ethic and a government that remained largely free of robber-baron infiltration. The American tycoons were still investing in their own country. Russia's robber barons are stifling their homeland's economic growth by stealing from Russia and investing abroad. In the late 1990s, Russia has no emerging middle class, and the oligarchy, which is deeply involved in the government, can alter policy for its private benefit.

In the meantime, while the big boys—they are all men—fight over an ever larger piece of the Russian economic pie, the government has been unable to create economic conditions in which the majority of Russians can thrive. The problem is not only that the majority of Russians remain worse off than before the economic transition began, but that they cannot become better off. The economy is stagnating at half its 1989 level. Real incomes have fallen by a third, and living standards in most regions have deteriorated to levels not seen in decades. Government attempts to curb inflation resulted not only in tremendous wage and pension arrears, but also in the government's inability to pay its bills for the goods and services it consumed. This led to total disarray in payments, with up to 75 percent of goods and services either paid in kind, or by promissory notes that cannot be cashed, or transacted through illegal channels to dodge taxes entirely. In real terms, government pensions and wages were cut to 40 percent or less of their original value, and the government still cannot collect enough taxes to cover these expenses. Tax receipts have fallen to less than 20 percent of the country's GDP. Meanwhile, external debt has skyrocketed, and domestic debt, which was next to nothing just a decade ago, has reached almost 15 percent of GDP. Servicing these debts, paid out to local bankers and foreign speculators at exorbitant interest rates, will take no less than 25 percent of total government expenditure in 1998. The current Russian market economy has created a handful of super-wealthy individuals while leaving the rest behind to struggle. It is no wonder that these economic policies resulted in some 250 communists and 50 ultranationalist Zhirinovskyites being elected to the 450-seat State Duma in 1995.

Furthermore, Russia is bedeviled by a corruption problem reminiscent of Latin America's in the 1970s and 1980s. The European Bank for Reconstruction and Development ranks Russia as the most corrupt major economy in the world. Graft permeates the country, from street crime to mafia hits to illegal book deals in Kremlin corridors to rigged bids for stakes of privatized companies. Recent polls by the Public Opinion Foundation show that Russians believe the best way to get ahead is through contacts and corruption. When asked to select criteria needed to become wealthy in today's Russia, 88 percent picked connections and 76 percent chose dishonesty. Only 39 percent said hard work. Anyone who attempts to start a small business in Russia will encounter extortion demands from the mafia, so there is no incentive for entrepreneurship. Better to stay home and grow potatoes at your dacha. A crime-ridden market cannot be effective. With no certainty about the future, with or without inflation, nobody will invest. Such a market can support the current level of consumption—which for the majority of the population means semi-pauperhood—for some time, but it does not and cannot provide any progress.

With such problems, despite the good news about the Russian economy over the last year, it is clear that the Russian market is still veering toward the corporatist, criminalist, oligarchic path.

AN UNFINISHED DEMOCRACY

Russia's current democratic institutions also deserve a mixed review. Certainly there are reasons for optimism. Russians are freer than at any time in their history. They can now read what they like, travel, talk, worship, and assemble. Russia's citizens have quickly grown accustomed to these liberties. Technological advances such as the Internet, fax machines, and mobile phones will make it impossible for any one source ever to monopolize information in Russia again. Through this continuous contact with the world, with each passing day, Russia becomes a more normalized society.

Perhaps the most often cited examples of successful Russian democracy are the Russian elections. Over the past three years, elections have become an accepted part of Russian life. This was hardly always the case. A mere three years ago, debate raged in Russia as to whether the ruling authorities would even allow elections to occur. But from the December 1995 Duma elections to the June 1996 presidential race to the subsequent gubernatorial and regional legislature elections, again and again elections have been successfully held in the Russian Federation. In many of those contests, notably the Duma election and some regional gubernatorial races, opposition candidates from the communist and other parties have won and taken office. With minor exceptions, voting and ballot counting have been peaceful and relatively free, while voter turnout has been higher than that of the United States.

Although the recent elections are a positive development in the creation of Russian democratic institutions, some disturbing trends point to trouble in the future. While international observers have cited Russian balloting as free and fair, Russian campaigns—most notably the 1996 presidential election—have been notoriously unfair. Spending limits are routinely ignored. While no actual figures have been disclosed, the 1996 Yeltsin presidential campaign is estimated to have cost at least $500 million. Some put it at an even $1 billion. (By comparison, Bill Clinton's primary and general election campaigns that year together cost $113 million.) Officially, Russian presidential campaigns could spend only $2.9 million, but Yeltsin's overspending neither elicited a major outcry nor started judicial proceedings.

Perhaps even more disturbing is the often cited European Institute on the Media survey that documents the media's flagrant pro-Yeltsin bias. According to the EIM, Yeltsin enjoyed 53 percent of all media coverage, while his closest competitor, Gennady Zyuganov of the Communist Party, received only 18 percent. Yeltsin appeared on television more than all the other candidates combined. Moreover, election coverage was extremely slanted in the president's favor. Giving candidates a point for each positive story and subtracting a point for each negative one, Yeltsin scored +492 before the first round of the election; Zyuganov earned –313. In the second round, Yeltsin had +247 to Zyuganov's –240, despite the fact that Yeltsin disappeared from the public eye a week before the election.

Electoral politics, like much else in Russia, are also at a fork in the road. As Russian political consultants learn more tricks of the trade, the danger increases that they might join with the robber barons to try to turn future Russian elections into nothing but window dressing for irremovable oligarchic rule—as was the case in the Soviet Union, where results were predetermined and the people were an afterthought.

Russia's democratic institutions have not developed as fully as its elections. As the recent cabinet firings show, the system of checks and balances is underdeveloped, leaving the country prone to the whims of a mercurial chief executive. The rule of law is often not respected. The judicial branch of government remains overly influenced by the executive branch. The lower house of parliament has made some headway in becoming more than a mere talking chamber in which the occasional fist-fight breaks out, and the executive branch now has to lobby the Duma to pass the budget, the start II treaty, and other crucial matters. But Yeltsin and his team still reserve the option of bypassing the Duma altogether—thereby ignoring the constitution—if the Duma disagrees with an executive initiative or is unwilling to be co-opted by promises of some new monthly leadership meeting with the president and prime minister. This strategy is routinely applied to the budget, where compromises are made to ensure passage and are then ignored throughout the year. Another example is the persistent rumor that Yeltsin will seek an unconstitutional third term as president.

No successful democracy functions without some kind of political party system, but attempts to develop such a system in Russia have been an unambiguous disappointment. Although political factions boasting varying degrees of regional activity exist within the Duma, a true functioning political party system in Russia has yet to develop, for a number of reasons. First, after 70 years of "party rule," Russians are understandably skeptical of political parties. Second, President Yeltsin's actions have actively undermined the development of a political party system. By rejecting any party affiliation, the president acts as if parties and party development are an afterthought in the consolidation of Russian democracy. Yeltsin accepts the assistance of like-minded parties when it is politically convenient and distances himself from them when it is not. So no party is the true party of the government, and Yeltsin cannot be held accountable to the people short of a general election. Third, for political reasons, Yeltsin sought in the past to limit the development of parties by trying to abolish the "party list" system that elects half the Duma, seating only parties that win over five percent of the popular vote. In 1995, only four parties did so, and over half of the Duma seats went to parties opposed to the Yeltsin administration. The list system ensures that parties will exist in some part of Russian society, but in 1998, Yeltsin renewed his call to change it. To better control the Duma, he advocates having the entire chamber elected from regional districts, similar to the system used in the U.S. House of Representatives. With more control over local leaders, Yeltsin believes he can influence who wins these Duma seats. In reality, however, organized crime would buy many of the seats. If Yeltsin succeeds in abolishing the party-list system, he will destroy the only arena in Russian society where parties currently exist without minimizing a major source of opposition. Such a strategy would hurt Yeltsin politically, but even worse, it would damage Russian democracy, which needs a functioning party system to allow people to express their views to the government.

The Russian media also earns a mixed review. On the one hand, Russians have a variety of news sources from which to choose. Opposition newspapers exist, and journalists are free to do investigative reporting and write their own opinions. The November book payment scandal, where senior members of Yeltsin's economic team were revealed to have accepted $500,000 for writing a book on privatization, first broke in the Russian media. Political leaders appear on programs like *Hero of the Day* and *Itogi* to explain their views to the people. Even so, in the past two years the media has become entirely controlled by the oligarchs, who are part of the government and use their editorial boards and programmers to promote their own selfish agendas. Nowhere was this more evident than in the Svyazinvest bid last summer, where the resulting "bankers' war" was played out in the media. By reading a certain paper or watching a certain television station, a Russian citizen got either one or another robber baron's version of the truth. Depressingly, the Russian service of Radio Free Europe/Radio Liberty remains the primary supplier of impartial news, just as it was in Soviet times.

In sum, Russian democracy still has a long way to go. True, elections are held, freedoms are respected, parties exist, and the media express divergent views, but such minimum democratic institutions exist in both Latin American and Western democracies. Russia is better off with its imperfect institutions than without them, but they do not yet properly reflect the people's needs and will.

THE WEST'S STAKE

In October 1996, Vladimir Nechai, the director of a nuclear complex near the Ural city of Chelyabinsk, killed himself because he lacked the money to pay his employees and could no longer ensure the safety of his plant's operations. His suicide underscored the most serious threat to all players in the post–Cold War world: loss of control of the Soviet arsenal of nuclear, biological, and chemical weapons. The increasing risks of chaos in a nuclear power are also evident in the rumors of nuclear smuggling. Russia has thousands of tons of nuclear, chemical, and biological material. Under the rule of a corrupt oligarchy, uranium and anthrax could become black market commodities available to the highest bidder. The control of Russia's weapons of mass destruction is an issue of world safety that cannot be ignored by Russia or the West.

Russia and the West face other common challenges. Russia borders some of the most unstable regions in the world. For centuries, it has acted as a buffer between those instabilities and Europe. Today this wall is of no less importance as drug trafficking, terrorism, and arms smuggling are becoming rampant. A Russian wall with holes would be dangerous for Europe.

Furthermore, Russia and the West share a desire for stability in order to promote economic development. In recent months, the West has focused on developing the Caspian Sea region's oil resources. Russia is a key player in the area, and finding a peaceful resolution to the Chechen issue will play a large role in determining how oil leaves the region. Moreover, Russia is arguably the greatest untapped economic market in the world. Stability makes possible the development of Russia's economy and presents a great opportunity for Western companies and economies.

A Western-style democracy in Russia would be a partner with the West in confronting the challenges of the 21st century. Russia and the West would work together better to maintain control over weapons of mass destruction and would be more likely to cooperate in containing regional conflict in explosive areas like the Caucasus and Middle East. Finally, the rule of law would govern business relations and allow for economic development and growth beneficial for both societies.

A corporatist Russian government would be more challenging and less stable. Realists may argue that a corporatist Russian government would value stability above all and therefore cooperate with the West to ensure the status quo. But such a system, although stable on the surface, would be built on false foundations, much like today's Indonesia, where any change of leadership could undermine the entire order. Nor would it necessarily be a status quo power. Another scenario has such a government becoming contentious and suspicious of Western actions and goals. Cooperation on important global issues would be less forthcoming, and rules and laws would change to fit personalities, hindering economic development.

Russia's choice will be heavily influenced by the West. Unfortunately, up to this point, the West has not always promoted the correct path. Nowhere is this more evident than in the debate over NATO expansion. If a military alliance moves closer to a country's borders without incorporating that country, it means that the country's foreign policy has dismally failed. Talk that this is a different NATO, a NATO that is no longer a military alliance, is ridiculous. It is like saying that the hulking thing advancing toward your garden is not a tank because it is painted pink, carries flowers, and plays cheerful music. It does not matter how you dress it up; a pink tank is still a tank.

The most important message of NATO expansion for Russians, however, is that the political leaders of Western Europe and the United States do not believe that Russia can become a real Western-style democracy within the next decade or so. In their eyes, Russia, because of its history, is a second-class democracy. Perhaps this is understandable. The combination of Chechnya (an arbitrary war in which Russia unnecessarily killed 100,000 people), the collapse of the Russian army, failed economic reforms, a semi-criminal government, and Yeltsin's unpredictability has given the West enough justification to conclude that Russia, for the time being, cannot be a dependable partner and that NATO expansion should therefore continue.

Ironically, if the United States explained its push for NATO expansion in these terms to the Russian people, they would at least understand why the alliance is expanding and respect the West for its honesty. But when the West says to Russians: "Russian democracy is fine, Russian markets are fine, Russia's relationship with the West is fine, and therefore NATO is expanding to Russia's borders," the logic does not work, leaving the Russian people and their leaders bewildered and bitter. This resentment will only be exacerbated if the West continues its two-faced policy.

Finally, the West's insistence on promoting personalities rather than institutions also hinders Russia from choosing the right path. The West plays favorites, and I recognize that I am one of them, even though I am not in power. The danger comes when the West, while promoting the rhetoric of democracy and capitalism, backs Boris Yeltsin, Anatoly Chubais, Viktor Chernomyrdin, Boris Nemtsov, and Yegor Gaidar even when they embark on actions that do not promote democracy or markets. When Yeltsin ordered tanks to fire at the Russian parliament, the West supported him, as it did—at least publicly—when he ordered the army to start the war in Chechnya. That led most Russians to believe that had Yeltsin canceled the presidential election in 1996, the West would have backed his choice, despite the fact that the decision would have ended Russia's nascent democratic experiment.

WHAT IS TO BE DONE?

A Russia that works for its citizens and plays a constructive role in world politics will be a Russia that has chosen well. To achieve such an outcome, a new set of rules must be established. The most important step is to separate business from political power in order to fight corruption. There must be a decisive break with the legacy of the past, when administrative power stood above the law. Individual businesses should be regulated by legislation, not by government officials or local barons who are often not easily distinguishable from gang leaders. The power of oil and gas tycoons, who generate huge profits using the country's natural resources, must be curtailed. They should be made accountable to parliament, and their activities should be made transparent and subject to public control.

The present system of economic management, where most large enterprises are run by insiders who disregard the owners' rights, must be radically reformed. "Collective" enterprises, whose management styles and responsibilities smack of the Soviet era, should be eliminated. In their place, the government must encourage responsible management based on a conception of private property that ensures and protects the owner's rights. Bankruptcy laws should be fully enforced to help eliminate incompetent managers, crooks, and Soviet-style directors who are unable to adapt to market realities. Enterprises that hold on to workers and produce nothing but debts should be closed or sold.

Open accounting that meets international standards is a prerequisite to controlling corruption. Also required is a strong, independent, and incorruptible judiciary that will hold crooked officials accountable. For easier oversight, senior government officials should sign a declaration of income, property, and expenses for themselves and their families twice a year for review by the independent judiciary. The law making Duma members immune from prosecution should be immediately repealed. The large number of criminals running for Duma seats to gain immunity is repulsive. How can a legislature fight corruption when its members have their own deals on the side?

Free competition must be promoted by encouraging small and medium-sized businesses and by removing the red tape and excessive regulation that stands in their way. Former Soviet monopolies should be destroyed to eliminate domination by a small group of large companies that account for half the country's GDP while employing only three percent of its labor force. Land reform is also essential, since there can be no stable development in the agricultural sector until the major part of the country's land is taken from hands of the oligarchic landlords who "inherited" it from the Soviet state. Finally, both power and financial resources must be decentralized. Russia will be doomed to instability and underdevelopment as long as 85 percent of the nation's money remains concentrated in Moscow. Local initiatives and entrepreneurship should be encouraged if the fruits of economic growth are to be shared among Russia's numerous regional, social, and ethnic groups.

To ensure that an established middle class emerges, an open market economy must appear based on private property and competition.

Unregulated prices, low inflation rates, and a stable currency are absolutely necessary. In Russia, however, these are not sufficient conditions for a competitive economy. Lower and simpler taxes, fiscal controls on oligarchs' incomes from the use of natural resources, incentives for entrepreneurship, a trustworthy news service, an independent judiciary, and fully developed political parties are also indispensable.

For its part, the West should hold those in power in Russia accountable for undemocratic deeds, in much the same way as it is willing to criticize its allies. Western leaders should apply to Russia the same criteria for evaluating the health of its democracy and the strength of its market economy that they apply to themselves. The West should not give Russia advice it is not willing to take itself. This is especially important because, in the 21st century, competition will occur between civilizations and not countries. Although Russia and the West have different histories, they belong to the same civilization. The old rivalries need not endure—if Russia chooses wisely.

Issue 14
Political Islam

INTRODUCTION

Just as the Cold War was driven by the competing clash of ideologies, it is not uncommonly thought that the post–Cold War future will be driven by the competing clash of civilizations. Many theorists who entertain this scenario believe that, if a clash is to occur, it is most likely to happen between the West and the Islamic world.

This argument is predicated on the assumption that Islamic culture is incompatible with Western democratic values—an assumption that is vigorously denied by both the authors in this section. David G. Kibble cites the Islamic scholar Aziz Al-Azmeh, who regards Islamic fundamentalism as a transitory phase in a highly conflictual process of evolutionary change in the Islamic world toward freer and more democratic societies. Ali A. Mazrui's argument is much more proactive in defense of Islamic civilization. His points are well made, such as when he argues that "of all the value systems in the world, Islam has been the most resistant to the leading destructive forces of the twentieth century" or "while Islam may generate more political violence than Western culture, Western culture generates more street violence than Islam."

As you read the articles, consider the following questions.

Discussion Questions

1. Is fundamentalism, Islamic or otherwise, a reaction to westernization or modernization?
2. Is Islam incompatible with democracy? With capitalism?
3. Does Islam place too high a premium on community and consensus? Aren't these important democratic values as well?

4. Will the driving force of twenty-first century international politics be clashes between civilizations?

For more information on this topic, visit the following websites:

http://www.mesa.arizona.edu
Middle East Association of North America

http://www.wings.buffalo.edu/sa/muslim/isl/isl.html
Islamic Texts and Resources Metapage

http://www.mideasti.org
Middle East Institute

Islamic and Western Values

ALI A. MAZRUI

Democracy and the humane life.

Westerners tend to think of Islamic societies as backward-looking, oppressed by religion, and inhumanely governed, comparing them to their own enlightened, secular democracies. But measurement of the cultural distance between the West and Islam is a complex undertaking, and that distance is narrower than they assume. Islam is not just a religion, and certainly not just a fundamentalist political movement. It is a civilization, and a way of life that varies from one Muslim country to another but is animated by a common spirit far more humane than most Westerners realize. Nor do those in the West always recognize how their own societies have failed to live up to their liberal mythology. Moreover, aspects of Islamic culture that Westerners regard as medieval may have prevailed in their own culture until fairly recently; in many cases, Islamic societies may be only a few decades behind socially and technologically advanced Western ones. In the end, the question is what path leads to the highest quality of life for the average citizen, while avoiding the worst abuses. The path of the West does not provide all the answers; Islamic values deserve serious consideration.

THE WAY IT RECENTLY WAS

Mores and values have changed rapidly in the West in the last several decades as revolutions in technology and society progressed. Islamic countries, which are now experiencing many of the same changes, may well follow suit. Premarital sex, for example, was strongly disapproved of in the West until after World War II. There were laws against sex outside marriage, some of which are still on the books, if rarely enforced. Today sex before marriage, with parental consent, is common.

Homosexual acts between males were a crime in Great Britain until the 1960s (although lesbianism was not outlawed). Now such acts between consenting adults, male or female, are legal in much of the

Ali Mazrui is Director of the Institute of Global Cultural Studies at the State University of New York at Binghamton.

Reprinted by permission. *Foreign Affairs*, Sept.–Oct. 1997. Vol. 76, No. 5, p. 118.

West, although they remain illegal in most other countries. Half the Western world, in fact, would say that laws against homosexual sex are a violation of gays' and lesbians' human rights.

Even within the West, one sees cultural lag. Although capital punishment has been abolished almost everywhere in the Western world, the United States is currently increasing the number of capital offenses and executing more death row inmates than it has in years. But death penalty opponents, including Human Rights Watch and the Roman Catholic Church, continue to protest the practice in the United States, and one day capital punishment will almost certainly be regarded in America as a violation of human rights.

Westerners regard Muslim societies as unenlightened when it comes to the status of women, and it is true that the gender question is still troublesome in Muslim countries. Islamic rules on sexual modesty have often resulted in excessive segregation of the sexes in public places, sometimes bringing about the marginalization of women in public affairs more generally. British women, however, were granted the right to own property independent of their husbands only in 1870, while Muslim women have always had that right. Indeed, Islam is the only world religion founded by a businessman in commercial partnership with his wife. While in many Western cultures daughters could not inherit anything if there were sons in the family, Islamic law has always allocated shares from every inheritance to both daughters and sons. Primogeniture has been illegal under the sharia for 14 centuries.

The historical distance between the West and Islam in the treatment of women may be a matter of decades rather than centuries. Recall that in almost all Western countries except for New Zealand, women did not gain the right to vote until the twentieth century. Great Britain extended the vote to women in two stages, in 1918 and 1928, and the United States enfranchised them by constitutional amendment in 1920. France followed as recently as 1944. Switzerland did not permit women to vote in national elections until 1971—decades after Muslim women in Afghanistan, Iran, Iraq, and Pakistan had been casting ballots.

Furthermore, the United States, the largest and most influential Western nation, has never had a female president. In contrast, two of the most populous Muslim countries, Pakistan and Bangladesh, have had women prime ministers: Benazir Bhutto headed two governments in Pakistan, and Khaleda Zia and Hasina Wajed served consecutively in Bangladesh. Turkey has had Prime Minister Tansu Ciller. Muslim countries are ahead in female empowerment, though still behind in female liberation.

CONCEPTS OF THE SACRED

Censorship is one issue on which the cultural divide between the West and Islam turns out to be less wide than Westerners ordinarily assume. The most celebrated case of the last decade—that of Salman Rushdie's novel *The Satanic Verses*, published in Britain in 1988 but banned in most Muslim countries—brought the Western world and the Muslim world in conflict, but also uncovered some surprising similarities and large helpings of Western hypocrisy. Further scrutiny reveals widespread censorship in the West, if imposed by different forces than in Muslim societies.

As their civilization has become more secular, Westerners have looked for new abodes of the sacred. By the late twentieth century the freedom of the artist—in this case, Salman Rushdie—was more sacred to them than religion. But many Muslims saw Rushdie's novel as holding Islam up to ridicule. The novel suggests that Islam's holy scripture, the Koran, is filled with inventions of the Prophet Muhammad or is, in fact, the work of the devil rather than communications from Allah, and implies, moreover, that the religion's founder was not very intelligent. Rushdie also puts women characters bearing the names of the Prophet's wives in a whorehouse, where the clients find the blasphemy arousing.

Many devout Muslims felt that Rushdie had no right to poke fun at and twist into obscenity some of the most sacred symbols of Islam. Most Muslim countries banned the novel because officials there considered it morally repugnant.[1] Western intellectuals argued that as an artist, Rushdie had the sacred right and even duty to go wherever his imagination led him in his writing. Yet until the 1960s *Lady Chatterley's Lover* was regarded as morally repugnant under British law for daring to depict an affair between a married member of the gentry and a worker on the estate. For a long time after Oscar Wilde's conviction for homosexual acts, *The Picture of Dorian Gray* was regarded as morally repugnant. Today other gay writers are up against a wall of prejudice.

The Satanic Verses was banned in some places because of fears that it would cause riots. Indian officials explained that they were banning the novel because it would inflame religious passions in the country, already aroused by Kashmiri separatism. The United States has a legal standard for preventive action when negative consequences are feared— "clear and present danger." But the West was less than sympathetic to India's warnings that the book was inflammatory. Rushdie's London publisher, Jonathan Cape, went ahead, and the book's publication even in far-off Britain resulted in civil disturbances in Bombay, Islamabad, and Karachi in which some 15 people were killed and dozens more injured.

Distinguished Western publishers, however, have been known to reject a manuscript because of fears for the safety of their own. Last year Cambridge University Press turned down *Fields of Wheat, Rivers of Blood* by Anastasia Karakasidou, a sociological study on ethnicity in the Greek province of Macedonia, publicly acknowledging that it did so because of worries about the safety of its employees in Greece. If Jonathan Cape had cared as much about South Asian lives as it said it cared about freedom of expression, or as Cambridge University Press cared about its staff members in Greece, less blood would have been spilled.

Targets, sources, and methods of censorship differ, but censorship is just as much a fact of life in Western societies as in the Muslim world. Censorship in the latter is often crude, imposed by governments, mullahs and imams, and, more recently, militant Islamic movements. Censorship in the West, on the other hand, is more polished and decentralized. Its practitioners are financial backers of cultural activity and entertainment, advertisers who buy time on commercial television, subscribers of the Public Broadcasting System (PBS), influential interest groups including ethnic pressure groups, and editors, publishers, and other controllers of the means of communication.[2] In Europe, governments, too, sometimes get into the business of censorship.

CENSORING AMERICA

The threat to free speech in the United States comes not from the law and the Constitution but from outside the government. PBS, legally invulnerable on the issue of free speech, capitulated to other forces when faced with the metaphorical description in my 1986 television series "The Africans" of Karl Marx as "the last of the great Jewish prophets." The British version had included the phrase, but the American producing station, WETA, a PBS affiliate in Washington, deleted it without authorial permission so as not to risk offending Jewish Americans.

On one issue of censorship WETA did consult me. Station officials were unhappy I had not injected more negativity into the series' three-minute segment on Libya's leader, Muammar Qaddafi. First they asked for extra commentary on allegations that Libya sponsored terrorism. When I refused, they suggested changing the pictures instead—deleting one sequence that humanized Qaddafi by showing him visiting a hospital and substituting a shot of the Rome airport after a terrorist bombing. After much debate I managed to save the hospital scene but surrendered on the Rome airport addition, on condition that neither I nor the written caption implied that Libya was responsible for the bombing. But, ideally, WETA would have preferred to cut the whole segment.

WETA in those days had more in common with the censors in Libya than either side realized. Although the Libyans broadcast an Arabic version and seemed pleased with the series as a whole, they cut the Qaddafi sequence. The segment also offended Lynne Cheney, chair of the National Endowment for the Humanities, who demanded that the endowment's name be removed from the series credits. After she stepped down from her post, she called for the NEH to be abolished, citing "The Africans" as an example of the objectionable liberal projects that, she said, the endowment had tended to fund.

In another case of decentralized censorship that affected my own work, Westview Press in Boulder, Colorado, was about to go to press with my book *Cultural Forces in World Politics* when editors there announced they wanted to delete three chapters: one discussing *The Satanic Verses* as a case of cultural treason, another comparing the Palestinian intifada with Chinese students' 1989 rebellion in Tiananmen Square, and a third comparing the South African apartheid doctrine of separate homelands for blacks and whites with the Zionist doctrine of separate states for Jews and Arabs. Suspecting that I would have similar problems with most other major U.S. publishers, I decided that the book would be published exclusively by James Currey, my British publisher, and Heinemann Educational Books, the American offshoot of another British house, which brought it out in 1990. Not even universities in the United States, supposed bastions of intellectual freedom, have been free from censorship. Until recently the greatest danger to one's chances of getting tenure lay in espousing Marxism or criticizing Israel or Zionism.

The positive aspect of decentralized censorship in the West, at least with regard to books, is that what is unacceptable to one publisher may be acceptable to another; what is almost unpublishable in the United States may be easily publishable in Britain or the Netherlands. With national television, the choices are more restricted. Many points of view are banned from the screen, with the possibility of a hearing only on the public access stations with the weakest signals.

In Western societies as in Muslim ones, only a few points of view have access to the national broadcast media and publishing industry or even to university faculties. In both civilizations, certain points of view are excluded from the center and marginalized. The source of the censorship may be different, but censorship is the result in the West just as surely as in the Islamic world.

LIFE AMONG THE BELIEVERS

Many of the above issues are bound up with religion. Westerners consider many problems or flaws of the Muslim world products of Islam and pride their societies and their governments on their purported secularism. But when it comes to separation of church and state, how long and wide is the distance between the two cultures?

A central question is whether a theocracy can ever be democratized. British history since Henry VIII's establishment of the Church of England in 1531 proves that it can be. The English theocracy was democratized first by making democracy stronger and later by making the theocracy weaker. The major democratic changes had to wait until the nineteenth and twentieth centuries, when the vote was extended to new social classes and finally to women.[3] The Islamic Republic of Iran is less than two decades old, but already there seem to be signs of softening theocracy and the beginnings of liberalization. Nor must we forget Muslim monarchies that have taken initial steps toward liberalization. Jordan has gone further than most others in legalizing opposition groups. But even Saudi Arabia and the smaller Gulf states have begun to use the Islamic concept of shura (consultative assembly) as a guide to democracy.

The West has sought to protect minority religions through secularism. It has not always worked. The Holocaust in secular Germany was the worst case. And even today, anti-semitism in Eastern Europe is disturbing, as are anti-muslim trends in France.

The United States has had separation of church and state under the Constitution for over 200 years, but American politics is hardly completely secular. Only once has the electorate chosen a non-Protestant president—and the Roman Catholic John F. Kennedy won by such a narrow margin, amid such allegations of electoral fraud, that we will never know for certain whether a majority of Americans actually voted for him. Jews have distinguished themselves in many fields, but they have so far avoided competing for the White House, and there is still a fear of unleashing the demon of anti-Semitism among Christian fundamentalists. There are now more Muslims—an estimated six million—than Jews in the United States, yet anti-Muslim feeling and the success of appeals to Christian sentiment among voters make it extremely unlikely that Americans will elect a Muslim head of state anytime in the foreseeable future. Even the appointment of a Muslim secretary of commerce, let alone an attorney general, is no more than a distant conjecture because of the political fallout that all administrations fear. When First Lady Hillary Rodham Clinton entertained Muslim leaders at the White House last year to mark a special Islamic festival, a *Wall Street Journal* article cited that as evidence that friends of Hamas had penetrated the White House. In Western Europe, too, there are now millions of Muslims, but history is still awaiting the appointment of the first to a cabinet position in Britain, France, or Germany. Islam, on the other hand, has tried to protect minority religions through ecumenicalism throughout its history. Jews and Christians had special status as People of the Book—a fraternity of monotheists. Other religious minorities were later also accorded the status of protected minorities (dhimmis). The approach has had its successes. Jewish scholars rose to high positions in Muslim

Spain. During the Ottoman Empire, Christians sometimes attained high political office: Suleiman I (1520–1566) had Christian ministers in his government, as did Selim III (1789–1807). The Moghul Empire integrated Hindus and Muslims into a consolidated Indian state; Emperor Akbar (1556–1605) carried furthest the Moghul policy of bringing Hindus into the government. In the 1990s Iraq has had a Chaldean Christian deputy prime minister, Tariq Aziz. And Boutros Boutros-ghali, a Coptic Christian, would never have been appointed secretary-general of the United Nations if not for his long and distinguished service in the foreign ministry of an otherwise Muslim government in Egypt.

The Republic of Senegal in West Africa, which is nearly 95 percent Muslim, had a Roman Catholic president for two decades (1960–1980). In his years presiding over that relatively open society, Leopold Sedar Senghor never once had to deal with anti-Christian disturbances in the streets of Dakar. His political opponents called him a wide range of derogatory names—hypocrite, stooge of the French, dictator, political prostitute—but virtually never taunted him for being a kafir (infidel).

When Senghor became the first African head of state to retire voluntarily from office, Abdou Diouf, a Muslim, succeeded him, and he remains president today. But the ecumenical story of Senegal did not end there; the first lady is Catholic. Can one imagine an American presidential candidate confessing on *Larry King Live*, "Incidentally, my wife is a Shiite Muslim"? That would almost certainly mark the end of his hopes for the White House.

One conclusion to be drawn from all this is that Westerners are far less secular in their political behavior than they think they are. Another is that Muslim societies historically have been more ecumenical, and therefore more humane, than their Western critics have recognized. Islamic ecumenicalism has sometimes protected religious minorities more effectively than Western secularism.

BETWEEN THE DAZZLING AND THE DEPRAVED

Cultures should be judged not merely by the heights of achievement to which they have ascended but by the depths of brutality to which they have descended. The measure of cultures is not only their virtues but also their vices.

In the twentieth century, Islam has not often proved fertile ground for democracy and its virtues. On the other hand, Islamic culture has not been hospitable to Nazism, fascism, or communism, unlike Christian culture (as in Germany, Italy, Russia, Czechoslovakia), Buddhist culture (Japan before and during World War II, Pol Pot's Cambodia, Vietnam, North Korea), or Confucian culture (Mao's China). The Muslim world has never yet given rise to systematic fascism and its organized brutalities. Hafiz al-Assad's Syria and Saddam Hussein's Iraq have been guilty of large-scale violence, but fascism also requires an ideology of repression that has been absent in the two countries. And apart from the dubious case of Albania, communism has never independently taken hold in a Muslim culture.

Muslims are often criticized for not producing the best, but they are seldom congratulated for an ethic that has averted the worst. There are no Muslim equivalents of Nazi extermination camps; nor Muslim conquests by genocide on the scale perpetrated by Europeans in the Americas and Australia, nor Muslim equivalents of Stalinist terror, Pol Pot's killing fields, or the starvation and uprooting of tens of millions in the name of Five Year Plans. Nor are there Muslim versions of apartheid like that once approved by the South African Dutch Reformed Church, or of the ferocious racism of Japan before 1945, or of the racist culture of the Old South in the United States with its lynchings and brutalization of black people.

Islam brings to the calculus of universal justice some protection from the abyss of human depravity. Historically, the religion and the civilization have been resistant to forces that contributed to the worst aspects of the twentieth century's interludes of barbarism: racism, genocide, and violence within society.

First, Islam has been relatively resistant to racism. The Koran confronts the issue of national and ethnic differences head on. The standard of excellence it sets has nothing to do with race, but is instead moral and religious worth—what the Koran calls "piety" and what Martin Luther King, Jr., called "the content of one's character." An oft-quoted verse of the Koran reads:

> O people! We have created you from a male and a female, and have
> made you nations and tribes so that you may know one another. The
> noblest among you is the most pious. Allah is all-knowing.

In his farewell address, delivered on his last pilgrimage to Mecca in A.D. 632, Muhammad declared: "There is no superiority of an Arab over a non-Arab, and indeed, no superiority of a red man over a black man except through piety and fear of God . . . Let those who are present convey this message to those who are absent."

Unlike Christian churches, the mosque has never been segregated by race. One of Muhammad's most beloved companions was an Ethiopian, Bilal Rabah, a freed slave who rose to great prominence in early Islam. Under Arab lineage systems and kinship traditions, racial intermarriage was not discouraged and the children were considered Arab regardless of who the mother was. These Arab ways influenced Muslim societies elsewhere. Of the four presidents of Egypt since the revolution of 1952, two had black African ancestors—Muhammad Nagib and Anwar al-Sadat.[4]

Islam has a doctrine of Chosen Language (Arabic) but no Chosen People. Since the conversion of the Roman Emperor Constantine I in A.D. 313, Christianity has been led if not dominated by Europeans. But the leadership of the Muslim world has changed hands several times: from the mainly Arab Umayyad dynasty (661–750) to the multiethnic Abbasid dynasty (750–1258) to the Ottoman Empire (1453–1922), dominated by the Turks. And this history is quite apart from such flourishing Muslim dynasties as the Moghuls of India and the Safavids of Persia or the sub-Saharan empires of Mali and Songhai. The diversification of Muslim leadership—in contrast to the Europeanization of Christian leadership—helped the cause of relative racial equality in Islamic culture.

Partly because of Islam's relatively nonracial nature, Islamic history has been free of systematic efforts to obliterate a people. Islam conquered by co-optation, intermarriage, and conversion rather than by genocide. Incidents in Muslim history, it is true, have caused large-scale loss of life. During Turkey's attempt in 1915 to deport the entire Armenian population of about 1,750,000 to Syria and Palestine, hundreds of thousands of people, perhaps up to a million, died of starvation or were murdered on the way. But—though this does not exonerate Turkey of its responsibility for the deaths—Armenians had provoked Turkey by organizing volunteer battalions to help Russia fight against it in World War I. Nor is the expulsion of a people from a territory, however disastrous its consequences, equivalent to the Nazi Holocaust, which systematically took the lives of six million Jews and members of other despised groups. Movement of people between India and Pakistan after partition in 1947 also resulted in thousands of deaths en route.

Saddam Hussein's use of poison gas against Kurdish villages in Iraq in 1988 is more clearly comparable to Nazi behavior. But Saddam's action was the use of an illegitimate weapon in a civil war rather than a planned program to destroy the Kurdish people; it was an evil incident rather than a program of genocide. Many people feel that President Harry S Truman's dropping of atomic bombs on Hiroshima and Nagasaki was also an evil episode. There is a difference between massacre and genocide. Massacres have been perpetrated in almost every country on earth, but only a few cultures have been guilty of genocide.

Nor did Islam ever spawn an Inquisition in which the burning of heretics at the stake was sanctioned. Cultures that had condemned human beings to burn and celebrated as they died in the flames, even hundreds of years before, were more likely to tolerate the herding of a whole people of another faith into gas chambers. Islam has been a shield against such excesses of evil.

THE ORDER OF ISLAM

Against Western claims that Islamic "fundamentalism" feeds terrorism, one powerful paradox of the twentieth century is often overlooked. While Islam may generate more political violence than Western culture, Western culture generates more street violence than Islam. Islam does indeed produce a disproportionate share of mujahideen, but Western culture produces a disproportionate share of muggers. The largest Muslim city in Africa is Cairo. The largest westernized city is Johannesburg. Cairo is much more populous than Johannesburg, but street violence is only a fraction of what it is in the South African city. Does Islam help pacify Cairo? I, along with many others, believe that it does. The high premium Islam places on umma (community) and ijma (consensus) has made for a Pax Islamica in day-to-day life.

In terms of quality of life, is the average citizen better off under the excesses of the Islamic state or the excesses of the liberal state, where political tension may be low but social violence has reached crisis proportions? Tehran, the capital of the Islamic Republic of Iran, is a city of some ten million. Families with small children picnic in public parks at 11 p.m. or midnight. Residents of the capital and other cities stroll late at night, seemingly unafraid of mugging, rape, or murder. This is a society that has known large-scale political violence in war and revolution, but one in which petty interpersonal violence is much rarer than in Washington or New York. Iranians are more subject to their government than Americans, but they are less at risk from the depredations of their fellow citizens. Nor is dictatorial government the explanation for the safe streets of Tehran—otherwise, Lagos would be as peaceful as the Iranian capital.

The Iranian solution is mainly in the moral sphere. As an approach to the problems of modernity, some Muslim societies are attempting a return to premodernism, to indigenous traditional disciplines and values. Aside from Iran, countries such as Sudan and Saudi Arabia have revived Islamic legal systems and other features of the Islamic way of life, aspects of which go back 14 centuries. Islamic movements in countries like Algeria, Egypt, and Afghanistan are also seeking revivalist goals. A similar sacred nostalgia is evident in other religions, such as the born-again Christian sects in the United States and Africa.

Of all the value systems in the world, Islam has been the most resistant to the leading destructive forces of the twentieth century—including AIDS. Lower levels of prostitution and of hard drug use in conservative Muslim cultures compared with other cultures have, so far, contributed to lower-than-average HIV infection rates.[5] If societies closer to the sharia are also more distant from the human immunodeficiency virus, should the rest of the world take a closer look?

One can escape modernity by striving to transcend it as well as by retreating from it into the past. Perhaps the Muslim world should explore this path, searching for postmodern solutions to its political tensions and economic woes, and pursuing the positive aspects of globalization without falling victim to the negative aspects of westernization.

THE DIALECTIC OF CULTURE

Western Liberal democracy has enabled societies to enjoy openness, government accountability, popular participation, and high economic productivity, but Western pluralism has also been a breeding ground for racism, fascism, exploitation, and genocide. If history is to end in arrival at the ultimate political order, it will require more than the West's message on how to maximize the best in human nature. Humankind must also consult Islam about how to check the worst in human nature—from alcoholism to racism, materialism to Nazism, drug addiction to Marxism as the opiate of the intellectuals.

One must distinguish between democratic principles and humane principles. In some humane principles—including stabilizing the family, security from social violence, and the relatively nonracial nature of religious institutions—the Muslim world may be ahead of the West.

Turkey is a prime example of the dilemma of balancing humane principles with democratic principles. In times of peace, the Ottoman Empire was more humane in its treatment of religious minorities than the Turkish Republic after 1923 under the westernizing influence of Mustafa Kemal Atatiirk. The Turkish Republic, on the other hand, gradually moved toward a policy of cultural assimilation. While the Ottoman Empire tolerated the Kurdish language, the Turkish Republic outlawed its use for a considerable period. When not at war, the empire was more humane than the Turkish Republic, but less democratic.

At bottom, democracy is a system for selecting one's rulers; humane governance is a system for treating citizens. Ottoman rule at its best was humane governance; the Turkish Republic at its best has been a quest for democratic values. In the final years of the twentieth century, Turkey may be engaged in reconciling the greater humaneness of the Ottoman Empire with the greater democracy of the Republic. The current Islamic revival in the country may be the beginning of a fundamental review of the Kemalist revolution, which inaugurated Turkish secularism. In England since Henry VIII, a theocracy has been democratized. In Turkey, might a democracy be theocratized? Although the Turkish army is trying to stop it, electoral support for Islamic revivalism is growing in the country. There has been increased speculation that secularism may be pushed back, in spite of the resignation in June, under political pressure from the generals, of Prime Minister Necmettin Erbakan, the leader of the Islamist Welfare Party. Is Erbakan nevertheless destined to play in the Kemalist revolution the role that Mikhail Gorbachev or Boris Yeltsin played in the Leninist revolution? Or is Erbakan a forerunner of change? It is too early to be sure. The dialectic of history continues its conversation with the dialectic of culture within the wider rhythms of relativity in human experience.

NOTES

1. In citing the Rushdie case as evidence of Islamic society's repressive nature, Westerners point to the 1989 fatwa, or legal ruling, by the Ayatollah Khomeini of Iran indicting Rushdie for blasphemy and the capital crime of apostasy and sentencing him to death in absentia. Iran, however, was the only Muslim country to decree the death penalty for Rushdie. Bangladesh said that Rushdie's crime, if proved, was a capital offense, but that he would have to be tried in a Muslim country to ascertain his guilt. There is a broad consensus that the book is blasphemous (even the Vatican agrees that it is), but Iran stands alone with the fatwa.
2. American writers such as Carl Bernstein, Howard Fast, Erica Jong, and Peter Maas have spoken of both overt and covert censorship; see Midge Decter, "The Rushdiad," *Commentary*, vol. 87, no. 6 (June 1989), pp. 20–21.
3. See Leonard Binder, *Islamic Liberalism: A Critique of Development Ideologies*, Chicago: University of Chicago Press, 1988, especially Chapter 9, "Conclusion: The Prospects for Liberal Government in the Middle East," pp. 336–60.
4. Like most other religions and civilizations, Islam tolerated the ownership and trade of slaves for centuries. But slavery among Muslims was almost race-neutral. In contrast to the racially polarized transatlantic slave system—white masters, black slaves—slaves in the Islamic world could be white, black, brown, or other, and so could masters. Moreover, slavery among Muslims allowed for great upward social mobility. Both Muslim India and Muslim Egypt produced slave dynasties; the former slaves who became Mamluk rulers of Egypt dominated the country from 1250 to 1517.
5. Studies by researchers in Ivory Coast of Muslim countries in Africa have shown that approximately half as many Muslims as non-Muslims are likely to be infected with HIV. See Catherine Tastemain and Peter Coles, "Can a Culture Stop AIDS in Its Tracks?" *New Scientist* (London), vol. 139, no. 1890.

Islamic Fundamentalism: A Transitory Threat?

DAVID G. KIBBLE

Islamic fundamentalism is never far from the news. A protrayal of what Islamic fundamentalism can mean in practice was provided by the graphic media accounts of life in Kabul after it was overrun by the Taliban Militia in October 1996. Public transport was ordered to halt five times a day to allow people to report to the mosque for prayer. Kabul radio announced, "All drivers of taxis, buses and lorries are asked to park their vehicles at the nearest mosque and to offer congregational prayers along with their passengers."[1] Women were banished from the workplace, girls' schools closed and women doctors sent home. Soccer was declared to be against Islam. Even chess was forbidden! Men were given six weeks to grow a beard, while women were asked to cover themselves in strict Islamic dress so that no part of the face could be seen. A spokesman for the Taliban commented: "We will punish all those who do not follow Islamic teachings, whether educated or uneducated."[2] Even Iran complained that the Taliban were going far beyond what Islam required.[3]

Other events keep Islamic fundamentalism in the news. In the summer of 1996 there was an abortive coup in Bahrain by a fundamentalist group calling themselves *Hezbollah Bahrain*. In June of the same year 19 U.S. servicemen were killed and 386 wounded in an attack on a military complex in Dhahran, Saudi Arabia. It is assumed that a fundamentalist group carried out the attack. Shortly after the victory of the Taliban Militia in Afghanistan, there was an attack in December on the Paris Metro, killing four. This was assumed to be an act of the GIA, the *Groupe Islamique Armée*, following on from the Algerian government's victory in a referendum which outlawed political parties based on religion.

1997 saw 250 people killed in January by the GIA in Algiers and 3 people killed and 42 injured in March in Tel Aviv as a result of a *Hamas* suicide bombing. In July, 2 further *Hamas* suicide bombers killed 15

David G. Kibble, a theology graduate of Edinburgh University, is a Deputy Headteacher at Huntington School in York, England. A former Naval Reservist and Commanding Officer of HMS *Ceres*, he has written on both sides of the Atlantic on defense issues, particularly on the Islamic background to problems in the Middle East and on the ethics of nuclear deterrence.

Reprinted by permission. *Strategic Review*, Spring 1998, Vol. xxvi, No. 2, p. 11–18.

people and wounded 170 in an attack on the Mahane Yehuda food market in Jerusalem, while more than 300 people died in attacks by the GIA in and around Algiers in one week at the end of August. Attacks in Algeria continued with 400 killed in December 1997 and over 10 massacred in Relizone province at the beginning of 1998. 1997 also saw the Egyptian fundamentalist terrorist group, *Gama al-Islamiya,* murdering 58 tourists at Luxor.

At the beginning of 1998 Muslim fundamentalist Ramzi Ahmed Yousef was sentenced to 240 years in prison for masterminding the 1993 bombing of the World Trade Center in New York and an unsuccessful plot to blow up a dozen U.S. planes in Asia. He went to jail defiantly proclaiming, "I am a terrorist and I am proud of it."

Yet, while Islamic fundamentalism may regularly hit the newspaper headlines, it is only a temporary phenomenon. Its internal contradictions and weaknesses combined with its passage into the new millennium cannot but ensure its demise in the longer term. Islamic fundamentalism may therefore be said to be "here today, gone tomorrow."

FUNDAMENTALIST ISLAM

Islam, like any other faith or political party, has many different hues. Islam contains people of many different nations and backgrounds and of many different persuasions within the umbrella of Islam. One of the most important differences between Muslims, in addition to the well-known division between Shiite and Sunni, lies in their interpretation of the Qur'an. On the one hand lies the modernist Muslim who wishes to take the Qur'an and to interpret it in the light of the twentieth century. The sacred text, the modernist argues, originally written some fourteen hundred years ago, needs adapting to the twentieth century. The Qur'an speaks of a literal creation by God, for example: the modernist would wish to update the concept of creation in the light of twentieth century scientific ideas and would wish to say that Allah created the universe through the process of evolution. One of the founding fathers of modernism was Muhammad Rashid Rida. He made the following comment concerning science and the Qur'an: "Human history contained in the Qur'an is like the natural history of animals, plants, and inanimate objects in it. . . . What is intended by all this is to demonstrate by example the omnipotence of the Creator and His Wisdom and not to set forth in detail the natural sciences or astronomy which God has enabled man to understand through study, contemplation and experiment. . . ."[4] In other words, the Qur'an is to be read not as a scientific text book, as the fundamentalist reads it, but as a religious document revealing religious truth. Similarly the modernist would argue that the Qur'anic requirement that thieves have a limb amputated is a requirement conditioned by its time: nowadays, such a barbaric punishment is no longer appropriate.

The fundamentalist, on the other hand, would argue that the Qur'an is the literal, absolute and final Word of God and must therefore be understood just as it stands without interpretation. What Allah said fourteen hundred years ago was said for all time. The concept of the book being interpreted for modern times is alien to the fundamentalist. According to the fundamentalist, the Qur'an is "the supreme norm for human life, the chief source of guidance. This means subordination of all other sources of knowledge to the Divine Revelation."[5] For the fundamentalist, literal creation by Allah means just that, and if the Qur'an demands amputation, then that is what shall be given, for that is what Allah is demanding. Such a literal reading of the Qur'an by fundamentalists results in ideas that are ". . . the product of a highly specific reading of a small range of sources, interpreted politically to favour right-wing, fascist and hypernationalist ideology."[6]

The fundamentalist understanding of the Qur'an has another aspect to it: if it is the direct Word of God to his people and should be interpreted exactly as it stands, then the assumption is that the text can be understood, or at the very least interpreted, directly by each individual Muslim. The fact that no adaptation to modern times is necessary and that the text is in itself plain can have the additional corollary that anyone can interpret the text and can do so directly and correctly. No priest, mullah or imam needs to interpret the book for the believer: it is in itself directly apprehensible. In this respect commentators have pointed out a similarity between fundamentalist Islam and the ideas of Martin Luther in the Christian rebellion.[7] Dale Eickelman and James Piscatori point out that the concept of each individual Muslim being the interpreter of the Qur'an, this concept of individual access to the divine, means that each individual Muslim is endowed with authority. There is no intermediary necessary between the believer and the Qur'an to say that his interpretation is incorrect. What the Muslim believer interprets directly must be the correct interpretation. The fundamentalist Muslim is therefore, in one sense, his own authority.

In essence, therefore, the fundamentalist Muslim regards the Qur'an as the direct revelation of God. It is to be interpreted by the individual believer exactly as it stands without any need for updating or setting in context.

Fundamentalist Muslims share certain ideas. They are committed to the cause of social action. The Qur'an commands: "Serve God . . . and do good—to parents, kinsfolk, orphans, those in need, neighbors who are near, neighbors who are strangers, the companion by your side, the wayfarer. . . ."[8] When Cairo was hit by an earthquake in 1992, it was the fundamentalist Muslim Brotherhood which provided relief centers in the poor neighborhoods. Similarly in Algeria the Islamic Salvation Front (FIS) earned goodwill when it provided tents and blankets after an earthquake near Tipaza. The Lebanese fundamentalist *Hizbullah* (Party of God) has developed an extensive social welfare system in Lebanon that involves educational, agricultural, medical and housing assistance. In Beirut's Bir al-Abid quarter it has run a supermarket co-operative, selling produce at below retail cost, and provides scholarships, runs health clinics and subsidizes housing for the needy. A recent British newspaper report highlighted the charitable works of Muslim fundamentalist groups among North African immigrant families in the poor areas of French cities, including rehabilitation work with drug addicts.[9] Raphael Israeli's study of fundamentalist groups in Palestine paints a similar picture.[10] Such charitable work is done not only for its own sake but also to serve fundamentalist groups' power-seeking strategies in the local and national political arena.

THE LEGITIMACY OF VIOLENCE: DIFFERENCES BETWEEN THE FUNDAMENTALISTS

Although Muslim fundamentalists agree on certain issues, there are some over which they differ. Chief among these differences is their stance towards a non-Muslim government. Fundamentalists agree that the Muslim ideal is a country run according to the precepts of the Qur'an and the *Sunnah* (sayings and deeds of the prophet Muhammad). It means the implementation and application of the law code known as *Sharia*, that is, law derived from the Qur'an and *Sunnah*.[11] In contradistinction to the non-Muslim state, fundamentalists see an Islamic country as one that is in one sense inevitable in that it conforms to the pre-existent divine pattern. Rational argument can be used with little effect to buttress the fundamentalist position, since the whole concept rests purely on divine command. But how should the Muslim fundamentalist react in the face of a government which rejects such an ideal?

The majority of fundamentalists would wish to pursue a peaceful path of progress towards their ideal, a path marked by persuasion and socail action. Such a path is one espoused by the moderate fundamentalist Egyptian Muslim Brotherhood. In the West Bank the moderate fundamentalist Sheikh Abdallah Nimr Darwish wants a Muslim state but denounces terrorism as an acceptable means of achieving that end even under Israeli domination. He believes that any struggle with the Israeli government must be undertaken within the limits of Israeli law. Just as most fundamentalists wish to achieve a Muslim state by peaceful means, so most Palestinian fundamentalists wish to see the return of the West Bank and its development into a Muslim state by a similar peaceful process.

On the other hand there are more militant Muslims at the other end of the spectrum who see violence as an acceptable tool. In Egypt groups such as *Takfir wal-Hijra* (Excommunication and Flight), *Jamaat al-Jihad* (Holy War Society) and Salvation from Hell are all prepared to use violence as a means of achieving their ends. At the heart of *al-Jihad's* message and mission is the belief that Egypt has regressed to the state of *Jahiliyya*, the pre-Islamic time of ignorance and unbelief.[12] The only cure the fundamentalist group sees is *Jihad* or Holy War. One of the group's tracts declares, "There is no doubt that the idols of this world can only disappear through the power of the sword."[13] At a conference in 1968 Sheikh Abdullah Ghoshash, Supreme Judge of the Hashemite kingdom of Jordan, pronounced that "[it] is unlawful to give up *Jihad* and adopt peace and weakness. . . . War is the basis of the relationship between Muslims and their opponents unless there are justifiable reasons for peace such as adopting Islam or making an agreement with them to keep peaceful."[14] Similar thoughts were expressed by the Ayatollah Khomeini: "The Qur'an commands: wage war until all corruption and all disobedience [of divine law] are wiped out! The wars that our prophet—blessed be his soul—waged against the infidels were divine gifts to humanity. Once we have won the war [against Iraq] we shall turn to other wars. . . . We have to wage war until all corruption, all disobedience of Islamic laws cease. . . . A religion without war is a crippled religion."[15]

THE NATURE OF ISLAMIC GOVERNMENT: A LACK OF CLARITY

Just as there is no unanimity concerning the use of violence, so there is a lack of unanimity concerning the nature of Muslim government.[16] The balance between given Divine Law and a democratic procedure, for example, is unclear. The Ayatollah Khomeini was clear concerning his vision: "What the nation wants is an Islamic republic. Not just a republic, not a democratic republic, not a demcratic Islamic republic. Just an Islamic republic. Do not use the word 'democratic.' That is Western and we do not want it."[17] Saleh Sirriyah, the mastermind behind the attempted seizure of the Heliopolis Military Academy in Egypt in 1974, offers a similar analysis: "Democracy . . . is a way of life which contradicts Islam's way; for in Democracy the people have the power to legislate and to permit and forbid what they will . . . while in Islam people have no such competence over what is *halal* [permitted by Allah] and what is *haram* [prohibited by Allah], even if they were to achieve total unanimity over the matter. Combining Islam and Democracy is, then, like combining Islam and Judaism. . . ."[18] A document by *Islamic Jihad* in Egypt argues that democracy can never be the correct form of government as it allows equal rights to all citizens, whereas Islam regards Christians and Jews as second-class citizens, having to pay the special *Jizzyah* tax. Non-Muslims would be effectively second-class citizens with limited rights and opportunities.

Other fundamentalists give more weight to a possible democratic procedure within a Muslim state. In Islam there exists the concept of *Ijma*. *Ijma* is the consensus of religious leaders who may decide courses of action, provided they remain within the guidelines set down in the Qur'an and the *Sunnah*, the sayings and deeds of the prophet. *Ijma* should be informed by *Shura*, a process of consultation with the people. In this way fundamentalists can argue that there is a place for at least a limited form of democracy within an Islamic regime. Contrary to popular opinion, such a form of government exists in Iran, where there are democratic elections for the *Majlis* (Parliament) and for the President of the Republic. That having been said, however, all legislation is subject to examination by the Council of Guardians, who can veto measures if they are deemed not to be in conformity with Islam. Some form of democracy has been advocated by the Muslim Brotherhood movements in Egypt and Jordan, Algeria's Islamic Salvation Front and Kuwait's *Jamiyyat al-Islah* (Reform Society), among others.

Defining the precise nature of governmental authority using and balancing such concepts as *Sharia* (that is law based on the Qur'an and *Sunnah*),[19] *Ijma* and *Shura* is not easy. One might argue that Islam itself has no fully clear guidelines on the matter: at the very least it lacks clarity. One commentator on religious law has said, concerning *Shura*, "To do any collective work without any prior mutual consultation is not only a way of the ignorant but it is also a clear defiance of the regulation laid down by Allah."[20] What would happen, one might ask, if *Shura* took place, the people were consulted and they pressed for the dissolution of a Muslim state? One critic of fundamentalist Islam comments that much of the Islamic political ideal is little more than a rejection of what it sees as the corrupt Western model. In other words it knows what it does not want, but lacks a coherent picture or vision of what it does want. He concludes that "there is no concrete political . . . model inherent in Islam."[21]

If fundamentalist Islam is not fully clear on what constitutes a truly Muslim government, it is even less clear on the question of economics. According to Olivier Roy the problem with fundamentalist Islamic economics is that it offers no socio-economic analysis and presents nothing in the way of a proper economic system. It concentrates so much on the relationship of the individual Muslim to his God that there is a resulting absence of anything of real substance when it comes to society, either in terms of government or in terms of basic economic policy.[22]

FUNDAMENTALIST ISLAM: PRESENT AND FUTURE

Those of us who remember the days of the Ayatollah Khomeini will remember seeing on our television screen streets full of Iranians demonstrating against the West: the United States was denounced as the "Great Satan" and the crowds chanted "*Allaho Akbar*" ("God is Great"). Amuzegar's study of contemporary Iran concludes that while there is an ingrained faith in Allah, an adulation for the prophet Muhammad, an enthusiasm for some of the Shia religious rites and a concurrence with many Islamic symbols, there is at the same time a resistance to ecclesiastical coercion, a resentment of Islam's undue infringements on one's private life and a rejection of thought control. He notes that despite the Islamic dress code with its head covering for the women and tieless, bearded men, there is in some sections of society the regular consumption of alcohol and what some fundamentalists would consider improper partying. Many Iranians listen to broadcasts by the BBC and by CNN rather than listen to their own indigenous networks; there is a black market for modern popular music, CDs and denim jeans.[23]

Discontent among some sections of Iranian society over economic hardship and particularly over activities of the Islamic moral police recently forced authorities to relax a number of fundamentalist measures: male students may now wear short sleeved shirts to university, and floral headscarves and raincoats are now tolerated in lieu of the traditional *abayya,* the black, head-to-toe covering for women. Yet the fundamentalists still hold the reins of power: religious scholars recently pronounced it forbidden for women to ride bicycles because bicycle seats resemble saddles and women should not ride horses; therefore they should not ride bicycles. None of the 1,500 novels sent to censors in the past year have been approved. Uprisings against the fundamentalist regime were crushed in three separate Iranian states in 1996. One Iranian commented, "That is what we have here, a totalitarian country ruled by religious clerics with no idea of how economies work and what people want." The leader of an underground pro-democracy movement made his feelings clear: "The ideals of the revolution have been betrayed. We wanted justice and social equality then. We are back to where we started with this regime."[24]

In that last comment there is a telling sentiment. The pro-democracy leader intimates that the Iranian revolution was supported not just for its Islamic basis, but more for its ability to release the Iranians from an unjust regime. What the people wanted, he implies, was not simply an Islamic regime: they wanted a regime that was more democratic in style and which would do away with the injustices of the Shah. It may be that for many support of fundamentalist Islamic movements is given not so much for religious reasons but for reasons of democracy and social justice. When they find that the fundamentalist regime is unpalatable in its religious strictures, they cry out again for what they really wanted in the first place: social justice and a greater measure of democracy. In other words, fundamentalist Islam is accepted by many mainly because it is seen as a vehicle for other things.[25]

It is therefore not surprising that in the recent Iranian presidential election the people voted for a more liberal figure, Mohammed Khatami. Although the reason for his victory was not simply anti-fundamentalist sentiment, it is clear that many Iranian people are not in favor of many of the measures brought in by the leaders of the Islamic republic.[26] Observers will also note the result of the recent Algerian election in which only 6% of the population voted for parties who suggested that the fundamentalist FIS should be re-integrated into Algerian politics. While the election was not entirely perfect, the result certainly demonstrated the peoples' lack of motivation for an Islamic state.[27]

Fundamentalist Islam with its punishments that many would confine to the Middle Ages and with its outdated strictures on dress and recreation sits uneasily in the latter part of the twentieth century. As a result many are suggesting that fundamentalist Islam as we have come to know it cannot survive in the longer term. Amuzegar points out that in Iran the rising strength of the middle classes, the development of new forms of communication, especially satellite television, and contacts with foreign nations can only serve to bring the future of the fundamentalist Islamic regime into question. He concludes that "The peoples' free spirit and their instinctive preference for progress and prosperity over retrogression and deprivation are bound to pave the way for the emergence of a more moderate, secular government."[28] Measures such as the Iranian *Majlis'* ban in 1994 on satellite dishes and a similar ban by the Ministry of the Interior in Saudi Arabia cannot keep the twenty-first century at bay forever. Young people in particular are not going to tolerate such retrograde measures, especially when they see the alternative a short distance away in the Mediterranean. Fundamentalist Islam has an "inability to incorporate modernity."[29]

FUNDAMENTALIST ISLAM: A TEMPORARY PHENOMENON

Muslim fundamentalists require that not only their personal beliefs be shaped by their religion but also their government. For the fundamentalist a Muslim government is a necessary part of their belief in the supremacy of Allah and of his revelation in the Qur'an. Despite this they cannot agree on the legitimacy of violence in achieving their objective, on the precise nature of a Muslim government or on its economic system. In addition there is, in Iran at least, a significant body of Muslim opinion which rejects an Islamic fundamentalist government from the inside.

These disagreements with regard to policy and practice are so significant that we may question the sustainability of fundamentalist Islam in the longer term. If a religion has a directly revealed text which is supposed to require a government determined by that text, it would seem to be a significant source of weakness that its adherents cannot agree on what that text requires. Fundamentalist Muslims have an Achilles heel in their inability to determine the shape of what is a major part of their belief.

It might be pointed out that Christians, for example, are not united with regard to their political beliefs. That is true, but the Christian faith never suggested that there should be the unity of church and state that the fundamentalist Muslim faith requires. Jesus' suggestion that the Christian should render unto Caesar that which Caesar requires, would seem to call for some element of separation between church and state. In fundamentalist Islam there is to be a distinctly Muslim state.

It is therefore concluded that the internal divisions within fundamentalist Islam will weaken it so significantly that it will, in the longer term, cease to be the major force in foreign affairs that it is at present. It would also seem difficult to see how a faith which involves barbaric punishment which might have been accepted in the Middle Ages, can continue in the twenty-first century. It seems difficult to see how a faith that cannot accept many of the ideas of modern science and of modern society can continue for much longer. Aziz Al-Azmeh's study of the various types of movement within Islam suggests that fundamentalism is essentially unreasonable and as such unworthy of the twentieth century. He concludes with the proposition that the use of reason can only have one end in Arab states: the demise of fundamentalist Islam and its replacement by secularism.[30] He sees the establishment of the democratic process as historical, developmental and as highly conflictual: fundamentalist Islam is just an element in this conflict but one which will eventually succumb to demise. Fundamentalist Islam is "an eminently historical player subject to the ruse of history."[31]

Partly because of these weaknesses, it is difficult to see how fundamentalist Islam can be seen as a long term "threat" to the West. To suggest, as former U.S. Secretary of Defense William Perry suggested, that the spread of Islamic fundamentalism in the Middle East represents a threat to Western survival is an arguable construct at best.[32] Similarly, the comment from former Secretary General of NATO Willy Claes that Islamic fundamentalism "is just as much of a threat to the West as Communism was" is judged to be equally inaccurate.[33]

A more reasonable argument is that Islamic fundamentalism could be better seen as representing steps toward democracy in some of the more authoritarian regimes of the Middle East. As such it could represent a liberating force in many respects.[34] In many areas of the Middle East where free speech is absent, political debate and movement often takes place through professional associations. These include syndicates of doctors, engineers and teachers—such as Kuwait's University Graduates Society, Qatar's Jassrah Cultural Club, and the United Arab Emirates' Association of Social Professions. Although technically nonpartisan, such associations are becoming increasingly politicized, with many being dominated by fundamentalist Muslims. Egypt's medical, engineering and legal associations had their 1992 elections dominated by the activities of the fundamentalist Muslim Brotherhood. Such groups deserve our support if we are in favor of opening up countries in the Middle East to greater democracy and promoting greater human rights. We should therefore be supporting elements of Muslim fundamentalism rather than blindly campaigning against all of them, particularly when the latter course of action means that we are effectively campaigning for regimes which leave much to be desired in the way of human rights and democracy.[35] However, to support Islamic fundamentalism in the short term as a matter of political expediency should not blind us to the fact that in the long term fundamentalist Islam has only a limited future.[36] The changing world in which we live can only reject a faith that is by its very fundamentalist nature resistant to change.

NOTES

1. Reported in *Daily Telegraph*, October 4, 1996, p. 17.
2. Ibid.
3. For background on the Taliban movement, see K. Clark, "Afghanistan Under the Taliban," *Middle East International*, No. 538, November 22, 1996, pp. 16–17.
4. Quoted in Aziz Al-Azmeh, *Islams and Modernities* (London: Verso), p. 119.
5. T. B. Irving, K. Ahmad, M. M. Ahsan, *The Qur'an: Basic Teachings* (Leicester, UK: The Islamic Foundation, 1979), p. 27.
6. Al-Azmeh, op. cit., p 52.
7. Dale F. Eickelman and James Piscatori, *Muslim Politics* (Princeton, NJ: Princeton University Press, 1996), pp. 70–71; S. J. Al-Azm, "Islamic Fundamentalism Reconsidered: A Critical Outline of Problems, Ideas and Approaches," *South Asian Bulletin*, XIV, 1994, pp. 73–88.
8. Qur'an, 4:36
9. See K. Lang, "French Ghettos Breed Guerillas for Islam," *Sunday Times*, December 8, 1996, p. 16.
10. Raphael Israeli, *Muslim Fundamentalism in Israel* (London: Brasseys, 1993).
11. Al-Azmeh contends that in reality no such codified law exists. "The *sharia* itself has evolved in parallel with the [Muslim] societies; and as far as one

can tell from an objective examination of History, it is not now—nor has it ever been—a unanimously accepted code, but only a collection of principles and guidelines on what is legal." Op. cit., p. 54.

12. The term *Jahiliyya* was popularized by the radical Egyptian fundamentalist of the mid 1900s, Sayyid Qutb.

13. Quoted in J. L. Esposito, *The Islamic Threat: Myth or Reality* (New York: Oxford University Press, 1992), p. 135.

14. Quoted in J. Laffin, *The Dagger of Islam* (London: Sphere), pp. 54–55.

15. Quoted in A. Taheri, *Holy Terror* (London: Hutchinson, 1987), p. 113.

16. Modernist Muslims would want to challenge the idea that Islam as a way of life necessarily involves an Islamic state. For details and for a bibliography, see Eickleman and Piscatori, op. cit., pp. 51–57.

17. Quoted in Laffin, op. cit., p. 125. With regard to the Ayatollah Khomeini, it is interesting that in 1988 he himself suggested in a letter to the then President, Ayatollah Khameini, that the government of Iran, as part of the "absolute vice-regency of the Prophet of God . . . has priority over all other secondary injunctions, even prayers, fasting, and *hajj*. . . . The government is empowered to unilaterally revoke any *Sharia* agreements which it has concluded with the people when those agreements are contrary to the interest of the country or to Islam." Quoted in F. Halliday, *Islam and the Myth of Confrontation* (London: I. B. Tauris, 1996), p. 69. In other words Khomeini says on the one hand that Iran is to be an Islamic country and then says on the other that the government has the power to overrule fundamental Islamic provisions where it deems this to be necessary. It seems that there is an unresolved contradiction here.

18. Quoted in Al-Azm, op. cit., p. 110.

19. *Sharia* consists of legislation based on the Qur'an and *Sunnah* together with the consensus of opinions of learned judges (*Ijma*), anything deduced by analogy from these (*Qiyas*) and independent judgement similarly based (*Ijtihad*). See A. R. I. Doi, *Sharia: The Islamic Law* (London: Ta Ha, 1984), Chap. 4.

20. Ibid., p. 17.

21. O. Roy, *The Failure of Political Islam* (London: I. B. Tauris, 1994), p. 195.

22. Ibid., pp. 145–146.

23. Jahangir Amuzegar, "Islamic Fundamentalism in Action: The Case of Iran," *Middle East Policy*, IV, 1995, pp. 27–29.

24. A. Malone, "Mullahs Face Struggle to Maintain their Iron Grip," *Sunday Times*, September 22, 1996, p. 15.

25. Fred Halliday sees fundamentalist Islamic politics consisting of a religious "front" for a body of mainly secular political ideals. He maintains that much of the history, development and future of fundamentalist Islamic movements should be understood in secular terms using the secular tools of historical, political and sociological analysis. See F. Halliday, op. cit., esp. Chaps. 1 & 2.

26. See M. Colvin, "Iran Votes for a Reverse Revolution," *Sunday Times*, May 25, 1997, p. 19; S. Barzin, "Khatami's Shock Victory," *Middle East International*, 551, May 30, 1997, pp. 5–6; S. Bakhash, "Iran's Remarkable Election," *Journal of Democracy*, 9, 1998, pp. 80–94. For details of Khatami's call for a review of Iran's relationship with the United States, see S. Barzin, "Respect for America," *Middle East International*, 556, 1998, pp. 9–10. For Washington's response, see D. Neff, "Washington's Upbeat Analysis," *Middle East International*, 566, 1998, pp. 10–11.

27. See H. Salen, "A Perfect Election," *Middle East International*, 552, June 13, 1997, p. 12.
28. J. Amuzegar, op. cit., p. 32.
29. O. Roy, op. cit., p. 203.
30. A. Al-Azmeh, op. cit., p. 58.
31. Ibid., p. 77.
32. Quoted in J. King, "A Clash of Civilizations. Pentagon Rhetoric on the Islamic Threat," *Middle East International*, 495, March 3, 1995, p. 16.
33. Quoted in ibid. For other representations of an Islamic threat, see F. A. Khavari, *Oil and Islam: the Ticking Bomb*, (Malibu: Roundtable, 1990). Part of the problem of seeing fundamentalist Islam as a threat is that it simply substitutes the old communist threat with another. The two are very different and should not be interpreted in the light of each other.
34. See H. A. Hawad, "Islam and the West: How Fundamental is the Threat?" *Royal United Services' Institute Journal*, 140, 1995; M. Azzam, "Islamism, the Peace Process and Regional Security," ibid.; J. Esposito, op. cit.; D. G. Kibble, "The Threat of Militant Islam: a Fundamental Reappraisal," *Studies in Conflict and Terrorism*, 19, 1996.
35. See Clarence J. Bouchat, "A Fundamentalist Islamic Threat to the West," in *Studies in Conflict and Terrorism*, 19, 1996.
36. Supporting Islamic fundamentalism in this way does not mean that we should support it lock, stock and barrel. We should criticize those elements of it with which we disagree. See D. G. Kibble, "Tomahawks for the Terrorists? A Considered Response to Fundamentalist Islamic Terrorism," *Naval Review*, 85, 1997. But also see F. Halliday, op. cit., p. 127 ff, who takes a different point of view.

PART V
Conflict Resolution

Issue 15
Intervention or Isolation?

INTRODUCTION

Should the United States, the world's sole remaining superpower, intervene militarily in disputes abroad? This question is especially pertinent in view of American-led intervention by air forces of NATO (the North Atlantic Treaty Organization) in the conflict in Serbia. Haunting pictures of forlorn Kosovo refugees, who were driven from their homes into neighboring countries, captured the world's attention. The NATO campaign of air bombardment was aimed at punishing the Serbs and stopping their policy of "ethnic cleansing" of Muslims from Kosovo. From a longer-term perspective, this conflict is yet another expression of long-standing animosity between the dominant Christian Orthodox Serbs and the Islamic Kosovars of Albanian descent.

If the Serb-Kosovar conflict is deeply rooted in history, so is the inclination of the United States to intervene in such disputes. The latter point is clear in the first selection by former State Department official Robert Kagan. As Kagan notes, although Americans often have expressed considerable reticence to become embroiled in foreign disputes, in the end the United States has usually intervened out of necessity.

Kagan supports a policy of intervention, even in relatively minor disputes, arguing that "the way one handles the small threats is likely to determine the way one handles the larger threats." Moreover, he contends that "once appeasing adversaries and wishing away problems becomes a habit, it becomes a hard habit to break." In essence, Kagan takes the psychological concept of habitual learning—a characteristic of individuals—and applies it to a nation, the United States.

Is American intervention abroad a learned habit? To provide an insight, we compare the contemporary intervention in Serbia with an ill-fated intervention several years ago in Somalia. The second selection, from the conservative magazine *Human Events*, presents a graphic description of the failed intervention in Somalia. Has the United States learned from the Somalian experience and adjusted its behavior in Serbia? In one sense, the answer seems to be "no," in that ill-defined goals with no clear exit strategy appear to characterize both interventions. On the other hand, the use of ground troops to drive Serb forces out of Kosovo has been avoided, since President Clinton no doubt recalled the scene of the bodies of dead American soldiers being dragged through the streets of Mogadishu, the Somalian capital.

As you read the articles, consider the following questions.

Discussion Questions

1. In this post–Cold War world under what circumstance should the United States intervene militarily in other countries? Should critical American national interests always be at stake? Suppose, for example, the goal is to feed starving people in an area where the U.S. has no national interests. Can military intervention be justified then?

2. Suppose that Russia were still a strong superpower. Would the U.S. be as likely to intervene abroad as it has in recent years? Why?

3. Suppose that Lyndon Johnson had faced today's international political and military environment in the mid-1960s, rather than the situation that existed then. Do you believe that the Vietnam War would have occurred?

      For more information on this topic, visit the following websites:

      http://hdc-www.harvard.edu/cfia/
      (web site of the venerable Center for International Affairs at Harvard University)

      http://www.csis.org
      (web site of the Center for Strategic and International Studies in Washington, a private think tank which has produced policy studies on U. S. post–Cold War role)

      http://www.sipri.se/
      (web site of Sweden's Stockholm International Peace Research Institute, which generally takes a skeptical view of U. S. foreign policy activism)

The Case for Global Activism

ROBERT KAGAN

Future historians will record—perhaps in astonishment—that the demise of the Soviet Union ushered in an era of American worldwide engagement and armed intervention unprecedented in scope and frequency. Despite a widespread conviction that, in a post-cold-war world, the American role would diminish, in a brief four years the United States has: launched a massive counteroffensive against the world's fourth largest army in the Middle East; invaded, occupied, and supervised elections in a Latin American country; intervened with force to provide food to starving peoples in Africa; and conducted punitive bombing raids in the Balkans.

Nor is this all. The United States has sent troops on another humanitarian mission in Africa, and volunteered troops to serve as peacekeeping forces in the Middle East and in the former Yugoslavia. It has worked in the UN Security Council to enact punitive sanctions against at least a half-dozen international scofflaws. It has seriously considered extending military protection to several important nations of Eastern Europe that have never before been part of an alliance with the United States. And it has interceded in disputes among the former republics of the Soviet Union.

How is this increased activity to be explained? The answer is rather easily found in the new relations of power in the post-cold-war world. The fall of the Soviet Union removed restraints on foreign leaders unhappy with the order imposed by the cold war and unleashed new struggles for power in areas hitherto under the former superpower's thumb. Some would-be challengers of the old order were encouraged by the belief that the United States would not step in. The United States, however, itself freed from the restraints of the cold war, began to fill the gap left by the absence of Soviet global power and continued a historical tradition of using its influence to promote a world order consistent with its material needs and philosophical predilections.

But if the course America has followed has been natural enough, to many American strategists, policy-makers, and politicians it seems also to have been unexpected—and unwelcome. Today, a scant two years after

Robert Kagan, who served in the State Department from 1984 to 1988, has recently completed a book about U.S. policy in Nicaragua, which is to be published by the Free Press.

Reprinted by permission of Robert Kagan. Published in *Commentary*, Sept. 1994. Vol. 98, Issue 3, p. 40.

the intervention in Somalia, three years after the Gulf war, and four years since the invasion of Panama, foreign-policy theorists continue to write of the need for a "global retrenchment" of American power. Before and after each venture abroad, they have argued that such high levels of American engagement cannot be sustained, politically or economically, and that a failure to be more selective in the application of American power will either bankrupt the country or drive the American public further toward the isolationism into which, they warn, it is already beginning to slip.

This political judgment has found intellectual buttressing in the so-called "realist" approach to foreign policy, which asserts that the United States should limit itself to defending its "core" national interests and abandon costly and unpopular efforts to solve the many problems on the "periphery."* During the cold war, realists fought against efforts by Presidents from Truman to Kennedy to Reagan to equate American interests with the advancement of a democratic world order. In the post-cold-war era, they have gained new prominence by again recommending a retreat from such ambitions and the definition of a far more limited set of foreign-policy goals.

Yet the realist view remains inadequate, both as a description, precisely, of reality—of the way the world really works—and as a recommendation for defending America's interests, either on the "periphery" or at the "core." When Americans have exercised their power in pursuit of a broad definition of interests—in pursuit, that is, of a more decent world order—they have succeeded in defending their "vital" interests as well. When they have sought to evade the dangers of global involvement, they have found themselves unexpectedly in a fight for national survival.

Throughout this century, the United States has faced the problem of its expanding power—and has responded with ambivalence. Americans are perhaps more suspicious of power than most people on earth, but just like others they have nonetheless sought it, guarded it, and enjoyed its benefits. As products of a modern, nonmartial republic, Americans have always tended to cherish the lives of their young more than the glories to be won on the battlefield; yet they have sacrificed their young for the sake of honor, interest, and principle as frequently as any nation in the world over the past 200 years. Again, as the products of a revolution against an imperial master, Americans have always abhorred imperialism; yet where their power was preponderant, they have assumed hegemony and have been unwilling to relinquish it.

The common view of American foreign policy as endlessly vacillating between isolationism and interventionism is wrong: Americans in

*See, for example, "The Core vs. the Periphery," by Fareed Zakaria, in the December 1993 *Commentary*.

this century have never ceased expanding their sphere of interests across the globe, but they have tried to evade the responsibility of defending those interests, until they had no choice but to fight a war for which they were unprepared. The American conception of interest, moreover, has always gone beyond narrow security concerns to include the promotion of a world order consistent with American economic, political, and ideological aspirations.

It was Theodore Roosevelt, paradoxically a President admired by realists for his shrewd understanding of power politics, who first grafted principled ends to the exercise of power. Roosevelt insisted that it was America's duty to "assume an attitude of protection and regulation in regard to all these little states" in the Western hemisphere, to help them acquire the "capacity for self-government," to assist their progress "up out of the discord and turmoil of continual revolution into a general public sense of justice and determination to maintain order."

For Roosevelt, American stewardship in the Western hemisphere was more than a defensive response to European meddling there; it was proof that the United States had arrived as a world power, with responsibilities to shape a decent order in its own region. When Woodrow Wilson, the quintessential "utopian" President, took office later, his policies in the hemisphere were little more than a variation on Roosevelt's theme.

The same mix of motives followed the United States as it reached out into the wider world, especially Europe and Asia. Growing power expanded American interests, but also expanded the risks of protecting them against the ambitions of others. After the 1880s, America's navy grew from a size comparable to Chile's to become one of the three great navies of the world. That increase in power alone made America a potential arbiter of overseas conflicts in a way it had never been in the 18th and 19th centuries. Greater power meant that if a general European war broke out, the United States would no longer have to sit back and accept dictation of its trade routes. It also meant, however, that the United States could not sit back without accepting a diminished role in world affairs.

Nor could Americans escape choosing sides. Although German and Irish-Americans disagreed, most Americans in the 1910s preferred the British-run world order with which they were familiar to a prospective German one. Wilson's pro-British neutrality made conflict with Germany almost inevitable, and America's new great-power status made it equally inevitable that when the German challenge came, the United States would not back down.

It was the growth of American power, not Wilsonian idealism and not national interest narrowly conceived, that led the United States into its first European war. A weak 19th-century America could not have conceived of intervening in Europe; a strong 20th-century America, because it could intervene, found that it had an interest in doing so.

After World War I, Americans recoiled from the new responsibilities and dangers which their power had brought. But they did not really abandon their new, broader conception of the national interest. Throughout the "isolationist" years, the United States still sought, however half-heartedly and ineffectually, to preserve its expanded influence and the world order it had fought for.

Although they refused to assume military obligations, Presidents from Harding to Franklin Roosevelt tried to maintain balance and order in Europe and in Asia through economic and political agreements. In Central America and the Caribbean, the Republican Presidents found themselves endlessly intervening, occupying, and supervising elections only so that they might eventually withdraw. (Only FDR decided that the best way to be a "good neighbor" in the hemisphere was to allow dictatorship to flourish.)

Americans, then, did not shun international involvement in the interwar years. Rather, they tried to enjoy the benefits of such involvement while hoping to avoid its inevitable costs. They resisted Japanese attempts to swallow China, but they did not believe the national interest required them to fight in Asia. They were unwilling to see France and England defeated by an increasingly dangerous Germany, but they did not see an interest in risking American lives in Europe. Through arms control and the theoretical banning of war, the United States sought ever more utopian mechanisms for pursuing its interests without risk. In the end, of course, this refusal to acknowledge the need to defend its expanded interests helped make war inevitable. Americans allowed the world order to collapse only to realize that this was a result they could not afford.

But if World War II marked the destruction of the old world order, it also extended the reach of American power beyond Theodore Roosevelt's capacity to imagine. And it offered American leaders another chance to confront the new responsibilities which the expansion of power had created.

We often forget that the plan for world order devised by American leaders in the last years of the war was not intended to contain the Soviet Union. Their purpose was to build a more stable international system than that which had exploded in 1939. They hoped that the new system, embodied in the United Nations, would eventually become a self-regulating mechanism, protecting American interests without requiring the constant exercise of American power. But they also understood that American power had become the keystone in the arch of any world order.

The threat to the new system which soon emerged in the form of the Soviet Union quickly changed Americans' sense of what the U.S. was trying to accomplish. The original goal of promoting and defending a decent world order became conflated with the goal of meeting the challenge of Soviet power—and in the minds of many people it remains so to this day.

Thus, all the policies that the United States would have continued to pursue without the existence of a Soviet Union—seeking a stable international economic system, exercising dominant influence in the Western hemisphere, insisting on an ever-increasing role in Europe, Asia, and the Middle East, demanding adherence to international agreements, preferring dictatorship to disorder but also preferring democracy to dictatorship—became associated with the strategy of containment. This had the effect, unfortunate in retrospect, of obscuring the essential continuities in American foreign policy since the beginning of the century.

The fact is that America was simultaneously pursuing two goals during the cold war—promotion of a world order and defense against the biggest threat to it. Characteristically, each of them was beset by ambivalence. There is a common presumption today that the choices of that era were somehow easier, that there was a broad consensus about at least a few basic certainties. Nostalgia for these alleged "certainties" obscures from memory the long, bitter debates over the proper definition of American interests during the cold war. But it is worth remembering that even the now-hallowed doctrine of containment was denounced as dangerous and impossibly ambitious by clear-headed "realists" of the time. (Walter Lippmann, for example, called containment a "strategic monstrosity" because it seemed to require an American response to every conceivable Soviet thrust anywhere in the world.)

There were, as it happens, few certainties in the cold war. The gray areas in which the hardest decisions had to be made were much like the gray areas of today. The two major American wars of that era were fought in regions and involved conflicts—Korea and Vietnam—where the direct interests of the United States were at least debatable. Throughout the cold war, indeed, fighting took place almost entirely on the "periphery," and was often conducted in the name of universal ideals that transcended the strategic importance of the plot of ground being contested.

The end of the cold war has required the United States once again to face the old dilemmas. As in the aftermath of World War II, the areas of the world where America exerts influence have expanded, not contracted. So, too, have the burdens of promoting and sustaining a world order that serves American material and spiritual needs.

The demise of the Soviet Union has not eliminated the threat to that order; it has only changed its form. Instead of arising from a single, large adversary, the threat has devolved into a large number of smaller but collectively serious challenges. As in the past, many experts have come forward to argue that resources are lacking for a globally active policy designed to meet those challenges, that the American public would be unwilling to support it, and even that American power is declining.

The evidence does not support these claims.

The percentage of the American economy devoted to military spending has dropped to the small digits. This is too low to allow the United States to carry out the many new tasks it will face in the post-cold-war era, but the increases that will be necessary will hardly bankrupt the country.

Nor is the assumption warranted that the American public does not support the overseas commitments and interventions undertaken in these past four years, or opposes further commitments today. Americans have rarely been enthusiastic about extensive overseas involvements, but the public has clearly been more willing to support them in the 1990s than it was in the 70s and 80s, as is demonstrated by the popularity of successful actions in such places as the Persian Gulf and Panama. Even in Bosnia and Somalia, ordinary Americans have complained not about action, but about confused and half-hearted policies and weak and incompetent execution.

We have also learned that the use of force need not be tied to unmistakable and narrowly defined security interests in order to win public support. A Latin American dictator cancels elections and helps Colombian drug dealers sell cocaine; a Middle Eastern despot invades a tiny neighboring country in order to control its oil wells; an African country dissolves into civil war and chaos, and famine threatens millions with starvation; one ethnic group tries to drive another ethnic group off its land and commits atrocities; an unfriendly Asian power develops nuclear weapons in violation of international agreements. Among these various events, only the Iraqi invasion of Kuwait qualified as a direct threat to American economic interests. In general, the issues that have invited an American response—aggression, political illegitimacy, genocide, mass starvation, nuclear proliferation, violations of international agreements—are all matters that fall under the general heading of threats to the kind of world order Americans value.

Can we sustain a policy of active response? Henry Kissinger has recently argued that, contrary to appearances, American power is actually in decline relative to other nations. While he admits that it "will remain unrivaled for the foreseeable future," nevertheless, because all power in the world has become more "diffuse," America's ability "to shape the rest of the world has actually decreased."

But surely the same level of American power applied to a world where opposing power is more diffuse should be more, not less, effective. America's problem today is not that its power is in relative decline but, on the contrary, that the places where it can exert potentially decisive influence have increased in number, and so have the choices we must confront.

Do "losses" on the periphery matter? Indeed, can there even be American "losses" on the periphery if America does not choose to become involved? Should America resist all those who oppose its view of world order? Or should the United States keep its powder dry for the really serious threats to its existence—the dominance of Europe or Asia, for instance, by a single power? Such is the nature of the questions Americans have faced throughout this century, and have answered in two different and historically instructive ways.

It would seem to make sense to heed the realists' assertion that a nation may become distracted, or exhaust itself by lesser endeavors, and thus fail to guard that which is most important. But this in fact is the path the United States followed in the 1930s, and lived to regret. First it failed to respond to the peripheral Italian invasion of Ethiopia, the peripheral Spanish Civil War, and the peripheral Japanese conquest of Manchuria, and then it failed to respond as well when the big threat to "core" interests did finally emerge in the figure of Hitler's Germany. The big threats and vital interests, as it turned out, were no less debatable than the small threats and lesser interests.

American policy during the cold war provides an interesting contrast. Despite a terrible debacle on the periphery, the United States did not lose sight of the core. On the contrary, concern about the core and concern about the periphery seem to have been mutually reinforcing. The "lesson of Munich," which dominated cold-war thinking until its temporary replacement by the "lesson of Vietnam," taught that a failure of will on small matters eventually led to a failure of will on more vital matters as well. This proved to be a sound strategy for defending American interests, both large and small, and it was this strategy that made possible a peaceful victory in the cold war.

There is no certainty that we can correctly distinguish between high-stakes issues and small-stakes issues in time to sound the alarm. In the past we did not know for sure whether an invasion of Ethiopia was merely the whim of an Italian despot in an irrelevant part of Africa or the harbinger of fascist aggression in Europe, whether a North Vietnamese victory was a signal of national reunification or the prelude to a hostile takeover of Southeast Asia. So today we do not know whether Serbian aggression is "ethnic turmoil" or the first step in the breakdown of European order.

But the way one handles the small threats is likely to determine the way one handles the larger threats. It does not take much imagination to envision what those larger threats may be: the rise of militant anti-American Muslim fundamentalism in North Africa and the Middle East, a rearmed Germany in a chaotic Europe, a revitalized Russia, a rearmed

Japan in a scramble for power with China in a volatile East Asia. If the goal is a United States capable of meeting these more serious threats when they do arise, then the best policy is one that seeks involvement rather than shuns it. Once appeasing adversaries and wishing away problems becomes a habit, it becomes a hard habit to break. Confrontation with the next Nazi Germany or Soviet empire, the tests of American strength, character, and endurance, essential to the preservation of a more stable world order, will continue to come in such unlikely places as Bosnia, Haiti, Somalia, and Korea. If we cannot plug every breach in the world order, we also cannot allow potential challengers of that order to act in the confidence that the United States will stand aside.

The post-cold-war era is a time of readjustment. Relationships of power change constantly, but how Americans respond to crises, even small ones, in this time of transition will affect the nature of the changes yet to come. Only if it is ready to engage its power when and as needed can the United States hope to shape the character and direction of the forces of change rather than be overwhelmed by them.

Finally, a political question that needs to be asked: who among us, Democrat or Republican, is prepared to rise to the challenge and follow the demanding (if in the long run safer) course of global activism?

On the Democratic side, even those Clinton-administration officials who appear willing to assert American leadership find it hard to overcome the instinctive aversion to the use of power which still burdens them twenty years after Vietnam. They seek the fruits of American intervention, yet seem incapable of doing what is necessary to secure them. Democrats today are paying the price for their years of opposition to Republican assertions of American strength abroad.

Since the Vietnam war, indeed, only the Republican party has had the understanding and the confidence to use American power in defense of the nation's interests. Yet the Republican party itself is now teetering on the edge of a historic transformation. Increasing numbers of Republican politicians, policy-makers, and intellectuals agree with Minority Whip Newt Gingrich's judgment that the United States is now "overextended around the world." There are fewer Republican calls for increases in the defense budget, and more Republican calls for decreases in overseas commitments. The Republican party is less and less recognizable as the party of Ronald Reagan or the George Bush who sent troops to Panama and the Persian Gulf.

In the same way, 75 years ago the Republicans transformed themselves from the party of the internationalist Theodore Roosevelt into the party of the isolationist Senator William Borah. In defeating Woodrow Wilson's brand of utopian internationalism, Republicans also killed the more practical internationalism of men like Henry Cabot Lodge, who believed American power had a critical role to play in preventing another war in Europe. When that disaster finally loomed, it was not Lodge but Borah who spoke for the party.

Victory in the cold war came when Republicans vehemently rejected the idea that the United States had to accept a diminished capacity to shape the world and adjust to the increasing power of its strategic and ideological adversaries. Such a prescription is as disastrous today as it was then, and shows the same lack of faith in the American people and their acceptance of responsibility. It took confidence and determination to take the United States safely through the end of the cold war. It will take no less confidence and determination to move America through this next, dangerous phase of history.

Somalia Debacle Shows Idiocy of Unbridled Interventionism

THE EDITORS OF HUMAN EVENTS

In the wake of the catastrophe visited upon American soldiers in Somalia last week, is there anyone left who wants the U.S. to play the role of world policeman?

No doubt there are a few globo-cop enthusiasts left, but the Somalia lesson should be clear: The United States has no business patrolling the planet for bad guys and undertaking "nation building," particularly when no U.S. vital interests are at stake. (Isn't this what many conservatives, and Pat Buchanan more loudly than most, have been saying all along?)

Nor should we begin to expand the number of American soldiers to be placed under United Nations command, as the Clinton Administration has been poised to do in a formal way with its long-awaited, but not quite finalized, Presidential Decision Directive 13.

In our effort to "rebuild" Somalia, 100 elite U.S. infantrymen, hoping to nab fugitive warlord leader Mohamed Farah Aidid on October 3, suffered 70% casualties, a figure, noted the Washington Post, "compared by sickened officers . . . to a 1965 massacre in Vietnam's Ia Drang Valley.

Reprinted by permission. Human Events, Oct. 16, 1993. Vol. 53, Issue 42, p. 1.

So badly pinned down were the Americans in Mogadishu that they could not evacuate their wounded, including Ranger commander Lt. Col. Danny McKnight, for nine hours."

(United Nations reinforcements took more than nine hours to reach the Rangers, reported the New York *Times*, because the American component of the rescue team, the Quick Response Force, "did not have the proper equipment and their Pakistani and Malaysian counterparts were not trained to carry out such a rescue operation. . . .")

During the course of the 15-hour battle, Aidid's forces, in confronting the Rangers unit and U.S. reinforcements, shot down two U.S. Blackhawk helicopters, killed 12 U.S. soldiers, wounded another 78 and captured an American pilot.

Toronto Star photographer Paul Watson—no American reporters were on the scene—was quoted as saying that the dead soldiers littered the landscape, with the corpse of one U.S. serviceman being dragged through the street by ropes tied to his feet and another stripped naked and surrounded by a joyful mob chanting, "Victory!" and telling reporters, "Come, look at the white man!"

Another dead U.S. serviceman was trundled through the streets in a wheelbarrow, with 200 Somalis cheering the spectacle.

This disastrous mission, the *Washington Post* noted, "seemed to epitomize the challenges of U.N. 'peace operations' in the disorderly new world order: An uncertain chain of command, disparities in language and skills among contributing national forces and a political reach that for months has exceeded its military grasp."

But not all of what went wrong, apparently, could be blamed on the U.N. factor alone. First off, President Clinton agreed that the U.S. role should be shifted from a famine rescue operation to that of a belligerent against Aidid. Then, Gen. Colin Powell, who has just retired as chairman of the Joint Chiefs of Staff, is reliably reported to have *twice* in the month of September asked Defense Secretary Les Aspin for tanks and armored vehicles to protect U.S. forces in Somalia, but was twice turned down for political reasons.

An Army official, reported the *Washington Times*, said that Pentagon officials—including highly controversial designated Assistant Secretary of Defense Morton Halperin—"opposed the military's request because they feared it 'would appear too offensive oriented.'" Shades of Vietnam all over again. (So damaging was the report that GOP Sen. Al D'Amato of New York called for Aspin's resignation.)

While Americans on all sides of the political spectrum were inundating their lawmakers with urgent calls for a U.S. withdrawal, the Clinton Administration's response was to up the ante, with the President deciding to pour another 1,500 troops into Somalia, even while Aidid was inflicting further casualties on American forces. White House officials, furthermore, said the President did not want to pull out our troops until at least March 31 of next year.

In the meantime, supposedly, American forces may—or may not—continue to hunt down Aidid, but will continue to "nation-build," even though U.S. aides admit they have "no hope" of constructing a permanent government in Somalia, only "an interim" one.

But being dragged down in the Deep Muddy in Somalia, it seems, has not especially dampened the Clinton Administration's enthusiasm for additional global adventures under U.N. auspices.

As former U.N. Ambassador Jeane Kirkpatrick points out . . . , the Clinton Administration—at least judging from various official speeches just prior to the October 3 debacle—is making "no retreat from the globalist, multilateralist, activist agenda."

The Clinton Administration, she stresses, is still committed to "global multilateralism, conceived, directed and administered through the United Nations," yet many of the outlined tasks are not "even remotely relevant to American interests."

"Few Americans," she said, "apparently noticed that in the same speech that laid down 'tough' conditions for new U.N. peacekeeping operations, Clinton also announced U.S. support for creating a 'genuine peacekeeping headquarters, with a planning staff, with access to timely intelligence, with a logistic unit that can be deployed on a moment's notice, and a modern operations center with global communications.'

"Few noticed—and virtually no media reported—that within days of the speeches signaling a [supposed] 'retreat' from multilateralism, the U.S. joined in adopting or extending mandates for 'peacekeeping' in Angola, Somalia, Liberia, Georgia and Haiti and was actively engaged in planning a massive peacekeeping effort in Bosnia."

Indeed, last week, Assistant Secretary of State Stephen Oxman—after the October 3 disaster—was telling the Senate Foreign Relations Committee that the U.S., under U.N. authority, was willing to put 25,000 American troops into war-torn Bosnia.

Even Charles Krauthammer, a hawkish interventionist turned surprisingly dovish in the case of Bosnia, exclaimed in his syndicated column: "Don't do it, Mr. President."

There just aren't good enough reasons, he went on, "to send 25,000 Americans into a zone of dangerous instability and constant combat. One reason that the United States and the Soviet Union rarely engaged their troops in U.N. peacekeeping during the Cold War is that superpowers make too large a target.

"An American patrol taken hostage is of far greater value than a Moroccan one. Shooting an American helicopter is a far greater prize than ambushing a Pakistani patrol.

"You would be sending 25,000 targets."

Yes, this would be sending 25,000 targets. But it is not particularly surprising that this kind of mindless interventionism, taken without regard to our strategic interests and without regard to the advice of our military, would be espoused by the Clinton folk.

This is an Administration, after all, whose top ranks are filled with a collection of draft dodgers, Vietnam doves, Marxist revisionists, ACLU "defense" experts and a National Security Adviser who opposed the bombing of Hanoi's sanctuaries in Cambodia.

How, then, could we reasonably expect this '60s group to successfully conduct military policy abroad?

Issue 16
Military Intervention: Kosovo

INTRODUCTION

Only a short time ago the vast majority of Americans had never heard of Kosovo. Now, nearly everyone is aware of the region, and most people have at least a vague idea of its location in eastern Europe. But few people understand the issues in this conflict.

To the American administration and its NATO allies, the "lesson of Munich" is most applicable. From the bitter experience of attempted British appeasement of Hitler in the early days of World War II came the lesson that national bullies cannot go unchallenged by the world community. Such bullies must not be permitted to abuse others, particularly ethnic minorities. From this perspective, Serbian "ethnic cleansing" of Albanians from Kosovo must not be allowed to continue. This lesson is particularly vivid for U.S. Secretary of State Madeleine Albright, who, as a young girl in Czechoslovakia, personally experienced the consequences of Hitler's aggressive behavior.

On the other hand, the Serbian government of Slobodan Milosević in Yugoslavia looks to the "lesson of Jerusalem." The central message of this lesson is that a nation must maintain control of the cradle of its culture. As Israelis insist that Jerusalem, site of the Wailing Wall, is an integral part of Israel, so Serbs insist that Kosovo, site of important shrines of Serb cultural origins, is an integral part of Serbia.

In the selections that follow, the two sides state their cases. First, in transcripts of two radio addresses to the nation, President Clinton makes the American case for the air campaign against Yugoslavia. The second selection, which is a statement prepared by the Yugoslav government, presents the case for the importance of Kosovo to the Serbs and condemns Kosovo Albanian groups that seek independence.

As you read the articles, consider the following questions.

Discussion Questions

1. President Clinton pictures the US/NATO military action in Kosovo as a humanitarian effort to save the Muslim Kosovars. Do you believe that is the **real** reason that the US became militarily involved there?

2. During the NATO bombing of Yugoslavia, public opinion there seemed to rally around President Milosević, even though many Yugoslav Serbs evidently do not like him. Why?

3. With the benefit of hindsight, if the US had it to do over, would you advise President Clinton to take the military action that he did in Yugoslavia?

   For more information on this topic, visit the following websites:

   `http://www.antiwar.com`
   (web site of the Committee against U. S. Intervention, which opposed US action in Yugoslavia)

   `http://www.gov.yu/terrorism/index.html`
   (Yugoslavia federal government's web page on "Albanian Terrorism in Kosovo")

   `http://kosovoapress.com`
   (web site of the Kosovo Liberation Army)

Radio Addresses of The President to the Nation

PRESIDENT BILL CLINTON

The White House Office of the Press Secretary

FOR IMMEDIATE RELEASE, MARCH 27, 1999

THE PRESIDENT: Good morning. Three days ago I decided the United States should join our NATO allies in military air strikes to bring peace to Kosovo. In my address to the nation last Wednesday, I explained why we have taken this step—to save the lives of innocent civilians in Kosovo from a brutal military offensive; to defuse a powder keg at the heart of Europe that has exploded twice before in this century with catastrophic results; to prevent a wider war we would have to confront later, only at far greater risk and cost; to stand with our NATO allies for peace. Our military operation has been underway for several nights now. In this time, Serb troops have continued attacks on unarmed men, women and children. That is all the more reason for us to stay the course. We must, and we will, continue until Serbia's leader, Slobodan Milosević, accepts peace or we have seriously damaged his capacity to make war. As always, America's military men and women are performing with courage and skill. Their strength comes from rigorous training, state of the art weaponry and hard-won experience in this part of the world. This is the same brave and tested force that brought stability to Bosnia after four years of vicious war. I am confident they will once again rise to the task. Some of them are fighter pilots, some are bombers, some are mechanics, technicians, air traffic controllers and base personnel. Every time I visit our troops around the world I am struck by their professionalism, their quiet, unassuming determination. They always say, this is the job I was trained to do. They don't see themselves as heroes, but we surely do. I've also been deeply impressed by the solidarity of NATO's purpose. All 19 NATO nations are providing support, from Norway to Turkey, from England to Italy, from Germany and France to our neighbors in Canada, including our three allies from Central Europe, the new NATO members: Poland, Hungary, the Czech Republic. And we should remember the courage of the Kosovar people today, still exposed to violence and brutality. Many Americans, now, have heard the story of a young Kosovar girl trying to stay in touch with a friend in America by e-mail, as a

Serb attack began in her own village. Just a few days ago she wrote, "at the moment, just from my balcony, I can see people running with suitcases, and I can hear some gunshots. A village just a few hundred meters from my house is all surrounded. As long as I have electricity, I will continue writing to you. I'm trying to keep myself as calm as possible. My younger brother, who is nine, is sleeping now. I wish I will not have to stop his dreams." We asked these people of Kosovo to accept peace, and they did. We promised them we would stick by them if they did the right thing, and they did. We cannot let them down now. Americans have learned the hard way that our home is not that far from Europe. Through two World Wars and a long Cold War, we saw that it was a short step from a small brushfire to an inferno, especially in the tinder box of the Balkans. The time to put out a fire is before it spreads and burns down the neighborhood. By acting now, we're taking a strong step toward a goal that has always been in our national interest—a peaceful, united, democratic Europe. For America there is no greater calling than being a peacemaker. But sometimes you have to fight in order to end the fighting. Let me end now by repeating how proud all Americans are of the men and women in uniform risking their lives to protect peace in the Balkans. Our prayers are with them. And our prayers are with all the people of the Balkans searching for the strength to put centuries of divisions to rest, and to join Europe and North America in building a better future together. Thanks for listening.

FOR IMMEDIATE RELEASE, APRIL 3, 1999

THE PRESIDENT: As we gather in our homes during this sacred week to observe Easter and Passover, let us take a moment to think about the plight of the people in Kosovo, who have been forced from their homes by a campaign of violence and destruction, and who look to us for help and hope. The tragedy in Kosovo has been mounting for over a year now. Over the last two weeks, Serbian forces have intensified their attacks against innocent civilians there, leaving no doubt about the cold, clear goal of their leader, Slobodan Milosević—to keep Kosovo's land while ridding it of its people. Nearly one out of every three people in Kosovo has been made homeless since the start of this conflict. Even before the recent surge, well over a quarter of a million people had been displaced. Every hour of every day more arrive at Kosovo's borders, tired, hungry, shaken by what they have been through. Among them are elderly people, who have lived their whole lives in peace with their neighbors, only to be told now to leave everything behind in minutes or to be killed on the spot. Among them are small children who walked for miles over mountains, sometimes after watching their fathers and uncles and brothers taken from them and shot before their eyes. Some have been shelled by artillery on their long trek to safety. Many have had their identity papers and family records stolen and destroyed, their history in Kosovo erased, their very existence denied. Our nation cannot do everything. We can't end all suffering; we can't stop all violence. But there are times when looking away simply is not an option. Right now, in the middle of Europe, at the doorstep of NATO, an entire people are being made to abandon their homeland or die—not because of anything they've done, but simply because of who they are. If there's one lesson we've learned in this century, it's that that kind of poison will spread if not stopped. If there's one pledge that binds the past and future generations, it is that we cannot allow people to be destroyed because of their ethnic or racial or religious groups—when we do have the power to do something about it. Our military mission in Kosovo is a difficult and dangerous one, but it's necessary and right, and we must stand with all our NATO allies to see it through.

Our goal is to exact a very high price for Mr. Milosevic's policy of repression and to seriously diminish his military capacity to maintain that policy. We also must open our hearts and our arms to the innocent victims of this conflict. This week I authorized the expenditure of $50 million in emergency funds to support the relief effort, and directed our military to do its part to get critical supplies to people in need. We'll work with the United Nations and with the many courageous volunteers working on the ground with non-governmental organizations from all around the world. You can help, too. I urge you to call your local Red Cross or church-based charity and ask them how you can get involved. Together we'll provide food, water, and medicine, blankets, clothing and shelter to Kosovar refugees. We'll remind the victims of this conflict that for all they have lost they have not been abandoned or forgotten. European countries are helping as well. Kosovo's neighbors, Macedonia and Albania, are taking the refugees in, despite the huge burden this places on these poor, struggling nations; so are Greece, Bosnia and Bulgaria— showing there's more mercy than madness in the Balkans, more compassion than cruelty in this troubled region of the world. All of us want to provide for the refugees; all of us want to make it possible for them to return home. Let us do our part for all the innocent people whose lives have been shattered by this conflict. And let us give our thanks to our men and women in uniform who are risking their lives today for our ideals, our interests, and their lives.

Let us keep in our prayers the three brave American servicemen now being held without justification in Belgrade that they may return to us soon. Let us do what we can—and what we must—for peace to prevail. And let us stay the course until it does. Thanks for listening.

Terrorism in Kosovo and Metohija

THE YUGOSLAV GOVERNMENT

The Albanian terrorism in the region of Kosovo and Metohija, directed to the persecution and exile of Serbian population lasted for centuries, but it was most prominent in the 19th century, when the number of Serbs was dramatically diminished by physical liquidations, by the usurpation of property and by other pressures, that resulted in forced exile.

The process of emigration continued with the same intensity in the 20th century. Between the two World Wars, the Kosovo Committee (established in 1918) was very active. Its activities were quite clear—terrorism, with the objective of "liberation of Kosovo and of other Albanian regions." During the Second World War, there were many terrorist organizations which cooperated with Italy and Germany (SS divisions Skenderbeg, Bali Kombetar, Albanian Fascist Party, etc.). The exodus of the Serbs and Montenegrins and the massive settlement of Albanians from Albania continued.

After the end of the Second World War, in the period 1941–1951, the terrorist organization of Shaban Paluzha was active in Kosovo and Metohija. In the following years, several terrorist organizations were established in Kosovo and Metohija, with the support of the Albanian migrants in Western Europe, and of Albania (The Front of National Liberation, Kosovo Movement, etc.).

Since 1990, when the Albanian separatist leaders proclaimed the Kosovo Republic in Kosovo and Metohija, the terrorist organization called the Kosovo Liberation Army was active. Its activities were not directed exclusively against the Serbian people and the authorities, but also against the Albanians who accept the Federal Republic of Yugoslavia as their country. The Islamic factor was strengthened since 1991, and it represents an important segment of the separatist and terrorist movement in this region.

From 1991, until March, 1998, there were 110 terrorists acts committed against the police and the buildings of the police. In those attacks, 18 police were killed and 54 were injured.

There were 68 attacks on civilian population in the period 1991–March 4, 1998, and 33 persons were killed.

During the period January–March 4, 1998, the number of terrorist attacks on citizens dramatically increased. There were 46 attacks, with 8 citizens killed and 6 injured.

In the period 1991–March 4, 1998, there were 45 terrorist attacks on the members of Albanian national minority, with 21 killed.

75 Terrorists were killed in the period 1991–1998.

The Serbs have been living in the territory of Kosovo and Metohija since the 6th century. That territory is of exceptional importance for the Serbian history and for the cultural-civilizational identity of Serbia—it was the centre of the Serbian statehood and it is important for the Serbs just as the Wailing Wall is important for the Jews. Many Serbian cultural monuments are situated in Kosovo and Metohija (200 medieval churches). There are no historical data saying that the Albanians populated that territory in the Medieval Ages. The Albanians in Kosovo and Metohija are mainly of Islamic religion, with a small number of Roman Catholics. The question of Kosovo is not only a question of territory or of the number of Serbian or Albanian population: it is an inalienable national treasury, indispensable for the identity of the Serbian people.

Kosovo and Metohija was the least developed region until the Second World War. Thanks to enormous investments of Serbia and Yugoslavia after the Second World War, an important prosperity was achieved in industry, agriculture and in social activities.

The political and terrorist's activities of the present separatists, members of the Albanian national minority in Kosovo and Metohija, follows consistently the project of the Prizren Ligue from 1878, which envisaged the unification of all, Albanians (from Albania, Greece, Macedonia and FRY) and the creation of Great Albania. This programme of unification is still a generally accepted national ideal and political objective of the Albanian extremists.

Over past several decades, the Albanians from Yugoslavia, Greece, and, recently, from Macedonia, present themselves to the world as the "part of the nation in jeopardy" and try to prove the "injustice" for, according to the Albanian interpretation, "one half of the Albanian ethnic territories" was left outside the borders of Albania.*

WHY A NEW ALBANIAN STATE

The main characteristics in Kosovo and Metohija are the absence of dialogue and a deep division between the ethnic groups. In spite of the fact that the Albanians achieved an enviable standard of living and a demographic explosion (the highest birth rate in Europe) in the FR of Yugoslavia, the Albanian separatists do not want the normalization of the life in Kosovo and reject every kind of dialogue which could contribute substantially to the normalization of the situation and to the lessening of the tensions.

The high degree of autonomy and of national rights did not satisfy the Albanian nationalists. They organized a separatist rebellion in 1981,

*Source: http://www.gov.yu/kosovo/terrorosm.html

with "Kosovo Republic" as their main slogan (separatist's demonstrations have been repeated a number of times until 1989). The slogan "Kosovo Republic" represents the main strategy of the Albanian separatism—the transformation of the Autonomous Province of Kosmet into a Republic which would have the right of secession. The Albanian separatist leaders in Kosmet never mention the question of the rights of national minorities, let alone the question of human rights and liberties. They request openly and unequivocally an independent state.

The Albanian separatist leaders organized elections in 1991, and established institutions of the "parallel authorities" which represent an alternative" to the FRY.

The selective non-recognition of the state in which they live and work is reflected in the:

—refusal to serve in the army

—non-participation in the elections—had they participated in the elections, the Albanians would have, bearing in mind the population, more than 30 out of 250 deputies in the Republican Parliament, around 12 out of 178 deputies in the Federal Parliament, and some 80% of the deputies in the Parliament of the Province. It is quite obvious that the members of the Albanian national minority would have practically the entire power in the Province.

—non-payment of all state taxes and duties. At the same time, they regularly pay to the "Parallel authorities" 3% of their income (very often that is a pure and simple blackmail of their compatriots).

—the establishment of "parallel schools," exclusively for the members of the Albanian national minority. The teaching is performed according to nationalist and separatist programmes, in non-adequate premises. The level of the knowledge acquired is best shown by the fact that their diplomas are not recognized anywhere in the world. Generations of the Albanian youth are handicapped educationally at the very start, and the "parallel schools" resulted in the final ethnic division among the young, in the closing of the young members of the Albanian national minority in the dogmas of extreme nationalism and separatism and the creation of the consciousness that common life with Serbs is impossible. The demonstrations and requests to return to the school buildings have as objective only the seizure of the buildings, and not the acceptation of the valid curriculum—as a matter of fact, they want to continue the "parallel schools" in the school buildings. The boycott of the educational system of the Republic of Serbia, which guarantees and assures conditions for teaching in Albanian prevents the application of the Declaration on the Rights of National, Ethnic, Religious and Language minorities, adopted by the LIN General Assembly in 1992. The manipulation of the young for the achievement of separatist objectives violates the UN Declaration on the Rights of Children and the International Convention on the Rights of Children.

Such a behaviour represents a violation of the provision 37 of the Final Document of the 2nd Meeting of the Conference on Human Dimension of the OSCE (Copenhagen, 1990), and of the Para.9 of the Preamble, of the articles 20 and 21 of the Framework Convention of the Council of Europe on the Protection of National Minorities. These provisions do not allow to the minorities any activities which would be contrary to the principles of the UN Charter, of the OSCE, and especially to the principle of respect of the territorial integrity, of the Constitution and the laws of the countries in which the minorities live.

At the same time, the Albanian minority uses all the benefits given by the state and the system they do not recognize, but which are suitable for them:

—health insurance

—employments in public and private sectors

—all rights in the field of information

—passports

—vaccination of the population, etc.

—the Albanian national minority has the Albanian Drama, a Section of the Academy of Science, an Authors' Association, a Musicians' Association and over 100 cultural and artistic associations. These institutions are financed by the Republic of Serbia.[†]

WHO REJECT THE DIALOGUE

The separatist leadership of the Albanian national minority, as established by their policy and practice since 1990 when "Kosovo Republic" was proclaimed, are substantially endangered by those who do not let them be equal citizens, not by the state. Albanian leaders have placed the citizens of their nationality in a political ghetto, depriving them of all rights which belong to them according to the Constitution and the Laws. The census was boycotted, in order not to establish the exact number for the Albanian national minority in Kosovo and Metohija, the elections were boycotted, jobs in factories, mines, schools, hospitals, were abandoned under the pressure of the nationalists. The abandonment of the state schools was justified by the idea that schools on whose certificates there is a title "Republika Srbija" were not acceptable.

[†] *Source:* http://www.gov.yu/kosovo/state.html

Parallel schools were established, the medical personnel of Albanian nationality was withdrawn into illegal and inadequate medical services, the use of services of state hospitals, which are free of charge and at a high professional level was prohibited. At the same time, the state regularly published textbooks in Albanian, provided medical protection, information in Albanian, issued passports, etc.

The Government of the FR of Yugoslavia submitted, in the framework of the Geneva Conference on Yugoslavia, a proposal for the overcoming of the problem of education in Kosovo and Metohija. The separatist leadership in Kosovo and Metohija rejected that proposal and prevented the resolution of the problem.

In a number of informal contacts the Albanian side did not show the wish for the normalization of the situation in Kosovo. A concrete agreement on the normalization of the schooling system was signed by President Slobodan Milosević and Rugova in September 1996. During the following months a meetings of the representatives of both sides was held with the intention to apply the agreement which had been achieved. The representatives of the Albanian minority demanded additional political concessions which were not mentioned in the political agreement. They demanded diplomas with the seal "Kosovo Republic," etc. Moreover, the demands concerned the taking of the university and college buildings in which the teaching would be performed outside the Yugoslav curricula, according to the curriculum of another state. Over 90% of the teaching in primary and secondary schools is in Albanian.

The Government of the Republic of Serbia invited, on March 11, 1998, the responsible representatives of the Albanian national minority to an open dialogue, for the solution of all concrete questions. The Government of the Republic of Serbia emphasized the fact that the dialogue is the only way to improve the political processes in order to solve the key problems of the citizens in this Province. All questions of Kosovo and Metohija should be solved in the framework of Serbia, by political means and according to international standards about the protection of the rights of national minorities, it was said in the communique from the meeting of the Government of the Republic of Serbia.

The Federal Government gave on March 12, 1998 its support to the invitation to open dialogue in order to find solutions for all concrete questions in Kosovo and Metohija.[††]

[††]*Source:* http://www.gov.yu/kosovo/dialogue.html

Issue 17
Humanitarian Intervention

INTRODUCTION

Discussions of military intervention for humanitarian purposes often involve two African countries: Somalia and Rwanda. A brief overview of recent history reveals the reasons for their involvement.

At present, Somalia has no government. According to the U.S Department of State's Background Notes, "The present political situation is one of anarchy, marked by inter-clan fighting and random banditry, with some areas of peace and stability." Since gaining independence from Britain and Italy in 1960, internal struggles for power have been continuous even for the period from 1979 to 1991, when a constitutional regime headed by Maj. Gen. Mohamed Said "Barre" gained some internal control. Barre was ousted by revolutionaries and died in exile in Nigeria in 1991. Dozens of warring factions competed for control. In 1992, in response to the continuing chaos and violence, the United States and other countries began Operation Restore Hope. According to the U.S. Department of State, a Unified Task Force (UNITAF) intervened in an operation that "was designed to create an environment in which assistance could be delivered to Somalis suffering from the effects of dual catastrophes—one man-made and one natural." Unfortunately, UNITAF was not able to bring the chaos under control, and as the State Department reports, "The United States played a major role in both operations until 1994, when U.S. forces withdrew after a pitched gun battle with Somali gunmen that left hundreds dead or wounded."

The story of Rwanda's tragedy is the story of the Tutsis and the Hutus. The Tutsis, a tribe of cattle herdsmen, moved north from South Africa to Rwanda in the 1400s. They quickly subjugated the native Hutu farmers, who became feudal vassals of the Tutsi nobility. In 1959 a Hutu rebellion ended in replacing the Tutsi monarchy with a Belgian-supported Hutu-led constitutional government. More than 150,000 Tutsis fled the country.

On July 5, 1973, Maj. Gen. Juvenal Habyarimana dissolved the National Assembly, but in 1978 his party called for an election in which he was elected president. On October 1, 1990, Tutsis in Uganda formed the Rwandan Patriotic Front (RPF) and invaded Rwanda. For two years the war raged, and then it was followed by an unstable cease-fire. On April 6, 1994, Habyarimana and the President of Burundi were both killed when the airplane in which they were flying was shot down as it prepared to land at Kigali. The Hutus used the incident to begin a fanatic campaign to exterminate the Tutsis. The U.S. Department of State reports that "the killing swiftly spread from Kigali to all corners of the country; between April 6 and the beginning of July, a genocide of unprecedented swiftness left up to 1 million Tutsis and moderate Hutus dead at the hands of organized bands of militia—Interahamwe. Even ordinary citizens were called on to kill their neighbors by local officials and government-sponsored radio."

The events in Somalia and Rwanda pose many problems. Although the Serbs conducted ethnic cleansing in Kosovo for months before NATO intervened, eventually NATO *did* intervene. Yet in Rwanda, in the same decade, ethnic cleansing of a much more substantial character occurred, and NATO did *not* intervene. Why? At least three explanations are possible.

The first explanation is that the United States has no vital interest at stake in Rwanda. The implication of this statement is that Americans simply do not care if thousands—even hundreds of thousands—of people are hacked to death with machetes, as long as the victims are not strategically located or the aggressors do not threaten our oil supplies.

A second explanation that has been offered is that the United States did not intervene because of racism. Perhaps we care enough to intervene only if the victims are white. We did not intervene in Cambodia in the mid-1970s when as many as two million Asians lost their lives to Pol Pot's regime.

Our experience in Somalia, however, at least partly refutes the first two explanations. Somalia is not of strategic importance to the United States, and most Somalians are not white; yet we intervened with humanitarian intentions.

The Somalian experience, however, poses a third possible explanation: Because we failed in Somalia, our failure makes us hesitant to enter countries with armed forces when we have no assurance that our intervention will actually save lives. Perhaps Somalia reminds us of a much more energetic and even more tragic intervention: that in Vietnam. Is Kosovo not, at least possibly, another Vietnam? Perhaps not. The third explanation implies that in some places, we may have a greater chance of success. Perhaps the Serbs are more vulnerable than the Hutus to the types of technological-surgical strikes that NATO is able to deliver.

Although the following two statements are not particularly recent, they are included in this volume not because they are precisely current, but because in some sense they are typical and unfortunately therefore timeless. New crises continue to arise around the world on a regular basis. In the articles in this section, a member of the U.S. House of Representatives berates the administration for not taking action. And the administration, irritated with its own impotence, pronounces its strongest denunciation of the perpetrators.

As you read the articles, consider the following questions.

Discussion Questions

1. What responsibility does the United States have for helping victims of atrocities in other countries?
2. What criteria can we use to determine whether intervention will be effective?
3. Is the U.S. national interest a legitimate criterion for intervention when humanitarian crises occur?

For more information on this topic, visit the following websites:

`http://info.acm.org/crossroads/xrds1-4/democracy.html`
Rwanda News

`http://www.rwandemb.org/`
Rwanda Embassy to U.S.

`http://www.usip.org/`
United States Institute of Peace

Representative Mica's
Speech on Rwanda:
In the House of Representatives, March 26, 1998

JOHN L. MICA

The SPEAKER pro tempore (Mr. Hulshof). Under a previous order of the House, the gentleman from Florida (Mr. Mica) is recognized for 5 minutes.

Mr. MICA. Mr. Speaker, I come before the House tonight to reflect on what we have seen on television and heard about, relating to the President of the United States' visit to Africa. I think all of us have witnessed the President as he has made his way across the African continent.

I read in this morning's *Washington Post,* and I know it was covered by other newspapers, an account of what the President said. And he was in Rwanda when he made this statement. He said, "We did not act quickly enough after the killing began." I believe he was talking to Rwandans.

I want to talk about that statement in a second. But President Clinton will not be going to Somalia on this trip. In Somalia, our President took a humanitarian mission initiated by President Bush, and turned it into a $3 billion disaster.

Remember, if you will, that President Clinton placed United States troops under United Nations command. Remember, if you will, that as Americans we watched in horror as our murdered troops were left under U.N. command, unable to defend themselves, were dragged through the streets of Mogadishu.

Today, Somolia has slipped back into chaos after this Clinton fiasco. We have to remember what took place in Africa and what the policies of this administration were. I protested the Clinton proposal for Somalia before that tragedy, time and time again, in the well and on the floor of this House.

Let me now turn to Rwanda. President Clinton, as I said in my opening statement, is quoted as saying, "We did not act quickly enough after the killing began." Pay particular attention to what the President said and what is printed in the papers.

Let me, if I may, as Paul Harvey says, tell you and repeat the rest of the story.

The President said we did not act quickly enough after the killing began. But what the President of the United States did not say to the world and to Africa is what we should now be remembering.

I saved the newspaper accounts of what the President said, because I was so stunned by the lack of action and actually the blocking of action by this administration, and brought them with me to the floor tonight. I saved them and had them blown up.

The Secretary General of the United Nations, Boutros-Ghali, begged President Clinton to allow an all-African U.N. force to go into Rwanda. Let me read what he said. This is what was in the newspaper.

When last year's peace agreement collapsed on April 7th and fierce fighting broke out between Hutu and Tutsi, the United Nations cut its 2,700-member force in Rwanda back to a few hundred at the urging of the Clinton administration.

I spoke out then, and I have spoken out afterwards on the floor when we saw what was happening with this administration and this policy before 1 million Africans were slaughtered.

Let me, if I may, recall some of the statements that I made on this floor. I made one statement on this floor, and I will read it. Let me, if I may, trace the history of this tragedy. Let me also, if I may, trace the history of our failed policy.

On April 6th, a plane with the presidents of Rwanda, and Burundi was shot down. We knew then the potential for violence, terror and mass killings.

On May 11th, the United States criticized a U.N. plan to send 5,500 multinational soldiers into Rwanda to protect refugees and assist relief workers. No U.S. troops would have been involved.

On May 16th, the U.S. forced the U.N. to delay plans to send 5,500 troops to end violence in Rwanda, an all-U.N. force.

So we see that the history of action and inaction by this administration, and history should so properly record it.

Press Statement on Rwanda:

U.S. Department of State, Office of the Spokesman,
February 6, 1997

NICHOLAS BURNS

RWANDA: TERRORIST VIOLENCE

The United States condemns in the strongest terms the terrorist attacks against Rwandans and expatriates in Rwanda.

On January 18, three Spanish aid workers were killed and an American seriously wounded in Ruhengeri province. On January 26, a Canadian priest was murdered as he celebrated mass in Ruhengeri prefecture. On February 4, two United Nations human rights monitors (one British citizen and a Cambodian citizen) and three Rwandan UN employees working with the human rights monitors, were killed in Cyangugu prefecture. All of these victims were unarmed civilians; and it appears that all were deliberately targeted.

These are not the first such attacks. Genocidal elements of the ex-FAR (former Rwandan Army) and the Interahamwe militia have been staging attacks into Rwanda, often killing innocent civilians, including government officials, persons of Hutu ethnicity who are cooperating with the Rwandan government and people who could be important witnesses in the ongoing genocide trials. These incidents appeared to increase in number and intensity during the first half of 1996.

We urge all Rwandans to put aside their differences, end the ceaseless violence, and work toward peace, justice, and reconciliation in their country.

Humanitarian aid workers are the first, and in some cases, the only means for the international community to provide emergency assistance to those in desperate situations. Their status under international law, and in common practice, has been clear—as non-combatants, they should be free from attack or intimidation. The United States deeply regrets these attacks upon unarmed humanitarian workers in Rwanda, as well as other recent attacks in Burundi and other parts of the world. When humanitarian aid workers are under attack, the international community loses its most potent tool in caring for vulnerable populations.

Issue 18
Sanctions

INTRODUCTION

Sometimes a nation may prohibit its citizens from having contact with persons in another nation. Trade, financial transactions, foreign investment, communication, travel, and other ties may be prohibited. The goal in imposing these penalties, or sanctions, may be to influence the other government, to punish it for objectionable actions previously taken, to cause an overthrow of the regime, or even to curry favor with influential domestic groups.

Sanctions are most effective if the country applying them is strong and if the target country is significantly dependent on the sanctioning country. No doubt this is one reason why sanctions have been a favored technique of influence among American leaders. The basic U.S. sanctions law, still on the books, is the 1917 Trading with the Enemy Act. That law makes it illegal for any person in the United States to trade with an "enemy" of the United States, defined as any person in a designated hostile country. In the years since 1917, Congress has added prohibitions against economic transactions other than trade, as well as restrictions on travel and cultural contacts. Various countries that are now on the U.S. enemies' list include Iran, Iraq, Libya, Sudan, and, of course, Cuba.

A strong proponent of U.S. sanctions, especially against Cuba, is the colorful chairman of the Senate Foreign Relations Committee, Jesse Helms. In 1995, Senator Helms authored legislation that extended the reach of U.S. sanctions to foreign companies that do business with Cuba, if they own assets there that had originally been seized from U.S. companies by the Castro government. In his irrepressible style, Senator Helms said: "Well, you cannot do business with Castro just as you could not do business with Adolph Hitler. . . . Cuba is controlled by the same Communist tyrant who has inflicted so much death and mayhem upon the Cuban people since he took over years ago. . . . We have condoned Fidel Castro long enough. It is time to get him out."

Fellow committee member Senator Paul Simon took an opposing position, arguing in favor of trade and contacts with Cuba:

> If you take a look at how we handle[d] the Soviet Union, we really had two courses; one by those who just wanted to isolate the Soviet Union completely, and the other by those who said, "Let us trade, let us have business back and forth, let us get them exposed to what democracy is all about."
>
> And that view prevailed and it, I do not need to tell you, was successful.
>
> I think we face the same two choices with Cuba. And my feeling is that what we ought to be doing is trading, exchanging visits, opening Cuba up, giving people of Cuba, like we gave people of the Soviet Union, a chance to see what things are like on the outside.

Do sanctions work, even when imposed by a country as powerful as the United States? Are they successful in causing policy changes by the targeted government or a change in the regime? And what are the costs of sanctions for a country's own companies that lose business in target countries—and for ordinary people in those countries who are deprived of needed imports?

In the articles that follow, David E. Weekman makes the argument for sanctions, using a more analytical style than that of Senator Helms. Richard N. Haass, director of foreign policy studies at the Brookings Institution, on the other hand, contends that sanctions are ill-advised.

As you read the articles, consider the following questions.

Discussion Questions

1. Now that you have read opinions on both sides of the sanctions issue, where do you stand? On balance, are sanctions a useful foreign policy tool, or not?
2. The United States government usually seems more interested in imposing economic sanctions on opposing regimes than do America's European allies. Why?
3. Suppose that you accept the proposition that sanctions could, at least potentially, be useful instruments of US policy. How would you change the American approach to sanctions to make them more effective?

    For more information on this topic, visit the following websites:

    http://www.treas.gov/ofac/
    (web site of Office of Foreign Assets Control of U.S. Treasury Department, which administers trade sanctions against target countries)

    http://www.sanctions.net
    (a web service by James Orr Associates, which lists national and even state and local laws imposing trade sanctions; free 1-month subscription available at site)

    http://www.usaengage.com
    (web site of USA Engage, a coalition of U.S. companies and agricultural interests that oppose U.S. trade sanctions)

Sanctions: The Invisible Hand
of Statecraft

DAVID E. WEEKMAN

Sanctions, when implemented as a result of an emerging U.S. foreign policy crisis, are usually evaluated in the public domain when the government is in a transitory phase somewhere between diplomacy and war. Analysis in the spotlight often drives the publicity-seeking politicians, pundits, and other sanctions "experts" to focus solely on the adverse impact of the sanctions and whether or not the sanctions have, to date, achieved the foreign policy objective. In most cases, the conclusion is that sanctions have "failed."

Similarly, in the aftermath of conflict, experts are usually quick to focus on the critical role that military force—or its threatened use—played in resolving the crisis. Thus, oftentimes, little attention is devoted seriously to examining the true role that sanctions played in helping to resolve—or at least manage—that crisis. The role that sanctions played in the 1994 Haitian crisis brings into question the conventional wisdom of those who claim the Haitian sanctions "failed." It can be argued that sanctions played a prominent, if not a key role in forcing the Junta to depart Haiti.

While this article is specifically about the 1994 intervention in Haiti, it is possible—and the author asks readers to consider the possibility—that the type of analytical approach taken here (e.g., viewing sanctions as one tool in the toolbox of statecraft, as opposed to viewing sanctions as the primary weapon employed), may be useful in further understanding the true role that sanctions are playing in the U.S. and UN's quest to contain Saddam Hussein and eliminate his weapons of mass destruction program. That, however, is the subject of another article.

THE UN. SANCTIONS

After close to thirty years of dictatorship, democracy in Haiti prevailed for the first time in 1990 with the election of Jean-Bertrand Alistide, a Roman Catholic priest, as President. The Haitian experience with democracy was

David E. Weekman is a Foreign Affairs Specialist with the U.S. Arms Control and Disarmament Agency.
Reprinted by permission. *Strategic Review*, Winter 1998.

short-lived, however. Aristide was ousted on September 30, 1991 by a military coup. The Junta was led by Lt. Gen. Raoul Cedras, Commander in Chief of Haitian Armed Forces, Brig. Gen. Phillippe Biamby, Army Chief of Staff, and Lt. Col. Michael François, Chief of Police.

The Organization of American States (OAS) imposed trade sanctions on Haiti in November 1991 in an attempt to punish the coup leaders and restore President Aristide to power. In May 1993, the United Nations Security Council (UNSC) enacted UN Resolution 841, which made the OAS trade embargo universal and imposed mandatory arms, oil, and financial embargoes on Haiti.[1] The Junta on July 3, 1993 agreed to the Governor's Island Accord (GIA), which called for the return of President Aristide to Haiti by October 30, 1993. In return, on August 27, 1993 the UNSC under Resolution 861 suspended the oil and arms embargo. However, after the Haitian generals were found to be in "serious and consistent non-compliance" with the GIA, the UNSC, under Resolution 873, reimposed the oil and arms embargo on October 13, 1993. Following the assassination of Justice Minister François-Guy Malary on October 14, the UNSC further tightened the embargo on October 16, 1993 under Resolution 875.[2]

However, President Clinton became increasingly frustrated with his inability to restore democracy to Haiti and by the increased reports from Haiti of judicial killings, arbitrary arrests, abductions, and rapes. As a result, the UNSC, acting on U.S. leadership, passed Resolution 917 on May 6, 1994, which was the strictest set of sanctions passed to date and designed to "tighten the noose" around the necks of the Junta and their inner circle of support.

Then, on July 22, 1994, the U.S. announced that it would push for a UN resolution to use "all necessary means" to restore exiled President Aristide to power.[3] On July 31, the UNSC passed Resolution 940 granting the United States that authority.

SANCTIONS IN ACTION

Prior to the embargo, the Haitian economy was driven by an export-based assembly industry, which produced baseballs, electronic goods, fishing lures, and clothing. These low-wage, low-skill assembly jobs, coupled with the fact that most Haitians farmed for sustenance, made Haiti one of the poorest countries in the Western Hemisphere. The plethora of sanctions imposed on Haiti from 1991 through 1994 had a devastating effect on the Haitian countryside, economy, and people.

International relief workers in Haiti observed that the most devastating impact of the embargo was a sharp increase in the price of propane gas, commonly used for cooking. The inability of most Haitians to afford propane drove up the demand for charcoal, the only readily available fuel substitute, which accelerated widespread deforestation and led to severe soil erosion.[4]

During the OAS embargo from 1991 to 1993, Haiti is said to have lost an estimated 150,000 jobs in the assembly sector. Unemployment estimates were as high as 70%. The government's deficit increased, trade fell, and Haitian currency plummeted. Real Gross Domestic Product declined by 14.8% in 1992, 5.2% in 1993, and 13.2% in 1994. Inflation for 1993 and 1994 was close to 50%.[5] A study that received a great deal of press during the embargo of Haiti was a 1993 report issued by the Harvard Center for Population and Development Studies that found that the deaths of 1,000 children per month in Haiti could be attributed to the sanctions.[6] Journalists never lacked anecdotal evidence detailing the devastating impact that the sanctions were having on the civilian population of Haiti, while the inner circle of the defacto government and its leaders apparently remained unaffected by the embargo, thus concluding that the sanctions were "failing." The reports often detailed incidents of malnutrition and starvation, while the wealthy elites and the generals sipped French champagne and ate salmon fillets and imported cheeses. The civilian population could not afford $10 for a gallon of gasoline, while Cedras and his ilk had full tanks in their land cruisers and access to all the fuel they needed. To pretend that the effects of sanctions against Haiti should be measured in strictly economic statistics, particularly with regard to the populace, is misleading and misses the point. To state that the sanctions had very little to do with the psychological, political, and diplomatic isolation of the Junta is to misconstrue the intended and actual effects of the sanctions. Imposing the sanctions on Haiti was a political act designed to have political effects. Furthermore, as an authority on economic sanctions, David Baldwin, argues, one must always be careful to recognize and acknowledge the degree of difficulty at hand—trying to dislodge a defacto government from power being one of the hardest.[7]

Sanctions, especially negative ones, are often believed to be, and frequently are viewed as instruments of coercion. Did the sanctions imposed by A result in B doing X? This begs the question for a yes (success) or no (failure) response. The literature on economic sanctions tends to be permeated with this school of thought.[8] Success in international politics, however, is usually a matter of degree. For instance, Baldwin has written that the costs of non-compliance with regard to X constitutes influence even though no change occurs in the policies of the target country.[9] Baldwin continues that not all influence is manifest in terms of changes in policy; changes in the cost of non-compliance also constitute influence. This increased cost of non-compliance can be a significant factor in the target government making some movement toward X. According to Baldwin, the relevant question is not whether economic measures were "decisive"—whatever that may mean—but whether they had a significant effect on the length, outcome, or intensity of the crisis.[10]

The pressure on Haiti's defacto government was dramatically increased in May 1994 with the passage of UNSC Resolution 917, which banned all travel to and from Haiti, denied visas to military, police, and other coup supporters, placed a total trade embargo on Haiti for non-humanitarian goods, and strongly urged all governments to freeze the financial resources of the coup leaders and their supporters.

Soon thereafter, the U.S. banned all financial transactions between the U.S. and Haiti and froze the assets, subject to U.S. jurisdiction, of 600 military leaders and other supporters of the Cedras regime. In June, the Clinton administration expanded the assets freeze to include all Haitian citizens. The implementation of Resolution 917 by various states increased the costs to the Junta for non-compliance with the terms of the GIA. Essentially, the regime had become internationally isolated. The defacto Haitian leaders, their families, and key supporters, accustomed to an opulent and aristocratic lifestyle, could no longer freely travel, found a sizable amount of their assets seized, and essentially were shunned by the international community. This last round of sanctions appeared to have the defacto authorities on the verge of buckling. Throughout the embargo, the border between the Dominican Republic and Haiti was very porous. Gasoline was a much needed commodity, and millions of gallons flowed freely into Haiti. Since the Junta's inner circle owned all the gas stations, trucks, and pumping stations, they experienced no shortage of fuel, even at exorbitant prices. They not only survived but prospered. Joaquin Balaguer, President of the Dominican Republic, repeatedly claimed that his country was enforcing the embargo, despite evidence to the contrary.

On May 16, 1994 there was a hotly disputed Presidential election in the Dominican Republic. This event, seemingly unrelated to the Haitian situation, did make a direct impact on the Haitian Junta and dramatically increased their costs for non-compliance with the sanctions. The election was marked by widespread accusations of fraud by international observers. The U.S. brokered a deal with Mr. Balaguer to achieve an understanding whereby the U.S. would not make an issue of the election irregularities, if President Balaguer would cooperate in "seriously" enforcing the embargo by sealing the Dominican border with Haiti.[11] Evidence exists that this understanding largely succeeded in having the Dominican armed forces deploy nearly half of the nation's army, shutting down a substantial number of once bustling smuggling centers along the border. The fuel supply of the defacto government began to dry up and this put increased pressure on the Junta.

In June, press reports began to surface of a split within and between the Junta and their wealthy supporters, who urged Cedras to resign, as well as reports which amazingly foretold the outcome of the crisis, stating that Cedras had agreed to resign as Commander of the Haitian Armed Forces when his term expired in October 1994.[12] It appears reasonable to conclude that the sanctions, rather than "failing," must have played some role in forcing the hand of Cedras to at least begin discussing and apparently deciding upon a retirement date—progress not evident before the imposition of sanctions.

THE THEORY OF SANCTIONS

"In discussing the role of sanctions . . . the pens often slip toward negative sanctions and almost never slip toward positive sanctions."—David A. Baldwin.[13]

Sanctions come in two forms, negative and positive. Negative sanctions can be defined as actual or threatened punishments to B; positive sanctions can be defined as actual or promised rewards to B. David Baldwin has observed that few analysts make a distinction between positive and negative sanctions because all threats imply promises and all promises imply threats; they are simply different ways of describing the same conditional influence attempt. In other words, a threat to punish B for noncompliance must imply a promise not to punish for compliance. Likewise, a promise to reward if B complies must imply a threat not to reward if B fails to comply.[14]

Baldwin moves beyond this "traditional" paradigm of positive sanctions and argues that in order to distinguish rewards from punishments, one must establish B's baseline of expectations at the moment A's influence attempt begins.[15] Positive sanctions then are actual or promised improvements in B's value position relative to his baseline of expectations. In other words, if A offers B $100 for doing X, and B is expecting to receive that $100, then this cannot be considered a reward. Whereas, if B is not expecting anything for doing X and suddenly A offers B $100 for doing X, then this can be considered a reward. In both episodes, B is operating from a different baseline of expectations—perhaps leading to a different outcome and a different timeframe within which that outcome occurs.

Baldwin, drawing upon Thomas Schelling's discussion of "compellent threats" to describe A's use of the stick to shift B's expectations, explains that A uses a negative sanction (the punishment) to lay the groundwork for the subsequent use of positive sanctions (the promise to withdraw the punishment if B complies).[16] Taking it a step further, if B's expectations are so low as a result of the negative sanctions imposed, A may gain increased leverage, and shorten the time frame in getting B to comply with X, by not only promising to withdraw the punishment, but by offering additional rewards for compliance.

Purchase, as an instrument of positive sanctions, is an often underused and frequently misunderstood form of economic statecraft. In *Economic Statecraft*, Baldwin argues that direct monetary payment is one of the most common ways for some people to get other people to do things they would not otherwise do.[17] The purchase of B by A to do X translates into a cost—perhaps, in some instances, a significant monetary expenditure. However, as Baldwin points out in his discussion on monetary costs, the cost of one instrument of statecraft must be carefully weighed against the costs and benefits of using other forms of statecraft to achieve that foreign policy goal.[18] Compared to military statecraft, economic statecraft is almost always cheaper. While a statesman using the power of positive sanctions risks being perceived by domestic audiences as soft, weak or lacking in toughness for "buying one's way out of a fight," only unimaginative statesmen would needlessly take their country to war if the foreign policy objective could be achieved by other means.

THE END GAME

Harold Lasswell has written that there are four types of statecraft: propaganda, diplomacy, military force, and economic statecraft.[19] Diplomacy and military force, or the threat of force, can be very powerful instruments of statecraft on the international stage, especially when employed at critical junctures of the crisis and when functioning in synergistic fashion. Policymakers tend not to give credit to, or publicly acknowledge, the role that other instruments may have played in solving a foreign policy problem. Even in the planning stages of a crisis, policymakers tend to focus exclusively on diplomacy and military force. The problem that the U.S. encountered in Haiti with these two levers of statecraft, at least up until the endgame, was that the threat to employ military force was not credible, thus weakening the hand of diplomacy. The U.S. lacked credibility on the threat to employ military force due largely to President Clinton's October 12, 1993, decision to withdraw the USS *Harlan County* from Port-au-Prince after mobs of gun-toting thugs demonstrated against the arrival of U.S. and Canadian military advisors.

The U.S. made no secret of its intent to return President Aristide to power by any means necessary. In testimony before the House Foreign Affairs Committee on June 8, 1994, William H. Gray III, President Clinton's Special Representative to Haiti, repeatedly refused to rule out military intervention as the means for restoring Aristide to power. Gray testified that "further steps will be taken in the coming days and weeks. No operations have been excluded. Democracy in Haiti will prevail."[20]

On September 15, 1994, in an Oval Office address, President Clinton stated, "Your time is up. Leave now or we will force you from power. . . . Our mission in Haiti, as it was in Panama and Grenada, will be limited and specific. . . . we will remove the dictators from power. . . ."[21]

During a meeting at the White House two days prior to the planned invasion, the 24-nation Multi-nation Force Coalition on Haiti issued a joint statement: "The dictators have . . . run out of time. . . . The Haitian military leaders should have absolutely no doubt about our resolve. We will show them that the international community stands by its word."[22]

Meanwhile, President Clinton dispatched a team, consisting of former Joint Chiefs of Staff Chairman General Colin Powell, former President Jimmy Carter, and former U.S. Senator Sam Nunn, to Haiti for face-to-face negotiations with the Junta. General Powell, in his memoirs, recounts his meetings with Haitian leaders and his perception of the effectiveness of the sanctions: "Our party retired to the Hotel Villa Creole in the hills above the City for a courtesy meeting with the Haitian parliamentarians. Later, we had dinner with prominent business leaders. What struck me was how sleek, well-fed, and well-dressed these men looked after almost three years of economic embargo had impoverished the rest of their countrymen. So much for sanctions."[23]

In discussions with General Cedras hours before the invasion, General Powell was unable to convince the Junta that the U.S. was ready to employ military force. Powell stated: "Let me make sure you understand what you are facing. Two aircraft carriers, two and a half infantry divisions, 20,000 troops, helicopter gunships, tanks and artillery."[24] General Cedras responded, "We used to be the weakest nation in the Hemisphere. After this, we'll be the strongest."[25]

The breakthrough came just as Carter, Powell, and Nunn were dead-locked with the Junta. Powell explains that General Biamby burst into the room and announced "the invasion is coming." Biamby had just been tipped off by a source at Fort Bragg. As Powell recounts, it was shortly thereafter that Haitian President Emile Jonassaint agreed to resign, which cleared the way for the resignation of Generals Cedras and Biamby.[26]

It is clear that the mission of the American troika, coupled with the departure of 61 planes from Fort Bragg bound for Haiti, were important factors in getting the Junta to step down.[27] It was a classic synergistic coupling of diplomacy and military force, well timed, and designed to achieve the desired foreign policy outcome.

The negative sanctions appeared, at the very least, to fracture the cohesiveness of the Junta and apparently even resulted in General

Cedras deciding on a date to retire. At the very least, the Junta was made more vulnerable to outside persuasion than they may otherwise have been. Furthermore, the Carter mission, coupled with the dispatch of the 82nd Airborne, only resulted in reaching an agreement, in principle, for the generals to step down on or before October 15, 1994.[28] This was an outcome that was no different than that apparently achieved by the severe negative sanctions. Moreover, this "coercive diplomacy" did not physically force the Junta to leave Haiti. Therefore, what did force them to depart the country? Perhaps it was the U.S. military sitting off the coast ready to invade at a moment's notice, or perhaps it is worth considering that positive sanctions, at least in part, also played a role in forcing the Junta to depart Haiti.

In the days preceding and following Cedras' departure from Haiti, a number of stories emerged, subsequently confirmed by the White House.[29] Reports indicated that General Cedras and other officials received a "golden parachute" from the U.S. in exchange for their departure from Haiti.[30] These reports suggest that there were several components to the deal.

1. Generals Cedras and Biamby gained immediate access to their share of the $79 million frozen in U.S. banks as a result of the sanctions.[31] Bank secrecy laws have prohibited the Treasury Department from saying exactly how much of the $79 million belonged to the two generals.

2. An agreement was reached whereby the U.S. would lease three rental properties in Haiti from Cedras, estimated to provide him with $60,000 paid one year in advance.[32]

3. Twenty-three of Cedras' relatives and associates were provided with safe passage to the U.S., plus transportation, housing, and living expenses.[33]

4. Cedras, Biamby and five others were provided with safe passage to Panama, plus transportation, housing, and living expenses.[34]

5. In Panama, Cedras was provided with a beach-side villa (believed to be at the Contadora Island Resort, which housed the exiled Shah of Iran), its rent paid one year in advance by the United States.[35]

6. Moving expenses for Cedras and his entourage are available, if he chooses to leave Panama (most likely to Spain, where he owns two homes).[36]

When the U.S. negotiated with Cedras on the terms of the golden parachute, Cedras was probably not expecting to be compensated for his departure. The severity of the sanctions under Resolution 917, the ever-increasing size of the U.S. military offshore, the fracturing of the Junta and the subsequent passage of Resolution 940, authorizing a

U.S.-led international invasion of Haiti, all led to a low and ever-decreasing baseline of expectations. The inducements to depart Haiti, in the eyes of Cedras, truly were a golden parachute, compensation or a reward for fleeing the country. Furthermore, the negative sanctions (e.g., the freezing of assets and denial of visas) became a positive sanction (their removal as a reward).

Clearly, the U.S. purchase of the Junta incurred a monetary cost to force their departure from Haiti. But, so what? As Baldwin would ask, "Would war have been cheaper?" The cost of fuel, spare parts, ammunition, food and medicine, equipment depreciation and replacement, combat pay—let alone the loss of human life to support a military intervention—would have far outweighed what the U.S. paid General Cedras for his departure from Haiti.

LESSONS FOR THE FUTURE

In the analysis of sanctions during a major foreign policy crisis, one must be careful not to become too enamored with analysis performed under a political spotlight. The Haitian sanctions did inflict tremendous pain on the Haitian population (as a military invasion would have as well), but that does not automatically translate into "failure." The negative sanctions, particularly those imposed under Resolution 917, resulted in severe discomfort to the Junta, if not an outright fracturing of the alliance, and apparently did help motivate Cedras to plan to resign in October 1994. If sanctions did not bring this about, what did?

The golden parachute deal received a fair amount of negative press.[37] The image of General Cedras living a pampered life in exile makes it understandable how one could believe that Cedras "won" (thus implying a U.S. loss) because he walked away with "silver rather than full of lead." As Baldwin reminds us, however, power is not a zero sum game.[38] If the adversary gains, the U.S. does not necessarily lose; such thinking impedes fruitful thinking about economic statecraft. Cedras and other international thugs can win, as long as the U.S. wins bigger. In the future, when policymakers jump to reap the political capital of a foreign policy victory, and as scholars and others write their post-mortems, it is hoped that they will view sanctions through Baldwin's lens rather than through General Powell's and let their pens slip toward positive sanctions and a more favorable view of negative sanctions.

Moreover, when future scholars review the history of the UN sanctions on Iraq (both pre- and post-Desert Storm), one hopes that they will critically examine the actual role that sanctions may have played in that crisis and not just arbitrarily conclude that sanctions "failed" because they did not oust Saddam Hussein from power.

Ejecting a government or dictator from power is no easy task, not even when military force is employed; witness the 1989 U.S. invasion of Panama and the 1993 U.S. intervention in Mogadishu, Somalia. For instance, it would be interesting to know what role sanctions played in impeding Saddam Hussein's ability to fight the coalition forces during Desert Storm (e.g., denial of spare parts, tank treads and tires). Likewise how robust would Saddam Hussein's military and weapons of mass destruction program be if there was no international oil embargo to deny him hard currency? What if there was no UN trade embargo on dual-use equipment, technologies, and chemicals? When viewed from this perspective, it would appear difficult to conclude that the sanctions on Iraq "failed."

NOTES

1. United Nations Security Council Resolution 841, June 16, 1993, paragraphs 5 & 8.
2. "Attaining Democracy: A Lengthy and Difficult Task," *UN Chronicle,* December 1993, pp. 20–22.
3. Daniel Williams and Julia Preston, "US Requests Open-ended Resolution from UN Backing Invasion of Haiti," *Washington Post,* July 22, 1994.
4. Lee Hockstader, "EmbargoTranslates into Ecological Disaster for Haiti," *Washington Post,* May 31, 1992, p. Al.
5. *Haiti Country Profile, 1995–1996* (London: Economic Intelligence Unit, 1995), pp. 38–40.
6. Sourced from: *World Disaster Report, 1995* (Geneva: International Federation of Red Cross and Red Crescent Societies, 1995) p. 24.
7. David A. Baldwin, *Economic Statecraft* (Princeton: Princeton University Press, 1985), p. 372.
8. See, for instance, Makio Miyagawa, *Do Economic Sanctions Work* (New York: St. Martin's Press, 1992); Gary Clyde Hufbauer, Jeffrey J. Schott, Kimberly Ann Elliott, *Economic Sanctions Reconsidered: History and Current Policy,* 2nd ed. (Washington DC: Institute for International Economics, 1990); Hufbauer, Schott, Elliott, *Economic Sanctions Reconsidered: Supplemental Case Histories,* 2nd ed. (Washington DC: Institute for International Economics, 1990); Lisa L. Martin, *Coercive Cooperation: Explaining Multilateral Economic Sanctions* (Princeton: Princeton University Press, 1992); Gunnar Adler-Karlsson, "The U.S. Embargo: Inefficient and Counterproductive," *Aussenwirtschaft* XXXV, June 1980, pp. 170–187; Peter A. G. Van Bergeijk, "Success and Failure of Economic Sanctions," *Kyklos,* vol. 42, 1989, pp. 385–403; Howard M. Fish, "The Problems with Sanctions," *Foreign Service Journal,* November 1990, p. 24; *Economic Sanctions* (U.S. General Accounting Office, NSIAD92-106, February 19, 1992).
9. Baldwin, *Economic Statecraft,* op. cit., pp. 132–133.
10. Ibid., p. 143.
11. See "Haiti: Tightening the Stranglehold," *The Economist,* August 6, 1994, p. 35; John Kifner, "Effort Is Begun by Dominicans to Seal Border," *Washington Post,* June 1, 1994, p. Al; Douglas Farah, "Balaguer Bars Cutting off Haiti," *Washington Post,* May 16, 1994; Robert S. Greenberger, "US Policy

on Haiti May Be Affected by Recent Vote in Dominican Republic," *Wall Street Journal*, June 27, 1994.

12. Douglas Farah, "Power in the Shadows in Haiti," *Washington Post*, June 20, 1994; Howard W French, "Split Reported in Haiti's Army with Chief Urged to Quit," *New York Times*, June 27, 1994, p. A2. Also see Gary Pierre-Pierre, "Haiti Strongman Reported to Set Retirement Date," *New York Times*, June 28, 1994, p. A6.
13. David A. Baldwin, "The Power of Positive Sanctions," *World Politics*, Volume XXIV, Number 1, October 1971, p. 22.
14. Ibid., p. 25.
15. Ibid., p. 23.
16. Ibid., pp. 24–25.
17. Baldwin, *Economic Statecraft*, p. 42.
18. Ibid., "Costs? Compared to What?" p. 140.
19. Harold D. Lasswell, *World Politics Faces Economics* (New York: McGraw Hill, 1945), p. 9.
20. "Give Sanctions Time to Bite, Gray Tells Lawmakers," *Congressional Quarterly*, June 11, 1994, p. 1540.
21. U.S. Department of State Dispatch, Vol. 5, No. 38, September 19, 1994, pp. 605, 607.
22. Ibid., pp. 607–608.
23. Colin L. Powell, with Joseph E. Persico, *My American Journey* (New York: Random House, 1995), p. 599.
24. Ibid., p. 600.
25. Ibid., p. 601.
26. Ibid., pp. 601–602.
27. Ibid., p. 612.
28. *Assessment Mission to Haiti, December 11–14, 1994* (Atlanta: The Carter Center of Emory University, 1995), Appendix 1.
29. Doyle McManus, "White House Defends Cedras Deal," *Los Angeles Times*, October 15, 1994, p. Al. Personal correspondence dated November 22, 1995, with Doron Bard, Desk Officer, Haiti Working Group, U.S. Department of State verified that an "arrangement" was made between the U.S. and Gen. Cedras.
30. The U.S. Department of State verified that ". . . all arrangements for Gen. Cedras' departure were made after the Carter Agreement was negotiated, immediately prior to Gen. Cedras' departure." See Note 29.
31. Douglas Jehl, "Haiti Generals Regain Access to $79 Million," *New York Times*, October 14, 1994, p. Al.
32. Douglas Farah, "U.S. Assists Dictators' Luxury Exile," *Washington Post*, October 14, 1994, p. Al. Kenneth Freed, "U.S. Gives Cedras a Lucrative Deal to Get Out of Haiti," *Los Angeles Times*, October 14, 1994, p. Al. This point was verified by the U.S. Department of State and negotiated ". . . on the eve of Gen. Cedras' departure from Haiti" (see Note 29).
33. Ibid., *Los Angeles Times*. The U.S. Department of State verified that the U.S. did fly Gen. Cedras and his family out of Haiti (see Note 29).
34. Ibid., *Los Angeles Times*.
35. "Not-so-pampered in exile," *The Economist*, October 22, 1994, p. 56. The U.S. Department of State denied that pre-paid rental housing awaited Gen. Cedras in Panama ". . . as far as the U.S. Government is concerned. We are unaware of any such arrangements in Panama" (see Note 29).
36. Ibid.

37. See for instance, Art Buchwald, "It Pays to Be a U.S. Enemy Nowadays," *Los Angeles Times*, October 18, 1994, E2; "Why Reward These Thugs? Payoff to Cedras Is a Blot on American Honor," *Los Angeles Times*, October 15, 1994, B7.
38. Baldwin, *Economic Statecraft*, p. 22.

Sanctioning Madness

RICHARD N. HAASS

A ROTTEN CORE

Economic sanctions are fast becoming the United States' policy tool of choice. A 1997 study by the National Association of Manufacturers listed 35 countries targeted by new American sanctions from to 1996 alone. What is noteworthy, however, is not just the frequency with which sanctions are used but their centrality; economic sanctions are increasingly at the core of U.S. foreign policy.

Sanctions—predominantly economic but also political and military penalties aimed at states or other entities so as to alter unacceptable political or military behavior—are employed for a wide range of purposes. The United States, far more than any other country, uses them to discourage the proliferation of weapons of mass destruction and ballistic missiles, promote human rights, end support for terrorism, thwart drug trafficking, discourage armed aggression, protect the environment, and oust governments.[1] To accomplish these ends, sanctions may take the form of arms embargoes, foreign assistance reductions and cutoffs, export and import limitations, asset freezes, tariff increases, import quota decreases, revocation of most favored nation (MFN) trade status, votes in international organizations, withdrawal of diplomatic relations, visa denials, cancellation of air links, and credit, financing, and investment prohibitions. Even U.S. state and local governments are introducing economic sanctions. Dozens have adopted "selective purchasing laws" that prohibit public agencies from purchasing goods and services from companies doing business with such countries as Burma and Indonesia.

Richard N. Haass is director of Foreign Policy Studies at the Brookings Institution. He was chairman of a Council on Foreign Relations study group on economic sanctions. This article is adapted from his forthcoming book, *Economic Sanctions and American Diplomacy*.

Reprinted by permission. *Foreign Affairs*, Nov.–Dec. 1997, Vol. 76, Issue 6, p. 74.

With a few exceptions, the growing use of economic sanctions to promote foreign policy objectives is deplorable. This is not simply because sanctions are expensive, although they are. Nor is it strictly a matter of whether sanctions "work"; the answer to that question invariably depends on how demanding a task is set for a particular sanction. Rather, the problem with economic sanctions is that they frequently contribute little to American foreign policy goals while being costly and even counterproductive. A recent study by the Institute for International Economics concluded that in 1995 alone, sanctions cost U.S. companies between $15 billion and $19 billion and affected some 200,000 workers. Secondary sanctions, levelled against third-party states that do not support a particular sanctions regime, add to this cost by jeopardizing the United States' trade relations. Thus, policymakers need to give more serious consideration to the impact of a sanction and weigh alternative policies more carefully.

THE SANCTIONS BOOM

Economic sanctions are popular because they offer what appears to be a proportional response to challenges in which the interests at stake are less than vital. They are also a form of expression, a way to signal official displeasure with a behavior or action. They thus satisfy a domestic political need to do something and reinforce a commitment to a norm, such as respect for human rights or opposition to weapons proliferation. Reluctance to use military force is another motivation. As the National Conference of Catholic Bishops points out, "Sanctions can offer a nonmilitary alternative to the terrible options of war or indifference when confronted with aggression or injustice."

The frequency with which the United States uses sanctions is also a result of the increased influence, especially on Congress, of single-issue constituencies, notably those promoting human rights, environmentalism, or ethnic, religious, or racially oriented causes. The media, too, plays a part. The so-called CNN effect can increase the visibility of problems in another country and stimulate Americans' desire to respond. Sanctions offer a popular and seemingly cost-free way of acting. The end of the Cold War and the demise of the Soviet Union have also contributed to the sanctions boom. Sanctions can now usually be introduced without opposition from Moscow, which in the past meant a veto in the U.N. Security Council or a Soviet subsidy for a target of U.S. sanctions.

Some evidence supports the efficacy of economic sanctions. One influential study concludes from analysis of more than 100 cases that economic sanctions have worked to some extent about a third of the time.[2] Other advocates are more selective in their views of history. For groups on the left, it is an article of faith that sanctions helped dismantle apartheid, just as the right argues that sanctions played a major role in the demise of the "evil empire."

Under the right circumstances, sanctions can achieve, or help achieve, various foreign policy goals ranging from the modest to the fairly significant. Sanctions introduced against Iraq after the Persian Gulf War have increased Iraqi compliance with U.N. resolutions calling for the elimination of its weapons of mass destruction. They have also diminished Baghdad's ability to import weapons and related technology. Iraq today is considerably weaker militarily and economically than it would have been without these sanctions.

Sanctions were one reason for the Serbs' decision to accept the Dayton agreement in August 1995 ending the fighting in Bosnia. The threat of sanctions may have also deterred several European firms from investing in Iran's oil and gas industry. Sanctions have burdened the economies of Iran, Cuba, and Libya, and may eventually contribute to change in those societies or in their behavior. U. S. sanctions against Pakistan, while having little discernible effect on that country's nuclear weapons program, have hurt Islamabad both economically and militarily, possibly influencing Pakistan's future actions as well as those of other would-be proliferators.

MORE HARM THAN GOOD

The limitations of sanctions are more pronounced than their accomplishments. Sanctions alone are unlikely to achieve results if the aims are large or time is short. Even though they were comprehensive and enjoyed almost universal international backing for nearly six months, sanctions failed to compel Saddam Hussein to withdraw from Kuwait in 1990. In the end, it took nothing less than Operation Desert Storm.

Other sanctions have also fallen short of their stated purposes. Despite sanctions against Iran, Tehran remains defiant in its support of terrorism, its subversion of its neighbors, its opposition to the Middle East peace process, and its pursuit of nuclear weapons. Fidel Castro still commands an authoritarian political system and a statist economy. Pakistan's nuclear program is well advanced; it now has enough material for at least a dozen bombs. Libya has refused to hand over the two individuals accused of destroying Pan Am Flight 103 over Lockerbie, Scotland. Sanctions did not persuade Haiti's junta to honor the results of the 1990 election that brought Jean Bertrand Aristide to power, nor did they convince Serbia and the Bosnian Serbs for several years to call off their military aggression. Unilateral sanctions are particularly ineffective. In a global economy, unilateral sanctions impose higher costs on American firms than on the target country, which can usually find substitute sources of supply and financing. Unilateral sanctions did, however, prove more costly for Haiti and Cuba, which were heavily dependent on trade with the United States. They also hurt Pakistan, which had been receiving substantial U.S. military and economic aid. Such cases are the exception, though; most unilateral sanctions will be little more than costly expressions of opposition except in those instances in which the ties between the United States and the target are so extensive that the latter cannot adjust to an American cutoff.

Generating international support for sanctions is often extremely difficult. In most instances, other governments prefer minimal sanctions, or none at all. They tend to value commercial interaction more than the United States does and are less willing to forfeit it. In addition, the argument that economic interaction is desirable because it promotes more open political and economic systems normally has more resonance in other capitals, although it has been used successfully by both the Bush and Clinton administrations to defeat Congress' attempts to revoke China's MFN status. Such thinking makes achieving multilateral support for sanctions more difficult for the United States. It usually takes something truly egregious, like Saddam Hussein's occupation of Kuwait, to overcome this anti-sanctions bias. Even with Iraq, generous compensation for third-party states affected by the sanctions, including Egypt and Turkey, was a prerequisite for their support.

Trying to compel others to join a sanctions regime by threatening secondary sanctions can seriously harm U.S. foreign policy interests. Congress is increasingly turning to secondary sanctions to bolster ineffective unilateral sanctions regimes, as with Cuba, Iran, and Libya; in all three instances, sanctions now apply to overseas firms that violate the terms of U.S. legislation like the Iran-Libya Sanctions Act and Helms-Burton Act. This threat appears to have deterred some individuals and firms from entering into proscribed business activities, but it has increased anti-American sentiment, threatened the future of the World Trade Organization (WTO), distracted attention from the provocative behavior of the target governments, and made Europeans less likely to work with the United States in shaping policies to contend with post-Cold War challenges.

MISSING THE TARGET

Sanctions often produce unintended and undesirable consequences. Haiti is a prime example. Sanctions exacerbated the island's economic distress, causing a massive exodus of Haitians to the United States that proved life-threatening for them and expensive and disruptive for Florida. In Bosnia, the arms embargo weakened the Muslims, since

Bosnia's Serbs and Croats had larger stores of military supplies and greater access to outside sources. This military imbalance contributed to the fighting and to the disproportionate Muslim suffering. Military sanctions against Pakistan may actually have increased Islamabad's reliance on a nuclear option because they cut off its access to U.S. weaponry and dramatically weakened Pakistan's confidence in Washington.

All this demonstrates that sanctions can be a blunt instrument. Most sanctions do not discriminate within the target country. There is a rationale for this: funds and goods can easily be moved around, and governments can often command what is in the hands of others. The problem with such a broad-brush approach is that sanctions tend to affect the general population, while those in the government and the military are able to skirt the sanctions.

Thus, the tendency to see economic sanctions as "below" the use of military force on some imagined ladder of foreign policy escalation must be revised. Sanctions can be a powerful and deadly form of intervention. The danger inherent in broad sanctions—beyond missing the true target—is both moral, in that innocents are affected, and practical, in that sanctions that harm the general population can bring about undesired effects, including strengthening the regime, triggering large-scale emigration, and retarding the emergence of a middle class and a civil society. Mass hardship can also weaken domestic and international support for sanctions, as with Iraq, despite the fact that those sanctions have included from the outset a provision allowing Iraq to import humanitarian goods and services.

"NOT-SO-SMART" SANCTIONS

"Smart" or "designer" sanctions, which penalize leaders while sparing the general public, are only a partial solution. It is possible that Haiti's military leaders were bothered by the fact their families could no longer shop in Florida. And executives who risk being denied access to the United States under the 1996 Helms-Burton act may think twice before entering into proscribed business deals. But opportunities to employ effective sanctions with precision are rare. Gathering the necessary information about assets, and then moving quickly enough to freeze them, can often prove impossible. Leaders and governments have many ways to insulate themselves, and designing "smart" sanctions to target only them is extraordinarily difficult, especially with a totalitarian or authoritarian state run by a few people.

In addition, authoritarian, statist societies are often able to hunker down and withstand the effects of sanctions. There are several possible reasons: sanctions sometimes trigger a "rally around the flag" nationalist reaction; by creating scarcity, they enable governments to better control the distribution of goods; and they create a general sense of siege that governments can exploit to maintain political control. This conclusion is consistent with literature suggesting that market economic reform reinforces the development of civil society; by reducing the scope for independent action, sanctions can work against forces promoting political pluralism.

Last, but far from least, sanctions can be expensive for American business. There is a tendency to overlook or underestimate the direct costs of sanctions, perhaps because, unlike the costs of military intervention, they do not show up in U.S. government budget tables. Sanctions do, however, affect the economy by reducing revenues of U.S. companies and individuals. Moreover, this cost is difficult to measure because it includes not only lost sales but also forfeited opportunities: governments and overseas companies can elect not to do business with the United States for fear that sanctions might one day be introduced, wreaking havoc with normal commercial relations.

TAKING SANCTIONS SERIOUSLY

A fundamental change in thinking and attitude is required. Economic sanctions are a serious instrument of foreign policy and should be employed only after consideration no less rigorous than for other forms of intervention, including the use of military force. The likely benefits of a particular sanction to U.S. foreign policy should be greater than the anticipated costs to the U.S. government and the American economy. Moreover, the sanction's likely effect on U.S. interests should compare favorably to the projected consequences of all other options, including military intervention, covert action, public and private diplomacy, or simply doing nothing. Broad sanctions should not be used as a means of expression. Foreign policy is not therapy; its purpose is not to make us feel good but to do good. The same holds for sanctions.

For pragmatic more than normative reasons, multilateral support for economic sanctions should typically be a prerequisite for the United States' imposition of them. Such support need not be simultaneous, but it should be all but certain to follow. Except when the United States is in a unique position to exert leverage based on its economic relationship with the target, unilateral sanctions should be avoided. Building international support will require intense, often high-level diplomatic efforts and even then may not succeed. Policymakers must then consider whether some alternative would not be better than weaker or unilateral sanctions.

International compliance with sanctions regimes can be increased by providing assistance to third parties to offset the economic cost of implementing sanctions. Greater use should be made of Article 50 of the U.N. Charter, which allows such states to approach the Security Council for redress. In addition, a fund for this purpose should be established within the U.S. foreign assistance budget. The cost would be more than offset by the benefits of multilateral cooperation.

By contrast, secondary sanctions are not a desirable means of securing multilateral support. They are not only an admission of diplomatic failure but they are also expensive. The costs to U.S. foreign policy, including the damage to relations with major partners and U.S. efforts to build an effective WTO, almost always outweigh the potential benefits of coercing unwilling friends to join sanctions regimes.

Sanctions should focus, as far as possible, on those responsible for the offending behavior and on limiting penalties to the particular area of dispute. Such limited sanctions would avoid jeopardizing other interests or an entire bilateral relationship. They would cause less collateral damage to innocents, and make it easier to garner multinational support. Sanctions designed to stem the proliferation of weapons of mass destruction are a prime example. Where there are transgressions, the United States should direct any sanctions toward nuclear or weapons-related activity, for example by cutting off associated technological cooperation or trade. Similarly, political responses such as event boycotts and visa denials might be the best way to signal opposition to objectionable behavior when no appropriate economic or military sanction is available or as a complement to something as specific as freezing an individual's assets. Political sanctions should not, however, extend to breaking diplomatic relations or canceling high-level meetings. Such interactions help the United States as much as the targeted party.

Sanctions should not hold major or complex bilateral relationships hostage to one or two issues. This is especially true with a country like China, where the United States has to balance interests that include maintaining stability on the Korean peninsula, discouraging any support for "rogue" states' weapons of mass destruction or ballistic missile programs, managing the Taiwan-China situation, and promoting trade, market reform, and human rights. Similarly, the United States has a range of interests with Pakistan that go well beyond nuclear matters, including promoting democracy, economic development, and regional stability. The principal alternative to broad sanctions in such instances is sanctions that are narrow and germane to the issue at hand. With Pakistan, for example, sanctions could focus on specific defense articles and technologies but exempt all economic assistance and military education and training.

Humanitarian exceptions should be part of any comprehensive sanctions regime. In part this is a moral judgment, that innocents should not be made to suffer any more than is absolutely necessary. But it is also pragmatic, since it is easier to generate and sustain domestic and international support for sanctions that allow the importation of food and medicine. Sanctions, however, should not necessarily be suspended if the humanitarian harm is the direct result of cynical government policy, such as Iraq's, that creates shortages among the general population in order to garner international sympathy.

Any imposition of sanctions should be swift. As with other forms of intervention, including military action, gradual escalation allows the target to adapt and adjust. Such an approach forfeits shock value and allows asset shifting, hoarding, and other arrangements to circumvent sanctions—as Libya and Iran found. This recommendation is easier said than done, since gaining international support for sanctions will in many cases require that the United States move slowly and gradually, further limiting the potential effectiveness of economic sanctions in today's world.

GETTING IT RIGHT

Policymakers should be required to prepare and send to Congress a policy statement similar to the reports prepared and forwarded under the 1973 War Powers Act before or soon after a sanction is put in place. Such statements should clearly explain the sanction's purpose, the legal or political authority supporting its use, the expected impact on the target, retaliatory steps the target or third parties may take, the probable humanitarian consequences and what is being done to minimize them, the expected costs to the United States, prospects for enforcement, the expected degree of international support or opposition, and an exit strategy, including the criteria for lifting the sanction. In addition, policymakers should be able to explain why a particular sanction was selected over other sanctions or policies. If necessary, portions of this report could be classified to avoid providing information that would be useful to the target. Any sanction Congress initiates should be approved only after the relevant committees have carefully considered the matter; members being asked to vote on the proposal would then be able to refer to a report that addresses their questions.

All sanctions embedded in legislation should allow the president to suspend or terminate them in the interest of national security. Beyond being consistent with the Constitution's bias in favor of executive primacy in foreign affairs, such latitude is needed if relationships are not to fall hostage to one interest and if the executive is to have the flexibility to explore whether limited incentives could bring about a desired policy result. The benefits of this latitude outweigh any diminution of automatic sanctions' deterrent power. Current legislation that mandates sanctions in specific circumstances should be repealed or modified.

The federal government, together with affected firms, should challenge in court states' and municipalities' right to institute economic sanctions against companies and individuals operating in their jurisdiction. This practice is eliciting protests not just from the targeted countries but from the European Union, which argues convincingly that such sanctions violate commitments made by the U.S. government to the World Trade Organization. The Constitution may not settle the struggle between the executive and legislative branches in foreign affairs, but it limits it to the federal branch of government.[3] State and local sanctions undermine the flexibility necessary for the executive branch to effectively carry out foreign policy. To paraphrase Justice Louis Brandeis, states may be laboratories of democracy, but not of diplomacy. Unfortunately, the Clinton administration—like the Reagan administration, which never challenged the more than 100 state and local sanctions targeting firms involved with South Africa—has chosen not to confront this issue. Beyond using the legal system, companies might consider deploying their economic power and avoid investing in states that have a history of supporting sanctions. Firms would also be wise to build broader coalitions (including labor unions) that would have a stake in opposing certain state and local sanctions.

Any sanction should be the subject of an annual impact statement, prepared by the executive branch and submitted in unclassified form to Congress, which would provide far more information and analysis than the pro forma documents written to justify many current sanctions. Like the report that would accompany a new sanction, the annual statement would introduce much-needed rigor into the sanction's decision-making process. A more careful calculation of economic costs would also provide a basis for determining payments to workers and companies being asked to bear a disproportionate share of the sanctions burden. Such seriousness has not been the hallmark of the American embrace of sanctions, which are often imposed and maintained with only cursory analysis of likely or actual effects.

The consequences of what is recommended here—less frequent and more modest use of economic sanctions—would risk creating something of a policy vacuum. In Washington it is difficult to beat something with nothing. So how does one beat economic sanctions?

Sometimes military force will be required. This was the lesson of Desert Storm and Bosnia. In Cuba, for example, instead of tightening sanctions—which increased the misery of the Cuban people and going along with Congress' introduction of secondary sanctions against U.S. allies, the Clinton administration might have been wiser to launch a cruise missile salvo or use stealth aircraft to take out the MiGs that in

1996 shot down the unarmed plane flown by Cuban exiles from the group Brothers to the Rescue.

In other instances, focused sanctions could be useful. A more appropriate response to Pakistan's nuclear program would have been export controls designed to slow missile and nuclear bomb development. With Haiti, narrow sanctions aimed at the illegitimate leadership would not have triggered the human exodus that pressured the administration into an armed intervention that could well have proved far more costly than it did. China was stung by the U.S. decision to oppose Beijing's bid to host the Olympic games in the year 2000 and is bothered by being singled out in various international bodies for its treatment of its citizens.

The principal alternative to economic sanctions is best described as constructive or conditional engagement. Such an approach, involving a mix of narrow sanctions and limited political and economic interactions that are conditioned on specified behavioral changes, might be preferable, especially if the goal is to weaken the near-monopoly of an authoritarian leadership over a country like Cuba, Iran, or China. Such an approach is not as simple as imposing economic sanctions; nor does it yield as dramatic a sound bite. Its principal advantage is that it might have a more desirable impact at less cost to Americans and American foreign policy.

NOTES

1. Excluded here are sanctions introduced to ensure market access or compliance with trade pacts. Economic sanctions for economic purposes tend to be used pursuant to the rules that guide trade. By contrast, economic sanctions for political purposes work in the absence of any agreed-on political or legal framework.
2. Gary Clyde Hufbauer, Jeffrey J. Schott, and Kimberly Ann Elliott, *Economic Sanctions Reconsidered: History and Current Policy*, 2nd ed., Washington: Institute for International Economics, 1990. This relatively positive assessment is hotly disputed on the grounds that the authors were overly generous in judging what constitutes "success" and in not properly disaggregating the effects of sanctions from the impact of the threat or use of military force. See Robert A. Pape, "Why Economic Sanctions Still Do Not Work," *International Security*, Fall 1997, pp. 90–136.
3. David Schmahmann and James Finch, "The Unconstitutionality of State and Local Enactments in the United States Restricting Business Ties with Burma (Myanmar)," *Vanderbilt Journal of Transnational Law*, March 1997, pp. 175–207.

Issue 19
China

INTRODUCTION

What challenges will U.S. world leadership face in the new millennium? Certainly not Russia, we think. The new European community? Perhaps. More and more, however, concern for the future focuses on China. The central problem is that China's 1.25 billion people, as they face the twenty-first century, are struggling to complete the tasks of the twentieth.

For example, China lacks the electrical power it needs to build a solid industrial base and to meet growing demands of homes and businesses. To supply its power, China expects to burn coal in dozens of new power plants. These new coal emissions would substantially set back global clean air standards and would contribute to global warming. Furthermore, as China's economic growth plans succeed, it is not clear how much the United States stands to lose. Will the advantage of new Chinese markets exceed competition from Chinese firms?

In addition to potential economic and environmental problems, China could pose a growing military threat to NATO, and it is this threat that is addressed in the two articles in this section. What is in China's military future? First, China is attempting to modify its military structure. Rather than employing a large land-oriented force, army planners are developing a more limited but more mobile and technologically sophisticated armed service. Progress in this plan is slow, for most Chinese armaments are significantly out-of-date. The air force has mainly F7s that were acquired in the 1960s, and most of the navy's technology is older still.

Chinese nuclear weapons development is a continuing concern. Early in 1999, news services revealed the leaking to the Chinese of American nuclear secrets kept at the Los Alamos, New Mexico laboratories. This incident was only the latest in a series of similar attempts to bring Chinese nuclear capabilities up-to-date.

Optimistic observers, like Wang Hao, author of the first article, note that China has taken some serious steps towards limiting nuclear arms proliferation and development. China signed the Nuclear Nonproliferation Treaty (NPT) in 1992 and then the Comprehensive Test Ban Treaty in 1996. In 1997, the Chinese government instituted strict regulations for nuclear exports.

Pessimistic analysts, however, like Stephen R. Aubin, the author of the second article, say that we have good reason to fear Chinese nuclear development. Mao Zedong started the Chinese nuclear weapon program, with Soviet assistance, in 1955. China's first nuclear test in 1964 led to eventual deployment of a formidable array of both sea- and land-based intermediate and long-range missiles. Even more threatening, perhaps, is the fact that China exported conventional arms to many other countries in the 1980s.

Is China a threat to U.S. interests of world peace?

As you read the articles, consider the following questions.

Discussion Questions

1. To what extent are U.S. and Chinese interests inherently compatible or conflictual?
2. To what extent should human rights issues affect our policies toward China?
3. Should our policies toward China emphasize strength and competition, or cooperation?

For more information on this topic, visit the following websites:

http://www.china.org.cn/
China Information Center

http://www.chinatoday.com/
China Today

http://www.odci.gov/cia/publications/factbook/ch.html
CIA World Factbook: China

China Is No Threat

WANG HAO

A few Western analysts have expressed great concern about "the China threat," especially last spring when tensions over the Taiwan issue peaked. These analysts argue that as China grows more powerful, economically and militarily, it will adopt a policy of expansion, menacing its neighbors. A few others believe that it is inevitable that China will move to fill the power vacuum in the Asia-Pacific region created by the retreat of the superpowers.

It is true that China is growing stronger. Its economy is soaring—growing at an average annual rate of 9 percent since reforms were instituted in 1978. That alone would put it in the spotlight. Add to that the fact that China has a population of 1.2 billion and is the world's third largest nation in land area, it seems natural that China will be influential in the region and on the world stage. On the other hand, despite these analysts' claims, China is not spending inordinate amounts on its military, nor is it inclined to threaten its neighbors.

MILITARY SPENDING

China's military spending is comparatively low. Even if China's military expenditures were double its reported figures—as some Western security specialists claim—its defense budget would still be far lower than those of most developed countries or of Japan, Saudi Arabia, or South Korea, according to *The Military Balance*, published by the International Institute for Strategic Studies in London. China spends less than $12 per capita on defense. India spends $11.7; Japan, $336; the United States, $1,081. And China's spending per soldier is less than that of India, Thailand, or South Korea—China's defense spending per soldier is less than one-thirtieth that of the United States. China's military spending is equally low as a percentage of gross domestic product. Again, even if it were doubled to meet some Western estimates, at 1.26 percent it would still be lower than the percent of GDP spent on defense by Korea, Thailand, or Malaysia. It is well below the average of 3.4 percent.

Wong Hao is chief sub-editor of *China Daily* in Beijing.

Reprinted by permission. *Bulletin of the Atomic Scientists*, July–Aug. 1996. Vol. 52, No. 4, p. 19.

China's defense spending remains low, both proportionately and in absolute terms. And although China regards upgrading national defense as one of the goals of modernization, it is unlikely to make a greater investment in its military. According to an official Chinese government "white paper" on defense, issued in November 1995, China "has placed defense spending in a position subordinate to and in the service of overall national economic construction."

That government report indicated that defense spending increased at an annual rate of 6.22 percent from 1979 through 1994. But the general retail price index grew at an annual rate of 7.7 percent over the same term.

Army officers received an across-the-board increase in monthly wages in 1994; senior officers received an increase of more than 50 percent. One might argue that most of the increase in defense spending in 1994 was designed to restore living standards for armed services personnel by compensating for price hikes.

Western critics also complain that Chinese reports of military expenditures are incomplete because they do not include the costs of military research and development, modernization of defense industry, plants and equipment, or the revenues that the army derives from commercial enterprises or weapons sales. However, according to the Stockholm International Peace Research Institute (SIPRI), which compiles and publishes military spending information, most nations' defense spending reports show a similar pattern: there is a "dearth of desegregated military spending data for most countries." SIPRI itself follows NATO guidelines; it does not regard government investments in military enterprises as defense expenditures.

This is particularly appropriate in the case of China where, as part of industrial reform, most defense industries no longer "belong" to the military and many are slated for conversion. On July 28, 1995, Hu Ping, a senior researcher from China's Institute for International Strategic Studies, explained in *People's Daily:*

"In recent years, orders for military materials have dropped, and quite a number of military enterprises have been running under capacity. The government has to give them financial aid and help them convert to the production of civilian goods. This money should be categorized as expenditures to reform state enterprises, not as national defense funds."

Like other state enterprises, China's military industrial enterprises practiced a "contract responsibility system," which required them to pay the government both taxes and a portion of their profits. Remaining profits from the production of civilian goods were used mostly to expand production and increase wages. Hu said that Chinese armies were now withdrawing from most of their civilian businesses, with the exception of traditional farming and some sideline production.

Counting receipts from weapon sales abroad would not change the picture much, either. Alfred Wilhelm, executive vice president of the Atlantic Council, testified before the U.S. Senate Subcommittee on East Asian and Pacific Affairs on October 11, 1995, saying: "Arms sales by defense-related corporations are commonly viewed outside China as a major source of income. However, most major weapons manufactures are not owned or operated by the Peoples Liberation Army (PLA), but by one of the civilian ministries. The proceeds from most foreign arms sales go to the originating ministry and not the PLA.

"Furthermore, a review of arms, sales from 1985–92 shows that China's arms sales averaged little more than $1.5 billion a year. Even if the entire amount were profit and all went to the PLA, the addition to the military coffers would be minimal. According to the Chinese government, at least one-third of state-owned enterprises are operating at a loss and only one-third are breaking even. Arms industries are all state-owned and like the rest many are unprofitable, and all are attempting to convert their excess capacity to civilian production. Of those making a profit, at least half of the profits are being reinvested in defense conversion or modernization as part of the state's massive effort to create new jobs."

MEETING NEEDS

China has realistic defense needs. China's borders, which it shares with 15 countries, extend for more than 22,000 kilometers. As security expert Harry Harding, quoted by Gerald Segal in *Defending China*, points out: "Few other major powers have felt as threatened, for such a long period of time, and by such powerful adversaries, as China has." For the past 46 years, especially during the Cold War era, the country faced direct threats to its security from almost all directions.

China has built up its military forces over the past four decades. Despite the size of its forces, China's limited economy and relative isolation have meant that the quality of its armaments is relatively low. China's military research and development is generally believed to be at least 15 years behind the West. Although China has tried to import better equipment, it takes considerable time to digest advanced weaponry. Western policies that restrict technology transfer have also made it difficult for China to modernize its military. Although China's military strength is now—and will remain in future—on a level that meets defensive needs, China is not in a position to adopt an expansionist policy or pose a threat to Asia-Pacific stability.

China's strategic perceptions can be best understood by reviewing the military thinking of Deng Xiaoping, the designer of China's reform and opening. For a long period of time following its founding, the People's

Republic was subject to isolation, blockade, and subversion. As a result, the nation was often on alert, preparing for an "early, massive, and even nuclear world war." But in the mid-1980s, Deng concluded that war was not inevitable and that it was possible to realize a long-standing peace. In November 1984, Deng told a meeting of the Central Military Commission: "We should make a real sober-minded judgment . . . [which] will keep our mind on economic construction. . . . We do not have to spend more money on military spending, so we can spare more money for economic construction. We should make up our mind now." Within the year the Central Military Commission issued new guidelines, moving from preparing against the threat of invasion to peacetime constraction. Simultaneously, the commission reduced the military by one million men. A move of this scale—made even before the Cold War was over—is a rare example of contemporary arms control and disarmament. Since 1986 the army has been reduced from 4.25 million to 3.2 million men, a decrease of more than 24 percent, and the defense industry has been gradually transformed from a monolithic producer of military products to a diversified producer of both military and civilian products.

China's decision in the 1990s to establish diplomatic ties with South Korea and Israel, moves that would have been unthinkable in the past, are also reflections of changing perceptions. The country has played an important role in alleviating tension on the Korean peninsula.

In the past 15 years, China has integrated itself into the international trade and financial communities. It is a member of the World Bank and the Asian Development Bank, and it is applying for membership in the World Trade Organization. According to World Bank statistics, China's imports and exports accounted for about 30 percent of gross national product in the 1990s, up from about 10 percent in 1978. China is now a full participant in the global and regional political, economic, and security arenas.

China's modernization requires a peaceful international environment, and China opposes the threat or use of force to settle international disputes.

Last October, Russia and China reportedly settled their long-running border dispute by demarcating the last 54 contested kilometers along their 4,380-kilometer border. China and India have also reached a peaceful agreement, and border problems with Vietnam are nearly resolved. At a meeting in Shanghai in late April, China and four of its neighbors—Russia, Kazakhstan, Kyrgyzstan, and Tajildstan—signed a confidence-building agreement specifying notification and sharply limiting the scale, scope, and number of border-area military exercises.

Apart from questions on the ultimate disposition of Taiwan and the governance of Hong Kong, which China regards as internal concerns, the only outstanding dispute between China and other Southeast Asian countries concerns the ownership of the Nansha (Spratlys) Islands. There are four other claimants: Vietnam, Malaysia, the Philippines, and Brunei. But all sides have behaved with restraint. In August 1995, China and the Philippines held talks in Manila that concluded with a code of conduct. Both sides vowed to refrain from force or the threat of force to resolve the dispute.

China's relations with its neighbors are the best they have been since the People's Republic was founded. As China's senior military scholar Xu Xiaojun said at a 1994 symposium in Beijing, "China enjoys the [best] security environment since 1949. It is not facing any real military threats. There is no obvious danger of a major attack . . . [and] there is not a single country in its neighboring or surrounding area that China defines as an antagonist."

THE FUTURE

It is only 16 years since China opened itself to the outside world and began its drive for reform. When a new but rising power enters the international arena, it is crucial to build an environment of trust and to correct misperceptions.

In terms of both its capabilities and its intentions, China is not a threat to its neighbors in the Asia-pacific region. There is no doubt that China intends to achieve influence through economic rather than military power. China regards the fall of the Soviet Union as a powerful object lesson—no matter how powerful a country's military, it will not last long without a strong economy.

Any country of the size and population of China will cause concern among its neighbors. Compared to the forces of powers like the United States, Russia, Britain, and France, China's military is weak. But it is a giant in Asia.

China still remains something of a mystery to other countries, and Western analysts believe that China should increase its transparency on strategic doctrine, intentions, and military spending. Last fall's publication of a major white paper on defense was a significant move in that regard.

In Asia, economic prosperity has paved the way for regional economic cooperation. Continued economic growth will require greater cooperation, including agreements in the security area. This may not necessarily lead to the establishment of a European Union–style organization, but there is a move toward a multilateral mechanism for dialogue. Chinese Foreign Minister Zian Zichen took part in the July 1993 inaugural meeting of the ASEAN Regional Forum in Singapore.

The best way to make a friend is to treat someone like a friend. This is also true in international relations. China and its Asia-Pacific neighbors have every reason to remain mutually trusted and understood. It is vital for them to view each other as partners, not enemies. Confrontation serves no one's interest.

China: Yes, Worry about the Future

STEPHEN R. AUBIN

In his article, "China as a Strategic Threat: Myths and Verities," John J. Schulz catalogues the Chinese People's Liberation Army's "long list of systemic problems," concluding that concern about China's military is warranted but "panic, overreaction, dramatic military preparation and response are not."

Schulz is right on many counts, but current U.S. policy toward China is completely devoid of "concern" over China's efforts at military modernization and its regional ambitions. And, while Schulz and others find solace in China's past failure to develop advanced military weapons systems indigenously, there is a danger in ignoring the possibility that China might be able to effectively modernize its military, thanks in part to its own economic and industrial progress, foreign military assistance, and commercially available technologies that have military applications.

Indeed, the "weak" and vulnerable Chinese dragon has been selectively laying the groundwork for a gradual military transformation that could alter the balance of power in the region and adversely affect U.S. interests much sooner than the 20 to 30 year time frame many China watchers and U.S. policymakers are predicting.[1] A number of trends and developments are just beginning to converge:

- A dramatic shift in Chinese military leadership and the growing professionalization of the PLA;
- Changes in operational doctrine that emphasize high technology and asymmetric warfare;
- A focused research and development effort, combined with purchases of foreign military technology, that reflects new doctrinal approaches;

Stephen P. Aubin is an adjunct fellow of the Alexis de Tocqueville Institution and is Director of Comminications for the Air Force Association.
Reprinted by permission. *Strategic Review.* Winter 1998, Vol. xxvi, No. 1, pp. 17–20.

- and improved access to commercial technologies that have military applications.

As Schulz suggests, U.S. policy should be crafted to ensure that an emergent Great Power China is a responsible regional and global actor—not an enemy of the United States. But without due attention to regional and global security considerations, political and economic "engagement" will likely fall short.

While the United States figures into Chinese military thinking as the principal future threat, U.S. government experts on China who might shed light on potential Chinese threats have been largely muzzled in an effort to avoid offending China's leaders and needlessly creating an enemy out of a "friend." In fact, the Clinton administration opposed a provision in the House version of the 1998 Defense Authorization Act (eventually stripped from the conference bill) that would have established a Center for the Study of Chinese Military Affairs at the National Defense University in Washington, DC. Such a center would have helped U.S. decisionmakers and members of Congress better understand many of the recent developments that seem to foreshadow an entirely new look for the PLA.

A NEW GENERATION COMES TO POWER

At the 15th Party Congress, held in September 1997, a number of decisions were made that firmly place the PLA on the road toward a leaner force with greater emphasis on high technology in key pockets, including the navy, air force, and 2nd Artillery, which oversees China's strategic nuclear missiles and has been expanding into conventional missiles.[2] The retirement of the two most senior military elders, Generals Liu Huaqinq and Zhang Zhen, also completed a dramatic shift in military leadership that has been underway for several years now.

The elevation of Generals Zhang Wannian, 69, and Chi Haotian, 68, to the top rung of the Central Military Commission, the key military decisionmaking body headed by Chinese President Jiang Zemin, follows a series of leadership changes that have spanned the General Staff Department, General Logistics Department, the air force, navy, and most of the military regions.[3]

Zhang Wannian, who holds the top position in the PLA, helped develop the doctrine of "limited war under high technology conditions," and Chi has served as defense minister and is responsible for the expanding military cooperation with Russia.[4] Both are proponents of modernization and the continuing professionalization of the PLA.[5]

While much has been said about the lack of education and training in the PLA, a sea change has been underway since 1977, when Deng Xiaoping stressed the strategic importance of education and training.[6] Deng reopened military schools closed during the Cultural Revolution and pushed reforms that revamped the entire military education system and tied promotion to military education.

In his study of China's officer corps, James Mulvenon cited a 1987 People's Daily article that reported an increase in college-educated officers at the army level from 1% in 1982 to 58% by 1987. The increase at the division level was similar, going from 2% to 66% .[7] More recent statistics state that 43% of today's officers have received technical secondary school education and 43% have received college or university education—with less than 1% in the lowest category of junior middle school or primary school education, and another 13% in the senior middle school education category.[8] According to this same report, there have been 260,000 graduates of military institutes and academies since 1980, and by the year 2000, 70% of all officers will have been college educated. The bottom line: China's military and political leaders recognize the need for professional, quality troops in the high-tech era.

HIGH-TECH AND ASYMMETRIC WARFARE

One advantage of more than a decade of U.S.-Chinese military contacts has been increased access to a wide range of recent Chinese military writings. The U.S. National Defense University published one collection in 1997, which reveals a clear focus on high-tech weapons and the Revolution in Military Affairs.[9] Given China's penchant for secrecy, Western analysts can only speculate on the extent to which theoretical writings actually influence policy. However, if nothing else, these writings show a determined attempt by the Chinese military to analyze how current and emerging technologies will affect future military operations.

One theme in many of these writings is the central role of information technology. Chinese military leaders have taken the lessons of the Gulf War to heart and are focusing on ways to counter U.S. military strengths, from stealth and long-range strike capabilities to space systems and computers, mainly by attacking what some Chinese writers have termed the enemy's military "brain centers." As one strategist wrote, "the operational objectives of the two sides on attack and defense are neither the seizing of territory nor the killing of so many enemies, but rather the paralyzing of the other side's information system and the destruction of the other side's will to resist. . . . Once a computer system is damaged so that it cannot operate normally, cruise missiles and other precision-guided weapons become arrows without targets; and high-tech performance aircraft, tanks, warships, radar, and activated command systems will be totally in the dark about what to do."[10]

Attacking U.S. vulnerabilities is part of an asymmetric strategy designed to create the conditions for a weaker power to prevail over a stronger one.[11] Chinese writers emphasize the fast pace of future operations and the need to launch preemptive strikes. For example, one theorist wrote, "Through a preemptive strike, China can put good timing and geographical location and the support of the people to good use by making a series of offensive moves to destroy the enemy's ability to deploy high-tech weapons and troops and limit its ability to acquire a high-tech edge in the war zone, thus weakening its capacity to mount a powerful offensive."[12]

Just before the 15th Party Congress, the Chinese Commission of Military Sciences published a book that contained papers by the commanders of the military regions and the major armed services. Among the themes were: streamlining the military (which will be cut by 500,000 troops over the next 3 years); a focus on modernization that will "increase the proportion of arms that have a higher content of science and technology"; building rapid-response mobile operation units or "fist" units composed of air units, airborne troops, armored units, motorized infantry, and signal troops; further raising the fighting capability of the 2nd Artillery, which will become the "decisive weapon"; building a compact, capable, effective and tough air force for offensive and defensive operations; and building a navy with an emphasis on coastal mobile combat armament, electronic warfare equipment, and "decisive" weapons.[13]

Another key point made was the need "to selectively import a small amount of advanced armament that is urgently needed, make a good job of technical assimilation and absorption, and raise the starting point of the development of China's new generation main battle armament."[14]

R&D, PROCUREMENT ARE FOCUSED

The third piece of the Chinese military puzzle—after the emphasis on more technically competent troops and new operational concepts—is a focused indigenous research and development effort combined with the acquisition of foreign technologies and expertise. According to Mark Stokes, an Air Force analyst who has researched the Chinese military-industrial complex, beginning in the early 1980s the PLA's Commission of Science, Technology, and Industry for National Defense (COSTIND) established the 863 Program, which focused China's science and technology establishment on seven key areas: space, lasers, automation, biotechnology, information systems, energy, and new materials.[15]

Stokes has concluded that China is pursuing information dominance by developing a wide range of space- and ground-based sensors to cue long-range precision strike assets and provide advanced warning of impending attacks on its territory.[16] In fact, China has deployed or is actively developing a number of systems, including ELINT satellites, electro-optical reconnaissance satellites, synthetic aperture radar satellites, missile early warning satellites, navigational satellites, weather satellites, strategic and tactical unmanned aerial vehicles, airborne early warning, space surveillance, counterstealth radars, SIGINT sites, tactical reconnaissance vehicles and ships, and special forces (infiltrated into enemy territory).[17]

China's weapons development and acquisition have also seemed to follow operational concepts outlined in recent writings. Cruise missiles provide asymmetric advantages against U.S. naval ships. Submarines, with their advantage of stealth, are touted as the dominant naval weapon.[18] Ballistic missiles are at the heart of China's nuclear deterrent, and conventional missiles offer asymmetric advantages against countries with superior air forces, like Taiwan.

Foreign purchases and technical assistance are helping China move more quickly in these and other high priority areas. Purchases of Russian M10-class submarines that can challenge U.S. Los Angeles–class subs; Russian Sovremenny-class missile destroyers with SSN-22 supersonic anti-ship missiles that could threaten the current defenses of the U.S. Navy's Aegis cruisers and destroyers; SA-10 surface-to-air missiles and Russian Su-27 fighters with world class AA-11 Archer air-to-air missiles that can seriously threaten U.S. F-15 air superiority fighters have been widely reported but not viewed in terms of a larger Chinese strategy of focused technology acquisition. Israel has also transferred the technology from its canceled Lavi fighter to China for its F-10 fighter, and Russia may supply the engine. Russia and Israel are also involved in a joint venture to supply an airborne warning and control system (AWACS) to China.[19]

Unlike past reluctance by China to become dependent on Russia, which grew out of the 1960 split between the two communist powers, today's cooperation is being viewed as less risky because it is not based on ideology but on commercial considerations.[20] And, if Russian cooperation does not work out, there is plenty of competition from countries like Israel and France.

The other aspect of foreign technology acquisition is related to commercial purchases that have military applications, from computers to satellites. One China analyst argues that unplanned consequences of market reform are resulting in a commercial sector technical infrastructure that could support a future revolution in military affairs.[21] According to Stokes, by 1995, China had ten of the largest communication networks in the world. As China has opened its market to leading telecommunications firms, it has emphasized high-capacity fiber optics, switching systems, and systems integration and data fusion—all of which could lead to one of the most sophisticated information systems in the world.[22]

OUTLOOK

None of these developments threaten the United States in the near future. But lack of attention now could lead to serious threats to U.S. and allied interests in the region in the medium and long term. U.S. presence in East Asia could be diminished, resulting in serious economic consequences, and the United States' ability to defend its regional interests might be denied by a modern Chinese military capable of exploiting U.S. vulnerabilities.

As the United States "engages" China and emphasizes cooperation, it should also prudently maintain the security system that has created a favorable balance of power in the region. That means taking the Chinese military seriously, maintaining the U.S. technological edge through modernization, and being more open about the military dimension of the U.S.-China relationship.

NOTES

1. The author wishes to thank Jason E. Bruzdzinski of the House National Security Committee staff for his insights and research assistance.
2. See "Major modernisation sees slimmer giant," *Jane's Defence Weekly*, December 10, 1997, pp. 24–26.
3. See David Shambaugh, "China's Post-Deng Military Leadership," Paper for the Seventh Annual Conference on the People's Liberation Army, September 14–16, 1997, Aspen Institute/Wye Woods Conference Center, University of Maryland, pp. 2–4.
4. Ibid., pp. 11–18.
5. Ibid.
6. See James C. Mulvenon, *Professionalization of the Senior Chinese Officer Corps: Trends and Implications* (Santa Monica, CA: Rand, 1997), p. 12.
7. Ibid., p. 14.
8. Chen Hui, *Xinhua*, October 11, 1997, FBIS-CHI-97-286.
9. See *Chinese Views of Future Warfare*, ed. Michael Pillsbury (Washington, DC: National Defense University Press, 1997).
10. See Ch'en Huan, "Third Military Revolution Will Certainly Have Far-Reaching Effects," *Hsien-Tai Chun-Shih*, March 11, 1996, FBIS-CHI-96-169.
11. See, for example, Wu Migzhong, Zhao Zhensheng, and He Huahiu, "Status, Development of Stealth, Counterstealth Technologies," *Shanghai Hangtian*, June 1997, Vol. 14, No. 3, pp. 36–42, FBIS-CHI-97-272; and Liu

Xuejun, "Study of Measures to Counter Unmanned Aerial Vehicles," *Guoii Hongkong*, March 1, 1996, FBIS-CHI-96-176.

12. Lu Linzhi, "Preemptive Strikes Crucial in Limited High-Tech Wars," *Jiefangiun Bao*, FBIS-CHI-96-025.

13. Kuan Cha-chia, "Military Regional Commanders Express Support for Jiang Zemin, Military Works Out Development Plans for the 21st Century," *Kuang Chiao Ching*, September 16, 1997, FBIS-CHI-97-288.

14. Ibid.

15. Mark A. Stokes, "China's Strategic Modernization: Implications for U.S. National Security," October 1997 (FY 97 Research Project under the USAF Institute for National Security Studies), p. 11.

16. Ibid., p. 19.

17. Ibid., p. 20.

18. See, for example, Shen Zhongchang et al., "The Impact of the New Military Revolution on Naval Warfare and the Naval Establishment," *Zhongguo Junshi Kexue*, February 20, 1996, FBIS-CHI-96-136.

19. For the most comprehensive discussion of China's weapons acquisitions, see Richard D. Fisher, Jr., "Foreign Arms Acquisition and PLA Modernization," Paper for the Seventh Annual Conference on the People's Liberation Army, September 15, 1997, Aspen Institute/Wye Woods Conference Center, University of Maryland.

20. See *Jane's Defence Review*, op. cit., p. 28.

21. See Wendy Frieman, "The Understated Revolution in Chinese Science and Technology: Implications for the PLA in the 21st Century," Paper for AEI 1997 Conference on the People's Liberation Army, September 2, 1997.

22. Stokes, op. cit., p. 28.

PART VI
Environment and Health

Issue 20
Environment

INTRODUCTION

As reported at the annual meeting of the American Meteorological Society in Dallas, Texas, in January 1999, measurements taken by the National Oceanic and Atmospheric Administration revealed that in 1998 the earth's surface temperature rose to their highest levels since record-keeping began over one hundred years ago. Was this rise irrefutable evidence that global warming is occurring and that unless the increase in greenhouse gas emissions is reversed, global warming will continue and have devastating effects on global climate?

At the same meeting, a number of scientists gave reports of satellite measurements of global temperatures in the lower atmosphere over the past twenty years that did not detect any significant upward trend in temperatures.

As the evidence suggests, the scientific debate over global warming is far from over. Climatic change is an incompletely understood science at best. Eons-long cycles of global warming and cooling are poorly understood, and the significance in the increase in surface temperatures is surrounded by much controversy. This lack of scientific consensus over the existence of global warming, much less of its likely consequences, is a major reason why vocal political disagreement exists over what, if anything, to do about it. The indecision and inaction on global warming to date can be contrasted to the relatively swift reaction of the global community to the depletion of the ozone layer, a finding over which there was little scientific disagreement.

The two articles presented here do not so much debate the scientific evidence for or against the existence of global warming as they do the economic reasoning of proposed approaches to deal with it. Jonathan H. Alder, editor of *The Costs of Kyoto: Climate-Change Policy and Its Implications,* is highly critical of recent multilateral efforts to reduce levels of carbon dioxide emissions. His criticisms fall mainly in two areas: (1) the costs of complying with the Kyoto Protocols of 1997, and (2) the grace period given to the developing world to meet emission standards. Alder sees the costs as both economic and political. On the economic side, he cites Clinton administration estimates ranging from $7 to $12 billion annually, arguing that the anticipated economic benefits are far from certain. But it is perhaps the political side of the cost issue that is central to his argument. As he contends, "Controlling emissions of green house gases requires controls on energy use: energy taxes, supply controls, or other regulatory mandates." Combating global warming would, in other words, require bigger government.

Thomas C. Schelling is not as critical as is Alder regarding those arguments in support of the global warming hypothesis. He does, however, also question the economic costs of the proposed measures to reduce greenhouse gas emissions. His criticism focuses on trade-offs between spending to reduce emissions versus assisting developing economies to develop more rapidly. His rationale is that, in the long run, helping economies to develop more rapidly may be a more effective way of reducing levels of emissions than employing strategies that focus on reducing current levels in the developed world.

Underlying the argument of both authors is the well-known dilemma of collective goods. Simply put, the atmosphere is a global commons where everyone's emissions mix with everyone else's, with the result that impact is not proportionately borne by those most responsible. The collective goods dilemma asks how countries can cooperate on an issue of mutual interests when it is in no one country's interest to change its behavior.

As you read the articles, consider the following questions.

Discussion Questions

1. Assuming that a scientific consensus were to emerge over global warming, are the economic costs of reducing emissions worth the investment when the climatic impact is still poorly understood?
2. Is it fair to argue, as Senator Chuck Hagel of Nebraska does (as quoted in Alder) that "for the first time, the United States would give control of our economy to an international bureaucracy within the United Nations"?
3. Should the developing world be given a grace period to allow it to achieve higher levels of development before being required to take measures to reduce their greenhouse gas emissions?
4. Does the argument of Schelling, that it would be better to promote development more actively as a strategy to reduce long-term emission, make economic sense? Does it make political sense?

    For more information on this topic, visit the following websites:

    http://www.gcrio.org/
    The US Global Change Research Information Office (GCRIO)

    http://www.cnie.org/
    Committee for the National Institute for the Environment

    http://www.ciesin.org/
    Center for International Earth Science Information Network

The Cost of Combating Global Warming:

Facing the Trade-offs

THOMAS C. SCHELLING

At international conferences, people speaking for the developing world insist that it is the developed nations that feel endangered by carbon emissions and want to retard elsewhere the kind of development that has been enjoyed by western Europe, North America, and Japan. A reduction in carbon emissions in the developing world, they assert, will have to be at the expense of the rich nations. Their diagnosis is wrong, but their conclusion is right. Any costs of mitigating climate change during the coming decades will surely be borne by the high-income countries. But the benefits, despite what spokespeople for the developing world say, will overwhelmingly accrue to future generations in the developing world. Any action combating global warming will be, intended or not, a foreign aid program. The Chinese, Indonesians, or Bangladeshis are not going to divert resources from their own development to reduce the greenhouse effect, which is caused by the presence of carbon-based gases in the earth's atmosphere. This is a prediction, but it is also sound advice. Their best defense against climate change and vulnerability to weather in general is their own development, reducing their reliance on agriculture and other such outdoor livelihoods. Furthermore, they have immediate environmental problems—air and water pollution, poor sanitation, disease—that demand earlier attention.

There are three reasons the beneficiaries will be in the developing countries, which will be much more developed when the impact of climate change is felt. The first is simple: that is where most people live—four-fifths now, nine-tenths in 75 years.

Second, these economies may still be vulnerable, in a way the developed economies are not, by the time climate change occurs. In the developed world hardly any component of the national income is affected by climate. Agriculture is practically the only sector of the economy affected by climate, and it contributes only a small percentage—three percent in the United States—of national income. If agricultural productivity were drastically reduced by climate change, the cost of living would rise by one

Thomas C. Schelling is Distinguished University Professor of Economics and Public Affairs at the University of Maryland.
Reprinted by permission. *Foreign Affairs*, Nov.–Dec. 1997. Vol. 76, No. 6 p. 8(7).

or two percent, and at a time when per capita income will likely have doubled. In developing countries, in contrast, as much as a third of GNP and half the population currently depends on agriculture. They may still be vulnerable to climate change for many years to come.

Third, although most of these populations should be immensely better off in 50 years, many will still be poorer than the rich countries are now. The contribution to their welfare by reduced climate change will therefore be greater than any costs the developing world bears in reducing emissions.

I say all this with apparent confidence, so let me rehearse the uncertainties, which have remained essentially the same for a decade and a half. Arbitrarily adopting a doubling of greenhouse gases as a benchmark, a committee of the U.S. National Academy of Sciences estimated in 1979 that the change in average global surface atmospheric temperature could be anywhere from 1.5 to 4.5 degrees Celsius. (Note that the upper estimate is three times the lower.) This range of uncertainty has still not officially been reduced.

More important than the average warming is the effect it may have on climates. Things will not just get warmer, climatologists predict; some places will, but others will get cooler, wetter, drier, or cloudier. The average warming is merely the engine that will drive the changes. The term "global warming" is mischievous in suggesting that hot summers are what it is all about.

The temperature gradient from equator to pole is a main driving force in the circulation of the atmosphere and oceans, and a change in that gradient will be as important as the change in average temperature. Climatologists have to translate changes in temperature at various latitudes, altitudes, and seasons into changes in weather and climate in different localities. That is another source of uncertainty. Mountains, for example, are hard to work into climate models. Not many people live high in the mountains, so why worry? But India, Pakistan, Bangladesh, and Burma depend on snowfall in the Himalayas for their irrigation.

A further question gets little attention: what will the world be like 75 years from now, when changes in climate may have become serious? If we look back to 1920 and conjecture about what environmental problems then might be affected by climate changes over the coming 75 years, one problem high on the list would be mud. This was the era of muddy roads and narrow tires. Cars had to be pulled out by horses. People could not ride bicycles, and walking in the stuff was arduous. One might think, "If things get wetter or drier the mud problem will get worse or better." It might not occur to anyone that by the 1990s most of the country would be paved.

If the climate changes expected 75 years from now were to happen immediately, the most dramatic consequences would be in the incidence of parasitic and other tropical diseases. Temperature and moisture affect malaria, river blindness, schistosomiasis, dengue fever, and infantile diarrhea, all vastly more dangerous than the radioactive and chemical hazards that worry people in the developed countries.

Alarmists have weighed in with dire predictions of how a warming of tropical and subtropical regions will aggravate the scourge of tropical diseases. But any changes in temperature and moisture need to be superimposed on those areas as they are likely to be 50 or 75 years from now, with better sanitation, nutrition and medical and environmental technology, cleaner water, and the potential eradication of vector-borne diseases.

Malaysia and Singapore have identical climates. There is malaria in Malaysia, but hardly any in Singapore, and any malaria in Singapore gets sophisticated treatment. By the time Malaysia catches up to where Singapore is now, many tropical diseases may have been tamed. One invasive tropical creature, the guinea worm, is already expected to follow smallpox into extinction.

THE MARSHALL MODEL

The modern era of greenhouse concern dates from the 1992 Rio Conference, attended by President Bush, which produced a "framework convention" for the pursuit of reduced carbon emissions. A sequel is set for Kyoto in December. Countries from the Organization for Economic Cooperation and Development (OECD) are groping for criteria and procedures to determine "targets and timetables." There are proposals for the formal allocation of enforceable quotas, possibly with trading of emission rights. There is disappointment with the lack of convincing progress in the five years since Rio. Many people wonder whether Kyoto will settle anything.

It will not. But five years is too soon to be disappointed. Nothing like a carbon emissions regime has ever been attempted, and it is in no country's individual interest to do much about emissions: the atmosphere is a global common where everybody's emissions mingle with everybody else's. The burden to be shared is large, there are no accepted standards of fairness, nations differ greatly in their dependence on fossil fuels, and any regime to be taken seriously has to promise to survive a long time.

There are few precedents. The U.N. budget required a negotiated formula, but adherence is conspicuously imperfect, and the current budget, even including peacekeeping, is two orders of magnitude smaller than what a serious carbon regime would require. The costs in reduced productivity are estimated at two percent of GNP—forever. Two percent of GNP seems politically unmanageable in many countries.

Still, if one plots the curve of U.S. per capita GNP over the coming century with and without the two percent permanent loss, the difference is about the thickness of a line drawn with a number two pencil, and the doubled per capita income that might have been achieved by 2060 is reached in 2062. If someone could wave a wand and phase in, over a few years, a climate-mitigation program that depressed our GNP by two percent in perpetuity, no one would notice the difference.

The only experience commensurate with carbon reduction was division of aid in the Marshall Plan. In 1949–50 there was $4 billion to share. The percentage of European GNP that this amounted to depends on hypothetical exchange rates appropriate to the period, but it was well over two percent, although differing drastically among the countries. The United States insisted that the Europeans divide the aid themselves, and gave them most of a year to prepare.

The procedure was what I call "multilateral reciprocal scrutiny." Each country prepared detailed national accounts showing consumption, investment, dollar earnings and imports, intra-European trade, specifics like per capita fuel and meat consumption, taxes, and government expenditures—anything that might justify a share of U.S. aid. There was never a formula. There were not even criteria; there were "considerations." There was no notion that aid should be allocated to maximize recovery, equalize standards of living, balance improvements in consumption levels, or meet any other objective. Each country made its claim for aid on whatever grounds it chose. Each was queried and cross-examined about dollar-export potential, domestic substitutes for dollar imports, dietary standards, rate of livestock recovery, severity of gasoline rationing, and anything pertinent to dollar requirements. The objective was consensus on how to divide the precious $4 billion.

Although they did not succeed, they were close enough for arbitration by a committee of two people to produce an acceptable division. After the Korean War, when NATO replaced recovery as the objective, the same procedure was used. Again consensus was not reached, but again there was enough agreement for arbitration by a committee of three to decide not only the division of aid but military burdens to be assumed. Multilateral reciprocal scrutiny proved effective, no doubt because an unprecedented camaraderie had been cultivated during the Marshall Plan. And remember, consensus had to be reached by countries as different in their development, war damage, politics, and cultures as Turkey, Norway, Italy, and France. A similar procedure recently led to the European Union's schedule of carbon reductions for its member countries. A difference is that in the Marshall Plan it was for keeps!

Did the Marshall Plan succeed despite, or because of, its lack of formal quantitative criteria and its reliance on looser, more open-ended, pragmatic modes of discourse and argument? In the time available, plan participants could not have agreed on formal criteria. In the end they had to be satisfied with a division. Any argument over variables and parameters would have been self-serving arguments once removed; arguing explicitly over shares was more direct and candid. Had the process gone on several years, more formal criteria might have been forged. The same may occur eventually with carbon emissions.

SETTING THE CEILING

Two thousand American economists recently recommended that national emission quotas promptly be negotiated, with purchase and sale of emission rights allowed to assure a fair geographic distribution of reductions. This appears to be the U.S. position for the meeting in Kyoto. It is an elegant idea. But its feasibility is suspect, at least for the present.

One cannot envision national representatives calmly sitting down to divide up rights in perpetuity worth more than a trillion dollars. It is also hard to imagine an enforcement mechanism acceptable to the U.S. Senate. I do not even foresee agreement on what concentration of greenhouse gases will ultimately be tolerable. Without that, any trajectory of global emissions has to be transitory, in which case renegotiation is bound to be anticipated, and no prudent nation is likely to sell its surplus emissions when doing so is clear evidence that it was originally allowed more than it needed.

The current focus of international negotiation is extremely short-term. That is probably appropriate, but the long term needs to be acknowledged and kept in mind. If carbon-induced climate change proves serious, it will be the ultimate concentration of greenhouse gases in the atmosphere that matters. The objective should be to stabilize that final concentration at a level compatible with tolerable climate change. Emissions of the carbon-based gases are the current focus of attention, but the question of concentration is what needs to be settled.

If scientists knew the upper limit to what the earth's climate system could tolerate, that limit could serve as the concentration target. It would probably not matter much climatically how that limit was approached. The optimal trajectory would probably include a continuing rise in annual emissions for a few decades, followed by a significant decline as the world approached a sustainable low level compatible with the ceiling on concentration. That is no argument for present inaction: future technologies that people will rely on to save energy or make energy less carbon-intensive 10, 20, or 30 years from now will depend on much more vigorous research and development, much of it at public expense, than governments and private institutions are doing or even contemplating now.

The ceiling is variously proposed as 450, 550, 650, or 750 parts per million, compared with about 360 parts per million today. The Intergovernmental Panel on Climate Change, the scientific advisory body associated with these conferences, has rendered no opinion on what level of concentration might ultimately become intolerable. Without that decision, there can be no long-range plan.

In the short run, there will almost certainly be innumerable modest but worthwhile opportunities for reducing carbon emissions. National representatives from the developed countries are counting on it. They are proposing reductions of 10 or 15 percent in annual emissions for most developed countries during the coming decade or so. If such reductions are seriously pursued—an open question—a rising trend in emissions would be superimposed on a short-term effort to limit actual emissions.

A program of short-term reductions would help governments learn more about emissions and how much they can be reduced by different measures. But the prevailing sentiment seems to be that emissions can be brought down and kept down in the OECD countries. It is not yet politically correct to acknowledge that global emissions are bound to increase for many decades, especially as nations like China experience economic growth and greater energy use.

When the OECD countries do get serious about combating climate change, they should focus on actions—policies, programs, taxes, subsidies, regulations, investments, energy technology research and development—that governments can actually take or bring about that will affect emissions. Commitments to targets and timetables are inherently flawed. They are pegged some years into the future, generally the further the better. Moreover, most governments cannot predict their policies impact on emissions.

To pick an unrealistic example, if the United States committed itself to raising the tax on gasoline by ten cents per gallon per year for the next 15 years, any agency could discern whether the tax actually went up a dime per year, and the U.S. government would know exactly what it was committed to doing. But nobody can predict what that tax would do to emissions by the end of 15 years.

GREENHOUSE POLITICS

Slowing global warming is a political problem. The cost will be relatively low: a few trillion dollars over the next 30 or 40 years, out of an OECD gross product rising from $15 trillion to $30 trillion or $40 trillion annually. But any greenhouse program that is not outrageously inefficient will have to address carbon emissions in China, whose current emissions are half the United States' but will be several times the U.S. level in 2050 if left unchecked. The OECD countries can curtail their own emissions through regulation, which, although inefficient, is politically more acceptable than taxes because the costs remain invisible. The developed-country expense of curtailing Chinese emissions will require visible transfers of budgeted resources. It will look like the foreign aid it actually is, although it will benefit China no more than India or Nigeria. Building non-carbon or carbon-efficient electric power in China will look like aid to China, not climate relief for the world.

There remains a nagging issue that is never addressed at meetings on global warming policy. The future beneficiaries of these policies in developing countries will almost certainly be better off than their grandparents, today's residents of those countries. Alternative uses of resources devoted to ameliorating climate change should be considered. Namely, does it make more sense to invest directly in the development of these countries?

There are two issues here. One is whether, in benefits three or four generations hence, the return for investing directly in public health, education, water resources, infrastructure, industry, agricultural productivity, and family planning is as great as that for investing in reduced climate change. The second is whether the benefits accrue earlier, to people who more desperately need the help. Is there something escapist about discussing two percent of GNP to be invested in the welfare of future generations when nothing is done for their contemporary ancestors, a third of whom are so undernourished that a case of measles can kill?

If there were aid to divide between Bangladesh and Singapore, would anybody propose giving any of it to Singapore? In 50 or 75 years, when climate change may be a significant reality, Bangladesh probably will have progressed to the level of Singapore today. Should anyone propose investing heavily in the welfare of those future Bangladeshis when the alternative is to help Bangladesh today? People worry that the sea level may rise half a meter in the next century from global warming and that large populated areas of Bangladesh may flood. But Bangladesh already suffers terrible floods.

The need for greenhouse gas abatement cannot logically be separated from the developing world's need for immediate economic improvement. The trade-off should be faced. It probably won't be.

Hot Air

JONATHAN H. ADLER

Global warming is not a threat to health or the economy. Plans to address it are.

Whether it's floods in North Dakota or hurricanes off the Florida coast, Vice President Al Gore never misses an opportunity to blame a disaster on global warming. In Florida on June 29 to announce stepped-up federal assistance to fight the wildfires, Gore attributed the fires to the greenhouse effect. "These fires offer a glimpse of what global warming may mean to families across America," he proclaimed, adding, "And that is why it is so critical that we get on with the job of cutting greenhouse-gas emissions. Working together, we can spare other communities like those we have seen here today."

Three weeks earlier, Gore had noted that five states set record temperatures in the first five months of 1998, proving beyond a doubt that global warming had arrived. Never mind that, according to climatologist John Christy of the University of Alabama at Huntsville, there are 37 states whose records were set before 1940—i.e., before modern industry started emitting substantial amounts of greenhouse gases.

There is a method to the Vice President's madness: repeatedly charge that the earth faces a crisis and, over time, the public will become more receptive to the United Nations global-warming treaty drafted last year in Kyoto. The Kyoto Protocol imposes legally binding caps on emissions of carbon dioxide and five other greenhouse gases. Under the treaty, the U.S. would be required to cut emissions by approximately one-third over the next 15 years.

The Kyoto Protocol is but the first step in a global campaign against the use of fossil fuels. Today's justification is global warming, but the policy prescription was the same when the threat was global cooling or resource depletion. Whatever the ostensible purpose, an international climate-change agreement would usher in governmental controls on all manner of energy use. In its willingness to turn ordinary people's lives upside down to suit intellectual fashions, it is the environmental equivalent of the Clinton health-care plan. Call it ClimateCare.

Mr. Adler is director of environmental studies at the Competitive Enterprise Institute (on leave) and a research fellow at the Political Economy Research Center in Bozeman, Montana. He is the editor of The Costs of Kyoto: Climate-Change Policy and Its Implications (CEI, 1997).

Reprinted by permission. National Review, Aug. 17, 1998. Vol. 50, Issue 15, p. 36, 4p.

The case for an international treaty is built upon four assumptions: 1) global warming poses a serious threat to human health and prosperity; 2) failure to act soon would increase the risks of warming; 3) existing policy options would substantially mitigate the threat at an acceptable cost; and 4) a global-warming agreement is enforceable on a global scale. Not one of these assumptions is valid. Americans, and indeed nearly everyone in the world save United Nations bureaucrats, have nothing to gain and a lot to lose by embracing Clinton's ClimateCare.

Do we even know that global warming is occurring? "The overwhelming balance of evidence and scientific opinion is that it is no longer a theory but now a fact that global warming is for real," announced President Clinton. The Vice President derides greenhouse skeptics as practitioners of "tobacco science." Questioning greenhouse pronouncements is "immoral" and "un-American," says Interior Secretary Bruce Babbitt.

Environmental activists and Administration officials cite the recent report of the UN Intergovernmental Panel on Climate Change, which purportedly represents the "consensus" of 2,500 scientists from around the globe. In reality, the bulk of the report was drafted by a handful of scientists, several with strong preferences for environmental regulation, and merely submitted to various committees for approval.

Moreover, the report merely concludes that "the balance of evidence suggests that there is a discernible human influence on global climate." Hardly a global call to arms. And yet even this equivocal statement was controversial. The report's editors inserted it at the last minute, after the text had already been approved, so that the report would conform with the much less cautious "policymaker's summary."

Surveys of climatologists suggest substantial disagreement about humanity's impact on the climate. In a 1997 poll, most state-government climatologists disputed the claim that "human activities are already disrupting the global climate." True, the environmental group Ozone Action got 2,600 scientists, including several Nobel Laureates, to sign a petition making that claim. But a counter-petition, circulated with a letter from Frederick Seitz, past president of the National Academy of Sciences, has garnered over 18,000 signatures, including many from physicists, geophysicists, climatologists, meteorologists, oceanographers, and environmental scientists. Scientific truth is not determined by majority vote, but there is clearly no "consensus" that human-induced warming is here.

Predictions of global warming in the future are largely based on computer models that can't even predict current temperatures accurately. And as the models improve, they consistently predict less warming. Last May, America's most prestigious scientific journal, *Science*, reported that "most [computer] modelers now agree that the climate models will not be able to link greenhouse warming unambiguously to human actions for a decade or more." One month later, the *Bulletin of the American Meteorological Society* published a paper suggesting that computer models exaggerate the climate's sensitivity to industrial emissions.

Highly accurate satellite measurements taken since 1979 find no warming trend. And independent measurements from weather balloons corroborate these readings. Environmentalists point to land-based records that show a warming of approximately 1° F. since the 1880s. But most of this warming preceded the buildup of greenhouse gases in the atmosphere. Also, land-based records cover only a small portion of the globe. Most are near cities, where temperatures are higher whatever the global climate.

Even if there were a significant amount of warming, there is no evidence for the doomsday scenarios of killer heatwaves, devastating hurricanes, and epidemic disease. What temperature increases have been observed have been in winter and at night; to the extent that they have an effect, it would be to prolong growing seasons and increase agricultural productivity, not produce heatwaves. Hurricanes? Higher temperatures don't correlate with them. And economic growth and technological advance have a much greater effect on the incidence of disease than climate change. Even the old standby—catastrophic flooding due to melting polar ice caps—is not likely, according to a recent study published in *Nature*. So much for the greenhouse apocalypse.

Set aside the ambiguous scientific case. Even on the apocalyptics' own models, postponing significant reductions in greenhouse-gas emissions by twenty years or so would scarcely affect the global climate at the end of the next century. And such a delay would substantially reduce the costs of emission reduction. Thomas Schelling, former president of the American Economic Association, points out that it is costly to replace or retrofit existing capital goods before the end of their useful life, and that emission-reducing technologies are likely to improve over time. Precipitate action, on the other hand, would entail substantial costs. Controlling emissions of greenhouse gases requires controls on energy use: energy taxes, supply controls, or other regulatory mandates. The Administration's own thumbnail analysis concluded that complying with the Kyoto Protocol would cost $7 to $12 billion annually. When challenged by Rep. James Talent (R., Mo.) to provide an estimate of Kyoto's cost "without the sweeteners," Janet Yellen, chairman of the Council of Economic Advisors, acknowledged that the Administration had "not attempted to derive a good solid estimate."

Studies by Wharton Econometric Forecasting Associates, Charles River Associates, and other groups place the price tag of the Kyoto Protocol in excess of $2,000 per household. Gasoline prices would rise by an estimated 50 cents per gallon or more, and home heating costs would rise as much as 70 per cent.

Restrictions on energy use "will affect people in every aspect of their lives," says Frances Smith, executive director of Consumer Alert, a pro-market consumer group. Mrs. Smith notes that Americans use energy from the moment they shut off their bedside alarms in the morning until they turn out the lights to go to bed. Increasing the cost of energy means increasing the cost of heating a home, cooking a meal, driving to work, lighting an office, and powering a factory. These costs would fall particularly hard on the poor. No wonder some economists, such as Gary Yohe of Wesleyan University, say that the Kyoto Protocol would be comparable to the 1970s energy crisis in its likely impact.

Some of the costs are less obvious. The Sierra Club claims that increasing federal fuel-economy standards from 27.5 miles per gallon to 40 or more is the single most important step against global warming. That would raise the price of new cars and also make them smaller and lighter, thus less safe. A Harvard-Brookings study estimates that existing standards already cause up to four thousand highway fatalities a year. Raising the standards could increase this death toll by as much as 50 per cent.

Finally, it is well established that wealthier is healthier and poorer is sicker. Insofar as climate-change policy reduces economic growth, it will hurt human health. The potential costs of global warming, in short, are surpassed by the costs of global-warming policy.

And these costs would not necessarily yield any environmental benefit. On the apocalyptics' own computer models, preventing the buildup of greenhouse gases in the atmosphere would require reduction of emissions by approximately 70 per cent—a reduction several times greater than that called for by the Kyoto treaty.

Environmentalists are stepping up the pace of global conferences, each designed to tighten the screws a little more on industrial emissions. The next such conference is scheduled for November in Buenos Aires, at which point President Clinton hopes to announce that several developing countries have agreed to limit emissions.

If warming is a real threat, getting developing countries to sign on is essential. China will soon overtake the United States as the leading emitter of greenhouse gases. India and Brazil are close behind. Even if the U.S. and Western Europe were to disappear from the earth, global emissions would climb throughout the twenty-first century thanks to the industrialization of the developing world.

If the Third World does not agree to significant and enforceable emission limits, the Kyoto Protocol could actually increase emissions by encouraging industry to flee from America. A Department of Energy study concluded that if the United States faces tighter controls than developing nations, energy-intensive industries such as aluminum and paper manufacturing will migrate.

But there are substantial doubts about whether the treaty can be enforced. If the UN cannot control the proliferation of nuclear or biological weapons, how is it supposed to control the most common industrial emissions?

Environmentalists point to the success of the Montreal Protocol, which banned chlorofluorocarbons and other substances believed to affect the ozone layer. But the Montreal Protocol banned only a handful of chemicals. Carbon dioxide is a ubiquitous by-product of industrial activity.

Where the treaty might have real bite is in the U.S., where Senate ratification makes treaties the law of the land. Other countries are less scrupulous. Moreover, the United States is one of only a handful of countries where current emission estimates are remotely reliable. Thus, approving the Kyoto treaty could impose obligations on the U.S. that would be ignored in the rest of the world.

Governments are not allowed to include reservations when ratifying the Kyoto Protocol. Thus the Senate could not condition approval of the treaty upon the excision of particular clauses. This is important because once the treaty is in effect, binding amendments can be passed by a three-fourths vote of the parties—and more than three-fourths of the world's countries are classified as developing countries, which are not required to reduce their emissions under the treaty. Thus U.S. obligations under the treaty could escalate without the Senate's, or even the President's, consent. "For the first time, the United States would give control of our economy to an international bureaucracy within the United Nations," warns Sen. Chuck Hagel of Nebraska.

The Administration is in no rush to send the Kyoto Protocol to the Senate, where there is strong bi-partisan opposition. Just before the Kyoto conference, the Senate passed, by 95 to 0, the Byrd-Hagel resolution opposing any treaty that does not impose restrictions upon developing countries or that would harm the U.S. economy. But if treaty opponents rest on their laurels, momentum will shift against them. Clinton officials are aiming for a vote just before the 2000 presidential election. In the meantime, they will work, as Vice President Gore has been doing, to build support for the treaty.

The Clinton budget contains $6.3 billion in research subsidies and tax credits designed to co-opt industry opposition with taxpayer dollars. The EPA has funneled hundreds of thousands of dollars over the past few years to environmental groups and trade associations that support the treaty. Already some corporations, such as Enron and the members of the Business Council for a Sustainable Energy Future, are pushing for treaty implementation.

Similarly, the Administration is maneuvering to feign compliance with the Byrd-Hagel conditions. While the resolution explicitly rejects any treaty that does not require developing countries to make "specific scheduled commitments to limit or reduce greenhouse-gas emissions," the Administration has already redefined this condition as "significant" developing-country participation—a much lower standard. Toward this end, Administration officials are promising foreign aid and investment in developing countries that agree to "participate" in the treaty.

Several Republicans, notably Reps. David McIntosh (Ind.) and Joe Knollenberg (Mich.) and Sens. Hagel and John Ashcroft (Mo.), have spoken out forcefully against the treaty. There have been more than a dozen committee hearings since December, and the House of Representatives has voted to bar the Environmental Protection Agency from spending any money preparing to implement the Kyoto treaty. But news coverage of these efforts has been limited and has echoed the Administration line.

ClintonCare was defeated not by proposing a watered-down alternative or placing conditions on the Clinton plan, but by the courageous efforts of Sen. Phil Gramm and others in fighting the very idea of a federal takeover of America's health care. Fighting ClimateCare requires similar resolve. Americans have no desire to pay higher fuel prices or subject domestic industrial decisions to international control. If the case is made against the treaty on economic, scientific, and moral grounds, it can be defeated. It's time for opponents to turn up the heat.

IMPROVING THE ENVIRONMENT

LINDA BRIDGES

For the last thirty years, but especially since the advent of the Clinton Administration, the Greens have been gathering power into their hands, and conservatives have had precious little success in stopping them. Behind the scenes, though, much work has been done, and the time is ripe for a counterattack. For the Philadelphia Society's annual meeting, society president M. Stanton Evans put together a program that offered some tips for our soldiers in the field.

1. Don't concede the argument. As Bill Dennis of the Liberty Fund put it, if someone starts talking about "the environment," stop him right there: "there are many environments; some of them are good for some things, others for others."

Fred Smith of the Competitive Enterprise Institute listed several scares that were completely manufactured (acid rain, dioxin, Alar) but of whose fictiveness the general public is unaware. It is the job of the scientists to uncover the falsehood, but the job of journalists and concerned citizens to spread the word.

Meanwhile, to say, "Something needs to be done," does not answer the question "What needs to be done?" Molecular biologist Bruce Ames talked about the government's response to the "cancer epidemic," which is to spend billions of dollars on Superfund cleanup and other efforts to reduce "carcinogens." The government evidently hasn't noticed that the 25 per cent of Americans who eat the smallest amount of fruits and vegetables have twice the incidence of cancer as the 25 per cent that eat the largest amount. Professor Ames suggests that money spent on nutrition for poor children would do much more to reduce cancer than money spent by the EPA.

2. Don't go into denial mode. As climatologist Patrick Michaels put it, "If you want to lose this argument, say, 'Human activity contributes only 3 per cent of the atmosphere's greenhouse gases.'" Instead, point to the very real flaws in the Kyoto model (as Jonathan Adler does, above).

3. Concentrate on tradeoffs. Perfect cleanliness is costly, and it is often not "the rich" who pay. Steven Milloy, publisher of the Junk Science home page, told of the EPA's war on CFC-powered asthma inhalers. The amount of CFCs used in inhalers is minuscule, but that did not matter to the EPA in its enforcement of the Montreal Protocol. Nor did the fact that non-CFC inhalers cost more, and the burden would have fallen disproportionately on children of the inner cities, where asthma is rife. Only action by Congress prevented the Food and Drug Administration from doing the EPA's bidding.

4. Don't expect fair play. Many people have a vested interest in the Green program and can't be expected to go quietly. Mr. Adler alludes above to the petition circulated by Frederick Seitz. Fred Singer, the co-engineer of that petition, was our keynote speaker at the Philadelphia Society meeting; that very weekend, the National Academy of Sciences dissociated itself from the petition, and a lengthy article in the *New York Times* referred to the Kyotoists as "mainstream" scientists and insinuated that Seitz, Singer, et al. take the positions they take because they are in the pay of "industry opponents of a treaty to fight global warming."

In a less personal vein, Mr. Milloy detailed some of the differences between science and "science policy." If normal doses of a substance do not produce cancer in lab rats, a researcher interested in science would conclude that there is no evidence that the substance is carcinogenic; a researcher interested in science policy would increase the dosage. If something that has been thought to cause cancer when inhaled does not do so when inhaled by rats— well, inject the little fellows with the sniff. And if it still doesn't cause cancer—try prolonging the study until the rats, whose normal lifespan is two to three years, start developing cancers as an effect of old age.

5. Don't gratuitously alienate the people you're trying to convince. John Baden of the Foundation for Research on Economy and Environment reminded us that the average citizen has no vested interest; he is simply concerned with his children's well-being, or his duty more generally to those who came before and those who will follow after. Don't denigrate his concern; instead, explain why the posited threat is not real, or the proposed solution not likely to be effective.

6. Tell what works. R.J. Smith of the Competitive Enterprise Institute told us about wood ducks. A hundred years ago they were nearly extinct for the same reason the EPA is now concerned about spotted owls: the old-growth forests in which they nested were being cut down. Friends of the Wood Duck brought the wood duck back. By putting forests off limits? No, by building artificial nesting places, which the ducks liked just fine.

7. Keep your perspective. Promoters of the Kyoto Protocol say carbon-dioxide levels have risen 30 per cent in the last century. True, agrees Fred Singer, but 15 million years ago there was 20 times as much CO_2 as there is now; CO_2 levels dropped precipitously at the beginning of the Ice Age.

As P. J. Hill of Wheaton College put it, many Greens see man as being of less value than other animals—forgetting that man is the only animal that can think about CO_2 or the fate of the spotted owl.

Issue 21
Health

INTRODUCTION

In a recent travel program on television, the back-packing film crew crossed a border into a country in south-central Africa. A large sign stared down at everyone entering this country: "Warning! 1 in 7 young people in [this area] has AIDS." The World Health Organization reports that in some African countries the infection rate is even higher.

The first of the following two articles, from the British biweekly magazine *The Economist,* recounts the sad facts. AIDS is decimating the populations of many countries in Africa and elsewhere in the developing areas. Many babies are born with AIDS, contracted from infected mothers. Children are becoming orphans after the deaths of their parents. As an official of World Vision, a private relief organization, told a congressional committee,

> I personally visited two districts of Uganda, Rakai, and Masaka. There I saw families with no breadwinners. The 20-to-45 age group has been decimated, leaving behind a disproportionate number of small children and old people who are all dependents. This scenario was repeated in village after village. . . .

Of course, expensive life-extending drugs available in developed counties are not an option for these destitute people.

Does the rest of the world have an obligation to help? Most people would say "yes." But is significant outside assistance getting through to countries facing this crisis? Many leaders in the most affected countries say that it is not, and they place primary blame on industrialized nations for failure to provide adequate resources.

In the face of such criticism, what has the United States done to help? The second selection is taken from a study of efforts by the U.S. foreign aid program (USAID) to help developing countries combat AIDS. It concludes that the United States is offering effective assistance. This study was done by the General Accounting Office, which reports to Congress, not to the administration. Its positive assessment of USAID's anti-AIDS programs thus has more credibility than had the evaluation been made by USAID itself.

As you read the selections, consider the following questions.

Discussion Questions

1. Suppose you were given $100,000 to spend in fighting AIDS in Kenya. What would you do with this money?
2. On balance, how effective have efforts of the world community been in fighting AIDS in developing countries? Are the right programs being undertaken?
3. Why should the US feel obligated to help countries in far-away central Africa fight AIDS?

   For more information on this topic, visit the following websites:

   `http://news.bbc.co.uk/hi/english/health/background_brief-ing/aids/`
   (overview of world AIDS problem by the British Broadcasting Corporation)

   `http://www.us.unaids.org/highband/index.html`
   (web site of UNAIDS, the Joint UN program on HIV/AIDS)

   `http://www.msnbc.com/modules/aids_in_africa/aids_in_africa_front.asp`
   (photos of AIDS victims in Africa; by MSNBC cable network)

A Global Disaster

THE EDITORS OF *THE ECONOMIST*

The AIDS virus has infected 47m people, and shows no signs of slowing. It cannot be cured. Can it be curbed?

DATELINE: PIETERMARITZBURG, HARARE, KAMPALA

In rich countries AIDS is no longer a death sentence. Expensive drugs keep HIV-positive patients alive and healthy, perhaps indefinitely. Loud public-awareness campaigns keep the number of infected Americans, Japanese and West Europeans to relatively low levels. The sense of crisis is past.

In developing countries, by contrast, the disease is spreading like nerve gas in a gentle breeze. The poor cannot afford to spend $10,000 a year on wonder-pills. Millions of Africans are dying. In the longer term, even greater numbers of Asians are at risk. For many poor countries, there is no greater or more immediate threat to public health and economic growth. Yet few political leaders treat it as a priority.

Since HIV was first identified in the 1970s, over 47m people have been infected, of whom 14m have died. Last year saw the biggest annual death toll yet: 2.5m. The disease now ranks fourth among the world's big killers, after respiratory infections, diarrhoeal disorders and tuberculosis. It now claims many more lives each year than malaria, a growing menace, and is still nowhere near its peak. If India, China and other Asian countries do not take it seriously, the number of infections could reach "a new order of magnitude," says Peter Piot, head of the UN's AIDS programme.

The human immuno-deficiency virus (HIV), which causes acquired immune deficiency syndrome (AIDS), is thought to have crossed from chimpanzees to humans in the late 1940s or early 1950s in Congo. It took several years for the virus to break out of Congo's dense and sparsely populated jungles but, once it did, it marched with rebel armies through the continent's numerous war zones, rode with truckers from one rest-stop brothel to the next, and eventually flew, perhaps with an air steward, to America, where it was discovered in the early 1980s. As American homosexuals and drug injectors started to wake up to the dangers of bath-houses and needle-sharing, AIDS was already devastating Africa.

So far, the worst-hit areas are east and southern Africa. In Botswana, Namibia, Swaziland and Zimbabwe, between a fifth and a quarter of people

Source: Reprinted by permission. *The Economist*, Jan. 1. 1999. Vol. 350, Issue 8100, p. 42, 3p.

aged 15–49 are afflicted with HIV or AIDS. In Botswana, children born early in the next decade will have a life expectancy of 40; without AIDS, it would have been nearer 70. Of the 25 monitoring sites in Zimbabwe where pregnant women are tested for HIV, only two in 1997 showed prevalence below 10%. At the remaining 23 sites, 20–50% of women were infected. About a third of these women will pass the virus on to their babies.

The region's giant, South Africa, was largely protected by its isolation from the rest of the world during the apartheid years. Now it is host to one in ten of the world's new infections—more than any other country. In the country's most populous province, KwaZulu-Natal, perhaps a third of sexually active adults are HIV-positive.

Asia is the next disaster-in-waiting. Already, 7m Asians are infected. India's 930m people look increasingly vulnerable. The Indian countryside, which most people imagined relatively AIDS-free, turns out not to be. A recent study in Tamil Nadu found over 2% of rural people to be HIV-positive: 500,000 people in one of India's smallest states. Since 10% had other sexually transmitted diseases (STDs), the avenue for further infections is clearly open. A survey of female STD patients in Poona, in Maharashtra, found that over 90% had never had sex with anyone but their husband; and yet 13.6% had HIV. China is not far behind.

No one knows what AIDS will do to poor countries' economies, for nowhere has the epidemic run its course. An optimistic assessment, by Alan Whiteside of the University of Natal, suggests that the effect of AIDS on measurable GDP will be slight. Even at high prevalence, Mr Whiteside thinks it will slow growth by no more than 0.6% a year. This is because so many people in poor countries do not contribute much to the formal economy. To put it even more crudely, where there is a huge over-supply of unskilled labour, the dead can easily be replaced. Some people argue that those who survive the epidemic will benefit from a tighter job market. After the Black Death killed a third of the population of medieval Europe, labour scarcity forced landowners to pay their workers better.

Other researchers are more pessimistic. AIDS takes longer to kill than did the plague, so the cost of caring for the sick will be more crippling. Modern governments, unlike medieval ones, tax the healthy to help look after the ailing, so the burden will fall on everyone. And AIDS, because it is sexually transmitted, tends to hit the most energetic and productive members of society. A recent study in Namibia estimated that AIDS cost the country almost 8% of GNP in 1996. Another analysis predicts that Kenya's GDP will be 14.5% smaller in 2005 than it would have been without AIDS, and that income per person will be 10% lower.

THE COST OF THE DISEASE

In general, the more advanced the economy, the worse it will be affected by a large number of AIDS deaths. South Africa, with its advanced industries, already suffers a shortage of skilled manpower, and cannot afford to lose more. In better-off developing countries, people have more savings to fall back on when they need to pay medical bills. Where people have health and life insurance, those industries will be hit by bigger claims. Insurers protect themselves by charging more or refusing policies to HIV-positive customers. In Zimbabwe, life-insurance premiums quadrupled in two years because of AIDS. Higher premiums force more people to seek treatment in public hospitals: in South Africa, HIV and AIDS could account for between 35% and 84% of public-health expenditure by 2005, according to one projection.

AIDS, THE KILLER

Little research has been done into the effects of AIDS on private business, but the anecdotal evidence is scary. In some countries, firms have had to limit the number of days employees may take off to attend funerals. Zambia is suffering power shortages because so many engineers have died. Farmers in Zimbabwe are finding it hard to irrigate their fields because the brass fittings on their water pipes are stolen for coffin handles. In South Africa, where employers above a certain size are obliged to offer generous benefits and paid sick leave, companies will find many of their staff, as they sicken, becoming more expensive and less productive. Yet few firms are trying to raise awareness of AIDS among their workers, or considering how they will cope.

In the public sector, where pensions and health benefits are often more generous, AIDS could break budgets and hobble the provision of services. In South Africa, an estimated 15% of civil servants are HIV-positive, but government departments have made little effort to plan for the coming surge in sickness. Education, too, will suffer. In Botswana, 2–5% of teachers die each year from AIDS. Many more take extended sick leave.

At a macro level, the impact of AIDS is felt gradually. But at a household level, the blow is sudden and catastrophic. When a breadwinner develops AIDS, his (or her) family is impoverished twice over: his income vanishes, and his relations must devote time and money to nursing him. Daughters are often forced to drop out of school to help. Worse, HIV tends not to strike just one member of a family. Husbands give it to wives, mothers to babies. This correspondent's driver in Kampala lost his mother, his father, two brothers and their wives to AIDS. His story is not rare.

OBSTACLES TO PREVENTION

The best hope for halting the epidemic is a cheap vaccine. Efforts are under way, but a vaccine for a virus that mutates as rapidly as HIV will be hugely difficult and expensive to invent. For poor countries, the only practical course is to concentrate on prevention. But this, too, will be hard, for a plethora of reasons.

- *Sex is fun* . . . Many feel that condoms make it less so. Zimbabweans ask: "Would you eat a sweet with its wrapper on?"
- *. . . and discussion of it often taboo.* In Kenya, Christian and Islamic groups have publicly burned anti-AIDS leaflets and condoms, as a protest against what they see as the encouragement of promiscuity. A study in Thailand found that infected women were only a fifth as likely to have discussed sex openly with their partners as were uninfected women.
- *Myths abound.* Some young African women believe that without regular infusions of sperm, they will not grow up to be beautiful. Ugandan men use this myth to seduce schoolgirls. In much of southern Africa, HIV-infected men believe that they can rid themselves of the virus by passing it on to a virgin.
- *Poverty.* Those who cannot afford television find other ways of passing the evening. People cannot afford antibiotics, so the untreated sores from STDs provide easy openings for HIV.
- *Migrant labour.* Since wages are much higher in South Africa than in the surrounding region, outsiders flock in to find work. Migrant miners (including South Africans forced to live far from their homes) spend most of the year in single-sex dormitories surrounded by prostitutes. Living with a one-in-40 chance of being killed by a rockfall, they are inured to risk. When they go home, they often infect their wives.
- *War.* Refugees, whether from genocide in Rwanda or state persecution in Myanmar, spread HIV as they flee. Soldiers, with their regular pay and disdain for risk, are more likely than civilians to contract HIV from prostitutes. When they go to war, they infect others. In Africa the problem is dire. In Congo, where no fewer than seven armies are embroiled, the government has accused Ugandan troops (which are helping the Congolese rebels) of deliberately spreading AIDS. Unlikely, but with estimated HIV prevalence in

the seven armies ranging from 50% for the Angolans to an incredible 80% for the Zimbabweans, the effect is much the same.

- *Sexism.* In most poor countries, it is hard for a woman to ask her partner to use a condom. Wives who insist risk being beaten up. Rape is common, especially where wars rage. Forced sex is a particularly effective means of HIV transmission, because of the extra blood.
- *Drinking.* Asia and Africa make many excellent beers. They are also home to a lot of people for whom alcohol is the quickest escape from the stresses of acute poverty. Drunken lovers are less likely to remember to use condoms.

HOW TO FIGHT THE VIRUS

Pessimists look at that list and despair. But three success stories show that the hurdles to prevention are not impossibly high.

First, Thailand. One secret of Thailand's success has been timely, accurate information-gathering. HIV was first detected in Thailand in the mid-1980s, among male homosexuals. The health ministry immediately began to monitor other high-risk groups, particularly the country's many heroin addicts and prostitutes. In the first half of 1988, HIV prevalence among drug injectors tested at one Bangkok hospital leapt from 1% to 30%. Shortly afterwards, infections soared among prostitutes.

The response was swift. A survey of Thai sexual behaviour was conducted. The results, which showed men indulging in a phenomenal amount of unprotected commercial sex, were publicised. Thais were warned that a major epidemic would strike if their habits did not change. A "100% condom use" campaign persuaded prostitutes to insist on protection 90% of the time with non-regular customers.

By the mid-1990s, the government was spending $80m a year on AIDS education and palliative care. In 1990–93, the proportion of adult men reporting non-marital sex was halved, from 28% to 15%; for women, it fell from 1.7% to 0.4%. Brothel visits slumped. Only 10% of men reported seeing a prostitute in 1993, down from 22% in 1990. Among army conscripts in northern Thailand, a group both highly sexed and well-monitored, the proportion admitting to paying for sex fell from 57% in 1991 to 24% in 1995. The proportion claiming to have used condoms at their last commercial entanglement rose from 61% in 1991 to 93% in 1995.

People lie about sex, so reported good behaviour does not necessarily mean actual good behaviour. But tumbling infections suggest that not everyone was fibbing. The number of sexually transmitted diseases reported from government clinics fell from over 400,000 in 1986 to under 50,000 in 1995. Among northern conscripts, HIV prevalence fell by half between 1993 and 1995, from over 7% to under 3.5%.

Most striking was the government's success in persuading people that they were at risk long before they started to see acquaintances die from AIDS. There was no attempt to play down the spread of HIV to avoid scaring off tourists, as happened in Kenya. Thais were repeatedly warned of the dangers, told how to avoid them, and left to make their own choices. Most decided that a long life was preferable to a fast one.

Second, Uganda. Thailand shows what is possible in a well-educated, fairly prosperous country. Uganda shows that there is hope even for countries that are poor and barely literate. President Yoweri Museveni recognised the threat shortly after becoming president in 1986, and deluged the country with anti-AIDS warnings.

The key to Uganda's success is twofold. First, Mr Museveni made every government department take the problem seriously, and implement its own plan to fight the virus. Accurate surveys of sexual behaviour were done for only $20,000–30,000 each. Second, he recognised that his government could do only a limited amount, so he gave free rein to scores of non-governmental organisations (NGOs), usually foreign-financed, to do whatever it took to educate people about risky sex.

The Straight Talk Foundation, for example, goes beyond simple warnings about AIDS and deals with the confusing complexities of sex. Its staff run role-playing exercises in Uganda's schools to teach adolescents how to deal with romantic situations. Its newsletter, distributed free, covers everything from nocturnal emissions to what to do if raped. Visiting AIDS workers from South Africa and Zimbabwe asked the foundation's director, Catharine Watson, how she won government permission to hand out such explicit material, and were astonished to hear that she had not felt the need to ask.

The climate of free debate has led Ugandans to delay their sexual activity, to have fewer partners, and to use more condoms. Between 1991 and 1996, HIV prevalence among women in urban ante-natal clinics fell by half, from roughly 30% to 15%.

Third, Senegal. If Uganda shows how a poor country can reverse the track of an epidemic, Senegal shows how to stop it from taking off in the first place. This West African country was fortunate to be several thousand miles from HIV's origin. In the mid-1980s, when other parts of Africa were already blighted, Senegal was still relatively AIDS-free. In concert with non-governmental organisations and the press and broadcasters, the government set up a national AIDS-control programme to keep it that way.

In Senegal's brothels, which had been regulated since the early 1970s, condom use was firmly encouraged. The country's blood supply was screened early and effectively. Vigorous education resulted in 95% of Senegalese adults knowing how to avoid the virus. Condom sales soared from 800,000 in 1988 to 7m in 1997. Senegalese levels of infection have remained stable and low for a decade—at around 1.2% among pregnant women.

Contrast these three with South Africa. On December 1st, World AIDS Day, President Nelson Mandela told the people of KwaZulu-Natal that HIV would devastate their communities if not checked. The speech was remarkable not for its quality—Mr Mandela is always able to move audiences—but for its rarity. Unlike Mr Museveni, South Africa's leader seldom uses his authority to encourage safer sex. It is a tragic omission. Whereas the potholed streets of Kampala are lined with signs promoting fidelity and condoms, this correspondent has, in eight months in South Africa, seen only two anti-AIDS posters, both in the UN's AIDS office in Pretoria.

HOW TO DITHER AND DIE

South Africa has resources and skills on a scale that Uganda can only marvel at. It even has an excellent AIDS prevention plan, accepted by the new cabinet in 1994. But the plan was never implemented. The government likes to consult every conceivable "stakeholder," so new plans are eternally drafted and redrafted. Local authorities cannot act without orders from the central government. NGOs, many of them dependent on the powers-that-be for their finance, waste months making sure that enough of their senior management posts are filled with blacks to satisfy the ruling African National Congress. And they have minimal freedom to experiment.

"There's an idea that if you disagree with the government, you are betraying the liberation struggle," says Mary Crewe, head of the Greater Johannesburg AIDS project. As a result, soldiers in the South African army are so ignorant that they snip the tips off their free condoms, and HIV has spread through South Africa as fast, according to Dr Neil Mc-Kerrow of Grey's Hospital in Pietermaritzburg, as if no preventive measures at all had been taken.

Such bungling is not unique to South Africa. Most governments have been slow to recognise the threat from AIDS. From Bulawayo to Beijing, apathy and embarrassment have hamstrung preventive efforts.

In anarchic countries, such as Congo and Angola, there have been almost no preventive efforts. Many people believe that the cause—a bid to restrain one of the most basic human instincts—is hopeless. As a Zimbabwean novelist, Chenjerai Hove, puts it with disturbing fatalism: "Since our women dress to kill, we are all going to die." But if the sexual drive is basic, so is the desire to live. If governments in poor countries wake up to the need to persuade their citizens that unprotected sex is Russian roulette, Mr Hove could be proved wrong.

This article is indebted to a number of UNAIDS reports, including AIDS epidemic update (December 1998), AIDS in Africa (November 1998), and "A measure of success in Uganda" (May 1998).

HIV/AIDS: U.S. Aid and UN Response to the Epidemic in the Developing World

UNITED STATES GENERAL ACCOUNTING OFFICE

JULY 1998: EXECUTIVE SUMMARY

PURPOSE

The Human Immunodeficiency Virus/Acquired Immunodeficiency Syndrome (HIV/AIDS) epidemic is spreading rapidly throughout the developing world, where over 90 percent of the 30 million people living with the disease reside. In these countries, the epidemic has begun to erode gains in health, child survival, education, and economic development.

Since the mid-1980s, the U.S. Agency for International Development (USAID) and the United Nations have established efforts to address the epidemic. USAID primarily uses private voluntary organizations to implement HIV/AIDS prevention activities in developing countries. In 1996, the United Nations reorganized its HIV/AIDS program in response to donor concerns that the U.N. effort was too heavily focused on the medical and public health aspects of the disease and did not sufficiently address the social, economic, and developmental issues affecting the spread of HIV/AIDS. In light of the importance of these efforts to address the HIV/AIDS epidemic in the developing world, the Chairman, House Committee on International Relations, and Representative Jim McDermott asked GAO to examine USAID and U.N. programs. This report examines (1) the contributions USAID has made to the global effort to prevent HIV/AIDS and the methods USAID uses to provide financial oversight over its HIV/AIDS prevention activities; and (2) the extent to which the Joint United Nations Programme on HIV/AIDS (UNAIDS) has met its goal of leading an expanded and broad-based, worldwide response to the HIV/AIDS epidemic.

BACKGROUND

UNAIDS and the World Health Organization (WHO) estimate that over 30 million people were living with the HIV infection at the end of 1997. Most people living with HIV/AIDS reside in the developing world—two-thirds live in sub-Saharan Africa—where the disease continues to spread rapidly. According to the UNAIDS Secretariat, the number of new infections increased from 3.1 million in 1996 to 5.8 million in 1997. International donors contribute about $250 million a year to support HIV/AIDS prevention activities in the developing world. The United States has been the largest single donor, contributing $117 million a year, through USAID and in support of the U.N. HIV/AIDS program.

USAID and the United Nations have been important contributors to the fight against HIV/AIDS since the mid-1980s. While both the United Nations and USAID have sought to reduce the spread of the epidemic, they have somewhat different, yet mutually supporting, roles and objectives. As a bilateral agency, USAID works in partnership with governments, other donors, and private organizations to support research and implement HIV/AIDS interventions in countries. The U.N.'s role is in advocating, mobilizing, and coordinating the international response worldwide in addition to managing HIV/AIDS activities in 152 countries.

USAID began its HIV/AIDS assistance program in 1986, when very little was known about the epidemic or how to fight it. USAID's initial efforts primarily consisted of research on the causes, extent of the problem, and ways to prevent the disease's spread and of short-term technical assistance to more than 74 countries. In the 1990s, Congress began appropriating more money specifically to combat the HIV/AIDS problem, and it was elevated to a USAID priority for planning and budgeting. USAID developed an agencywide goal to reduce the number of new HIV infections by identifying and applying interventions to prevent HIV transmission. It designed targeted programs to meet this goal and, by 1997, USAID was directly supporting major HIV/AIDS programs in 28 countries. USAID relied heavily on cooperative agreements[1] with the private sector to implement its program. Under the terms of these agreements, the primary financial oversight responsibility is on the funding recipient.

The U.N. efforts to address HIV/AIDS began in 1987 under the auspices of WHO. WHO provided technical and financial support to fight the epidemic worldwide, primarily focusing on the medical and public health aspects of the disease. By the early 1990s, the United Nations and donors agreed that a more comprehensive approach was needed. On January 1, 1996, UNAIDS replaced WHO's Global Program on AIDS in an attempt to draw upon the experience and skills of all U.N. agencies.

UNAIDS is composed of six U.N. agency cosponsors[2] and a Secretariat, which is the coordinating unit. When forming UNAIDS, the cosponsor agencies agreed to increase resources devoted to HIV/AIDS activities; to mobilize resources for HIV/AIDS in affected countries, including increased private sector involvement; and to coordinate with other cosponsor agencies at the country level. The UNAIDS Secretariat was expected to (1) advocate increased political and financial support for HIV/AIDS activities; (2) develop a framework for measuring the performance and objectives of HIV/AIDS activities; (3) organize entities at the country level—called "theme groups"—as the forum for coordinating U.N. efforts; and (4) provide technical support and information to theme groups on what activities work best to facilitate development and implementation of national HIV/AIDS strategies. The biennial budget for the UNAIDS Secretariat in 1996–97 was $120 million, of which the United States contributed $34 million, or about 28 percent.

RESULTS IN BRIEF

Despite the continued spread of HIV/AIDS in many countries, USAID has made important contributions to the fight against HIV/AIDS. USAID-supported research helped to identify interventions proven to curb the spread of HIV/AIDS that have become the basic tools for the international response to the epidemic. Applying these interventions, USAID projects have increased awareness of the disease; changed risky behaviors; and increased access to treatment of sexually transmitted diseases and to condoms, which have helped slow the spread of the disease in target groups.

Under the terms of cooperative agreements with private implementing organizations, USAID managers are expected to closely monitor projects, but the major responsibility for internal financial management and control rests with recipient organizations. USAID's financial oversight primarily consists of conducting pre-award evaluations of prospective funding recipients, reviewing quarterly expenditure reports, and requiring audits. Officials from USAID's Office of the Inspector General said that there were no indications of systemic problems from audits conducted.

In its first 2 years of operation, UNAIDS has made limited progress in achieving its goal of leading a broad-based, expanded global effort against HIV/AIDS. While available information indicates that spending by the cosponsors has not increased, data are not yet available to measure UNAIDS' progress in increasing spending by donor countries, the private sector, or affected countries.[3] Moreover, theme groups, the forum for coordinating U.N. efforts in the field, have had a difficult start and, in some countries, cosponsor agencies are just beginning to work together. Finally, the UNAIDS Secretariat has not been successful in providing technical assistance and other support to facilitate theme group activities and has only recently begun to establish a framework for developing performance measures for the U.N.'s HIV/AIDS programs. Despite UN-AIDS' limited progress in meeting its broader coordination and resource mobilization objectives, GAO observed innovative activities that were implemented by cosponsor agencies.[4]

PRINCIPAL FINDINGS

USAID Funded Development and Implementation of Effective Interventions

The interventions developed, in part, by USAID-supported efforts, have become the basic tools for HIV/AIDS prevention. They are

— information, education, and counseling to raise awareness of the threat of HIV/AIDS in an effort to promote behavior changes, such as abstinence, that will reduce risk;

— treatment of sexually transmitted diseases which, if untreated, can facilitate transmission of the HIV virus; and

— promotion of increased condom use through condom "social marketing," or advertising the availability and appeal of using condoms.

In elevating HIV/AIDS prevention to an agency priority, USAID devised a strategy that relies on development and application of interventions in target groups based on specific country needs. Programs in countries GAO visited focused on the high-risk groups that spread the disease and used proven interventions to change behavior and reduce the chance of infection.

These interventions have been proven to have an impact on HIV/AIDS because they result in behavior changes that reduce the risk of disease transmission. However, it is difficult to determine the link between a particular activity or program and reductions in the incidence of HIV/AIDS because of the long incubation period for the disease; a person can be infected as a result of activity from 7 to 10 years previously. Thus, in addition to blood testing to measure the impacts of its HIV/AIDS activities in target groups, USAID also relies upon proxy indicators, such as behavioral change. Public health experts agree that the proxy indicators used by USAID are reasonable indicators of changes in HIV incidence.

GAO's review of internal and external evaluations, conducted by technical experts from the public and private sectors and academia, and other data collection efforts, as well as discussions with representatives of high-risk groups, found that USAID projects have increased knowledge of HIV, changed risky behaviors, and increased access to treatment for sexually transmitted diseases and to condoms, thus helping slow the spread of the disease in targeted groups such as commercial sex workers. Evaluations conducted for USAID's largest project, the AIDS Control and Prevention Project (AIDSCAP), determined that its activities were successful in the countries where it had projects. For example, in the Dominican Republic, USAID found that commercial sex workers and tourist resort staff were the primary conduits for HIV/AIDS. USAID focused its efforts on these groups, providing information about the disease to the workers, distributing condoms, and counseling them on alternative employment options. The percentage of HIV-positive commercial sex workers at one clinic funded by USAID slowed from 5.8 percent in 1995 to 3.3 percent in 1996.

NATURE OF USAID'S FINANCIAL OVERSIGHT

Following direction from Congress, USAID primarily relies on U.S.-based private voluntary organizations and indigenous nongovernmental organizations to implement its HIV/AIDS programs. USAID has mainly used cooperative agreements to fund these organizations' efforts. Under these agreements, project managers are expected to be substantially involved in planning and monitoring project progress; however, recipient organizations have the primary responsibility for their internal financial management and control. According to USAID officials, these agreements provide maximum flexibility to USAID and its private partners to design, implement, and change work plans without a formal process for review and approval.

USAID's financial oversight generally consists of (1) conducting pre-award evaluations to determine if a recipient has appropriate financial and management systems in place to handle the USAID financing; (2) reviewing quarterly expenditure reports submitted by the funding recipient to monitor the level of funds expended; and (3) obtaining annual external audits which, in accordance with the Single Audit Act,[5] provide information to oversight officials and program managers on whether funding recipients' financial statements are fairly presented. The audits are also intended to provide reasonable assurance that federal assistance programs are carried out in accordance with applicable laws and regulations. The annual single audit reports of USAID's $200 million, 6-year AIDSCAP project did not indicate any financial management or reporting problems. The

Office of the Inspector General determined that there were no indications from audits conducted that systemic problems existed.

UNAIDS HAS MADE LIMITED PROGRESS TOWARD MEETING ITS GOAL

UNAIDS has made limited progress toward achieving its goal of leading a broad-based, expanded global response to HIV/AIDS. Expenditure data for cosponsor agencies indicate that U.N. spending has not increased since the establishment of UNAIDS, but data are not available to measure spending from other sources. At the country level, the success of theme groups has been uneven. The UNAIDS Secretariat has not provided support to facilitate country programs.

HIV/AIDS SPENDING BY COSPONSOR AGENCIES HAS NOT INCREASED

Although one of UNAIDS' objectives was to increase resources devoted to HIV/AIDS by cosponsor agencies, spending on HIV/AIDS has not risen since the creation of UNAIDS. Instead, spending declined from $337 million in 1994–95 to $332 million in 1996–97. While UNFPA and UNDP increased spending for HIV/AIDS after UNAIDS was established and UNESCO began programming for HIV/AIDS activities, these increases were outweighed by decreased expenditures by the World Bank and UNICEF. The decline in U.N. spending for HIV/AIDS occurred despite an increase in overall spending by cosponsor agencies of 6.5 percent.

DATA ARE NOT AVAILABLE TO MEASURE PROGRESS IN MOBILIZING RESOURCES FROM OTHER SOURCES

One of UNAIDS' objectives was to increase spending by donors and affected countries and to increase private sector involvement in fighting the epidemic. However, the UNAIDS Secretariat is still analyzing survey data that should assist in developing a baseline to measure UNAIDS' progress in mobilizing donor and affected country resources.[6]

Preliminary data from the survey indicate that contributions from major donors[7] remained relatively stable between 1993 and 1996 at about $250 million a year. Data for 1997 were not available. Despite Secretariat efforts at the international level to encourage private sector involvement in the fight against HIV/AIDS, the UNAIDS Secretariat reports that private sector HIV/AIDS activities have remained limited to date. GAO's work in the field and the Secretariat's reports indicate that at the country level U.N. agencies have only made limited efforts to encourage private sector support of HIV/AIDS activities. U.N. officials offered several reasons for the lack of private involvement, including inadequate information about the impact of the disease on its workforce and the lack of government encouragement.

DIFFICULT BEGINNING FOR THEME GROUPS

The UNAIDS Secretariat was expected to organize theme groups as the forum for coordinating cosponsor agency activity in the field. Cosponsor agencies were expected to work together in the theme groups to support national governments' HIV/AIDS programs. UNAIDS' surveys of theme groups and GAO's work in the field indicate that cosponsor agencies met regularly and even conducted joint projects in some countries, such as the Dominican Republic. In others, such as Honduras and India, representatives rarely met. Despite the presence of World Bank projects in three of the five countries GAO visited, the World Bank representative did not attend any of the theme group meetings. A 1997 survey of theme groups, compiled by the Secretariat after GAO conducted its fieldwork, showed that theme groups were making some progress in working together. However, in areas where the groups reported progress, such as national resource mobilization, less than half of the theme groups that responded to the survey were operating effectively. U.N. officials reported several reasons for theme group difficulties: (1) lack of guidance to agency field representatives regarding how theme groups should operate and what the scope of their mission should be, (2) lack of individual accountability for theme group success, and (3) lack of commitment to working together in theme groups because of concerns held by some cosponsor representatives about the role of UNAIDS as the organizational vehicle for the U.N. response. Officials from the UNAIDS Secretariat said that they met with cosponsor agencies in March 1998 to address these problems and develop strategies to improve theme group coordination.

UNAIDS SECRETARIAT HAS NOT PROVIDED SUPPORT REQUIRED TO FACILITATE COUNTRY PROGRAMS

Despite being directed by its governing board to develop a framework for measuring the performance of the U.N.'s HIV/AIDS programs within a year of UNAIDS' establishment, the UNAIDS Secretariat has been slow to create an evaluation framework. Only recently has the Secretariat: (1)

staffed the evaluation unit that is charged with developing performance measures and (2) funded a survey to gather data on spending by donors and affected countries on HIV/AIDS. The survey data are necessary to measure UNAIDS' progress toward meeting its objectives. In addition, in countries GAO visited, cosponsor agency officials did not think that best practices information and technical support available from the UNAIDS Secretariat were useful. For example, U.N. officials told GAO that the best practices information was too theoretical and lacked project implementation guidance. Cosponsor agency officials also said they rarely used technical support from the Secretariat because it was not tailored to their specific needs and, in some cases, they were not aware of its availability. Secretariat officials acknowledged deficiencies in its country support activities and have begun to develop more country-specific materials that include implementation guidance.

RECOMMENDATIONS

GAO is making no recommendations in this report.

AGENCY COMMENTS AND GAO'S EVALUATION

USAID, the Department of State, the Department of Health and Human Services, and the UNAIDS Secretariat provided written comments on a draft of this report. These agencies emphasized the unique and important role UNAIDS plays in the global fight against HIV/AIDS. USAID, the UNAIDS Secretariat, and State had concerns about information GAO presented on UNAIDS. The agencies' comments and GAO's detailed evaluation of them are included in the report where appropriate.

USAID shared GAO's concerns about the areas in which UNAIDS has not made sufficient progress and noted that it is working with UNAIDS to strengthen UNAIDS' role. USAID, State, and the UNAIDS Secretariat noted that UNAIDS has only been in existence for 2-1/2 years and were concerned that it may have been too early to assess the program. State also said it was disappointed at the very negative tone in the report concerning UNAIDS' activities and believed that the report did not give any credit to UNAIDS for what it had achieved. Furthermore, State said that GAO implied that U.N. agencies and the U.S. government should stop supporting UNAIDS. The UNAIDS Secretariat stated that it was pleased with the overall presentation and objectivity of the report but was concerned that GAO's presentation of USAID's and

UNAIDS' programs obscured the important distinctions between them. The Secretariat also noted that it had expected a more positive perspective on the program.

GAO agrees that UNAIDS plays an important and unique role in the global response to HIV/AIDS and clarified the report to better reflect the distinction between the UNAIDS and USAID's program. While GAO recognizes that UNAIDS has been in existence for only 2-1/2 years, GAO did not evaluate the program's impact on the HIV/AIDS epidemic. In its report, GAO presents the facts as it found them to be, including areas needing improvement and areas that have worked well. In fact, the report specifically identifies UNAIDS' accomplishments, including information on innovative grassroots interventions. Also, GAO did not evaluate whether support for UNAIDS should be continued. GAO's objective, as stated in the report, was to examine the program's progress, since its inception, in meeting established objectives such as increasing resources devoted to HIV/AIDS and working together in theme groups at the country level.

ABBREVIATIONS

AIDS—Acquired Immunodeficiency Syndrome. AIDSCAP—AIDS Control and Prevention Project. AZT—Azidothymidine.

GPA—Global Program on AIDS.

HIV—Human Immunodeficiency Virus. HIV/AIDS—Human Immunodeficiency Virus/Acquired Immunodeficiency Syndrome.

NGO—non-governmental organization.

OIG—Office of the Inspector General. OMB—Office of Management and Budget.

PVO—private voluntary organization.

STD—sexually transmitted disease.

UNAIDS—Joint United Nations Programme on HIV/AIDS. UNDP—United Nations Development Program. UNESCO—United Nations Educational, Scientific, and Cultural Organization. UNFPA—United Nations Population Fund. UNICEF—United Nations Children's Fund. USAID—U.S. Agency for International Development.

WHO—World Health Organization

NOTES

1. A cooperative agreement is a funding mechanism used by a federal agency to transfer funds to an organization to support an agency program.
2. UNAIDS consists of the following six agencies: the United Nations Children's Fund (UNICEF); the United Nations Development Program (UNDP);

the United Nations Population Fund (UNFPA); the United Nations Educational, Scientific and Cultural Organization (UNESCO); WHO; and the World Bank.

3. Throughout this report, reference to U.N. funding for HIV/AIDS activities is limited to the six cosponsoring agencies and the Secretariat.

4. GAO conducted fieldwork in the Dominican Republic, Honduras, India, the Philippines, and Zambia.

5. The Single Audit Act of 1984 (31 U.S.C. 7501-7507), requires organizations that meet a minimum threshold of federal funding to undergo a single, nonfederal audit each year.

6. Study on the National and International Financing of the National Response to HIV/AIDS, UNAIDS/PCB(6)/98.3 (Geneva, Switzerland: May 24, 1998).

7. Major donors were identified by the United Nations as Australia, Canada, Denmark, France, Germany, Japan, Luxembourg, the Netherlands, Norway, Sweden, the United Kingdom, and the United States.